International Relations Theory and the End of the Cold War

International Relations Theory and the End of the Cold War

RICHARD NED LEBOW
and
THOMAS RISSE-KAPPEN,
Editors

. . .
. .
.

Columbia University Press
New York

Columbia University Press

New York   Chichester, West Sussex

Copyright © 1995 Columbia University Press

R. Koslowski and F. Kratochwil, "Understanding Change in International Politics:
The Soviet Empire's Demise and the International System," and J. Gross Stein,
"Political Learning by Doing: Gorbachev as Uncommitted Thinker and Motivated Learn-
er," reprinted from *International Organization* 48, 2, by permission of The MIT Press,
Cambridge, Massachusetts, copyright © 1994 by I.O. Foundation
and Massachusetts Institute of Technology.

Library of Congress Cataloging-in-Publication Data
International relations theory and the end of the Cold War /
Richard Ned Lebow and Thomas Risse-Kappen.

p.   cm.

Includes bibliographical references and index

ISBN 0–231–10194–5 (cloth). — ISBN 0–231–10195–3 (pbk.)

1. International relations.   2. Cold War.   I. Lebow, Richard Ned.

II. Risse-Kappen, Thomas.

JX1391.I6384   1995

327.1'01—dc20   94–42569

C IP

Printed in the United States of America

c
10 9 8 7 6
5 4 3 2
1

p
10 9 8 7 6
5 4 3 2

TO OUR GRADUATE STUDENTS,
WHO ARE STRUGGLING TO MAKE SENSE
OF THE CHANGING WORLD

CONTENTS

The genesis of this book was a 1991 conference on international relations theory and the end of the Cold War at Cornell University. At the last session of our conference, a prominent international relations scholar expressed his dissatisfaction with the proceedings. We had not posed a theoretically interesting question, he insisted. The end of the Cold War was "a mere data point" that could not be used to test or develop theory. But by that logic, a graduate student countered, we should give up the study of the Big Bang; it too was a data point.

These statements represent two very different ways of looking at recent events. The first maintains that one anomalous case is irrelevant to the testing and development of theory. The second contends that the reconciliation of the two poles of a bipolar system is a remarkable development that is worth studying. The contributors to this volume adhere to the second point of view. Most of us also believe that the reorientation of Soviet foreign policy under Mikhail Sergeievich Gorbachev and the East-West reconciliation it promoted constitute formidable challenges to existing international relations theories. Neither realists, liberals, institutionalists, nor peace researchers recognized beforehand the possibility of such momentous change, and all of them have been struggling to find explanations consistent with their theories.

To improve our theories we need to know how and why they are inadequate. With this end in mind the Cornell University Peace Studies Program held a conference in October 1991 to address the implications of the end of the Cold War for international relations theory. The editors, who were also the conference organizers, invited prominent representatives of different paradigms and theories and asked them to prepare or comment on papers that evaluated the utility of their preferred approach in explaining the transformation of Soviet foreign policy and the end of the Cold War.

The conference was lively and contentious, with sharp disagreements about the purpose of theory, the most useful level of analysis, and the utility of case studies. To the delight of the graduate students, there was also a clash between paradigms. From the opening panel to the final summation, realists and their critics fought a running battle about the premise of the conference (realists in particular had their doubts) and the relevance of realism to the post–Cold War world (critics had their doubts). Equally interesting, and probably more fruitful, was the controversy within paradigms about how much existing theories needed reformulation in light of their failure to recognize the possibility of the kinds of changes that occurred in the world between 1986 and 1991.

With one exception, the conference papers were revised for publication in this volume, and one of the participants, Richard Herrmann, was asked to write a conclusion. The authors met a second time at Columbia University in February 1992 to plan the revisions and talk about how their individual contributions could be recast to fit together better in a book. Four of the revised papers were published in a symposium on international relations and the end of the Cold War in the spring 1994 issue of *International Organization*.

The book is based on the papers, but the papers and the conference benefited enormously from the observations and criticism of the other participants. These included John Lewis Gaddis, James Goldgeier, Robert Herman, Robert Jervis, Peter Katzenstein, Robert Keohane, Elizabeth Kier, Stephen Krasner, Judith Reppy, Nina Tannenwald, Shibley Telhami, Dan Thomas, Stephen Walt, and Kenneth Waltz.

Neither the conference nor the book would have been possible without the Hewlett Foundation and Cornell University Peace Studies Program. The foundation underwrote the cost of the conference, and the program looked after all the arrangements. Realists and nonrealists alike were unanimous in their gratitude and praise for both organizations. We are also indebted to John Odell, editor of *International Organization*, and Kate Wittenberg, senior editor at Columbia University Press, for their unflagging interest in our project. Thanks too to the several reviewers for *IO* and Columbia for their helpful suggestions and sometimes penetrating critiques, and to Victoria Stanly for preparation of the index.

We recognize that we are too close to the event to say anything definitive about the meaning and significance of the Cold War and its demise. But before definitive studies can be written, many less enduring but provocative works must appear. At best, our book falls into this latter category. We hope it will appeal to scholars and students of international relations and encourage some of them to take the next steps along the road of reflection and discovery.

Richard Ned Lebow and Thomas Risse-Kappen

Michael W. Doyle is Vice President of the International Academy of Peace and Professor of Politics and International Affairs in the Woodrow Wilson School at Princeton University. He has held a Research Fellowship at Harvard University (1988–1989) and an SSRC / MacArthur Foundation Fellowship in International Peace and Security Studies (1985–1989). His books include *Empires* (1986) and *Escalation and Intervention: Multilateral Security and Its Alternatives* (1986), coedited with Arthur Day. Recent essays include "Politics and Grand Strategy," in R. Rosecrance and A. Stein, eds., *The Domestic Bases of Grand Strategy* (1993); "Liberalism and International Relations," in R. Beiner and W. J. Booth, eds., *Kant and Political Philosophy: The Contemporary Legacy* (1993); and "An International Liberal Community," in G. Allison and G. Treverton, eds., *Rethinking America's Security* (1992).

Richard K. Herrmann is an Associate Professor in the Department of Political Science and Director of the Program in Foreign Policy Analysis at the Mershon Center for National Security Research, The Ohio State University. He is author of *Perceptions and Behavior in Soviet Foreign Policy* (1985). He has written articles in journals such as *World Politics, International Security, American Journal of Political Science*, and *International Studies Quarterly*. He is currently coeditor of *International Studies Quarterly*.

Rey Koslowski is a Ph.D. candidate in the Political Science Department of the University of Pennsylvania. His dissertation focuses on international migration and the conceptualization of domestic and international politics. His publications include "Migration and the Demographic Context of European Political Institutions," to appear in a forthcoming volume edited by Donald Puchala; "Intra-EU Migration, Citizenship, and Political Union," *Journal of Common Market*

Studies (1994); and "Market Institutions, East European Reforms, and Economic Theory," *Journal of Economic Issues* (1992).

Friedrich V. Kratochwil is a Professor in the Department of Political Science at the University of Pennsylvania. He has also taught at Maryland, Princeton, and Columbia. Dr. Kratochwil has published widely in American and European journals including *International Organization, World Politics, Archiv für Rechts und Social Philosophie*, and *Theoria Politica*. He is author of *Rules, Norms, and Decisions* (1988) and *International Order and Foreign Policy* (1978); coauthor of *Peace and Disputed Sovereignty* (1986); and coeditor of *International Law, a Contemporary Perspective*.

Richard Ned Lebow is Professor of Political Science and Director of the Program in International Affairs at the Graduate School of Public and International Affairs, University of Pittsburgh. His most recent publications include *We All Lost the Cold War*, coauthored with Janice Gross Stein (1994), and *The Art of Bargaining* (1995).

Kenneth A. Oye is Director of the MIT Center for International Studies and an Associate Professor in the Department of Political Science. He has served on the faculties of Harvard University, Princeton University, and Swarthmore College, and has been a Guest Scholar at the Brookings Institution. He is author of *Economic Discrimination and Political Exchange: World Political Economy in the 1930s and 1980s* (1992); coeditor of *Eagle in a New World: American Grand Strategy in the Post–Cold War Era* (1992) and *Eagle Resurgent: The Reagan Era in American Foreign Policy* (1987); and editor of *Cooperation Under Anarchy* (1986). He is a member of the Editorial Board of *World Politics* and the Program Advisory Committee of the Overseas Development Council.

Thomas Risse-Kappen is Professor of International Politics at the Fakultät für Verwaltungswissenschaft, University of Konstanz, Germany. He has also taught at Cornell and Yale Universities and the University of Wyoming. He is author of *Cooperation Among Democracies: Norms, Transnational Relations, and the European Impact on U.S. Foreign Policy* (1995); and the editor of *Bringing Transnational Relations Back In: Non-State Actors, Domestic Structures, and International Institutions* (1995). He has published articles in *International Organization, International Security*, and *World Politics*.

Jack Snyder is Professor of Political Science and Director of the Institute of War and Peace Studies at Columbia University. He is the author of *Myths of Empire: Domestic Politics and International Ambition* (1991).

Janice Gross Stein is Harrowston Professor of Conflict Management and Negotiation at the University of Toronto. She is coauthor, with Richard Ned Lebow, of *We All Lost the Cold War* (1994), and, with Richard Ned Lebow and Robert Jervis, of *Psychology and Deterrence* (1985); and coeditor, with Louis Pauly, of *Choosing to Cooperate: How States Avoid Loss* (1993).

International
Relations Theory
and the End
of the
Cold War

RICHARD NED LEBOW AND THOMAS RISSE-KAPPEN

I

Introduction:
International Relations Theory and
the End of the Cold War

The reorientation of Soviet foreign policy under Mikhail Sergeievich Gorbachev and the East-West reconciliation it brought about constitute a formidable challenge to international relations theory. Neither realists, liberals, institutionalists, nor peace researchers recognized beforehand the possibility of such momentous change, and they have all been struggling to find explanations consistent with their theories.[1]

The ongoing transformation of the international system represents a double surprise for the profession. Most theorists and policy analysts assumed that bipolarity and its associated Soviet-American rivalry would endure for the foreseeable future. In the unlikely event of a system transformation, the catalyst for it would be superpower war. This was a fundamental tenet of realist theories of power transition.[2] Some peace researchers also predicted that relative shifts in power were likely to prompt more aggressive behavior on the part of the disadvantaged hegemon.[3] Everybody was surprised when the Soviet Union changed course, retreated from Eastern Europe, and allowed constituent republics to secede — and did all this peacefully.

Stability Versus Change

To improve our theories we need to know how and why they are inadequate. The how is not hard to establish. Political scientists and their theories failed not only to anticipate any of the dramatic events of the last several years but also to recognize the possibility that such changes could take place.

Radical shifts in policy and their consequences are almost always difficult to foresee. Diplomats and journalists — as well as political scientists — were taken by surprise by Stalin's purges and pact with Hitler and by President Anwar el-Sadat's peace overture to Israel, just as they were by the direction, scope, and pace of change in Gorbachev's Soviet Union.

To be fair, we must acknowledge that macrotheories of international relations do not aspire to make specific predictions. They attempt to predict broad trends, or responses to those trends, and rarely concern themselves with the timing of either. Most theories of international relations are also probabilistic; they do not require every case to conform to their expectations. Some approaches, like chaos theory and poststructuralism, challenge the notion of linear causality or the possibility of prediction.[4] However, the majority of international relations theorists — including those working within the traditions of realism, liberalism, and institutionalism — share the epistemological conviction that causal inferences of a conditional or probabilistic kind are possible. It is entirely legitimate to hold these scholars to their own standards and evaluate the validity of their theories on the basis of their probabilistic predictions.

Measured by its own standards, the profession's performance was embarrassing.[5] There was little or no debate about the underlying causes of systemic change, the possibility that the Cold War could be peacefully resolved, or the likely consequences of the Soviet Union's visible decline. None of the existing theories of international relations recognized the possibility that the kind of change that did occur could occur. Because of the failure to recognize this theoretical possibility, practitioners remained insensitive to the change after it was well under way. Few expected major change in Eastern Europe even after the Soviet Union's foreign policy had undergone radical changes and Gorbachev had repeatedly stressed his belief in the "absolute independence" of "all fraternal countries."[6]

The why of our collective failure is also apparent. Intelligence analysts distinguish between simple and complex surprises. The former are idiosyncratic events that cannot be foreseen or whose prediction requires special information. The shooting down of a Korean airliner over the Soviet Union in September 1983 is a case in point. Western analysts had long been aware of the Soviet Union's sensitivity to unauthorized aerial incursions but could not have guessed that a Korean 747 would overfly the Kamchatka Peninsula or that Soviet air defense would mistake it for an American spy plane.

It is undeniable that scholars lacked precise data about the internal economic and political situation in the former Soviet Union and its Eastern European empire.[7] But indications of Soviet economic decline were ample, and Sovietologists carried on a lively debate about the future of the post-Brezhnev Soviet Union.[8] The failure of Soviet specialists and international relations scholars was not empirical but conceptual. Because they did not consider the possibility of a peaceful but radical transformation of the Soviet political system and its foreign policy, they did not grasp the significance of the data at their disposal.

Complex failures refer to events that could have been predicted if analysts had interpreted properly the information at hand. Examples include the Soviet missile deployment in Cuba in 1962, the 1973 attack against Israel by Egypt and Syria, and the steep rise in oil prices imposed by OPEC following the 1973 Middle East war. In retrospect, analysts recognized that they had had the information necessary to predict these developments. They were the victims of faulty conceptions that led them to ignore relevant information or to interpret it incorrectly.[9]

The failure to expect or seriously consider the possibility of far-reaching foreign policy change in the Soviet Union is a complex failure. International relations scholars were misled by widely shared and deeply ingrained conceptions about the behavior of great powers in general and the Soviet Union in particular. These conceptions determined the questions they thought important and researchable and directed scholarly attention toward the explanation of continuity and stability and away from the study of the prospect of change. Soviet and Eastern European specialists were similarly slow to grasp the revolutionary potential of Mikhail Gorbachev. They underestimated the possibility of significant political change in the Soviet Union and exaggerated the stability of Eastern Europe's communist regimes. Many scholars argued that the post-Brezhnev leadership would be unlikely to sponsor major political or economic reforms to address the Soviet Union's intensifying economic crisis.[10]

For international relations scholars, the preeminent intellectual question in the security field was "the long peace" between the superpowers. In international political economy, it was the survival of the postwar international economic order despite the declining hegemony of the United States. Both questions assumed that the robustness of the political and economic status quo was an anomaly that required explanation.[11] Security specialists deemed it remarkable that the superpowers had avoided war, unlike rival hegemons of the past. They were just as surprised by the seeming durability of superpower spheres of influence. "The very fact," John Gaddis wrote, "that the interim arrangements of 1945 have remained largely intact for four decades would have astonished — and quite possibly appalled — the statesmen who cobbled them together in the hectic months that followed the surrender of Germany and Japan."[12] Many political economists were equally surprised that neither Germany nor Japan had attempted to restructure international economic relations to suit their respective interests.[13]

The prolonged survival of the postwar political and economic orders had important intellectual consequences. Because these arrangements had successfully weathered so many challenges, scholars greatly exaggerated their stability. Expectations about the continued survival of the economic and political orders may have reinforced one other. Concern about America's economic decline predated theoretical interest in the Soviet Union's decline. The fact that the postwar economic order established by the United States survived its decline as a hegemon encouraged the belief that the political-economic order erected by the Soviet Union in Eastern Europe would survive the decline of its creator.

The evolution of superpower relations also encouraged this conclusion. Central Europe had been the most important arena of the Cold War; between 1947 and 1962, Moscow and Washington had approached the brink of war in a series of crises provoked by their efforts to extend, consolidate, or protect their respective spheres of influence. After the Berlin crisis of 1961, tensions eased, and an uneasy peace descended on the region. With the signing of the Final Act of the Helsinki Accords in August 1975, the Western powers formally acquiesced to the status quo. The United States and its principal European allies recognized the legitimacy of Eastern Europe's communist governments and the postwar boundaries imposed on them by the Soviet Union.

The unexpected stability of the postwar political and economic orders directed scholarly attention to the intriguing question of why they had endured. Attempts to explain this, and the controversy these explanations provoked, pushed the problem of change out of the pages of the principal journals and into the obscurity where it has lingered until quite recently.[14] No major theory of international relations made change its principal focus, and even theories that incorporated some concept of change made no attempt to specify the conditions under which it would occur.[15] In the absence of theoretical interest in change, there was no debate about how or why the postwar order might evolve or be transformed. Scholars became correspondingly insensitive to the prospect that this could occur.

In a deeper sense, our blindness may be attributable to the political assumptions that shaped our view of the world and directed our

4

research agenda. For example, the absence of superpower war seemed so anomalous because of the widely shared belief that the Soviet Union was an aggressive and expansionist adversary. If Soviet leaders had not been regarded as gain seeking and risk prone but as loss avoiding and risk averse — and much evidence from the time of Khrushchev on recommends this interpretation — the superpowers' success in avoiding war would not have required an extraordinary explanation.

Cold War critics were equally myopic. Those who considered the nuclear arms race and its escalatory potential to be the major source of tension in East-West relations directed their scholarly attention to the domestic and international causes of the arms race and the ways it might be halted or stabilized through arms control and security regimes. Once again, few recognized or studied the possibility that the underlying conflict might undergo — or indeed, had already undergone — a profound transformation.

The same myopia affected the study of political economy. For years, the reigning orthodoxy, imported from classical economics, was that states were rational and gain seeking. If scholars had started from the premise that the world's capitalist establishment, like its political leaders, was above all else anxious to preserve order and predictability — especially when that order had been so spectacularly successful — they would not have viewed the survival of the postwar international economic framework as anomalous.

Theory is supposed to free scholars from their political, generational, and cultural biases. But social theory inevitably reflects these biases. It does a disservice when it confers an aura of scientific legitimacy on subjective political beliefs and assumptions.

Dependent Variables

The end of the East-West conflict, the breakup of the Soviet Union, the wars in the former Yugoslavia, and the possible reconciliation of Israel and the Palestinians have rekindled theoretical interest in change and its causes. The contributors to this book are divided in their judgment about the ability of existing theories to account for the end of the East-West conflict and the ensuing transformation of the international system. All the authors acknowledge causal links among changes in the international environment, developments within the Soviet Union, the shift in Soviet foreign policy, the end of the East-West conflict, and the transformation of the international system. Their attempts to explore the nature of these links provide the book with theoretical coherence.

All our essays are about change and its causes. However, there is no consensus among the authors (or in the discipline) about the nature of those changes, their timing, their causes or relative importance. For some scholars, the critical change is the end of bipolarity. For others, it is the end of the East-West conflict. The two events are related but distinct: the former refers to a shift in the distribution of power within the international system; the latter to a specific international conflict.

Bipolarity

The polarity of the international system is of particular interest to realist scholars who maintain that it determines the fundamental character of interstate relations. Most realists agree that bipolarity has come to an end, although they disagree about when and why it happened. Some, like John Mearsheimer, maintain that bipolarity ended with the Soviet Union's political and military retreat from Eastern Europe.[16] Other realists attribute the end of bipolarity to the breakup of the Soviet Union as a state.[17] Kenneth Waltz, who originally concurred with Mearsheimer, now argues that the international system remains bipolar.[18]

These differences reflect realism's failure to develop an operational measure of polarity. Without such a measure, realists have no guidelines for distinguishing cause from effect. Some argue that the withdrawal from Eastern Europe or the collapse of the Soviet Union caused the end of bipolarity. Others insist that these developments were the result of the Soviet Union's decline and thus a consequence of the end of bipolarity. Both assertions are in any event problematic.

Realists who contend that the retreat from Eastern Europe or the breakup of the Soviet Union brought about the end of bipolarity have difficulty explaining these triggering events. Realist theories assert that states need to maintain their power relative to other states. According to Kenneth Waltz, it is axiomatic that states "try to arrest or reverse their decline."[19] The Soviet Union's willingness to give up what had been regarded until then as a vital sphere of influence and allow constituent Soviet republics to secede appears to contradict realism's core assumption that leaders are highly motivated to preserve their states and their states' power.

Some realists have tried to finesse this problem by portraying both developments as unintended and unforeseen consequences of bad policy decisions by Mikhail Gorbachev and Eduard Shevardnadze. But if wiser policies could have preserved the Warsaw Pact and the Soviet Union, the international system would by their definition still be bipolar. The argument of unintended consequences in effect divorces polarity from the international distribution of capabilities by which it is supposed to be determined. Moreover, the suggestion that Gorbachev's policies were ill-considered and counterproductive compels scholars to look outside realism – to ideas, domestic politics, or decision making – to explain Gorbachev's foreign policy and the resulting transformation of the international system it brought about.

Realists who maintain that the breakup of the Warsaw Pact and the Soviet Union were the result of the Soviet Union's decline avoid these conceptual problems. But they have no theoretical basis for making such a claim. Without operational definitions of polarity, there are no criteria for establishing the decline of bipolarity independent of its consequences.

The End of the Cold War

Realists and nonrealists alike are interested in why and how the East-West conflict was resolved. To answer this question, they need a more precise understanding of the nature of that conflict and the stages through which it passed. The dependent variable must be delineated before the search for independent variables can begin.

Most analyses of the end of the East-West conflict focus on the policies of Mikhail Gorbachev. This is understandable because his liberalization of the Soviet system, sponsorship of political change in Eastern Europe, and commitment to disarmament were the catalysts of accommodation. But as Kenneth Oye and Richard Herrmann acknowledge in their essays here, major improvements took place in East-West relations long before Gorbachev came to power in 1985.

The Cold War is generally assumed to have begun in 1947 and to have had twin peaks of tension. The first peak, between 1948 and 1954, was characterized by acute confrontations in Central Europe, Korea, and the Taiwan Straits. The second peak, between 1958 and 1963, witnessed renewed confrontation in the Taiwan Straits and Central Europe and a war-threatening crisis in Cuba. In between, Stalin's successors made two unsuccessful attempts to reach an accommodation with the West.[20]

By the late 1960s the Cold War had lost much of its intensity. American military involvement in Vietnam did not prevent the two superpowers, and the Soviet Union and Western Europeans, from exploring their common interest in war avoidance and trade. The resulting détente was short-lived, but the Cold War revival of the late 1970s and early 1980s was a pale imitation of its predecessor. *Ostpolitik* and the Helsinki Accords kept Central Europe free of confrontation, while strategic parity prevented another Cuba. In the Far East, American rapprochement with China reduced the threat of renewed confrontation in Korea or the Taiwan Straits. Cold War II was a search for strategic advantage and a limited competition for influence in the Third World.

By the time of Gorbachev, East-West relations were fundamentally stable. Twenty-three years had elapsed since the last war-threatening crisis. The superpowers took each other's commitment to avoid war for granted and had entered into a series of arms control and "rules of the road" agreements that regulated their strategic competition and interaction. These accords weathered the shocks of the Soviet invasion of Afghanistan and Reagan's commitment to Star Wars. Gorbachev's initiatives were built on this preexisting foundation.

This cursory review of the Cold War suggests that Gorbachev's policies initiated the final phase of a reconciliation that had been proceeding fitfully since the death of Stalin. Gorbachev would never have contemplated—or have been allowed to carry out—his domestic reforms, asymmetrical arms control agreements, and liberation of Eastern Europe if he or the majority of the Central Committee had expected a hostile West to respond aggressively to a visibly weaker Soviet Union. The willingness of Gorbachev and his key associates to make unilateral concessions indicates that for them the Cold War had already receded into the past. They were doing away with its atavistic institutional remnants to facilitate cooperation with their former adversaries and the benefits this was expected to bring.

This understanding of the Cold War was not unique to Gorbachev and his advisers; it was shared by a sizable percentage of elite opinion in Western Europe and the United States. In their essays, Thomas Risse-Kappen and Janice Gross Stein argue that Soviet "new thinkers," and through them, Gorbachev, had largely assimilated an interpretation of the East-West conflict that had been developed by Western critics of the arms race. They do not deny that Gorbachev's accomplishments were real and significant: he set in motion the process that in five years led to the near-total and totally unanticipated reconciliation of the two blocs. But students of Gorbachev's foreign policy must acknowledge—as Janice Stein does in her essay—that his remarkable opening to the West was only possible because of all of the changes in East-West relations that had already taken place. Nikita Khrushchev, who was also committed to ameliorating East-West relations, could never have carried through the radical changes in Soviet foreign policy that characterized the Gorbachev era.

Because Gorbachev's policies represent the final stage of a long-term process of reconciliation, they must be situated in a historical perspective. To do this, we need appropriate conceptions of the East-West conflict. Analysts need to identify the key stages and turning points of the East-West conflict, the reasons for this evolution, and then go on to assess the relative importance of the final stage ushered in by Gorbachev's initiatives.

Our argument draws attention to the deeper structures of the East-West conflict. But it should not be read to suggest that those structures were in any way determining. We suggest that certain kinds of conciliatory initiatives require preconditions, but these initiatives will not occur just because the associated preconditions are present. In their essays, Richard Ned Lebow and Janice Gross Stein argue that someone other than Gorbachev could have come to power with very different conceptions of internal reform and foreign policy. Grigory Romanov or Yegor Ligachev, other contenders for power in 1985, would probably have pursued a kinder and gentler version of Brezhnevism, as had Konstantin Chernenko and Yuri Andropov. East-West relations might have improved, but the two blocs probably would have retained their essential character and antagonism. Analyses of the East-West conflict must recognize the importance of both structure and agents in explaining its resolution.

Analysis must also go beyond the study of Soviet foreign policy. Resolution of the Cold War required the active collaboration of the governments of Western Europe and the United States. Their policies reflected a fundamental reconceptualization of East-West relations. This had been under way for some time in Western Europe; it was accelerated, not initiated by Gorbachev.

President Ronald Reagan's positive response to Gorbachev's overtures was critical to East-West accommodation. And Reagan's about-face was hardly foreordained. In 1953, the *troika* that followed Stalin—Malenkov, Bulganin, and Khrushchev—signaled its interest in winding down the Cold War. Dwight Eisenhower and John Foster Dulles recognized their objective but spurned most of their advances. Another American president might have responded differently to Gorbachev.

The evidence suggests that Eisenhower and Reagan acted differently because of their different assessments of long-term Soviet intentions. In the early 1950s, Eisenhower and Dulles regarded the

Soviet interest in accommodation as sincere but tactical. They were convinced that Bulganin, Khrushchev, and Malenkov were just as hostile to the capitalist West as Stalin had been but sought to ease Cold War tensions to safeguard the Soviet position in a period of growing Western strength. Eisenhower and Dulles accordingly decided to step up the pressure on the Soviet Union in the hope of further weakening Moscow's grip on Eastern Europe.[21]

Reagan and his secretary of state, George Schultz, were equally suspicious of Soviet intentions at first. Gorbachev's protestations of good will and his apparent interest in deep cuts in strategic forces flew in the face of their understanding of the Soviet Union and its goals. Even after Gorbachev's foreign and domestic policies had won widespread support and sympathy in the West, Reagan continued to adhere to his "evil empire" image of the Soviet Union and to express doubts about the Soviet leader's sincerity. After all, this was the same president who as late as 1980 had explained away the Sino-Soviet split as the result of "an argument over how best to destroy us."[22]

Gorbachev's commitment to withdraw Soviet forces from Afghanistan, his domestic reforms, and, above all, the personal impression he made on Reagan in their several meetings finally convinced the president of his sincerity. As a result of his "epiphany," Reagan was transformed from a doubting Thomas into the leading dove of his administration.[23]

We can speculate that Reagan's about-face was facilitated by the nature of his image of the Soviet Union. Cognitive psychologists find that simple, undifferentiated images are more susceptible to change, while complex images with more components interconnected through elaborate causal reasoning are more resistant to change.[24] Reagan's image of the Soviet Union, while pronounced in its hostility, was relatively simple and undifferentiated. Once he came to regard Gorbachev as a friend and committed to peace, he may have changed his image of the Soviet Union to make it consistent with his image of Gorbachev.[25]

The validity of any particular interpretation of the shift in Ronald Reagan's foreign policy is not the issue here. Rather, it is the existence of that shift, its importance for East-West accommodation, and the corresponding need somehow to account for it. To explain the Cold War and its ultimate demise, we need to develop conceptions of that conflict that identify critical structures, processes, and actors and their decisions. We need to ask the right questions before we can find the right answers.

Authors and Arguments

The nine essays in this book attempt to explain the changes that occurred in Soviet foreign policy, East-West relations, and the international system from 1985 to 1992. Their authors acknowledge the problems these changes create for their preferred approaches or theories, and some of them attempt to specify further or reformulate their key propositions. It is our collective hope that constructive self-criticism will lead to better theory.

The first four essays assess the capability of structural explanations—realism, liberalism, and functionalism—to explain the end of the Cold War and the resulting transformation of the international system. Despite their differences in approach, all the authors identify Mikhail Gorbachev's dramatic reorientation of domestic and foreign policy as the critical factor in ending the Cold War and explain that reorientation as a response to the failures of the Soviet economic and political system. Their essays recognize the importance of a benign international environment in conditioning and encouraging Gorbachev's reformist and accommodative policies.

Richard Ned Lebow begins with a critical examination of the explanations realists have offered for three of the most important international developments of the last half-century: the "long peace" between the superpowers, the Soviet Union's renunciation of its informal empire in Eastern Europe, and the post–Cold War transformation of the international system. Realist theories at the international level address the first and third of these developments, and realist theories at the unit level have made an ex post facto attempt to account for the second. Lebow maintains that all these explanations are unsatisfactory because of the conceptual failings of realist theories. He questions the overall utility of the realist paradigm.

Kenneth Oye acknowledges that realist theories are underspecified but believes that realism still offers the most compelling explanation for the changes in Soviet foreign policy under Gorbachev. Oye argues that the underlying cause of the end of the Cold War was economic decline, moderate in the United States and severe in the Soviet Union. The Soviet decline was attributable to the structure of the economy, disproportionate military spending, and costly foreign commitments. The Soviet response—glasnost, perestroika, and a conciliatory foreign policy—was conditioned by the specific character of the international environment. The stability that robust nuclear deterrence conferred to superpower relations allowed and encouraged policies that accepted short-term vulnerabilities in the expectation of strengthening the Soviet Union's economic and political situation in the longer term.

Michael Doyle examines the utility of three formulations of liberalism in accounting for the demise of communism in Eastern Europe and the Soviet Union. He contends that "democratic liberalization," identified with people's aspirations for freedom from arbitrary authority, provides a good underlying explanation for opposition to communism but tells us nothing about the timing or outcome of rebellions against communist regimes. "Liberal modernization" theory, which emphasizes the superiority of democracy and market economies over authoritarianism and command economies, helps to explain the failure of Soviet-type systems but not the timing. For this, we need "liberal internationalism" with its identification of commerce as a potent international source of the change. It was the combination of pressures from below, coming from dissident groups in Eastern Europe, and decisions at the top, made by Andropov and Gorbachev under the strain of Cold War competition, that brought about the revolutions of 1989. The reformist choices of Soviet leaders were also encouraged by the prospect of joining in the benefits of the "democratic peace."

Jack Snyder applies historical modernization theory in the tradition of Alexander Gerschenkron and Barrington Moore to the Soviet Union. As a "late, late industrializer," the Soviet Union developed highly centralized political and economic institutions to mobilize the resources necessary to catch up militarily with more advanced powers. While well suited for the early stages of extensive development, these institutions became increasingly dysfunctional because they prevented the innovations required for more intensive development. Modernization created a better-educated, urbanized, and increasingly dissatisfied middle class. To win support and legitimize the policies that further economic development required, "new thinkers" appealed to this constituency with a set of ideas and strategic myths.

Snyder believes that his explanation is compatible with realism and liberalism. He distinguishes between what he terms aggressive and defensive realism. The latter takes account of the security dilemma and recognizes that aggressive foreign policies can be counterproductive because they are likely to provoke balancing behavior. Gorbachev's foreign policy revolution could be described as a shift from aggressive to defensive realism. Snyder's explanation is liberal in the sense that he, like Michael Doyle, emphasizes the importance of the benign international environment for Gorbachev's initiatives and attributes that environment to the preference of liberal democracies for cooperative foreign policies.

The Oye, Doyle, and Snyder essays emphasize how structures at the international or state levels influence foreign policy. None of the authors is a structural determinist. Each maintains that structure creates powerful constraints and opportunities but acknowledges that choices of leaders are also shaped by personality, ideas, coalitions, and broader domestic political considerations. These disparate substate-level influences can prompt decisions to try to adapt foreign policy to the constraints and opportunities created by structures, as seemingly happened in the case of Gorbachev. They can also impede foreign policy change, as Oye suggests happened in the case of Brezhnev.

Lebow presents an avowedly antistructural perspective. He contends that leaders and elites have subjective understandings of their international and domestic environments that are rooted in their conceptions of the world and their own societies and reflect their political needs and agendas. He explains the different responses of Brezhnev and Gorbachev to the Soviet Union's economic decline in terms of their different expectations about the feasibility and consequences of domestic reform.

The next four essays focus on nonstructural determinants of foreign policy, making the case that norms, ideas, domestic agendas, and personality were primarily responsible for Gorbachev's foreign policy and the transformation of the international system.

Rey Koslowski and Friedrich Kratochwil argue that changes in beliefs and practices can bring about foreign policy and system change. They contend that the reinstitutionalization of civil society in Eastern Europe and its interaction with perestroika led to a redefinition of Soviet security interests that found expression in Gorbachev's repudiation of the Brezhnev Doctrine. They draw on models of imperial decay to analyze Gorbachev's reforms as an unsuccessful counterreformation strategy to save the Soviet empire. Koslowski and Kratochwil argue that the transformation of the international system is a response to changes in norms and conventions, not to changes in relative power capabilities or other so-called structural attributes of the international system.

In his second contribution, Richard Ned Lebow offers a critical assessment of his earlier work in which he argued that leaders faced with mounting international and domestic pressures tend to pursue aggressive foreign policies. Gorbachev's accommodative foreign policy indicates an alternative response. To explain it, Lebow reformulates his need-driven theory by specifying the conditions in which acute foreign and domestic threats prompt conciliatory responses. Leaders must be committed to domestic political and economic reforms whose success is seen to require accommodation abroad. They must recognize that the strategy of confrontation has failed in the past and is unlikely to work in the future. They must also entertain the expectation that conciliatory policies will be reciprocated. Lebow develops his argument by analyzing three historical cases of accommodation: France and Britain at the turn of the century, Egypt and Israel in the 1970s, and the recent Soviet-American experience. He finds striking similarities among the three cases, including evidence that the motivated biases that often blind leaders to the adverse consequences of confrontational policies can also lead them to minimize the risks associated with accommodation.

Thomas Risse-Kappen argues that neither the Gorbachev foreign policy revolution nor the Western responses to it can be adequately understood without taking into account the ideas that informed leadership decisions. He argues that many of the concepts associated with "new thinking" and "common security" were developed by American arms controllers and Western European peace researchers and left-of-center politicians and transmitted to Soviet leaders by analysts and scholars at Soviet institutes. "Common security" satisfied the Gorbachev coalition's need for consistent and coherent policy concepts and legitimized policies to which that coalition was attracted for other reasons. Ideas interacted with domestic structures and institutions and become politically relevant. Risse-Kappen contends that the benign Western response to the Gorbachev revolution was also shaped by the influence of these transnationally diffused ideas. The variation in domestic structures, especially between the United States and Germany, accounts for the differential impact of these ideas.

Janice Gross Stein also analyzes the reasons why Gorbachev and the key officials who helped to formulate or implement his foreign policy became proponents of "new thinking." She finds that propositions derived from cognitive psychology are less helpful than theories of political learning. Stein contends that Gorbachev came to power committed to domestic reforms but had few specific foreign policy beliefs. He was a prime candidate for learning and open to the ideas and policies promoted by *institutchiks* and Foreign Ministry officials, especially when they facilitated his domestic agenda. Gorbachev also learned by doing. He adjusted his policies in response to Western reactions to his initiatives. In contrast to rational or interest-based explanations that assume deductive thinking, Stein argues that Gorbachev was an inductive learner.

Among the authors of these four chapters, Risse-Kappen is most sympathetic to the approaches of Oye, Doyle, and Snyder. He considers systemic and state structures very important but also recognizes the significance of ideas and the domestic political context in which they play out. He urges a more integrated approach to the study of foreign policy that attempts to bridge the gap between international and domestic policy.

The other authors — Koslowski and Kratochwil, Lebow, and Stein — are highly critical of the analytical utility of any conception of structure. Koslowski and Kratochwil argue for a "constructivist" approach that acknowledges the central role ideas play in shaping foreign policy. Lebow and Stein, and Richard Herrmann in his concluding essay, emphasize the role of agents over structures. Their starting point is the perspective of leaders and how their policies take shape in reference to their goals and subjective understandings of their domestic and international policy environments. For these authors, and also for Risse-Kappen, the interesting analytical question is how the conceptions of leaders develop and change. In common with Koslowski and Kratochwil, they see ideas as central to both processes.

The end of the Cold War and bipolarity have touched off a major debate about the shape of the post–Cold War world and its propensity for conflict.[26] Several of our contributors join this debate.

Richard Ned Lebow challenges the applicability of the realist concepts of anarchy and polarity to the post–Cold War world. He argues that the international system is still technically anarchical because there is no enforcement authority but that the concept of anarchy offers little help in explaining the character of present-day relations among the developed democracies. Lebow argues, as do Rey Koslowski and Friedrich Kratochwil, that the allegedly inescapable consequences of anarchy have been largely overcome by a complex web of multilateral institutions that govern interstate relations and provide mechanisms for resolving disputes. These institutions reflect and help sustain a consensus in favor of consultation and compromise that mute the consequences of power imbalances among states. To the extent that the principles that govern relations among the industrial democracies come to characterize relations between them and many of the countries of the former Eastern bloc, Lebow contends, this cooperative pattern of international relations will encompass most of the developed world. It will coexist with the more traditional, conflict-prone pattern that continues to character-ize relations among other former communist states (e.g., Yugoslavia) and many lesser developed countries and between them and the developed world.[27]

Michael Doyle and Jack Snyder share the liberal expectation that international relations will become more peaceful if democracy takes root in more states. For Doyle, optimism must be tempered by the realization that liberal states have frequently engaged in impru-dent imperialism against authoritarian systems and that autarchy and nationalism remain powerful sources of conflict. He suggests that majority rule may be a necessary but not sufficient cause of international peace. Snyder points out the danger of an authoritari-an backlash in the successor states of the Soviet Union. He warns that such a reversal could be the consequence of rapid economic lib-eralization that destabilizes efforts to build democracy.

In his concluding essay, Richard Herrmann addresses three themes that are common to many of the other contributions: the utility of neorealism, the nature and timing of the Cold War, and the sources and motives of Soviet foreign policy.

Like Snyder, Herrmann criticizes realism for its monocausal focus on power. He acknowledges that multicausation introduces unit-level variations that neorealism was designed to avoid but con-tends that it is necessary to explain the evolution of Soviet foreign policy. That evolution and its Western counterpart, as Herrmann agrees with Koslowski and Kratochwil, were the result of mutual redefinitions of threats and interests. These redefinitions were inde-pendent of any shift in relative capabilities and contrary to realism's expectation that the condition of anarchy would make cooperation extraordinarily difficult to achieve and maintain. Herrmann also challenges realism's characterization of the state. He suggests that states are artificial constructs based on varying conceptions of legiti-macy and that the end of the Cold War has unleashed a new era in which the principle of national identity may compete more success-fully with territoriality as a basis for statehood.

Realists have depicted the Cold War as a bipolar security dilem-ma. However, Hans Morgenthau, the preeminent classical realist, viewed the Cold War as primarily an ideological struggle. He argued that the rise of mass politics and democracy had swept away the transnational aristocracy that had provided the common norms necessary for a balance-of-power system to work. Without these constraints, postwar international politics had become a Manichaean struggle between contending forms of nationalistic universalism.

Herrmann adduces evidence in support of Morgenthau — most notably the consistent willingness of the superpowers to invest heavily in geostrategically insignificant areas in the name of their respective crusades — but concedes that the ideological component of superpower relations declined sharply over time. Nevertheless, he contends, Morgenthau's characterization of the Cold War, offers important insights into the conflict, and it is imperative for students of the Cold War to come to an understanding of what that conflict was about before they attempt to explain its resolution.

To understand the nature of the Cold War, we must know something about the motives of its protagonists. Traditional realists sidestepped or denied this issue by assuming a common motivation for all states. Several of the contributors to this book argue that, since the motives of leaders of the same country can vary enormously, understanding the motives of different Soviet leaders is critical to understanding their respective foreign policies. Herrmann reviews some of the different explanations advanced to explain Soviet foreign policy, all of which he contends are nonfalsifiable as presently constructed. They can account for the end of the Cold War but could never have predicted its timing. Herrmann is cautiously optimistic that new information about the deliberations of Soviet leaders might permit us to discriminate more authoritatively among these competing explanations.

Herrmann insists that the importance of motivation makes it imperative to base inferences about a country's foreign policy on its elite's perceptions of its goals, the nature of the environment in which it operates, and the foreign and domestic constraints it faces. From such a perspective, the most critical feature of the international system is the distribution not of capabilities but of interests and aims. Such an orientation would compel theorists to engage in the interpretative debates that were at the heart of the Cold War.

NOTES

1   Some of the more interesting postdictive efforts include Daniel Deudney and G. John Ikenberry, "The International Sources of Soviet Change," *International Security* 16 (winter 1991 / 92): 74–118; Daniel Deudney and G. John Ikenberry, "Soviet Reform and the End of the Cold War: Explaining Large-Scale Historical Change," *Review of International Studies* 17 (summer 1991): 225–50; George W. Breslauer and Philip E. Tetlock, eds., *Learning in U.S. and Soviet Foreign Policy* (Boulder, Colo.: Westview, 1991); and James M. Goldgeier and Michael McFaul, "A Tale of Two Worlds: Core and

Periphery in the Post–Cold War Era," *International Organization* 46 (spring 1992): 467–91.

2   See A. F. K. Organski, *World Politics*, 2d ed. (New York: Knopf, 1967), 202–3; A. F. K. Organski and Jacek Kugler, *The War Ledger* (Chicago: University of Chicago Press, 1980); George Modelski, "The Long Cycle of Global Politics and the Nation-State," *Comparative Studies of Society and History* 20 (April 1978): 214–35; William R. Thompson, ed., *Contending Approaches to World System Analysis* (Beverly Hills, Calif.: Sage, 1983); Raimo Väyrynen, "Economic Cycles, Power Transitions, Political Management, and Wars Between Major Powers," *International Studies Quarterly* 27 (December 1983): 389–418; Robert Gilpin, *War and Change in World Politics* (New York and Cambridge: Cambridge University Press, 1981); Charles F. Doran and Wes Parsons, "War and the Cycle of Relative Power," *American Political Science Review* 54 (December 1960): 947–65; and Paul Kennedy, *The Rise and Fall of the Great Powers: Economic Change and Military Conflict from 1500 to 2000* (New York: Random House, 1987). This literature is reviewed by Jack S. Levy, "Declining Power and the Preventive Motivation for War," *World Politics* 40 (October 1987): 82–107; and by Richard Ned Lebow, "Thucydides, Power Transition Theory, and the Causes of War," in *Hegemonic Rivalry: From Thucydides to the Nuclear Age*, ed. Richard Ned Lebow and Barry S. Strauss (Boulder, Colo.: Westview, 1991), 125–68.

3   One of us made this point at the beginning of the 1980s. See Richard Ned Lebow, "Clear and Future Danger: Managing Relations with the Soviet Union in the 1980s," in *New Directions in Strategic Thinking*, ed. Robert O'Neill and D. M. Horner (London: Allen and Unwin, 1981), 221–45; and a subsequent revision, "The Deterrence Deadlock: Is There a Way Out?" in *Psychology and Deterrence*, Robert Jervis, Richard Ned Lebow, and Janice Gross Stein (Baltimore: Johns Hopkins University Press, 1985), pp. 180–202.

4   See, for example, Alan Beyerchen, "Clausewitz, Nonlinearity, and the Unpredictability of War," *International Security* 17 (winter 1992/ 93): 59–90; James Der Derian and Michael Shapiro, eds., *International-Intertextual Relations: Postmodern Readings of World Politics* (Lexington, Mass.: Lexington, 1989); and Richard Ashley and R. B. J. Walker, eds., "Speaking the Language of Exile: Dissidence in International Studies," *International Studies Quarterly* (special issue) 34 (September 1990): 259–68.

5   For an excellent overview, see Philip Everts, "The Events in Eastern Europe and the Crisis in the Discipline of International Relations," in *The End of the Cold War: Evaluating Theories of International Relations*, Pierre Allan and Kjell Goldmann (Dordrecht, Holland: Martinus Nijhoff, 1992), 55–81.

6   Mikhail S. Gorbachev, *Perestroika: New Thinking for Our Country and the World* (New York: Harper and Row, 1987), 165.

7   On the methodological problems of studying the former Soviet Union,

see Jack Snyder, "Richness, Rigor, and Relevance in the Study of Soviet Foreign Policy," *International Security* 9 (winter 1984 / 85): 89–103; and Jack Snyder, "Science and Sovietology: Bridging the Methods Gap in Soviet Foreign Policy Studies," *World Politics* 40 (January 1988): 93.

8   See, for example, George Breslauer, *Five Images of the Soviet Future: A Critical Review and Synthesis* (Berkeley: University of California, Institute of International Studies, 1978); Robert Byrnes, ed., *After Brezhnev: The Sources of Soviet Conduct in the 1980s* (Bloomington: Indiana University Press, 1983); and Robert Wesson, ed., *The Soviet Union: Looking to the 1980s* (Stanford: Hoover Institution, 1980).

9   For a good general treatment of this problem, see Richard K. Betts, *Surprise Attack: Lessons for Defense Planning* (Washington, D.C.: Brookings, 1982). On 1973, see Janice Gross Stein, "Calculation, Miscalculation, and Deterrence II: The View from Jerusalem," in *Psychology and Deterrence*, ed. Robert Jervis, Richard Ned Lebow, and Janice Gross Stein (Baltimore: Johns Hopkins University Press, 1985), pp. 60–88. On American intelligence and the placement of Soviet missiles in Cuba, see Richard Ned Lebow and Janice Gross Stein, *We All Lost the Cold War* (Princeton: Princeton University Press, 1994), chap. 14.

10 For a critical evaluation of the performance of Soviet studies with regard to the Gorbachev revolution, see the debate between Jerry Hough and George Breslauer in *Milestones in Glasnost and Perestroika*, ed. Ed Hewett and Victor H. Winston (Washington, D.C.: Brookings, 1991), pp. 465–95.

11 The focus of realism is great-power relations. In describing the postwar political order as stable, realists are referring to the stability of Europe and the de facto, and later de jure, acceptance of its division by East and West. The postwar political order in other regions of the world could hardly be called stable.

12 John Lewis Gaddis, *The Long Peace: Inquiries into the History of the Cold War Era* (New York: Oxford University Press, 1987), 218.

13 See Charles Kindleberger, *The World in Depression, 1929–1939* (Berkeley: University of California Press, 1973); and Gilpin, *War and Change in World Politics*. For critical discussions and alternate explanations, see Robert O. Keohane, *After Hegemony* (Princeton: Princeton University Press, 1984); Robert O. Keohane, *International Institutions and State Power* (Boulder, Colo.: Westview, 1989); Duncan Snidal, "The Limits of Hegemonic Stability Theory," *International Organization* 39 (autumn 1985): 579–614; and Volker Rittberger, ed., *The Study of Regimes in International Relations* (New York: Oxford University Press, 1993).

14 A literature search reveals that between 1970 and 1990 *International Organization*, *World Politics*, and *International Studies Quarterly* published no more than a half-dozen articles whose primary focus was major foreign policy or systemic change.

15 An exception is Gilpin, *War and Change in World Politics*. This point

is also made by three articles in Robert O. Keohane, ed., *Neorealism and Its Critics* (New York: Columbia University Press, 1986): John Gerard Ruggie, "Continuity and Transformation in the World Polity: Toward a Neorealist Synthesis," pp. 131–57; Robert O. Keohane, "Theory of World Politics: Structural Realism and Beyond," pp. 158–203; and Robert W. Cox, "Social Forces, States and World Orders: Beyond International Relations Theory," pp. 204–55. For a critique of cognitive psychology's failure to deal adequately with change, see Richard Ned Lebow and Janice Gross Stein, "Afghanistan, Carter and Foreign Policy Change: The Limits of Cognitive Models," in *Diplomacy, Force, and Leadership: Essays in Honor of Alexander L. George*, ed. Dan Caldwell and Timothy J. McKeown (Boulder, Colo.: Westview, 1993), pp. 95–128.

16   See John J. Mearsheimer, "Back to the Future: Instability in Europe After the Cold War," *International Security* 15 (summer 1990): 5–56. Mearsheimer appears to be making the same argument as Kenneth N. Waltz, "The Emerging Structure of International Politics," paper presented at the annual meeting of the American Political Science Association, San Francisco, August 30–September 2, 1990.

17   Stephen Walt to the author, October 20, 1993.

18   Kenneth N. Waltz, "The Emerging Structure of International Politics," *International Security* 18 (fall 1993): 44–79.

19   Kenneth N. Waltz, "The Emerging Structure of International Politics," third draft of a paper prepared for the annual meeting of the American Political Science Society, San Francisco, August 1990, pp. 7–8.

20   For the Soviet perspective on these early efforts at détente, see James G. Richter, "Perpetuating the Cold War," *Political Science Quarterly* 107 (summer 1992): 271–301; and Lebow and Stein, *We All Lost the Cold War*, chap. 3.

21   The best source on this is Matthew A. Evangelista, "Cooperation Theory and Disarmament Negotiations in the 1950s," *World Politics* 41 (July 1990): 502–28.

22   See Don Oberdorfer, The Turn from the Cold War to a New Era: The United States and the Soviet Union, 1983–1990 (New York: Poseidon, 1991), esp. chs. 1–4; and Robert Scheer's interview with Ronald Reagan during the 1980 primary campaigns in Scheer, With Enough Shovels: Reagan, Bush and Nuclear War (New York: Random House, 1982), p. 242.

23   See Oberdorfer, *The Turn*, chs. 4–7, on the Reagan-Gorbachev summit encounters.

24   Philip E. Tetlock, "Monitoring the Integrative Complexity of American and Soviet Policy Rhetoric: What Can Be Learned?" *Journal of Social Issues* 44 (summer 1988): 819–27; and Philip E. Tetlock, "Learning in U.S. and Soviet Foreign Policy: In Search of an Elusive Concept," in *Learning in U.S. and Soviet Foreign Policy*, ed. George W. Breslauer and Philip E. Tetlock (Boulder, Colo.: Westview, 1991), pp. 20–61.

25   For an alternate point of view, see Keith L. Shimko, "Reagan on the Soviet Union and the Nature of International Conflict," *Political Psychology* 13 (September 1992): 353–78.

26   See, for example, Mearsheimer, "Back to the Future"; Steven Van Evera, "Primed for Peace: Europe After the Cold War," *International Security* 15 (winter 1990 / 91): 7–57; Goldgeier and McFaul, "A Tale of Two Worlds"; Robert Jervis, "The Future of World Politics: Will It Resemble the Past," *International Security* 16 (winter 1991 / 92): 39–73; and Charles Kupchan and Clifford Kupchan, "Concerts, Collective Security, and the Future of Europe," *International Security* 16 (summer 1991): 114–61.

27   A similar argument has been made by Goldgeier and McFaul, "A Tale of Two Worlds."

2

*The Long Peace,
the End of the Cold War,
and the Failure of Realism

Nation-states are engaged in a never-ending struggle to improve or preserve their relative power positions.
—Robert Gilpin, *U.S. Power and the Multinational Corporation*

The greatness of the idea of European integration on democratic foundations consists in its capacity to overcome the old Herderian idea of the nation state as the highest expression of national life.
—Václav Havel, *New York Review of Books*

The dramatic events of 1989 to 1991 are widely recognized to have ushered in a new era in international relations. Prominent realists maintain that a shift from bi- to multipolarity is under way in the international system. Some of them predict that a multipolar world will be more conflictual and urge states to acquire nuclear weapons.[1] Realists and neorealists alike argue that superpower behavior since 1945 is consistent with their theories. I contend that it sharply contradicts them.

I develop my argument by looking at realist explanations for three of the more important international developments of the last half-century: the "long peace" between the superpowers, the Soviet Union's renunciation of its empire and leading role as a superpower, and the post–Cold War transformation of the international system. Realist theories at the international level address the first and third of these developments, and realist theories at the unit level have made an ex post facto attempt to account for the second. The weakness of these explanations raises serious problems for the realist paradigm.

*The author gratefully acknowledges the support of the Hewlett Foundation and the United States Institute of Peace. I would also like to acknowledge the helpful comments of Friedrich Kratochwil, John Odell, Kenneth A. Oye, Thomas Risse-Kappen, Janice Gross Stein, and Stephen Walt.

Evaluating Realism

The realist paradigm is based on the core assumption that anarchy is the defining characteristic of the international system. Anarchy compels states to make security their paramount concern. Security is a function of power, defined as capability relative to other states. Drawing on the core assumption of anarchy and the self-help system it allegedly engenders, realists have advanced a variety of sometimes contradictory propositions about international relations. Realists disagree, among other things, about the relative war-proneness and stability of multipolar versus bipolar international systems, the importance and consequences of nuclear weapons, and, more fundamentally, about the weight of power as an explanation of state behavior. The competing predictions of realist theories make realism difficult to falsify. Almost any outcome can be made consistent with some variant of realist theory.

Operationalization

Testable theories require careful conceptual and operational definitions of their dependent and independent variables. These definitions must be conceptually precise and stipulate how the variables are to be measured or their presence determined. Realist theories do not meet these conditions. They do not share common definitions of the core concepts they use to construct variables. Individual definitions of *national interest*, *power*, *balance of power*, and *polarity* allow for an unacceptably wide range of conceptual and operational meaning and make it difficult to test realist propositions against evidence drawn from specific cases. Neorealism, the most scientifically self-conscious of realist theories, is particularly inadequate in this regard, as my critique of its explanation for the "long peace" will demonstrate.

Specification

Theories must stipulate the conditions associated with predicted outcomes. If the conditions are met but repeatedly fail to produce the predicted outcomes, the theories can be rejected. If predicted and unpredicted outcomes occur, the theories have been inadequately specified.

Power transition theories constitute the branch of realism that analyzes great-power responses to decline. These theories failed to envisage the possibility of a peaceful accommodation between the two poles of a bipolar system or that one of them would voluntarily relinquish its core sphere of influence to bring about that accommodation. Such an anomalous outcome constitutes strong grounds for rejecting power transition theories. Realists have sought to save their core insights by treating the end of the Cold War as a special case and reformulating their propositions to take it into account.[2] Anomalous cases often serve as the catalyst for better theory. But as the second part of my critique will show, realist attempts ex post facto to explain Mikhail Gorbachev's reorientation of Soviet foreign policy are neither logically consistent nor empirically persuasive.

Utility

Good theory is based on good assumptions. Realists maintain that their core assumption of anarchy accurately captures the dynamics of the international system and generates powerful explanations of interstate behavior. Some recent literature contends that the assumption of anarchy has no theoretical content and cannot generate useful or testable propositions.[3] I contend that international structure is not determining. Fear of anarchy and its consequences encouraged key international actors to modify their behavior with the goal of changing that structure. The pluralist security community that has developed among the democratic, industrial powers is in part the result of this process. This community and the end of the Cold War provide evidence that states can escape from the security dilemma.

A Critical Case?

At the final session of a 1991 conference at Cornell University on international relations theory and the end of the Cold War, a prominent participant expressed his dissatisfaction with the proceedings. The end of the Cold War, he insisted, was "a mere data point" that could not be used to test or develop theory. However, neorealism drew on a single case of bipolarity to construct its theory. If that case does not fit the theory, it raises serious doubts about the validity of the theory. Other realist theories have cast their empirical nets more widely. But the end of the Cold War and the ongoing transformation of international relations also raise serious problems for these theories. This essay does not test in a formal sense any of these theories; such tests are precluded by the lack of specification as well as by my own reliance on only a few cases. Rather, I will attempt to demonstrate that historical evidence since 1945 contradicts many realist claims and expectations and suggests the need for alternative approaches to the study of international relations.

Realism and the Long Peace

Security specialists consider it remarkable that the superpowers did not go to war as did rival hegemons of the past. Many realist theories attribute the absence of war to the bipolar nature of the postwar international system, which they consider less war-prone than the multipolar world it replaced. All of them have poorly specified definitions of bipolarity. None of the measures of bipolarity derived from these theories sustains a characterization of the international system as bipolar before the mid-1950s at the earliest.

For the sake of brevity, I will discuss only two realist theories that emphasize the restraining effects of bipolarity, those of Hans Morgenthau and Kenneth Waltz. They are arguably the most influential international relations theories of the Cold War era.

Measures of Power and Polarity

The first edition of *Politics Among Nations* (1948) coincided with the beginning of the Cold War; in that and subsequent editions, Morgenthau worried that the United States and the Soviet Union would stumble into a nuclear war despite their mutual recognition of its destructiveness. For Morgenthau, the long peace was not an analytical puzzle but a desperate hope.[4]

Morgenthau believed that postwar international relations was shaped by bipolarity and nuclear weapons. Both were double-edged swords. Bipolarity was "a mechanism that contains in itself the potentialities for unheard-of good as well as for unprecedented evil." It "made the hostile opposition of two gigantic power blocs possible" but also held out the hope of regulating that opposition through an equilibrium of power maintained by moderate competition. Nuclear weapons made leaders more cautious and more insecure. The nuclear arms race reduced international politics to a "primitive spectacle of two giants eying each other with watchful suspicion." Human survival depended on mutual restraint. This was not a function of the international system's polarity but of the skill and commitment of leaders.[5]

Drawing on Morgenthau's insight that bipolarity had the potential to promote a more stable international order, Waltz built a formal deductive theory of international relations.[6] In an effort to create a parsimonious theory at the system level, he gave explanatory weight to the nature of the system, the number of actors, and the distribution of their capabilities and downplayed the explanatory power of state attributes, including leadership.

Writing in the late 1970s, Waltz was struck by the seeming stability of the postwar order and the success of the superpowers in defying earlier predictions that the Cold War would sooner or later turn hot. He attributed the absence of war to bipolarity, which, he maintained, was less war-prone than multipolarity. Waltz argued that war arose primarily because of miscalculation; states misjudged the relative power or the power and cohesion of opposing coalitions. The latter error was more common because of the difficulty of estimating accurately the power and cohesion of shifting and often unstable coalitions. In a bipolar world, where hegemons rely on their own vastly superior power for their security, coalitions are less important, and "uncertainty lessens and calculations are easier to make."[7]

Waltz regarded military technology as a unit attribute and outside his theory. He sought to minimize its consequences and insisted that the "perennial forces of politics" were more important than nuclear weapons in shaping the behavior of nations. Nuclear adversaries "may have stronger incentives to avoid war" than did conventionally armed states, but then the United States and the Soviet Union also found it more difficult to learn to live with each other "than more experienced and less ideological adversaries would have."[8]

Waltz's *Theory of International Politics* has one major dependent variable, the war-proneness of international systems, that is explained by one independent variable, the polarity of the system. The theory resides entirely at the system level: war-proneness is a system property, and polarity is a structural characteristic of the system. Waltz is unyielding in his contention that a theory of international relations should not incorporate variables at the unit level or use system-level properties to predict the behavior of individual units. Bipolarity affects state behavior only indirectly by structuring constraints and incentives for leaders.[9]

Many international relations scholars and historians contend that nuclear weapons have played a far more important role in preserving the peace than Waltz's theory acknowledged. Waltz has come to accept the contention of his critics. In 1981 he upgraded the role of nuclear weapons, arguing that they "have been the second force working for peace in the post-war world." In 1986 he conceded that the introduction of nuclear weapons, a unit-level change, had a system-level effect. In a 1990 essay, Waltz went further and argued that "the longest peace yet known has rested on two pillars: bipolarity and nuclear weapons." Nuclear weapons deterred attacks on states' "vital interests," and "because strategic weapons serve that end and no other, peace has held at the center through almost five postwar decades, while war has frequently raged at the periphery." Waltz reaffirmed this argument in 1993.[10]

Waltz's 1990 essay argued that the international system was undergoing a peaceful transition from bipolarity to multipolarity.

Neorealism recognized the possibility of system change — although not peaceful system change — but maintained that multipolar systems were more war-prone. While not rejecting this core proposition of neorealism, the essay indicated that it was no longer relevant. The long peace would endure because the superpowers possessed nuclear weapons. Waltz was arguing that nuclear weapons, by his definition a unit-level capability, can explain war-proneness, the most important system-level property. Such a reductionist argument vitiates the need for a theory of international relations whose principal purpose is to explain war-proneness. This may be why Waltz has subsequently backed away from his characterization of the international system as moving from bipolar to multipolar.

Waltz now insists that the international system remains bipolar even after the breakup of the Soviet Union.[11] His depiction of the post–Cold War world as bipolar is strikingly at odds with the views of other prominent realists. More to the point, it cannot be derived from the definition of power in his *Theory of International Politics*. Even before the collapse of the Soviet Union, U.S. Defense Department studies showed that the United States, Japan, and Western Europe were steadily increasing their lead over the Soviet Union in the development and application of almost all the technologies critical to military power and performance.[12] Post-Soviet Russia is in a demonstrably weaker position.

What Distribution? What Capabilities?

Realist definitions of power are imprecise, making it difficult to develop measures of polarity. The most thoughtful treatment of capabilities remains that of Hans Morgenthau. In his chapter in *Politics Among Nations* on the elements of national power, he reviewed the physical and political components of power. These include size, population, natural resources, industrial capacity, military preparedness, national character, morale, and the quality of diplomacy and government. The discussion is enlightening for the emphasis it placed on the less tangible and less easily measured political components of national power.

Morgenthau was adamant that no one factor adequately captures the power of a state and castigated previous authors for this fallacy. Nevertheless, in his discussion of industrial capacity, he described it as the defining characteristic of great powers and of bipolarity. The Soviet Union, he insisted, always had the potential of a great power, but only became one "when it entered the ranks of the foremost industrial powers in the 30s, and it became the rival of the United States as the other super power only when it acquired in the 50s the industrial capacity for waging nuclear war." [13]

Morgenthau's formulation of bipolarity offers little help to scholars interested in explaining the long peace. His equation of superpower status with "the industrial capacity for waging nuclear war" supports his judgment that the Soviet Union became a superpower sometime in the 1950s. There is a consensus among other realists that bipolarity and the long peace date from 1945. Morgenthau's characterization of superpower status is also vague because it leaves the threshold of nuclear capability undefined. If it is the capability to produce nuclear weapons, the Soviet Union could be considered a superpower in 1948. If it is the capability to produce significant numbers of nuclear weapons and the requisite means of their delivery, the Soviet Union did not achieve superpower status until sometime in the mid-1960s.

Waltz's conceptualization of power is similar to Morgenthau's, from which it is derived. Like Morgenthau, he insists that states do not become superpowers because they excel in one category of power. Rank is determined by how a state scores on all its components: size of population and territory, resource endowment, economic capability, military strength, political stability, and competence. Waltz ignores his own caveat, however, and reduces superpower status to one component. "In international affairs," he writes, "force remains the final arbiter," and the United States and the Soviet Union "are set apart from the others . . . by their ability to exploit military technology on a large scale and at the scientific frontiers." [14]

Waltz's use of military capability as the indicator of superpower status is puzzling. He is adamant that "nuclear weapons did not cause the condition of bipolarity." He insists that the world was bipolar in the late 1940s, when the Soviet Union had no nuclear weapons, and has not become multipolar since other states have acquired them. "Nuclear weapons do not equalize the power of nations because they do not change the economic bases of a nation's power." The superpowers are set apart "not by particular weapons systems but by their ability to exploit military technology on a large scale and at the scientific frontiers." Had the atom never been split, the superpowers would still "far surpass others in military strength, and each would remain the greatest threat and source of potential danger to the other." [15]

Waltz seems to argue, like Morgenthau, that superpower status is primarily a function of advanced scientific and industrial capability. It is this capability that permits the superpowers to deploy state-of-

RICHARD NED LEBOW

the-art weapons and to field large, well-equipped conventional forces. Nuclear weapons are a symbol not a cause of great-power status, and countries that develop these weapons in the absence of similarly advanced industrial and scientific infrastructures do not become superpowers.

On the basis of Waltz's criteria, the Soviet Union was not a superpower in the 1940s. At the end of World War II, and for a long time thereafter, its gross national product was a fraction of that of the United States. In 1947 its industrial base and output were roughly comparable to Britain's—each produced 12 percent of the world's steel in comparison to the United States' 54 percent, and 12 and 9 percent, respectively, of the world's energy in comparison to the United States' 49 percent. Britain had more engineers, a better and denser transportation network, and a highly developed financial base.[16] Soviet technology remained backward. The Red Army was equipped with inferior weapons. Its triumph over Germany was the result of sheer mass and the ability of an authoritarian regime to mobilize almost all available resources for its military effort. The Soviet Union did not produce a jet engine until the late 1940s, and that was a copy of a Rolls Royce engine obtained after the war. It exploded an atomic device in 1949, but Britain also possessed the knowledge to produce nuclear weapons.

What distinguished the Soviet Union from Britain was its population and size, but this had always been so and did not make the Soviet Union a superpower before World War II. The Soviet Union fielded a massive army, but it had proportionately larger forces than everyone else in 1939. The postwar Red Army was capable of little beyond its primary mission of occupation. American military estimates in the late 1940s depicted it as a poorly equipped, poorly trained, poorly led force without the logistical base to sustain a major offensive in Western Europe.[17] Until at least the mid-1950s, if not later, there was little the Soviet Union could do to damage the United States, while throughout this period it was vulnerable to nuclear attack by long-range American bombers. The Soviet Union remained a regional power until it developed a blue-water navy and airborne power projection capabilities in the early 1970s.

By Waltz's criteria, the international system must be considered unipolar in the late 1940s. It did not become bipolar until the mid-1950s at the earliest. This was the assessment of Hans Morgenthau, who used a similar definition of bipolarity. It is also the conclusion of Peter Beckman, who carried out the most rigorous attempt to date to measure relative power in this period.[18] Combining scores for most

30

of Waltz's components of power, Beckman ranked the United States first in 1947 with a score of 53, followed by the Soviet Union and Great Britain with scores of 9 and 6, respectively. By 1955 the Soviet Union had begun to narrow the gap: the United States led at 41, the Soviet Union was second at 15, and Britain and West Germany each scored 4. The United States was still more than twice as powerful as the Soviet Union. The Soviet Union had exploded a thermonuclear device, but it is questionable if it met Waltz's condition of being at the scientific frontiers of industrial and military technology.

The year the Soviet Union acquired superpower status is unimportant. What is relevant for our purposes is that by Waltz's definition, the Soviet Union was not a superpower in the late 1940s and early 1950s. The great-power peace that survived the tensest stage of the Cold War—the years of the Czech coup, the first Berlin crisis and blockade, and the Korean War—cannot be attributed to bipolarity.

In 1990 Waltz and John Mearsheimer argued that bipolarity was coming to an end or had already disappeared.[19] They predicted the emergence of a multipolar system with all its associated tensions or a system that would retain some of the benefits of bipolarity because of the presence of nuclear weapons. Their contention that the world was in the course of a system transformation was not derived from neorealist theory.

If power is a function of size of population and territory, resource endowment, economic capability, military strength, political stability and competence, then in 1985, when Gorbachev assumed office, the Soviet Union could be considered a superpower. Neorealists certainly argued that this was so. By 1990, when Waltz contended that the shift to multipolarity was under way, the Soviet Union still arguably met these criteria. Its economy had declined, but its relative standing was the same, and its population, territory, resource endowment, and military strength were unchanged. In 1990 the world remained bipolar. In the judgment of many prominent realists, it was not until the breakup of the Soviet Union that bipolarity came to an end.[20]

In 1990 Waltz and Mearsheimer each claimed that a system transformation was under way because of the Soviet Union's political and military retreat from Eastern Europe. Although this retreat was startling and dramatic, there are no theoretical grounds for using it as an indicator of a system transformation. By the criteria expounded in Theory of International Politics, it did not affect the distribution of capabilities. Neorealism, moreover, maintains that alliances are much less important in a bipolar world. The two hegemons were so powerful vis-à-vis third parties that they did not need alliances to guarantee their security. Gorbachev's retreat from Eastern Europe might even be interpreted as confirmation of this proposition and as evidence that the international system remains bipolar. Neorealist theory would not expect a great power to behave this way in a multipolar world.

Since 1990 the pace of change in the international system has accelerated. The Warsaw Pact and the Soviet Union have ceased to exist. Post-Soviet Russia is a smaller, less populous state, consumed with the problems of political instability, ethnic fragmentation, and precipitous economic decline. Its leaders have sought aid from their former adversaries to build housing in Russia for troops to be withdrawn from the Baltic republics and requested technical assistance to dismantle old nuclear weapons for which the blueprints have been lost. The Kremlin no longer attempts to expand its influence but instead uses what little leverage it has to extract economic concessions from the West.

Russia's nuclear arsenal remains robust—if considerably smaller because so much of it is in Ukraine or in the process of being dismantled—but its conventional forces have undergone a notable decline in size and effectiveness. Most armored divisions lack spare parts and effective maintenance, and much of the former Soviet navy is rotting in port and unable to put to sea. With the economic disruption that followed the breakup of the Soviet Union and the partial dismantling of its command economy, Russia has fallen further behind the West in the development and deployment of state-of-the-art weapons and has lost for the foreseeable future the ability to exploit military technology "on a large scale and at the scientific frontiers." Many of its leading scientists and engineers have gone abroad in search of employment.

Waltz's 1993 article acknowledges that "no state lacking the military ability to compete with the other great powers has ever been ranked among them." He nevertheless contends that Russia is a superpower and the international system bipolar.[21] By any reasonable application of Waltz's criteria, the international system has shifted in the direction of unipolarity.

Even this cursory review indicates that bipolarity cannot satisfactorily explain the long peace. When Waltz's definition of bipolarity is applied to the postwar international system, it lends support to Morgenthau's contention that the system did not become bipolar until at least the mid-1950s—after the most acute confrontations of the Cold War.[22] Different operational criteria of bipolarity do not provide a better fit with the long peace. No single measure—or combination of the components of power identified as important by realists—indicates the onset of bipolarity in 1945 and its passing from 1985 to 1990.

Waltz insists that the determination of polarity is a simple matter. "We need only rank [the powers] roughly by capability." The question of polarity "is an empirical one, common sense can answer it."[23] Yet differences among realists, and between the Waltz of 1990 and that of 1993 about when the international system became bipolar and when bipolarity ended (or if it did)—indicate that common sense offers no help in determining polarity. For this, well-specified definitions of polarity and measures of power are required.[24]

Realism and Declining Hegemony

Realist theories are found at the system and unit levels. Realist and neorealist theories that attempt to explain the absence of superpower war since 1945 operate at the system level. Realist theories that predict the foreign policy of individual states operate at the unit level, and it is to these theories I now turn to try to explain recent changes in the foreign policy of one of the two poles of a bipolar international system. For realists, these two levels of analysis are distinct but related. Changes in unit-level behavior can alter the distribution of capabilities and by doing so change the polarity of the international system. A transformation of the international system will in turn have important consequences for unit-level behavior.

Realism recognizes that great powers and superpowers can experience sharp relative declines. Some realist theories incorporate the Hegelian notion that successful expansion inevitably carries with it the seeds of subsequent decay.[25] All realist theories that address the question are unambiguous in their prediction that declining states, in the words of Kenneth Waltz, "try to arrest or reverse their decline."[26] Realists contend that states have no choice. Because of the anarchical character of the international system, they must maintain their relative power or risk being victimized by others.

Power Transition Theories and the Soviet Union

Within the realist paradigm, power transition theories focus specifically on the problem of hegemonic decline and its consequences.[27] Many of these theories argue that hegemonic war is most likely to occur when the power capabilities of a rising and dissatisfied challenger increase to the point where they approach those of the dominant state. They differ in their prediction about whether the challenger or the declining hegemon will initiate the war.[28]

Not all power transition theories maintain that hegemonic decline will inevitably lead to war. Robert Gilpin argues that the first and most attractive response is to launch a preemptive war against the rising power while the declining state still has a military advantage. A declining power can also expand against third parties in the hope of obtaining more secure frontiers and thereby reducing the burden of defense. The Romans were past masters at this strategy. The Austrian and Russian empires tried with less success: their efforts to expand in the Balkans was a major cause of war in 1914.[29]

Gilpin describes retrenchment as a more peaceful response to decline. A state can try to slow its decline and preserve the core of its power by abandoning some of its peripheral commitments. The Roman, Byzantine, and Venetian empires conducted strategic withdrawals at different times in their history, and Gilpin considers the Nixon Doctrine a possible modern analogue. Declining states can also retrench through alliance and accommodation with less threatening powers, sharing the benefits of hegemony in return for assistance in its preservation. Britain pursued this strategy with considerable success in the decade before World War I. The most difficult form of retrenchment is appeasement. It attempts to buy off a rising challenger through concessions. When appeasement conveys weakness, as it did at Munich in 1938, it can encourage further demands. Gilpin asserts that all forms of retrenchment are fraught with danger and less attractive than expansionist strategies.[30]

War and Change in World Politics was published in 1981. In analyzing hegemonic decline, Gilpin's focus was very much on the United States and the possible consequences of its continuing economic and military decline. He foresaw the possibility of a relative Soviet decline, brought about by an American resurgence and alliances with an increasingly powerful Japan, China, and Western Europe. He worried that a superpower in decline, facing the prospect of encirclement, would respond by behaving more aggressively.[31]

Until the late 1980s, Soviet foreign policy appeared consistent with realist theories. Moscow tried to expand its influence in the Third World and consolidate it in Eastern Europe. Soviet leaders suppressed rebellions in East Germany in 1953 and in Hungary in 1956, invaded Czechoslovakia in 1968 to restore hard-line communists to power, and used the threat of intervention in 1980 to keep Solidarity from power in Poland.

Under Gorbachev, Soviet foreign policy became increasingly inconsistent with power transition and other realist theories. Military disengagement from Afghanistan, carried out in 1988–1989, could be explained as retrenchment at the periphery. The 1987 treaty on intermediate nuclear forces was problematic because it clearly was not motivated by a concern for relative gain. The Soviet Union agreed to remove many more missiles from the European theater than did the United States, and the treaty was widely interpreted as advantageous to the West.

The Soviet withdrawal from Eastern Europe was more anomalous. Realists like Gilpin who recognize retrenchment as a possible response to decline expect it to occur at the periphery, not in a primary sphere of influence. In all of Gilpin's examples, states retrenched to marshal their resources against a rising challenger. The Soviet retreat, by contrast, appears to have been motivated by a combination of ideological and domestic political considerations.[32]

The Soviet Union retreated from a region whose control had always been regarded as essential to blunt attack from the West. The communist governments of Eastern Europe faced opposition, especially in Poland, but were firmly in control until they were undermined by Gorbachev's calls for reform and his promise not to use Soviet forces to interfere with democratization. Gorbachev may have been surprised by the pace of change but not by its results. He and his advisers had began discussing the possibility of cutting loose Eastern Europe as early as 1987.[33]

The Soviet retreat from Eastern Europe not only went far beyond any realist conception of retrenchment; it stands in sharp contrast to a core realist assumption: hegemons are expected to make every possible effort to retain their principal sphere of influence. This proposition can be traced back to Thucydides, from whom realists claim descent.[34] One of the most famous speeches in his history is the Athenian defense of their empire before the Spartan assembly. The Athenians made no pretense of their motives or the expected consequences of acting otherwise:

> And the nature of the case first compelled us to advance our empire to its present height, fear being our principal motive, though honour and interest afterwards came in. And at last, when almost all hated us, when some had already revolted and had been subdued, when you had ceased to be the friends you once were, and had become objects of suspicion and dislike, it appeared no longer safe to give up our empire, especially as all who left us would fall to you. And no one can quarrel with a people for making, in matters of tremendous risk, the best provision that it can for its interest.[35]

Joseph Stalin, Nikita Khrushchev, and Leonid Brezhnev would never have made such a revealing speech, but it captures their motives nicely. Like Cimon and Pericles before them, they ruled their alliance-cum-empire with an iron hand for fear that any defection would put the alliance as a whole at risk and constitute an intolerable threat to their security. Realists accepted these Soviet concerns as legitimate, and many deemed preservation of the Soviet position in Eastern Europe essential to superpower peace.[36] How then can they explain the Soviet retreat?

The Soviet response to relative decline confounds existing realist theories in other important ways. Instead of launching a preventive war, the Soviet Union sought an accommodation with the United States, its principal adversary and rival hegemon, and made concessions that greatly enhanced the relative power of the United States and its NATO ally, the Federal Republic of Germany. Under Gorbachev and Boris Yeltsin, Moscow has been content to play a subordinate role in international affairs.[37]

The Soviet response to decline is not captured by any realist theory. At the very least, those theories are underspecified. They need first to identify all the generic responses of great powers to decline and specify the conditions under which each will apply. Until they do, the realist paradigm consists of a fundamental axiom — that the pursuit of power is the principal objective of states — and a collection of loose propositions and underspecified theories that attempt to apply this maxim in diverse and sometimes contradictory ways. This makes it impossible for realists to predict much of anything before the fact but all too easy for them to explain anything once it has occurred.

Realism After the Fact

Some realists contend ex post facto that Soviet foreign policy after 1985 was not inconsistent with realist theories and is a logical and long overdue response to the Soviet Union's economic decline. Perestroika and glasnost were intended to revitalize the economy and provide the resources necessary for the Soviet Union to resume the role of a superpower. Foreign policy was temporarily subordinated to this goal. Gorbachev withdrew the Red Army from Afghanistan, negotiated nuclear and conventional arms control agreements with NATO, and retreated from Eastern Europe to free economic resources and labor for agriculture and industry. Withdrawal from Eastern Europe would also help secure loans and credits from West.[38]

This explanation is not persuasive. If Gorbachev had been a moderate reformer whose foreign policy was essentially an extension of Brezhnev's, the same realists who now advance this explanation would have regarded Soviet policy as entirely consistent with their theoretical expectations. None of them would have insisted that the Soviet Union's relative decline demanded a leader who would introduce Western-style democratic reforms, hold relatively free elections, acknowledge the legal right of republics to secede from the Soviet Union, encourage anticommunist revolutions in Eastern Europe, agree to dissolve the Warsaw Pact, withdraw Soviet forces from the territories of its former members, accept the reunification of Germany within NATO, and exercise restraint when confronted with growing demands for independence by constituent republics of the USSR. Such recommendations, let alone a prediction that all this would soon come to pass, would have been greeted derisively as the height of *un*realism.

Soviet foreign policy had been living beyond its means for a long time. Stalin, Khrushchev, and Brezhnev all pursued enormously expensive military and aid programs. Brezhnev did this well after the disparity between Soviet goals and resources had become painfully apparent. By the mid-1970s, the Soviet growth rate had declined to about 2 percent; by the end of the decade, growth had stopped. Throughout this period, military spending was relatively constant and consumed an increasing share of the gross national product.[39] How does a realist explanation that depicts Gorbachev's radical reorientation of Soviet domestic and foreign policy as a response to the country's declining economy account for the status quo under Brezhnev?

Realists might respond that their theories predict trends, not timing. Leaders and political systems vary enormously in their responsiveness to changing capabilities. Brezhnev was slow to recognize the country's economic problems and reluctant to initiate the necessary changes. As the economy deteriorated, dissatisfaction with the status quo mounted and facilitated the rise to power of a reformist leader.

This interpretation is belied by the evidence. Brezhnev allocated enormous sums to the military, weapons research and development, and foreign aid in the hope of making the Soviet Union a global power equal of the United States. He was nevertheless increasingly disturbed by the downward trend of the Soviet economy and its long-term implications for the Soviet Union's status as a superpower. By the early 1970s, he recognized that the Soviet economy was performing sluggishly and that the gap between the Soviet Union and the West was likely to increase. He tried to rectify this situation through a series of limited reforms intended to rationalize planning and investment. He also supported détente with the West to gain access to advanced foreign technology.[40]

Brezhnev's strategy failed. Administrative reform and massive investment in agriculture accomplished very little. The cumbersome command economy, which Brezhnev and his colleagues hoped to reform and make more efficient, was the cause of, not the solution to, the Soviet Union's economic malaise. Détente also failed to produce the expected transfer of technology from the West; this was the principal reason Brezhnev was willing to sacrifice it in pursuit of unilateral advantage in the Third World.

The stasis of Brezhnev's later years was not the result of political *immobilisme*. Far-reaching reforms or shifts in spending priorities would undeniably have antagonized some of the powerful interests, especially the military, that Brezhnev had initially co-opted to build and sustain his authority. However, Brezhnev had long since consolidated his authority to the point where he could have promoted major policy initiatives without fear of being overthrown. A more likely explanation is his inability, after the failure of his reforms, to see any alternative, or at least one that would not pose a challenge to the Soviet political system and the privileges of its *nomenklatura*. In his last years, ill health probably also took its toll.

Considering Brezhnev's goals and the constraints he faced, his foreign and domestic policies, while ultimately unsuccessful, were nevertheless a direct response to the Soviet Union's perceived decline. He attempted to manage that decline by strengthening central authority and providing the military with enough state-of-the-art technology to maintain the Soviet Union's claim to superpower status. To buttress Moscow's position in Eastern Europe, he sought and obtained Western recognition of the region's Soviet-imposed regimes and territorial boundaries. He allowed these regimes more latitude for economic experimentation, including trade and investment links with the West.

A more persuasive realist argument would recognize Brezhnev's attempt to cope with the relative decline of the Soviet Union and depict Gorbachev's strategy as a more extreme version prompted by the bleaker circumstances of the mid-1980s. Certainly, the programs of the two leaders share many similarities. Like Brezhnev, Gorbachev sought to revitalize the Soviet economy through domestic reform and accommodation with the West while preserving the core of Soviet state structure — its command economy and all-powerful Communist Party. Gorbachev's more radical domestic reforms

38

and his accommodation with the West might be explained as a response to the further decline in relative Soviet capabilities.

This interpretation of Gorbachev is equally problematic. The Soviet Union's economic decline was gradual if persistent during the years between the failure of Brezhnev's reforms and Mikhail S. Gorbachev's accession to power in 1985. Moreover, its relative decline was only marginal, because these were not years of great growth for the United States, which was itself a declining power relative to Japan and the European Economic Community. The sharp downturn in the Soviet economy came only after Gorbachev began his reforms, and largely as a result of them.

The shadow of the future might also be invoked to account for the differences between the two leaders. Brezhnev was pessimistic but anticipated only a gradual erosion of the Soviet Union's relative standing. By 1985, on the other hand, the Soviet political elite regarded the future with deep foreboding; the economy had stopped growing — budgetary shortfalls were anticipated — and the cost of military competition with the West had increased. There were compelling reasons for Gorbachev to adopt a more radical, if risky approach to economic reform.

Gorbachev was undeniably committed to revitalizing the Soviet economy. However, in his six years in power Gorbachev talked a lot about the need for economic restructuring but took few meaningful steps in that direction. Until 1989 he made no major cuts in defense spending. Between 1985 and 1989 defense consumed about the same percentage of GNP as it had under Brezhnev. After 1989 it consumed more.[41] Gorbachev never attempted to dismantle the command economy or to encourage private, capitalist ventures. He backed away from his most important initiatives in this direction when they encountered opposition from conservative party and public opinion. Until the unsuccessful coup of August 1991, he remained committed to the leading role of a reformed Communist Party in the political and economic life of the country. Gorbachev the reformer struggled to preserve archaic and dysfunctional domestic structures that stood in the way of the economic growth necessary to preserve the Soviet Union as a great power.

The realist contention that Gorbachev's domestic reforms were "an externally imposed necessity" is conceptually and empirically flawed.[42] It is outside of any realist theory and not derived logically from realist assumptions. Realists who make the argument contend that decline can be a catalyst for change. Granted that this is a valid proposition, it is not a helpful one. The policies of Brezhnev and

Gorbachev indicate different responses to decline. Other possibilities include a more aggressive foreign policy — as predicted by most power transition theories — or an ostrich policy that denies the problem — the apparent preference of Russia's current "red-brown" coalition between former communists and the nationalist right. As mentioned above, to account for Gorbachev, realist theories would have both to identify the range of responses to decline and specify the conditions under which each is likely to be adopted.

Even then, Gorbachev's foreign policy would still constitute a problem because it went way beyond the requirements of realism. In Eastern Europe, there was a range of options short of those the Soviet Union took (allowing pro-Western governments to come to power, dismantling the Warsaw Pact, withdrawing Soviet forces, and agreeing to the unification of Germany within NATO). For example, Gorbachev could have permitted domestic change in Eastern Europe but made it clear that the Soviet Union expected postcommunist governments to remain within the Warsaw Pact. Far from opposing such a compromise, the United States and the European members of NATO would almost certainly have welcomed it and displayed sensitivity to Soviet security concerns. Yet Gorbachev never seriously explored that option. On the contrary, in his famous April 1987 speech in Prague, he called on East Europeans to reform their own political systems and did nothing to dampen the resulting mass protests when they threatened the survival of many of the region's communist regimes.

It is very difficult to reconcile Soviet foreign policy in Eastern Europe with realism. Neorealists might argue that alliances are less important in a bipolar world because the superpowers do not depend on alliances for their security the way great powers do in a multipolar world. But this postulate applied equally well to the Soviet Union of Khrushchev and Brezhnev, both of whom went to great lengths to preserve the Soviet position in Eastern Europe. In two Berlin crises, Khrushchev even risked war with the United States to shore up the faltering authority of East Germany's communist regime.

Nuclear deterrence as an explanation is even more problematic. Some realists have argued that Gorbachev withdrew from Eastern Europe because of his confidence in nuclear deterrence; the Soviet Union no longer needed a defensive glacis to protect it from invasion.[43] But why then did Brezhnev invade Czechoslovakia and threaten to invade Poland to restore and preserve pro-Soviet governments? Nuclear deterrence was a reality in 1968 and was certainly as robust in 1980 as it was in 1985.

Nuclear deterrence is intended to protect a state or its protégés against attack. No realist contends that it is effective against internal threats to security arising from ideological or ethnic opposition. But this is a principal reason why past Soviet leaders maintained their authority in Eastern Europe. Before ordering the Warsaw Pact into Czechoslovakia, Leonid Brezhnev confided to Polish leader, Wladaslaw Gomulka, that all pact nations needed to participate in the invasion because in the absence of Eastern bloc solidarity, unrest might spill over into the Soviet Ukraine.[44] Brezhnev's remark indicates that Soviet leaders subscribed to a domino theory in Eastern Europe. They worried that the loss of any Warsaw Pact country would destroy the alliance and that the demise of the alliance would seriously weaken their hold on the western border provinces of the Soviet Union, whose peoples were unreconciled to Soviet rule and wanted independence or reunification with their compatriots across their borders. The events of 1990–1991 demonstrated the validity of Brezhnev's fears.

The most fundamental tenet of realism is that states act to preserve their territorial integrity. Gorbachev's decision to abandon Eastern Europe's communist regimes wittingly called the integrity of the Soviet Union into question. It triggered demands for independence from the Baltics to Central Asia that led to the demise of the Soviet state. Soviet foreign policy under Gorbachev is outside the paradigm. To explain it, the analyst too must go outside the paradigm and look at the determining influence of domestic politics, belief systems, and learning.[45]

The Emerging International System(s)

The Hobbesian world of realism recognizes only two ordering principles: anarchy and hierarchy. Unipolar worlds are characterized by hierarchy. Multi- and bipolar systems are anarchical, although there is likely to be more structure in a bipolar system because of the way each hegemon dominates its own bloc or alliance system. A tight bipolar world might even be described as two hierarchies competing under conditions of anarchy.

Stalin imposed a tight, hierarchical structure on the Soviet bloc. The Western alliance was always much looser. Paradoxically, the hierarchy of both blocs began to decline almost as soon as the international system became bipolar in the mid-1950s. By the late 1970s, the United States was at best primus inter pares within NATO. It had to negotiate changes in military doctrine, weapons deployments, and arms control policies with its allies, and consultations and negotiations frequently led to compromises that bore little relationship to the distribution of power within the alliance. The influence of the United States in NATO and with many of its non-NATO allies was constrained by norms of cooperation and consensus that benefited less powerful allies. On arms control and other issues, some of these allies also benefited from transnational coalitions that imposed constraints on the U.S. capacity to shape NATO policy.[46]

The international system is still technically anarchical because there is no enforcement authority. However, relations among the developed, democratic states of Western Europe, North America, Asia, and Oceania, can hardly be characterized as a self-help system. The allegedly inescapable consequences of anarchy have been largely overcome by a complex web of institutions that govern interstate relations and provide mechanisms for resolving disputes. These institutions reflect and help sustain a consensus in favor of consultation and compromise that mute the consequences of power imbalances among states. In the course of two generations, a community of nations has evolved that is bound together by the realization that national security and economic well-being require close cooperation and coordination with other democratic and democratizing states.[47]

In 1957 Karl W. Deutsch and colleagues developed the concept of a security community where "there is a real assurance that members of that community will not fight each other physically, but will settle their disputes in some other way." They distinguished between amalgamated security communities, characterized by the formal merger of two or more previously independent units, and pluralistic communities, in which separate governments retain legal independence.[48]

There is good reason to consider the community of developed nations identified above a pluralistic security community. Since 1945 there have been no wars or war-threatening crises among its members. The most serious conflicts, over Northern Ireland, Gibraltar, and fishing rights in the vicinity of Iceland are testimony to the restraint of the governments involved. Contrast, for example, the Republic of Ireland's careful and largely constructive response to the troubles in the north with the more interventionist and escalatory responses of Greece and Turkey in Cyprus or Pakistan in Kashmir.

Perhaps the best evidence for the existence of a pluralistic security community is the general absence of military plans by one community member for operations against another. In 1969, the Irish army developed a plan for the occupation of Northern Ireland, but it was shelved after a cabinet crisis.[49] Spain may retain an operational plan for the occupation of Gibraltar, but Spanish military authorities insist that it is not an option they think about, plan for, or rehearse. Military planning among security community members clearly reflects the expectation that relations among them will continue to be peaceful. Many of these plans are collaborative and tested in joint exercises. This is most evident in the NATO, but there is also close, if less publicized cooperation among the United States, South Korea, and Japan, and among the United States, Australia, and New Zealand.

Joint planning is only one of the military ties that bind together the members of the security community. They have also established many programs for common training and exchanges of military officers. They routinely share intelligence and have established bi- and multilateral agreements for the development of advanced military technology and weapons systems. In NATO, officers of different nationalities staff commands to which member states contribute or earmark forces. France and Germany have taken integration a step further and are establishing a joint brigade, something that would have been unthinkable a generation ago.

Within NATO, the impetus for integration was twofold: member states were responding to a perceived military threat from the Soviet Union but wanted to prevent the emergence of a strong, independent German military force. The Soviet threat has disappeared, but NATO governments and their publics remain strongly committed to the alliance and its efforts at military integration.[50] Defense officials and military officers indicate the widespread belief that NATO contributes to European stability in many ways. They emphasize the political reassurance that military integration provides, especially to those concerned about Germany's role in Europe. Many also stress NATO's contribution to building democracy in Portugal, Spain, and Greece through its efforts to professionalize and transform the worldviews of their military organizations. They hope NATO will play a similar role in the East.[51] Civilian and military authorities in non-NATO members of the security community also speak of the continuing importance of military cooperation.[52]

The nature and extent of postwar military cooperation and integration among the developed democracies are unprecedented. It is accordingly difficult to make confident judgments about their long-term political consequences. If analogies to economic integration are valid, military integration will create high exit costs. Cooperative training, deployment and coproduction of weapons encourage an economy of scale that maximizes the comparative advantages of participants. If integration has progressed sufficiently far, it may be extraordinarily difficult in the short term — and this is the critical time perspective in many conflicts — to disengage and develop equally capable fully national forces and the weapons industry necessary to support them. The very act of disengagement would sound a loud political alarm and encourage other states to take precautionary measures.

It is also reasonable to suppose that military cooperation, like its economic counterpart, builds a greater sense of community among participants. Armies that train together, like companies that work together, develop profitable ties and even loyalties that they are anxious to preserve. The French experience is a case in point. After President Charles de Gaulle withdrew from military participation in NATO, French military officials developed a dense network of informal links with their colleagues in NATO and kept cooperation alive as far as was politically feasible.[53]

Further evidence for the existence of a security community is the belief on the part of other states that such a community exists. In Eastern Europe, Hungary, the Czech Republic, and Poland seek membership in NATO and the European Community in the expectation that this will confer significant security and economic benefits. In the Far East, too, expanded efforts at multilateral cooperation in the economic and security spheres are under way.

The pluralistic security community that now includes Europe, North America, Australia, and some of the countries of the Pacific Rim began as at least two separate security communities — Canada–United States and Norway-Sweden — and Deutsch and his colleagues count Mexico and the United States as a third.[54] In the first decades of the twentieth century, the Canadian–U.S. security community was extended to the United Kingdom and Ireland, and the Norway-Sweden community grew to include all of Scandinavia. By 1957, Deutsch et al. believed that the security community was developing in the wider North Atlantic area. From the vantage point of 1994, the North Atlantic security community appears robust. It is also growing larger, with the accession of Spain and Portugal. Pluralistic security communities also have developed between Australia and New Zealand and between Japan and the rest of the developed world. One large pluralistic security community could eventually encompass all these countries, much of Eastern Europe, some of the former Soviet Union, and the countries of the rapidly developing Pacific rim.

Deutsch and his colleagues found two essential conditions for pluralistic security communities: the compatibility of major values relevant to political decision making and the capacity of participating political units to respond to each other's needs, messages, and actions quickly, adequately, and without resort to violence. A third condition, the mutual predictability of behavior, was also thought to be important.[55]

The most vital of these conditions is the first; shared values make responsiveness and predictability possible. The pluralistic security community of developed democracies is based on many common values and ideals. In a recent address to the General Assembly of the Council of Europe, Czech President Václav Havel identified the common values of Europe as "respect for the uniqueness and freedom of each human being, the principles of a democratic and pluralistic political system, a market economy, and a civic society with the rule of law. All of us [also] respect the principle of unity in diversity and share a determination to foster creative cooperation between the different nations and ethnic, religious, and cultural groups — and the different spheres of civilization — that exist in Europe."[56]

The appearance and spread of security communities closely parallels the development of democratic institutions and successful market economies.[57] But the Deutsch formulation indicates that democracy and capitalism, though necessary, are insufficient conditions for pluralistic security communities. Responsiveness and predictability are also essential, and they are encouraged by greater political participation within countries and more intense personal and economic interaction between or among them. Cross-national interaction also contributes to the development of a common bond among different peoples.[58]

Some of the countries of Eastern Europe, the former Soviet Union, and the Pacific rim appear committed to the development of pluralist democracy and free market economies. Their success would establish the essential precondition for a wider security community. To the extent that the principles that govern relations among the industrial democracies come to characterize relations between them and some or all of these countries, a single pluralistic security community could come to encompass most of the developed world. In its present or expanded form, it will coexist with the more traditional, conflict-prone pattern that continues to characterize relations among other former communist states (e.g., Serbia-Croatia-Bosnia, Armenia-Azerbaijan), among many less developed countries, and between them and the developed world.[59]

Adaptation Versus Learning

Realists and neorealists share a *structuralist* or *positional* ontology.[60] Units precede the system and generate its structure through their interaction. Structure is the unintended by-product of unit interaction. It is immune to efforts to modify it or mitigate its effects. Once structure is formed, Waltz insists, "the creators become the creatures of the market [that is, the system] that their activity gave rise to." And this is why "through all the changes of boundaries, of social, economic, and political form, of economic and military activity, the substance and style of international politics remain strikingly constant."[61]

For realists, states cannot escape from the predicament of anarchy; the best they can do is adapt to the underlying realities of international relations. The predictive claims of realist theories rest on the assumption that states on the whole do adapt and therefore respond in similar ways to similar constraints and opportunities. Neorealism maintains that adaptation is facilitated by an evolutionary process. Like Darwin, Waltz assumes that the environment (or international structure, in the language of neorealism) rewards certain adaptations in structure and behavior and punishes others. Through a process of natural selection, well-adapted units prosper, and the unfit decline or become extinct.[62]

For evolution to bring about a world of better-adapted units, the effects of natural selection must be cumulative. If giraffes with long necks have an advantage because they can reach more leaves, more of them will survive and reproduce. Their offspring will on average have longer necks than the generation to which their parents belonged, and the process will continue until the most advantageous neck length is reached. This is not true for states. Clever, adaptive leaders may mobilize their countries' resources and increase their power relative to other states. But their skills are not hereditary. Accomplished statesmen are just as likely to be followed by hacks or by leaders whose foreign policy is severely constrained by domestic considerations. Frederick the Great transformed Prussia from an inconsequential fiefdom into a great power. Bismarck and Frederick William IV made Prussia the dominant unit within an enlarged and extraordinarily powerful Germany. Kaiser Wilhelm and Adolf Hitler squandered Germany's resources and reduced its size and relative standing through poorly conceived bids for hegemony. Because bad leadership and domestic constraints are recurrent problems largely independent of the success or failure of the foreign policies of previous leaders, it is unrealistic to expect a significant improvement in the performance of units over time.

The twentieth century offers little support for the neorealist notion of evolutionary adaptation. We need only note one of the supreme ironies of neorealism: The previous system transformation, from multipolarity to bipolarity, was brought about by the blatant failure of key units to respond to structural imperatives. Germany, Japan, and the Soviet Union were grossly inept in their foreign policies. Germany and Japan challenged powers whose combined strength was many times theirs. The Soviet Union helped to unleash the world's most destructive war by refusing to balance against Germany but bandwagoning instead, in the hope of making territorial gains. Britain and France were equally culpable; they neglected their military power and tried to appease rather than oppose both Mussolini and Hitler. If one or more of these states had been better adapted, the world might still be multipolar.

Natural selection and interspecific competition do not require organisms to understand how they work. In fact, they work best when their mechanisms are unknown. This principle is well illustrated by the now-extinct Oligocene horned gopher, *Epigaulus*. In the mating season, males locked horns in combat, with the winner taking all the available females. Large horns seem to have conferred an advantage in combat, so larger horned animals reproduced, and over time the species developed larger and larger horns. The point was reached where the horns became dysfunctional: the gopher needed bigger and bigger burrows in which to hide and thus became more vulnerable to predators.

If *Epigaulus* had recognized the suicidal nature of sexual selection by combat, females might have chosen their mates on the basis of different criteria. Such a shift would have required a relatively sophisticated understanding of evolution and familiarity with the fate of overspecialized species, and individuals would have had to develop a longer-term perspective on both themselves and their environment. This was impossible given the limited intellectual capabilities of *Epigaulus*.

An understanding of structure creates the possibility of modifying it or of escaping from some of its apparent consequences. Human beings possess this capability. They have already affected the evolution of their own and other species in dramatic ways. Some of these changes are a direct result of our understanding of evolution. We have developed and maintain many farm animals and plants through selective breeding. Modern maize and camels cannot

47

reproduce without human assistance. Natural selection would have worked differently among humans if we did not care for or heal individuals who would not otherwise survive to reproduce. Modern technology raises the possibility of a more fundamental reshaping of our species through genetic engineering.

Knowledge of structure and process has also enabled human beings to alter their social environment in profound ways. Smith, Malthus, and Marx described what they believed to be inescapable laws that shaped human destiny. Their predictions were not fulfilled, at least in part because their analyses of population dynamics and economics prompted policies intended to prevent them from coming to pass.

A similar process is under way in international relations. Throughout the nineteenth and first half of the twentieth century, the great powers behaved on the whole like *Epigaulus*. Then, prodded by the examples of two destructive world wars and the possibility of a third that would likely be fought with nuclear weapons, leaders sought ways to escape from the deadly consequences of self-help systems. They developed and nurtured supranational institutions, norms, and rules that mitigated anarchy and provided incentives for closer cooperation among states. Gradually, the industrial democracies bound themselves together in a pluralistic security community.

Superpower leaders were also conscious of the destructiveness of modern warfare but nevertheless became entangled in an intense power struggle. In the late 1940s and early 1950s policymakers in both Moscow and Washington were pessimistic about their chances of avoiding war over the course of the next generation.[63] During these years, and again in the early 1960s, the superpowers came to the brink of war in tense confrontations in Berlin and Cuba.

The Cold War and its sometimes tense aftermath were characterized by crises and arms races but also by attempts to reduce the threat of war through accommodation, arms control, and reassurance. Soviet and American leaders gradually became convinced that their opposites were as anxious as they were to avoid war. Some influential figures in both camps came to the equally important realization that attempts to gain unilateral advantage through threatening weapons deployments invariably fail or even backfire.[64] Through a series of small steps, the superpowers moved back from the abyss. With the advent of Gorbachev, they took giant steps. Human intellect and a mutual commitment to avoid war gave the superpowers and their allies the understanding and courage to escape from their security dilemma.

A bipolar system is defined by its poles. Because the Soviet Union and the United States repudiated the notion of international relations as a self-help system and changed the rules by which they operated, they transformed their relationship and, by extension, the character of the international system. Elite learning at the unit level had systemic consequences. Superpower success in escaping the security dilemma indicates that units are not always victims of some abstract, foreordained structure but instead intelligent, reflective actors who, by their coordinated behavior, can and have transcended the consequences of anarchy as depicted by realism.

The postwar experience suggests that an *atomist* or *transformational* conception of structure is more appropriate to the study of contemporary international relations among the developed democracies. In this formulation, structure is both an antecedent and consequence of unit behavior. In the first instance, structure enables action and constrains its possibilities but is subsequently reshaped by that action. Language and its set of semantic and syntactic rules make certain kinds of communication possible. Speakers of any language gradually introduce new vocabulary and grammar and drop old words and forms: as a result of their behavior, the structure of the language evolves. Postwar leaders changed the structure of international relations by developing new institutions, norms, and rules. The altered structure encourages and rewards different kinds of behavior the way new semantic and syntactic rules facilitate a different use of a language.

Realism and the Future of Great-Power Relations

Realists maintain that this achievement is illusory.[65] In the absence of a hierarchical structure, humanity is doomed to repeat endlessly the cycle of expansion and decline and war and renewal. Only nuclear weapons, some realists aver, hold out the possibility of preventing great-power war.

The pessimism of realists derives from their view of the fundamental differences between domestic and international society. The former has a Leviathan. No matter how delicately governments encase their fists in velvet, they have the power to enforce their decrees and to maintain order. Such authority does not exist at the international level. I contend that the difference is overdrawn. Governments can only enforce laws and regulations when the vast majority of the population willingly complies. When compliance is absent — as during Prohibition or with current U.S. laws concerning marijuana and the fifty-five-mile-per-hour speed limit — law enforcement agencies are largely helpless. It is no exaggeration to say that police authority has more or less ceased to function in many sections of American cities where their authority is viewed as illegitimate by citizens and is forcibly opposed by well-armed drug dealers.

International relations among the developed democracies, on the other hand, has taken on many of the characteristics of relationships in domestic societies. An increasing number of states have begun to acknowledge the necessity of regulating their political and economic intercourse through rules, norms, and agreements. As in domestic relations, this high degree of compliance is motivated by enlightened self-interest.

The concept of evolutionary structure recognizes the possibility of change in different directions. It may be that the community of developed nations will become more peaceful and generate structures that encourage peaceful behavior. It is also possible that unforeseen developments could bring about a return to a self-help system and the kind of behavior identified with realism. Only time will tell. International relations scholars who work at the system level need to recognize both possibilities and to develop the intellectual tools that will enable them to monitor the evolution of international structure if they are to make predictions based on it.

Realism descends from a long and venerable intellectual tradition. Some of its most important twentieth-century luminaries like E. H. Carr and Hans Morgenthau embraced realism in the dark decades of the 1930s and 1940s because it appeared to offer the best hope of saving humankind from the ravages of a new and more destructive war. Contemporary realists remain committed to the goal of peace but find it difficult to accept that the postwar behavior of the great powers has belied their unduly pessimistic assumptions about the consequences of anarchy. Ironically, their theories and some of the policy recommendations based on them may now stand in the way of the better world we all seek.

NOTES

1   See John J. Mearsheimer, "Back to the Future: Instability in Europe After the Cold War," *International Security* 15 (summer 1990): 5–56; Kenneth N. Waltz, "The Emerging Structure of International Politics," paper presented at the annual meeting of the American Political Science Association, San Francisco, August 30–September 2, 1990. For an argument that the recent changes make realism and, in particular, realist scholars more relevant to the practice of international relations, see Stephen M. Walt, "The Renaissance of Security Studies," *International Studies Quarterly* 35 (June 1991): 211–39. For a critique, see Edward A. Kolodziej, "Renaissance in Security Studies? Caveat Lector!" *International Studies Quarterly* 36 (December 1992): 421–38.

2   See, for example, Daniel Deudney and G. John Ikenberry, "The International Sources of Soviet Change," *International Security* 16 (winter 1991 / 92): 74–118; Daniel Deudney and G. John Ikenberry, "Soviet Reform and the End of the Cold War: Explaining Large-Scale Historical Change," *Review of International Studies* 17 (summer 1991): 225–50; and the third essay in this book, Kenneth A. Oye, "Explaining the End of the Cold War: Morphological and Behavioral Adaptations to the Nuclear Peace?"

3   See Helen Milner, "International Theories of Cooperation Among Nations: Strengths and Weaknesses," *World Politics* 44 (April 1992): 466–96; and Alexander Wendt, "Anarchy Is What States Make of It: The Social Construction of Power Politics," *International Organization* 46 (spring 1992): 391–425.

4   Hans J. Morgenthau, *Politics Among Nations* (New York: Knopf, 1948).

5   Hans J. Morgenthau, *Politics Among Nations*, 4th ed. (New York: Knopf, 1966), pp. 347–49. All subsequent references to Morgenthau are to this edition.

6   See Kenneth N. Waltz, *Theory of International Politics* (Reading, Mass.: Addison-Wesley, 1979).

7   Ibid., pp. 168. See ibid., pp. 169–70. See also Kenneth N. Waltz, "The Stability of a Bipolar World," *Daedalus* 93 (summer 1964): 881–909. On the question of the relative stability of bi- and multipolarity, see also Karl W. Deutsch and J. David Singer, "Multipolar Power Systems and International Stability," *World Politics* 16 (April 1964): 390–406; Richard N. Rosecrance, "Bipolarity, Multipolarity, and the Future," *Journal of Conflict Resolution* 10 (September 1966): 314–27; and Thomas J. Christensen and Jack Snyder, "Chain Gangs and Passed Bucks: Predicting Alliance Patterns in Multipolarity," *International Organization* 44 (spring 1990): 137–68.

8   Waltz, *Theory of International Politics*, pp. 173, 174.

9   Ibid., esp. pp. 123–28.

10 Kenneth N. Waltz, *The Spread of Nuclear Weapons: More May Be Better*, Adelphi Paper no. 171 (London: International Institute for Strategic Studies, 1981), p. 3; Kenneth N. Waltz, "The Emerging Structure of International Politics," third draft of a paper prepared for the annual meeting of the American Political Science Society, San Francisco, August 1990, manuscript pp. 1, 13. See Kenneth N. Waltz, "Reflections on *Theory of International Politics*: A Response to My Critics," in *Neorealism and Its Critics*, ed. Robert O. Keohane (New York: Columbia University Press, 1986), p. 37; and Kenneth N. Waltz, "The Emerging Structure of International Politics," *International Security* 18 (fall 1993): 44–79.

11 Waltz, "The Emerging Structure of International Politics" (1993).

12 *Statement of the Under Secretary of Defense Research and Engineering, The FY 1987 Department of Defense Program for Research and Engineering, February 18, 1986*, 99th Cong., 2d sess., 1986, pt. 2:11; *The Department of Defense Critical Technologies Plan*, March 15,

1989; U.S. Congress, Office of Technology Assessment, *Arming Our Allies: Cooperation and Competition in Defense Technology*, OTA-ISC-449, May 1990; and *Aviation Week and Space Technology*, May 20, 1991, p. 57.

13   Morgenthau, *Politics Among Nations*, p. 114. For the components of national power, see ibid., pp. 106–44. For typical errors of evaluating power, see ibid., 149–54.

14   Waltz, *Theory of International Politics*, pp. 131, 180–81.

15   Ibid., pp. 180–81.

16   Statistics drawn from United Nations, *Statistical Yearbook 1948* (Lake Success, N.Y.: United Nations, 1949), table 1.

17   Matthew A. Evangelista, "Stalin's Postwar Army Reappraised," *International Security* 7 (winter 1982 / 83): 110–68.

18   Peter R. Beckman, *World Politics in the Twentieth Century* (Englewood Cliffs, N.J.: Prentice-Hall, 1984), pp. 207–9, 235–38.

19   See Waltz, "The Emerging Structure of International Politics" (August 1990), pp. 1–2, 29; Mearsheimer, "Back to the Future." See also Christensen and Snyder, "Chain Gangs and Passed Bucks."

20   Based on interviews with various scholars at the 1993 annual meeting of the American Political Science Association, Washington, D.C., September 1–4, 1993, and on a letter from Stephen Walt to the author, October 20, 1993.

21   Waltz, "The Emerging Structure of International Politics" (1993), p. 54.

22   Morgenthau, *Politics Among Nations*, p. 114.

23   Waltz, *Theory of International Politics*, p. 131.

24   The same point is made by R. Harrison Wagner, "What Was Bipolarity?" *International Organization* 47 (winter 1993): 77–106.

25   Robert Gilpin, *War and Change in World Politics* (New York and Cambridge: Cambridge University Press, 1981); and Paul Kennedy, *The Rise and Fall of the Great Powers: Economic Change and Military Conflict from 1500 to 2000* (New York: Random House, 1987), are the two most prominent examples.

26   Waltz, "The Emerging Structure of International Politics" (August 1990), pp. 7–8.

27   This literature is reviewed by Jack S. Levy, "Declining Power and the Preventive Motivation for War," *World Politics* 40 (October 1987): 82–107; and Richard Ned Lebow, "Thucydides, Power Transition Theory, and the Causes of War," in Richard Ned Lebow and Barry S. Strauss, eds., *Hegemonic Rivalry: From Thucydides to the Nuclear Age* (Boulder, Colo.: Westview, 1991), pp. 125–68.

28   See A. F. K. Organski, *World Politics*, 2d ed. (New York: Knopf, 1967), pp. 202–3; A. F. K. Organski and Jacek Kugler, *The War Ledger* (Chicago: University of Chicago Press, 1980), chs. 1 and 3; George Modelski, "The Long Cycle of Global Politics and the Nation-State," *Comparative Studies of Society and History* 20 (April 1978): 214–35; William R. Thompson, ed., *Contending Approaches to World System Analysis* (Beverly Hills, Calif.: Sage, 1983); Raimo

Väyrynen, "Economic Cycles, Power Transitions, Political Management, and Wars Between Major Powers," *International Studies Quarterly* 27 (December 1983): 389–418; and Gilpin, *War and Change in World Politics*. Charles F. Doran and Wes Parsons, "War and the Cycle of Relative Power," *American Political Science Review* 54 (December 1960): 947–65, argue that this is only one of the situations in which hegemonic war is likely.

29 Gilpin, *War and Change in World Politics*, pp. 191–92, 197.

30 Ibid., pp. 192–97.

31 Ibid., pp. 231–44.

32 Based on interviews with Mikhail Gorbachev, Anatoliy Dobrynin, Oleg Grinevsky, Vadim Zagladin, and Georgyi Shakhnazarov. See also Robert Herman, "Ideas, Institutions and the Reconceptualization of Interests: The Political and Intellectual Origins of New Thinking in Soviet Foreign Policy" (Ph.D. diss., Cornell University, 1994).

33 Ibid.

34 On the analogy, see Richard Ned Lebow, "Superpower Management of Security Alliances: The Soviet Union and the Warsaw Pact," in *The Future of European Alliance Systems*, ed. Arlene Idol Broadhurst (Boulder, Colo.: Westview, 1982), pp. 185–236; and the following three chapters in Richard Ned Lebow and Barry S. Strauss, eds., *Hegemonic Rivalry: From Thucydides to the Nuclear Age* (Boulder, Colo.: Westview, 1991): Robert Gilpin, "Peloponnesian War and Cold War," pp. 31–52; Lebow, "Thucydides, Power Transition, and the Causes of War," pp. 125–68; and Matthew A. Evangelista, "Democracies, Authoritarian States, and International Conflict," pp. 213–34.

35 Thucydides, *The Peloponnesian War*, trans. Richard Crawley (New York: Random House, 1982), p. 44. Gilpin cites this paragraph in support of his own argument; see Gilpin, *War and Change in World Politics*, p. 207.

36 See John Lewis Gaddis, "One Germany — in Both Alliances," *New York Times*, March 21, 1990; Stephen M. Walt, "The Case for Finite Containment: Analyzing U.S. Grand Strategy," *International Security* 14 (summer 1989): 5–49; Lawrence Eagleburger, speech at Georgetown University, September 13, 1989, reprinted in the *New York Times*, September 16, 1989, pp. A1, 6; and Mearsheimer, "Back to the Future." The last argues that because the West wants to maintain the peace, "it therefore has an interest in maintaining the Cold War order, and hence has an interest in the continuation of the Cold War confrontation; developments that threaten to end it are dangerous" (p. 52).

37 For a description of the several post–Cold War schools of foreign policy that have developed in Russia, see Alexei G. Arbatov, "Russia's Foreign Policy Alternatives," *International Security* 18 (fall 1973): 5–43. For the views of critics of the Gorbachev-Yeltsin accommodation with the West, see the interviews in David Remnick, *Lenin's Tomb: The Last Days of the Soviet Empire* (New York: Random House, 1993).

38   See Mearsheimer, "Back to the Future," pp. 53–54; Waltz, "The
      Emerging Structure of International Politics" (August 1990), p. 8;
      Valerie Bunce, "Soviet Decline as a Regional Hegemon: the Gor-
      bachev Regime and Eastern Europe," *Eastern European Politics and
      Societies* 3 (spring 1989): 235–67; Valerie Bunce, "The Soviet Union
      Under Gorbachev: Ending Stalinism and Ending the Cold War,"
      International Journal 46 (spring 1991): 220–41; and Oye, "Explain-
      ing the End of the Cold War."

39   On the Soviet economy and military spending in the 1970s, see U.S.
      Congress, House of Representatives, Permanent Select Committee on
      Intelligence, CIA *Estimates of Soviet Defense Spending* (Washington,
      D.C.: Government Printing Office, 1980); and Franklyn D. Holz-
      man, "Politics and Guesswork: CIA and DIA Estimates of Soviet Mili-
      tary Spending," *International Security* 14 (fall 1989): 101–31.

40   On Brezhnev and his response to the Soviet Union's economic prob-
      lems, see George W. Breslauer, *Khrushchev and Brezhnev as Leaders:
      Building Authority in Soviet Politics* (London: Allen and Unwin,
      1982), pp. 137–268; Harry Gelman, *The Brezhnev Politburo and the
      Decline of Détente* (Ithaca: Cornell University Press, 1984); and
      Richard Anderson, "Competitive Politics and Soviet Foreign Policy:
      Authority-Building and Bargaining in the Brezhnev Politburo"
      (Ph.D. diss., University of California at Berkeley, 1989).

41   Evangelista, "Stalin's Postwar Army Reappraised."

42   Waltz, "The Emerging Structure of International Politics" (August
      1990), p. 8.

43   See Oye, "Explaining the End of the Cold War," for such an argu-
      ment.

44   See *New York Times*, August 28, 1980, p. A4.

45   For attempts at such explanations, see Richard Ned Lebow, "The
      Search for Accommodation: Gorbachev in Comparative Perspec-
      tive"; and Janice Gross Stein, "Political Learning by Doing: Gor-
      bachev as Uncommitted Thinker and Motivated Learner," the sev-
      enth and ninth essays in this book.

46   See, for example, Douglas Stuart and William Tow, *The Limits of
      Alliance: NATO Out-of-Area Problems Since 1949* (Baltimore: Johns
      Hopkins University Press, 1990); Thomas Risse-Kappen, *The Zero
      Option: INF, West Germany, and Arms Control* (Boulder, Colo.:
      Westview, 1988); and Richard C. Eichenberg, "Dual Track and Dou-
      ble Trouble: The Two-Level Politics of INF," in *Double-Edged
      Diplomacy: International Bargaining and Domestic Politics*, ed.
      Peter B. Evans, Harold K. Jacobson, and Robert D. Putnam (Berke-
      ley: University of California Press, 1993), pp. 45–76.

47   I include the following countries in this community: Iceland, Ireland,
      the United Kingdom, Norway, Sweden, Denmark, Finland, Portugal,
      Spain, France, Belgium, Italy, Luxembourg, the Netherlands, Ger-
      many, Switzerland, Austria, Canada, the United States, Mexico,
      Japan, South Korea, the Philippines, Taiwan, Singapore, Australia,
      and New Zealand.

48 Karl W. Deutsch et al., *Political Community and the North Atlantic Area* (Princeton: Princeton University Press, 1957), pp. 5–6.

49 The Irish Army's plan called for a border incident to be staged as the pretext for invasion. A Republic ambulance, requested by a Catholic physician in Londonderry, was to be fired on while crossing the Craigavon Bridge. In response, the Sixth Brigade of the Irish Army was to secure the bridge and march into Londonderry. Meanwhile, an armored column would cross into the southern corner of Ulster and strike at Lurgan and Toome Bridge, cutting off Belfast from the rest of Ulster. The two forces were then to link up and "liberate" Belfast. The plan assumed noninterference by the British Army! See Richard Ned Lebow, "Ireland," in *Divided Nations in a Divided World*, ed. Gregory Henderson, Richard Ned Lebow, and John G. Stoessinger (New York: David McKay, 1974), p. 247. For the cabinet crisis, see ibid., p. 264.

50 See NATO Heads of Government, "Copenhagen Declaration," June 7, 1991; "New Strategic Concept," communiqué of the NATO summit, Rome, November 8, 1991; final communiqué of the ministerial meeting of the North Atlantic Council in Athens, Greece, June 10, 1993; statement issued at the meeting of the North Atlantic Cooperation Council in Athens, Greece, June 11, 1992. For public opinion data, see "Europabarometer 36 – Herbst 1991," *Frankfurter Allgemeine Zeitung*, December 9, 1991; and Ronald D. Asmus, "National Self-Confidence and International Reticence," document no. N-3522-AF (Santa Monica: RAND, 1992).

51 Based on interviews with various officials in Lisbon, Madrid, Paris, Brussels, the Hague, Bonn, Rome, and Copenhagen, 1991–1993.

52 Based on interviews in Wellington, Canberra, and Tokyo.

53 See Diego Ruiz Palmer, "French Strategic Options in the 1990s," Adelphi Paper no. 260 (London: International Institute for Strategic Studies, 1991); and Elizabeth Pond, *Beyond the Wall: Germany's Road to Unification* (Washington, D.C.: Brookings, 1993), p. 66, quoting interviews with NATO officials. See also David G. Haglund, *Alliance Within the Alliance? Franco-German Military Cooperation and the European Pillar of Defense* (Boulder, Colo.: Westview, 1991).

54 Deutsch et al., *Political Community in the North Atlantic Area*, pp. 28 and 68.

55 Ibid., pp. 66–67.

56 Václav Havel, "How Europe Could Fail," *New York Review of Books*, November 18, 1993, p. 3.

57 Considerable research argues that democratic governments do not fight other democratic governments. See, for example, Steve Chan, "Mirror, Mirror on the Wall . . . Are Freer Countries More Pacific?" *Journal of Conflict Resolution* 28 (December 1984): 617–40; Zeev Maoz and Nasrin Abdolai, "Regime Types and International Conflicts, 1816–1976," *Journal of Conflict Resolution* 33 (March 1989): 3–36; and Randall L. Schweller, "Domestic Structures and Preventive War: Are Democracies More Pacific?" *World Politics* 44 (January 1992): 235–69.

58   Deutsch et al., *Political Community and the North Atlantic Area*, pp. 117–61.

59   A similar argument has been made by James M. Goldgeier and Michael McFaul, "A Tale of Two Worlds: Core and Periphery in the Post–Cold War Era," *International Organization* 46 (spring 1992): 467–91.

60   For an elaboration, see Richard Ashley, "The Poverty of Neorealism," *International Organization* 38 (spring 1984): 225–86; Alexander Wendt, "The Agent-Structure Problem in International Relations Theory," *International Organization* 41 (summer 1987): 335–70; and David Dessler, "What's at Stake in the Agent-Structure Debate?" *International Organization* 43 (summer 1989): 441–73.

61   Waltz, *Theory of International Politics*, p. 90; idem, "Reflections on *Theory of International Politics*," p. 329.

62   See Waltz, *Theory of International Politics*, p. 118; and idem, "Reflections on *Theory of International Politics*," pp. 330–31.

63   Richard Ned Lebow, "Windows of Opportunity: Do States Jump Through Them?" *International Security* 9 (summer 1984): 147–86.

64   See McGeorge Bundy, *Danger and Survival: Choices About the Bomb in the First Fifty Years* (New York: Random House, 1988); John Lewis Gaddis, *The Long Peace: Inquiries into the History of the Cold War Era* (New York: Oxford University Press, 1987); and Richard Ned Lebow and Janice Gross Stein, *We All Lost the Cold War* (Princeton: Princeton University Press, 1994).

65   Waltz writes that "rules, institutions, and patterns of cooperation, when they develop in self-help systems, are all limited in extent and modified from what they might otherwise be" ("Reflections on *Theory of International Politics*," p. 336).

3

*Explaining the End of the Cold War:
Morphological and Behavioral Adaptations
to the Nuclear Peace?

To explain the transformation of the postwar order and the end of the Cold War, one must account for radical changes in both the behavior and the morphology of the former Union of Soviet Socialist Republics. The proximate sources of Soviet-American tension were alleviated by a series of increasingly dramatic Soviet foreign policy actions. Soviet withdrawal from Afghanistan, retreat from Africa, concessions on nuclear arms control, and, most centrally, relinquishment of control over Eastern Europe were reversals of traditional Soviet security policies. Then the underlying ideological conflict between the United States and Soviet Union was resolved by changes in the domestic structure of the Soviet Union, changes that followed from the displacement of Leninism by forms of political near-liberalism and by the partial displacement of centralized planning and state ownership by varieties of market capitalism. These changes in the structure of the Soviet Union and the Eastern bloc provided the clearest possible assurance that the transformation of Soviet foreign policy would endure.[1]

What theories of international relations provide insights into these developments? Which bodies of theory stand up, in retrospect, as broadly consistent with these revolutionary changes in Soviet foreign policy behavior and domestic structure? In the preceding essay, Richard Ned Lebow contends that traditional realism is broadly inconsistent with these developments. This essay joins several of the

*I acknowledge with gratitude the insights of Valerie Bunce, Michael Doyle, Kimberly Eliott, Andrei Kortunov, Stephen Krasner, Friedrich Kratochwil, Aleksei Kvasov, Richard Ned Lebow, Igor Malyshenko, Vladimir Popov, Judith Reppy, Lilia Shevtsova, and Jack Snyder; the research assistance and cite checking of Karen Alter and Byoung-Joo Kim; and the institutional support of the MacArthur Foundation and the Pew Charitable Trusts. None of these individuals or institutions bears responsibility for the content of this essay.

specific debates raised by Lebow without challenging his broad claim that the end of the Cold War proves realism wrong. Because realism is underidentified, it cannot be tested with reference to the end of the Cold War or any other sequence of events. Physicist Wolfgang Pauli might properly quip that, like bad science, realism and Marxism and liberalism are "not even wrong." However, specific theories commonly associated with realism may offer some insights into the end of the Cold War.

First, consider the relationship between the international environment and unit-level attributes. Kenneth Waltz argues that the international environment selects for some adaptations in structure and behavior and selects against others.[2] By contrast, Lebow contends that the developments that led to the transformation of the international system were not adaptations to a changing international environment. In his view, learning rather than environmental selection accounts for changes in domestic structures and foreign policy behavior. I argue that international environmental characteristics — specifically the development of nuclear weapons and the subsequent long central systemic peace — were a significant permissive cause of political and economic liberalization within the Soviet Union and the weakness of institutions within the Eastern and Western blocs. These morphological changes in turn fostered the learning that Lebow quite correctly asserts is critical to accounting for change in Soviet foreign policy.

Second, consider the problem of explaining Soviet responses to hegemonic decline. Robert Gilpin argues that a state may seek to reverse its decline by shedding peripheral commitments and lightening burdens of leadership.[3] By contrast, Lebow contends that the Soviet retreat from Eastern Europe and the Third World and its reductions in military spending cannot be explained as mere retrenchment. Lebow argues that because these acts compromised traditionally defined vital security interests, they were at variance with realism. I hold that each of these changes in Soviet behavior was in accord with prudential realism, albeit a prudential realism redefined to address the problems of an economically declining power in a nuclearized international environment. In fact, as the Soviet new thinkers revolutionized Soviet security policy, their specific arguments on the desirability and feasibility of retrenchment are virtually indistinguishable from the specific arguments of Robert Gilpin on the economic burdens of hegemony and of Robert Jervis on the virtues of defensive security strategies in a nuclear world.[4]

The first section of this essay centers on morphology. It examines the transformation of domestic and bloc structures that might otherwise have precluded radical revision of Soviet foreign and domestic policy. I argue that a relatively peaceful nuclearized environment fostered liberalization and decentralization within the Soviet Union and the Soviet bloc. The second section centers on behavior. It analyzes the changes in the content of Soviet policy that brought about an end to the Cold War. I argue that the lessons learned by the new thinkers and the policies that they proposed and that were adopted were framed in terms of theories associated with modern prudential realism.

Morphological Adaptations to the Nuclear Peace

As Otto Hintze observed, external insecurity breeds domestic illiberalism. A state's domestic organization is determined by what Hintze termed the necessities of defense and offense.[5] A Prussia exposed on the plains of Mitteleuropa, an England sitting across the channel from the continent, and a United States insulated from conflict by the Atlantic Ocean dwelled in markedly different security environments. Given eighteenth- and nineteenth-century military technologies, geographical location had significant and direct implications for the levels of security in these nations. Hintze argued that relative insecurity fostered development of the Prussian barracks state, while relative security bred English and American liberalism. What effect did changing security environments have on the evolution of American and Soviet political and economic systems? What effect did changing security environments have on the structure of the blocs that the United States and Soviet Union fashioned in the aftermath of the Second World War?

National Political and Economic Structures

Does a benign international security environment select for liberal political and economic structures? A relatively benign international security environment fostered the development of more liberal polities and economies by weakening domestic groups and bureaucracies that might otherwise have blocked movement toward liberalization. The characteristic Cold War activity of preparing for wars that did not come and the classical international activity of waging central systemic war have profoundly different effects on domestic political and economic structures. Consider the differing effects on domestic political and economic systems of preparing for war and of waging war.

The act of waging war has two opposed effects on the domestic characteristics of states. On the one hand, war can strengthen opponents and weaken proponents of political liberalism and economic decentralization. The economic centralization and political repression that I will argue reduced the economic efficiency of Eastern bloc nations in the 1970s and 1980s may be an asset in time of war. During the Second World War, the United States and Great Britain relied on systems of material balances and production quotas to mobilize and redirect resources to wage war. They turned to physical rationing to repress consumption. These liberal polities also curtailed freedom of movement and expression through preventive detention and censorship. During times of war, liberal capitalist democracies become more politically authoritarian and more economically centralized as the real or imagined necessities of war take precedence over individual freedoms.[6] On the other hand, war can have liberalizing consequences. When locked in struggles for national survival, authoritarian governments with relatively narrow bases of domestic support may arm and / or enfranchise classes and groups that had been excluded from governing coalitions. In the aftermath of war, a return to the domestic political status quo ante bellum can prove difficult or impossible. Under these conditions, postwar liberalization can be an unintended consequence of wartime mobilization. But the liberalizing consequences of war are not always enduring. For example, during the 1930s, political illiberalism and economic centralization went hand in hand is Stalinist Russia. During the Second World War, some of the worst excesses of Stalinism were held in check as the Soviet leadership stepped away from domestic political measures that reduced rather than enhanced Soviet military capabilities. After the war, however, Stalinism reemerged quickly. In short, war simultaneously narrows the range of discourse while broadening bases of political support. As a consequence, effects of war on domestic liberalism are complex, with these two effects partially offsetting each other.

How does preparing for wars that do not come affect the characteristics of domestic polities and economies? In a relatively peaceful world marked by perpetual preparation for war, rising security should be monotonically associated with increasing political and economic liberalism.

The 1940s and early 1950s saw the rise of a national security state within the United States and the reinforcement of the Stalinist Soviet system.[7] The initial development of nuclear weapons and of long-range delivery systems engendered what could plausibly be described as an insecure environment for both the Soviet Union and the United States. Intercontinental bombers with nuclear payloads transformed military geography. Neither America's Atlantic moat nor Russia's Eastern European glacis appeared to afford adequate security in the early years of the nuclear era. Although robust second strike capabilities may well be profoundly stabilizing, the early postwar period was marked by insecure deterrents and rapidly changing capabilities. Preemption and fear of preemption are characteristic of this and other periods of rapid transition. External insecurity was an important, though certainly not an exclusive, cause of attacks on civil liberties within a McCarthyite United States and of the postwar purges of the Stalinist Soviet Union. America's sense of heightened insecurity contributed directly to the purges of State Department China hands and Alger Hiss, the witchhunts of the House Un-American Activities Committee, and the McCarthy hearings. The Federal Bureau of Investigation moved back to a wartime footing while the Central Intelligence Agency adopted and expanded the missions of the wartime Office of Strategic Services. A large and centralized defense sector, dependent on government organization and subsidization of research and development and on guaranteed purchases of military products, developed within America's decentralized economy.

As for the Soviet Union, as argued above, the Second World War had had liberalizing effects on politics. However, during the postwar period, Stalin used external insecurity to legitimate a vicious round of purges that eradicated liberal and cosmopolitan tendencies tolerated during the war. During the immediate postwar period, the KGB and NKVD filled the gulags with real and imagined enemies. In the realm of economic affairs, Stalin relied on external insecurity to reinforce centralized planning and material balances. The Soviet economy continued to be organized to mobilize resources for the military sector.

As both the United States and the Soviet Union developed stable deterrents, years without central systemic war gradually assuaged early fears of attack. Soviet-American relations cycled between Cold War and détente. Both countries prepared for a war that did not come, and Soviet and American troops engaged in interventions on the periphery, but the existence of stable nuclear deterrents effectively guaranteed security while fears of possible uncontrollable escalation from conventional to nuclear war discouraged conventional challenges to traditionally defined vital interests. The central systemic peace engendered by these conditions contributed to the liberalization of American and Soviet polities and economies. First, the American and Soviet national security states softened. Immediate postwar movement toward the development of hardened national security states slowed and then reversed in the 1950s. Within the United States, the excesses of McCarthyism were followed by the domestic somnolence of the Eisenhower years. During the same period in the Soviet Union, Khrushchev denounced Stalinism and engaged in moderate domestic political reforms. Although the hard structure of the Communist Party and restrictions on freedom of speech and expression remained in place until very recently, the Soviet political system gradually became more open. Although periods of moderate liberalization were followed by periods of repression, the Soviet system evolved toward liberalization.

The liberalization of the Soviet polity was a factor permitting the emergence of the new thinkers and the foreign policy they devised. Before treating the content of their analysis in the next section, a caveat is in order. International environmental factors do not provide anything approaching a complete explanation of the rise of glasnost and the survival of Soviet new thinkers. The absence of central systemic war was one, though hardly the only, factor permitting these changes. Fortunately, we can only speculate on how central systemic war might have precluded or deferred domestic changes that in turn fostered learning in Soviet foreign policy.

Of course, the significance of domestic liberalization extends well beyond the fostering of the new thinkers and their foreign policy. This détente differs from all others in one critical respect: ideological context. For forty years, students have been asked to comment on the relative significance of bipolarity, nuclear weapons, and ideology as explanations of the Cold War. For forty years, students argued that the Cold War was overdetermined, that the simultaneous emergence of bipolarity, nuclear weapons, and ideological cleavages in the immediate postwar period precluded evaluation of the significance of any one of these factors. Today, multipolarity, bipolarity, and nuclear weapons exist, albeit in lopsided form, but the ideological component has changed, albeit in response to a benign security environment defined by these factors. Previous efforts to limit East-West competition proved to be ephemeral because they could not address the ideological division between the United States and the Soviet Union. The Yalta agreement and the Helsinki agreement foundered over ideology. A politically liberal United States could not accept Soviet authoritarianism at home and Soviet violations of the principle of self-determination. These agreements over spheres of influence sought to reconcile the irreconcilable by accepting Soviet dominance over Eastern Europe while guaranteeing self-determination within Eastern Europe. By with-drawing from its sphere of influence in Eastern Europe, the Soviet Union eliminated this long-standing political impediment to endur-ing détente.

Bloc Structures

The political liberalization of the Soviet domestic system is one important permissive factor in the radical redefinition of Soviet for-eign policy. A second is the absence of strong centralized institutions and loyalties within the Eastern bloc. The puzzle here is why the ini-tial reorganization of international politics into bloc politics after the Second World War did not prove to be self-sustaining. Had the blocs developed into strongly institutionalized orders, then the radi-cal restructuring of arrangements we have observed in the past two years would have encountered significantly greater resistance.

This section argues that the nuclear peace fostered looseness at the level of the blocs even as it promoted liberalization within the Soviet Union. For over four decades, the fundamental ordering prin-ciples of international politics and the basic elements of American grand strategy remained in stasis. Between 1945 and 1950, all advanced industrial societies were absorbed into one of two eco-nomically integrated military protectorates. The boundary between the Eastern and Western blocs came to define mutually exclusive zones of military protection, economic production, and relative political homogeneity. In subsequent years, this core system was projected onto the periphery as Soviet-American rivalry infused civil wars and regional conflicts throughout the Third World. Rou-tinized geopolitical rivalry between the United States and the Soviet Union legitimated these postwar military, economic, and political arrangements. The grand strategies of the United States and the Soviet Union operated largely in defense of the postwar status quo. The line through Germany, the Eurasian industrial heartland, and the developing world appeared to be as fundamental to the organi-zation of global political, military, and economic affairs as bound-aries between nation states.

The transient arrangements of the immediate postwar period persisted for forty years and then collapsed abruptly in the first years of the nineties. To analyze the end of the postwar order and the restructuring of American foreign policy, I combine institutionalist and environmental perspectives. As Stephen Krasner has observed, institutions persist in the face of environmental change. As a conse-quence, political life is commonly marked not by gradual adapta-tion to shifting environmental incentives but by long periods of stability followed by brief episodes of discontinuous change.[8] His general observation bears directly on the problems of explaining the end of the Cold War and the collapse of the postwar order.

In the weakly institutionalized postwar order, the domestic institutions and norms of bloc members, relics of the immediate postwar period, were a substantial source of inertia. Shifting international environmental incentives — specifically, continuing central systemic peace and widening disparities between economic and military strength — were a substantial force for the modification of the existing order. Although these factors impinged on the United States, their impact on the Soviet Union was acute. Tensions between the structures of the postwar order and shifting environmental incentives accumulated for forty years and then shattered the system in 1989.

Charles Tilly's analysis of the formation of the European state system bears on the problem of explaining the formation and collapse of the bloc system. He describes the transition from feudal to national order as a self-reinforcing macroinstitutional process. Nascent state builders protected or conquered feudal constituents and extracted resources to finance protection and conquest.[9] As Tilly observes: "Power holders' pursuit of war involved them willy-nilly in the extraction of resources for warmaking from the populations over which they had control and in the promotion of capital accumulation by those who could help them borrow and buy. War making, extraction, and capital accumulation interacted to shape European state making."[10] Preparation for war fostered development of national institutions and loyalties. Furthermore, war making and state making in one nation state reinforced war making and state making in its neighbors. In Tilly's pithy words, "If protection rackets represent organized crime at its smoothest, then war making and state making — quintessential protection rackets with the advantage of legitimacy — qualify as our largest examples of organized crime."[11]

Without implying that bloc making was a form of legalized extortion, I suggest that the process of bloc formation paralleled some aspects of state formation as described by Tilly. After the Second World War, rights to political and military protection and obligations to protect were defined at the level of the bloc. The Eastern and Western blocs were far more than mere alliances of convenience, and the boundary between East and West defined zones of political and military security as clearly as the national boundaries of sixteenth- and seventeenth-century Europe. Furthermore, the resulting duopolistic system legitimated the leadership of the United States and the Soviet Union. This self-reinforcing dynamic accounted for the stability of the bloc system.

But the bloc system was not as durable as the state system that preceded it. The extractive mechanisms and loyalties so central to the formation and maintenance of the modern nation-state were not to be found within the blocs. Both the United States and the Soviet Union bore a disproportionate share of the economic burdens of military rivalry. Neither the United States nor the Soviet Union could shift economic burdens onto allies or clients. As a consequence, both countries weakened economically relative to the other industrialized nations and the industrializing Pacific rim. Bloc makers in contemporary international relations offered protection without extracting protection payments.

Under conditions of central systemic peace, economic benefits derived from military strength were minimal. The United States and the Soviet Union faced a slowly widening gap between the international distribution of military and economic strength. For the latter, the disjunction between military and economic strength reached critical proportions and could not be addressed without a radical reversal of its foreign policies and a fundamental alteration of the postwar order. Existing institutional arrangements strained and ultimately broke in 1989.

The postwar blocs remained more integrated than late feudal orders but less institutionalized than traditional nation-states. In the absence of war, pressures for the development of centralized bloc institutions and loyalties proved insufficient to sustain further consolidation of the blocs. As a consequence, with the partial exception of the European Community, boundaries between nations define the effective limits of institutional capacity. National governments define economic policies, collect revenues, raise armies, and administer systems of justice or injustice. To be sure, national decisions were conditioned by bloc-level politico-military and economic processes. Since the inception of the blocs until 1989, Eastern European leaders governed within limits defined and enforced by the Soviet Union, whereas the much greater autonomy of leaders of Western industrial democracies has been reinforced by principles of popular and international sovereignty. But the blocs did not develop centralized institutions that further impinged on the autonomy of the nations within them. The blocs were integrated economies without mechanisms for effective economic management. They were military protectorates without monopolies on organized violence or effective mechanisms for extracting resources to finance protection. As a consequence, both the Soviet Union and the United States found it difficult to sustain their economic positions within their blocs.

Behavioral Adaptations to the Nuclear Peace and Hegemonic Decline

Constancy of bloc structure contrasted with two quite substantial yet undramatic changes in context: the continuing central systemic peace and the emergence of looming disparities between military and economic strength.[12] What John Gaddis calls "the long peace" and what John Mueller terms "history's greatest non-event" is the longest period without central systemic war since Roman times.[13] This peace coincided with a second development. Historically, pronounced disparities between military and economic strength have been relatively rare and short-lived. Since 1948, however, differentials between military and economic strength slowly but steadily increased. Western and Eastern military capabilities were roughly equivalent, but the Eastern economies decelerated and then stalled relative to the West, while the Soviet Union declined precipitously in economic strength. The United States remained the preeminent Western military power, but the American economy grew more slowly than most Western Europe economies and grew far less rapidly than the economies of Japan and the East Asian newly industrializing countries (NICs).[14] This conjunction of prolonged central systemic peace and widening disjunctions between military and economic strength differentiated the postwar period from earlier eras in international affairs.

Disparities between economic and military strength grew larger rather than smaller as long as the blocs existed. It is by now common to assert that military strength can come at the expense of economic performance, citing as evidence the economic collapses of military powers over the last five hundred years. I move one step beyond this position and contend that the terms of the trade-off may have deteriorated over time. Widening disjunctions between military and economic strength followed from the conjunction of technological advance and prolonged but uncertain central systemic peace.

First, exogenous general technological advance and associated specialization reduced the proportion of spending that can serve both military and economic ends. Consumption, investment, and defense are exhaustive but not necessarily mutually exclusive categories. At low levels of technology, common implements may be equally effective as weapons or tools. If spears and knives are state-of-the-art instruments of war and the hunt, no clear trade-off between security and growth exists. At intermediate levels of technology, common production facilities can produce differentiated weapons and tools. If shipyards produce men-of-war and merchantmen, investments in shipyards can serve military and economic ends. At high levels of technology, common technologies may serve military and economic ends even if instruments and assembly facilities are highly differentiated. If microprocessor technology is embodied in advanced avionics suites and compact disc players, research on microprocessor technology can serve military and economic ends. At each of these technological levels, positive effects blur the trade-off between military spending and investment. However, as technological levels and associated degrees of specialization rise, the proportion of military spending that can contribute directly to economic growth declines. As a consequence, especially when exacerbated by secrecy and compartmentalization, which inhibit diffusion of technology to the civilian sector, the simple trade-off between military strength and economic performance is more acute in contemporary international relations than during earlier epochs.[15]

Second, the continuing peace neutralized two mechanisms that have traditionally closed gaps between military and economic strength. One time-honored gap-closing mechanism—looting and enslavement—has not operated since the Red Army carted off a substantial proportion of Eastern Europe's industrial base and labor immediately after World War II. The other mechanism is the traditional effect of war on the relative economic position of conquerors and conquered. Although conquest was not necessarily cost-effective in any absolute sense, the economic consequences of military victory were generally preferable to those of defeat.[16] Less obviously, war traditionally spurred consolidation of the economically rich and the militarily strong by fostering the development of effective centralized institutions that tended to offset burdens within the larger polity. The centralized institutions and loyalties of the nation-state spread through military absorption and through emulation born of fear of conquest. As long as peace continued, further institutionalization and centralization of authority within the blocs was not feasible. Thus, since the immediate postwar period, contemporary gaps between military strength and economic performance have not been reduced through centralized and institutionalized redistribution of costs.[17]

Where do we stand today? The subtlety of American relative decline and access to external sources of financing have permitted the

United States to continue with old policies. No crisis compelled a radical redefinition of existing policies. Relative decline was more acute in the Soviet Union than it was in the United States. Consider gross indicators of this economic performance in the 1970s and 1980s — the period leading up to the reforms. The Soviet Union's growth trajectory fell far below the mediocre performance of the United States. Furthermore, as figure 3.1 indicates, Soviet productivity grew at only half the abysmal American rate of increase in productivity. When compared with the growth paths and productivity paths of the United States, much less with those of Japan and Western Europe, Soviet economic performance can only be described as poor.

What factors account for this abysmal economic performance?

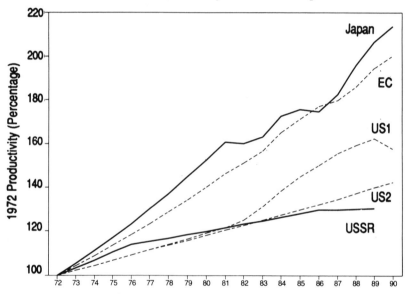

Figure 3.1: Manufacturing Cumulative Growth in Labor Productivity
US1 overestimates American productivity growth. During the 1980s, the U.S. Commerce Department erred by attributing value added by offshore production of intermediate products to American plants, in effect, inflating the numerator of productivity calculations — value of goods produced — and then dividing it by the denominator of person hours of American manufacturing labor. US2 is based on a 1991 Commerce Department series that corrects for this error. From International Monetary Fund, *World Economic Outlook* (Washington, D.C.: International Monetary Fund, October 1990), p. 122. Soviet productivity calculated from CIA, *Handbook of Economic Statistics 1989* (Washington, D.C.: National Foreign Assessment Service, 1989), table 36, p. 60. US2 curve drawn from Department of Commerce productivity reestimates. Based on anonymous source, Council of Economic Advisors.

Republican mythology holds that the Reagan administration defense buildup was indirectly responsible for Soviet retrenchment and democratization. In this view, Soviet efforts to match the U.S. military buildup overstrained the Soviet economy. By drawing resources from consumption and investment, the arms race with the United States served as the coup de grâce for an economically stagnant Soviet Union. This view is not sustained by the evidence. As figure 3.2 shows, the Soviet Union did not respond to the Reagan military buildup with a buildup of their own. In fact, Soviet military spending as a percentage of GNP was flat during most of the 1980s and then fell off moderately in 1988. Some portion of Soviet investment is hidden military spending; Soviet investment actually declined moderately during the Reagan years. In fact, the Soviet response to the Reagan military buildup was to spend a bit more on consumption. If Ronald Reagan did not engender reform by arms racing the Soviet Union into economic collapse, what factors do account for Soviet economic stagnation?

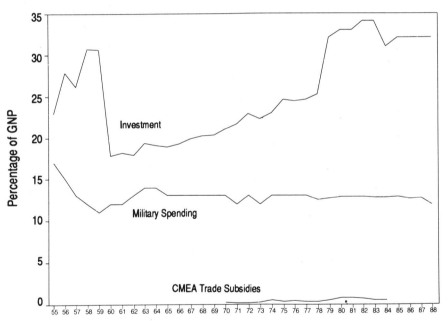

Figure 3.2: Soviet Military Spending and Investment as a Percentage of GNP
From CIA, *Handbook of Economic Statistics 1984* (Washington, D.C.: National Foreign Assessment Service, 1984), 66, 68; and CIA, *Handbook of Economic Statistics* (Washington, D.C.: National Foreign Assessment Service, 1990), 64–76.

In order of significance, the structure of the Soviet economy, the gross apportionment of resources within that economy, and external drains on Soviet resources account for flagging Soviet economic and productivity growth. The centralized command economy that had produced rapid increases in economic product and productivity during earlier phases of development were not well suited to modern conditions. Indeed, the slack and inefficiency engendered by the structure of the Soviet economy vitiated measures that might otherwise have enhanced economic performance.

Consider the Soviet Union's apportionment of resources to investment, defense, and consumption. As figure 3.2 indicates, Soviet investment levels ran at European and below Japanese levels during most of the 1960s, increased slowly through the middle 1970s, and then rose dramatically in the late 1970s. High and constant levels of military spending — roughly double American levels when expressed as a proportion of national product — tightened the trade-off between investment and consumption. This trade-off confronted Soviet planners as they sought to arrest flagging economic growth during the late 1970s. Asked to review figure 3.2, Vladimir Popov of the Academy of the National Economy noted that Soviet planners reacted in the simplest possible manner to flagging growth. As staunch advocates of material balances and centralized planning, they reasoned that raising levels of investment might overwhelm slack and inefficiency and restore Soviet growth to levels characteristic of the 1950s. In effect, they raised the investment quota. Investment levels rose dramatically in the late 1970s, ipso facto at the expense of consumption rather than military spending. The squeeze on Soviet consumption that followed from constant high levels of military spending and increasing levels on investment undercut incentives to work and did not attack the central problems of inefficient central planning. Popov further observes that increased investment probably reduced rather than raised rates of growth in the late 1970s and early 1980s.

The Soviet Union's relationship to other Council for Mutual Economic Assistance (CMEA) members increased, albeit marginally, these strains on the Soviet economy. Soviets extracted resources from Eastern European clients during the looting of the immediate postwar period, thereby accentuating unrest; then transferred substantial resources to clients to buy off discontent during the 1960s; and ultimately eliminated subsidies to clients to prop up the Soviet economy during the 1980s, again accentuating unrest. As the lowest line on figure 3.2 indicates, implicit trade subsidies from the Soviet

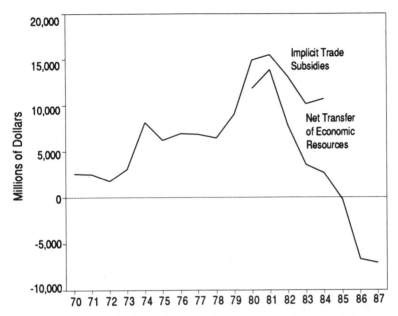

Figure 3.3: Soviet Subsidies and Economic Aid to Eastern European Nations
Information on implicit trade subsidies is from CIA, *Handbook of Economic Statistics 1990* (Washington, D.C.: National Foreign Assessment Service, 1990), table 9; information on net transfer of economic resources is from Michael Marrese, "CMEA: Effective but Cumbersome Political Economy," *International Organization* 40 (spring 1986): 302, table 3.

Union to Eastern European members of CMEA account for a small share of Soviet national product. Subsidies and economic aid to Cuba, Vietnam, Mongolia, North Korea, and other non-European clients roughly double the drain on Soviet resources. When viewed in absolute terms in figure 3.3, implicit trade subsidies to Eastern Europe amounted to roughly $15 billion at the 1980 peak. After 1980 Soviet net resource transfers to Eastern Europe fell dramatically, and by the end of the 1980s the Soviet Union was extracting approximately $1.5 billion in resources from Eastern Europe. The adjustments in levels of subsidies revealed in figure 3.3 resulted in large measure from the continuation of past policies rather than from radical rethinking of Soviet–Eastern European economic relations. Throughout most of this period, CMEA trade was governed by a five-year moving average of world prices. During 1973–74 and 1978–79, oil prices within CMEA lagged rising world prices and

Soviet implicit subsidies increased. During the early 1980s, oil prices within CMEA lagged behind falling world prices, and Soviet implicit subsidies fell. The levels of these estimates are somewhat suspect. Aleksei Kvasov, head of the economic department of the Ministry of Foreign Affairs, observes that Soviet exports of oil and raw materials to Eastern Europe are reasonably perfect substitutes for internationally traded raw materials while Soviet imports of manufactured goods from Eastern Europe were significantly inferior to manufactured products on world markets. As a consequence, valuation of products at world prices understates significantly the real level of Soviet subsidies.

The shifting pattern of real resource transfers had predictable effects on growth rates within Eastern Europe. Although these transfers were a small proportion of Soviet national product, they represented significant proportions of Eastern European national products. The levels of implicit price subsidies enjoyed by Eastern European nations amounted to as much as 5 percent of national product in 1980. The swing from effective subsidization in 1980 to the effective extraction of resources by 1987 squeezed Eastern European economies. The dramatic reductions in Eastern European rates of growth in the 1980s are in part a product of this swing. If the fragility of Western financial and monetary institutions imposes a constraint on the American ability to extract resources from Western allies, internal unrest imposed an even more significant constraint on the Soviet ability to extract resources from Eastern European clients.

National responses to prolonged peace and looming disparities between economic and military strength, most significantly the response of the Soviet Union, helped transform the bloc system that we took for granted. For forty years, strains between institutional sources of continuity and shifting environmental incentives accumulated. In 1989 the tension was relieved, and the Eastern bloc was transformed. The stability of the postwar order rested on policies that could not be sustained over the long term. Although enormous differences of both degree and kind existed between the Soviet and American systems, not least in terms of overall economic performance, adaptability, and viability, both superpowers found that all available options undercut the existing order.

The Soviet Union and the United States could simply have continued along the lines established during the first four decades of postwar history. But over the long term, differences in growth in economic productivity threatened American and Soviet economic viability. Relative deterioration in American and Soviet economic bases were certain to undercut their dominance. The existing bloc system slowly but surely eroded Soviet and American economic performance and contributed to the gradual collapse of global bipolarity. Neither the Eastern nor the Western bloc could survive indefinitely if the material bases of hegemony continued to dissipate. The conservative response — a return to strategies of the past — posed a significant long-term threat to the continuity of the postwar system and to the security of the Soviet Union.

These circumstances created a growing propensity for change. The sudden, discontinuous rush of events was touched off by a series of deliberate policy choices in Moscow. During 1988 and 1989, Gorbachev let it be known that internal political and economic choices were a matter for the individual countries of Eastern Europe to decide for themselves. In short, he explicitly renounced the Brezhnev Doctrine. Moreover, at critical junctures he made it clear to each of the regimes not only that Moscow favored reform but also that Soviet troops stationed in Eastern Europe would not leave their barracks to support the leaders of Poland, Hungary, East Germany, and Czechoslovakia against the mounting demands of their own citizens. As the Soviet Union withdrew the political and military backing that had sustained the East European regimes, each of these regimes came crashing down. Ultimately, Soviet democratization and Eastern European devolution and revolution eroded the political boundary between East and West. Over the same period, reductions in military and economic aid and withdrawals of troops eroded the significance of the military boundary. The United States and Soviet Union chose to reduce interbloc military and political rivalry to decrease the quantity of resources allocated to defense. Both the American fiscal squeeze and the severe Soviet economic crisis imposed limits on military spending. In particular, Soviet economic reforms required the higher levels of consumption and stable (but redirected) levels of investment that can only come at the expense of military spending. Reductions in military spending by one power strengthened tendencies toward reductions in the other, less through formal international negotiation than by weakening coalitions favoring sustained defense spending within the rival state. Finally, the Soviet and Eastern European search for Western markets, credits, and technology eroded the economic boundary. Political democratization, military retrenchment, and economic liberalization within what used to be termed the Eastern bloc ended the postwar system.

Soviet New Thinking: The Logic of Retrenchment and Reform

If the existence of the Soviet new thinkers is due, in part, to the liber-alizing effects of a benign security environment, the content of the new thinking is the recognition of that benign security environment and the derivation of implications for Soviet foreign policy. As Jef-frey Checkel has observed, the new thinking of Aleksandr Yakovlev and other key advisers to Gorbachev had far-reaching effects on the definition of Soviet interests and on Soviet behavior.[18] In this sec-tion, I focus on the origins and content of a reasonably representa-tive part of the wave of new thinking. Readers may wish to consult Checkel's fine study for a more extensive description and analysis of détente and the new thinking.

One of the seminal essays on the new thinking was written in late 1987 and published in *Kommunist* in January 1988.[19] In "Security Challenges: Old and New," Vitaly Zhurkin, Sergei Karaganov, and Andrei Kortunov recognized explicitly that continuing military rivalry with the United States would result in further deterioration of the Soviet economic position. They argued explicitly that both external retrenchment and internal reform were necessary to reverse the gradual deterioration of the Soviet position. Their essay was what we would call a trial balloon. Because it appeared in *Kommu-nist*, members of the broader Soviet foreign policy community quite properly interpreted its publication as a clear signal that its radical arguments had been vetted by the highest levels of the party and the state. Yet because Zhurkin, Karaganov, and Kortunov were from the Academy of Sciences, the essay was unofficial and could be dis-avowed if necessary. To secure approval of the Foreign Ministry and of Gorbachev's inner circle, conventional paragraphs were inserted into the draft. As a consequence, the essay is an interesting combina-tion of new thinking and ideological boilerplate. At a minimum, the arguments it contained were designated as within the legitimate realm of discourse. These arguments came to underpin the revolu-tion in Soviet foreign policy of 1989.

The new thinkers stated explicitly that a combination of external retrenchment and internal reform served two purposes — the direct goal of restoring Soviet growth and the indirect goal of easing West-ern fears of the Soviet Union. Their arguments rested on assump-tions about the Soviet economic predicament and the implications of a peaceful nuclearized international environment for Soviet for-eign policy that cannot be readily distinguished from the assumptions of Western advocates of hegemonic retrenchment and defensive military strategies Gilpin and Jervis.

The new thinkers noted

> a certain disparity between the tremendous foreign policy role and the relative economic and scientific and technical power of our country is lately becoming an increasing subject of concern, for it began to grow during the period of stagnation. The accumulation of negative trends in the economic development of the USSR in the 1970s and beginning of 1980s became more noticeable and has had a more dangerous impact on the dynamics of the correlation of forces between the two systems. The economic dimensions of the Soviet predicament were a consequence of . . . the economic exhaustion of socialism in the course of the arms race and, in particular, by imposing upon it unbearable military expenditures.

They argued that Soviet economic problems were so severe that nothing short of "the systematic implementation of the restructuring of the economic mechanism and social life and the acceleration of the socioeconomic development of socialism" offered much hope of renewal.[20]

The new thinkers' call for domestic restructuring is broadly consistent with a weaker strand in Soviet thinking in the early 1980s. Leslie Gelb reports on a 1983 conversation he had with Chief of the Soviet General Staff Marshal Nikolai Ogarkov. Ogarkov argued for an economic revolution within the Soviet Union and raised the question of whether the Soviets could have an economic revolution without a political revolution. Gelb notes that Marshal Ogarkov was purged less than a year later but that his logic was resurrected by Mikhail Gorbachev when he launched perestroika and glasnost several years later.[21]

If the new thinkers' statement of the need for internal restructuring echoed earlier themes, their arguments that "future security cannot be achieved by military means" were more radical. To lighten economic burdens and to enhance security, they argued, the Soviet Union should resist succumbing to American efforts "aimed at provoking the Soviet Union to develop its own SDI program and to engage in multibillion dollar expenditures to militarize outer space." They argued against heavy expenditures in conventional military capabilities that would only serve to reinforce "the myth of the Soviet military threat" without enhancing Soviet security. They argued against engagement in Afghanistan, Nicaragua, Angola, Ethiopia, and Mozambique on the grounds that the old way "assigns to the USSR much greater political responsibility and economic and military burdens compared to those of the United States."[22]

Most centrally, the new thinkers argued that the existence of nuclear weapons had eliminated "the main traditional threat of an invasion from the West." This substantially weakened the main traditional justification for the retention of the Eastern European glacis. The old specter of Western encirclement had been solved "once and for all and irreversibly" by "the threat of annihilation in the flames of nuclear war." They observed that "strategic nuclear parity, understood in terms of depriving either side of the hope of mounting an attack with impunity, is a great factor of stability." The authors went on to discuss the threat to Soviet security posed by American development of Pershing II missiles and concluded that "from the viewpoint of present military-political realities, such a nuclear attack would also mean, in the final account, an inevitable catastrophe for the attacker as well." In short, they argued that the nuclear peace is the reason that "we can speak of a substantially increased freedom of maneuvering both in domestic and foreign policy."[23]

This remarkable essay continued with a careful discussion of the effects of increased freedom on American security policy. The following passage could have been drawn from Robert Jervis's writings on the security dilemma and on deterrence and the spiral model: "It is only openness that allows us efficiently to make the peoples of other countries aware of our political tasks, to convince them of the peaceful intentions and plans of the USSR and to isolate reactionary and militaristic groups. That is why steps aimed at broadening the openness of our foreign political and military activities are of tremendous importance in strengthening the security of the Soviet Union. They reduce rather than increase the threat."[24] This parallels Jervis's argument that offensive strategies may have had the effect of reducing the security of adversaries and thereby eliciting offsetting responses that leave the aggressor less secure. Yet, as Jervis asserts, the problem of avoiding needless spirals of conflict is greatly complicated by inherent problems in signaling intent. The new thinkers' explanation of how openness might enhance Soviet security is by far the clearest quasi-official example of Jervis thought with which I am familiar.

The question of whether to label Gilpin, Jervis, and the new thinkers as realists is far less interesting than the emergence of virtually identical arguments on the advantages of retrenchment and defensive security polities in both declining hegemons at roughly the same time, a coincidence that appears to have contributed to the ending of the Cold War.[25] Although Gilpin's analyses of hegemonic decline and retrenchment and Jervis's analyses of the security dilemma and the perils of needless spiraling did not find a receptive audience within the American foreign policy establishment of the 1980s, the writings of the new thinkers were a product of the Soviet foreign policy establishment. There was nothing inevitable about the acceptance of these arguments. Under different political conditions, international and domestic, the new thinkers and their ideas could well have been ignored or eradicated. But it is fair to say, at least in retrospect, that their arguments provided the intellectual underpinnings of the radically revised Soviet foreign policies that brought about an end to the Cold War.

When I was asked to respond to Ned Lebow's argument on realism and the end of the Cold War, I found myself somewhat uneasy with the assignment. There is merit in seeking to devise explanations for the end of the Cold War. But there is also a risk of undue scholasticism if the problem is framed in terms of defending or attacking academic theories rather than grappling directly with a phenomenon of truly historic significance.

First, traditional realism is not a theory of international politics that can be confirmed or rejected on the basis of the end of the Cold War or any other specific event or sequence of events. Realism is more properly viewed as a worldview rather than explanatory theory. As explanatory theory, it is grossly underidentified. The ambiguity and plasticity of realism permits its advocates and critics to argue indefinitely over the fit between realism and virtually any specific sequence of events. As a consequence, the task of confirming or denying realism by examining the end of the Cold War is hopeless. However, specific subspecies of theory that are commonly viewed as realist are defined with sufficient precision to permit at least some assessment of the events that led to the end of the Cold War. I accept the task of reexamining theories that may be associated broadly with realism while rejecting the notion that realism as a whole is a theory that can be tested. Although specific realists such as Waltz, Gilpin, and Jervis may take solace in the fit between their theories and the end of the Cold War, realism cannot be confirmed or disconfirmed by that event.

Second, although this essay emphasizes international factors that facilitated the end of the Cold War, it should not be interpreted as rejecting the significance of Mikhail Gorbachev, the new thinkers, and Soviet domestic political institutions and processes. To grapple effectively with the sources of the end of the Cold War, we should not consider international, domestic, or individual factors to the exclusion of the others. The only analysts who must choose to defend one and only one approach to international relations are unfortunate graduate students confronting poorly drafted general examination questions, many of whom may be forced to read this volume to prepare for their exams.

Gorbachev and the new thinkers could have chosen to pursue the old policies and to defend the old domestic political and economic structures. Because there was nothing inevitable about the changes in Soviet behavior or morphology, the end of the Cold War is a monument to these individuals. Because political and economic turbulence within the Commonwealth of Independent States may yet sweep aside the reforms and the reformers, we can only hope that the monument will continue to honor living individuals and reforms.

NOTES

1   This paper focuses on the causes of the end of the Cold War and does not examine the subsequent disintegration of the Soviet Union or the evolution of the emerging interrepublican international subsystem on the territory of the former Soviet Union. The breakup of the Soviet Union into the Commonwealth of Independent States, the Baltic Republics, and the Republic of Georgia and the subsequent assertion of Russian authority over portions of the Caucasian region took place after the end of the Cold War.

2   Kenneth N. Waltz, "Reflections on *Theory of International Politics*: A Response to My Critics," in *Neorealism and Its Critics*, ed. Robert O. Keohane (New York: Columbia University Press, 1986).

3   Robert Gilpin, *War and Change in World Politics* (New York and Cambridge: Cambridge University Press, 1981).

4   Robert Jervis, "Cooperation Under the Security Dilemma," *World Politics* 30 (January 1978): 186–214.

5   See Otto Hintze, "Military Organization and the Organization of the State" in *The Historical Essays of Otto Hintze*, ed. Felix Gilbert (New York: Oxford University Press, 1975). For more general arguments on the effects of international economic and security contexts on domestic structures, see Peter Gourevitch, "The Second Image Reversed: International Sources of Domestic Politics," *International Organization* 32 (autumn 1978): 881–911; and Daniel Deudney and G. John Ikenberry, "The International Sources of Soviet Change," *International Security* 16 (winter 1991 / 92): 74–118. Deudney and Ikenberry stress the pacific character of liberal capitalist democracies in their discussion of the effects of security environments on domestic

Soviet liberalization. By contrast, my essay places greater emphasis on the consequences of the nuclear peace. Gourevitch, Deudney, and Ikenberry all provide clear derivations of the implications of the Gerschenkron early / late industrialization thesis for domestic structures.

6   Of course, not all repressive measures enhanced American military capabilities, the internment of Japanese-Americans being one obvious example.

7   A partial exception to the generalization about insecurity and war may be worth noting. The U.S. Army opposed the excesses of McCarthyism in part because of the debilitating effects of the witchhunt on the army's military efficiency.

8   See Stephen D. Krasner, "Sovereignty: An Institutional Perspective," *Comparative Political Studies* 21 (April 1988): 66–94.

9   In feudal societies, semisovereign lords, barons, junkers, and daimyo governed economically and militarily self-sufficient territories. The principalities, duchies, and estates of feudal Europe and Japan were nearly autarchic. Local artisans and peasants produced weapons, capital goods, clothing and food; trade was limited to luxury goods, salt, and small quantities of metal. To secure their domains against rebellious peasants, marauding brigands, and ambitious neighbors, local nobles erected fortifications, maintained troops of loyal retainers, and warred or negotiated with each other. To extract resources from their domains, nobles appropriated the labor and product of peasants, collected rents from local monopolies, and imposed taxes and tolls on trickles of trade. Kings, emperors, and shoguns operated as mere franchisers of protection and extraction, exchanging titles to territory for promises of blood and treasure. Their claims to national authority rested ultimately on the personal loyalty and self-interest of potential domestic rivals. Feudal armies were transient agglomerations of local armies, with each noble mustering, arming, provisioning, paying, and commanding his own unit. Although royalty drew resources directly from royal lands, they could not extract men or material directly from the manors. The politico-military problem of bypassing a semisovereign armed nobility, the economic problem of taxing autarchic nonmarket entities, and the administrative problem of creating an alternative extractive and coercive apparatus were mutually reinforcing.

The great consolidations of European and Japanese feudal societies into nation-states were driven by the quest for internal and external security. As in feudal times, nominal national patrons and entrepreneurial clients co-opted, disarmed, or beheaded actual and potential rivals. Nascent state makers went on to establish protectorates over territories where they controlled organized violence. In feudal orders, access to peak military technology was restricted to members of oligarchies and denied to members of the masses. During the transition from feudal to national order, access to peak military technologies and the right to maintain armed forces were restricted to central authorities and denied to local oligarchs. Central authorities secured monopolies on organized violence gradually. For example, in Japan, local armies were thinned and remanded to central control, and firearms not secured in central armories were melted and converted into religious artifacts. Local lords retained small bands of swordsmen and archers. In France, small *compagnies d'ordonnance* with allegiance to Charles VII formed the core of what became a national army. In seventeenth-century Prussia and Switzerland, the constant formation and dissolution of central forces from foreign mercenaries gave way to small standing forces loyal to central authorities. In England, the New Model Army of 1645 became a centralized army. In each case, national forces were initially supported through solicitation of resources from local authorities. In each case, the creation of national armies permitted the gradual displacement of local authorities.

As nascent state makers replaced the local monopolies of lords with the national monopolies of kings, barriers to trade within national protectorates fell. Finally, as the size of protectorates increased, the centralized differentiated institutions of the state replaced administration through personalism and patronage. Each of these innovations increased the war-making capacity of nations. Domestic violence no longer dissipated blood and treasure, economic integration spurred growth, and the emergence of centralized differentiated institutions eased constraints on extracting economic resources and converting them into military strength. Because increased war-making potential in one nation jeopardized the security of other nations, these innovations diffused across international boundaries. Nation-states conquered and absorbed some neighbors, while fears of conquest legitimated state making in others. Once this self-reinforcing process began, it deepened until the last vestiges of feudalism were all but eradicated, and it spread to encompass virtually every nation in the world.

This discussion of an ideal typical feudalism does not take account of the many variations on these general themes. See Marc Bloch, *Feudal Society* (Chicago: University of Chicago Press, 1961); Rushton Coulbourne, ed., *Feudalism in History* (Princeton: Princeton University Press, 1956); John W. Hall and Jeffrey P. Mass, eds., *Medieval Japan: Essays in Institutional History* (New Haven: Yale University Press, 1974); Noel Perrin, *Giving Up the Gun: Japan's Reversion to the Sword, 1543–1879* (Boston: Godine, 1979); and Peter Duus, *Feudalism in Japan* (New York: Knopf, 1976).

10 Charles Tilly, "War Making and State Making as Organized Crime," in *Bringing the State Back In*, ed. Peter B. Evans, Dietrich Rueschemeyer, and Theda Skocpol (New York: Cambridge University Press, 1985), p. 172. For an earlier presentation of this logic of state making with application to state formation in the Third World, see Youssef Cohen, Brian Brown, and A. F. K. Organski, "The Paradoxical Nature of State Making: The Violent Creation of Order," *American Political Science Review* 75 (December 1981): 901–10. Tilly offers a

convincing explanation of the durability of the state system once the process of war making and state making began but does not offer a similarly persuasive explanation of the timing of the transition from feudal to national order.

11   Tilly, "War Making and State Making," p. 168.

12   Portions of this section are drawn from Kenneth A. Oye, "Beyond Postwar Order and New World Order: American Foreign Policy in Transition," in *Eagle in a New World: American Grand Strategy in the Post–Cold War Era*, ed. Kenneth A. Oye, Robert Lieber, and Donald Rothchild (New York: Harper Collins, 1992).

13   See John Gaddis, "The Long Peace: Elements of Stability in the Postwar International System," *International Security* 10 (spring 1986): 99–142; and John Mueller, *Retreat From Doomsday: The Obsolescence of Major War* (New York: Basic, 1989). As these authors note, central systemic peace is not synonymous with global peace. Their observations do not extend to regional conflicts or to interventions within or outside spheres of influence.

14   For works on the causes and / or implications of asymmetries between military and economic strength, see Gilpin, *War and Change in World Politics*; Richard Rosecrance, *The Rise of the Trading State: Commerce and Conquest in the Modern World* (New York: Basic, 1986); and Paul Kennedy, *The Rise and Fall of the Great Powers: Economic Change and Military Conflict from 1500 to 2000* (New York: Random House, 1987). These views are attacked as "declinist" by Samuel Huntington in "The U.S.—Decline or Renewal?" *Foreign Affairs* 67 (winter 1988 / 89): 76–96. Other works attacking the notion of American decline include Bruce Russett, "The Mysterious Case of Vanishing Hegemony; or, Is Mark Twain Really Dead?" *International Organization* 39 (spring 1985): 207–231; Joseph S. Nye, Jr., *Bound to Lead: The Changing Nature of American Power* (New York: Basic, 1991); and Henry Nau, *The Myth of America's Decline: Leading the World Economy into the 1990s* (New York: Oxford University Press, 1990).

15   Unfortunately, I cannot test this conjecture on the effects of technological advance on the magnitude of spillover effects. Estimates of investment, growth, and military spending for tribes of hunters through early twentieth-century nation-states are unreliable even when they are available.

       One can measure, albeit imperfectly, positive military spillover. Regressing economic growth against investment yields residual growth not explained by investment. Residual growth can then be regressed against military spending. I have tested for military spillover in eleven OECD Office for Economic Cooperation and Development countries in exactly this way. I could find no association between economic growth and military spending from 1951 to 1984 after controlling for investment.

16   On the relative efficiency of economic and military modes of extraction, see David A. Baldwin, *Economic Statecraft* (Princeton: Prince-

ton University Press, 1985) and Rosecrance, *The Rise of the Trading State.*

17 If state making was, in Charles Tilly's words, a protection racket in which state makers collected protection payments, bloc making was a protection racket in which extortionists failed to collect.

18 Jeffrey Taylor Checkel, *Ideas and International Politics: Foreign Policy Change and the End of the Cold War* (Department of Political Science, University of Pittsburgh, 1994, unpublished manuscript). For an abridged version of his argument, see Jeffrey Checkel, "Ideas, Institutions and the Gorbachev Foreign Policy Revolution," *World Politics* 45 (January 1993): 271–300.

19 Translation in Joint Publications Research Service Report JPRS-UKO-88–006, Arlington, Va.: Foreign Broadcast Information Service, March 24, 1988, pp. 25–31.

20 JPRS-UKO-88–006, pp. 29–30.

21 Leslie Gelb, "Who Won the Cold War?" *New York Times*, August 20, 1992, p. A27.

22 JPRS-UKO-88–006, p. 30. In August 1988 Alexei Izyumov and Andrei Kortunov elaborated on this position, arguing that "objective conditions of our development require that we should clearly define the spheres and priorities of our economic interests abroad and examine all pros and cons of any major international move. In other words, Soviet foreign policy must gradually introduce 'cost-accounting and self-financing.' In particular, the gratuitous subsidizing of the economies of some of our allies should be replaced" ("The Soviet Union in the Changing World," *International Affairs* [Moscow] 8 [August 1988]: 54).

23 JPRS-UKO-88–006, pp. 26–27.

24 JPRS-UKO-88–006, p. 27. The New Thinkers did not rely exclusively on the stabilizing properties of nuclear weapons to make their case for revolutionary change in Soviet foreign policy. They also noted that "the very nature of the industrial society operating there [in Western Europe] operates as a war-restraining factor" and that "bourgeois democracy provides a certain obstacle to the outbreak of war" (JPRS-UKO-88–006, pp. 27, 28). In effect, a modified version of Doyle thought coexists side by side with Jervis thought. In October 1991, Jack Snyder and I asked two of the new thinkers to explain why they believed that the West would not exploit Soviet retrenchment. Igor Malyshenko, then a personal aide to Gorbachev, and Andrei Kortunov, director of American foreign policy studies at the USA and Canada Institute (ISKAN) and coauthor of the 1987 *Kommunist* essay, began their discussion with what they termed the significance of nuclear weapons. Both argued that the existence of a stable nuclear deterrent effectively guaranteed the security of both the Soviet Union and the United States while fears of possible uncontrollable updraft from conventional to nuclear war discouraged conventional challenges to traditionally defined vital interests. Both observed that Soviet control of Eastern Europe, interventions in the periphery, and

investment in war-fighting nuclear capabilities did not and could not enhance Soviet security. Igor Malyshenko, the son of a Soviet General, stressed the impossibility of maintaining a firebreak between conventional and nuclear holocaust as he made the case for why the West would not exploit retrenchment. Both also mentioned the relatively unaggressive character of liberal democracies as an important secondary factor in their analysis of contemporary security relations.

25   To be fair, the October 1991 conversation with Soviet new thinkers on the irrelevance of traditional territorial indices of security and of nuclear counterforce may reflect blowback from American proponents of these views such as Robert Jervis and Stephen Van Evera. Georgi Arbatov of ISKAN has spoken at MIT of his first exposure to Scandinavian defensive security analysis, pointing explicitly to his contacts with the Palme Commission in the late 1970s and early 1980s.

4

Liberalism and the End of the Cold War

The Cold War is over. President Yeltsin has explicitly declared that he (also the Russians?) no longer regards the United States as an enemy and no longer targets missiles in our direction. President Bush celebrated the victory — by "the Grace of God" — in the 1992 State of the Union Address in the name of the "G.I. Joes and Janes" and even more nameless U.S. taxpayers to whom he wished to credit the demise of communism, which "died this year."[1] President Clinton embraced the Russian leader at the recent Vancouver Summit and, together with the other members of the Group of Seven industrial democracies, reaffirmed a commitment to the financial backing of Russian democracy.

Graceful as well as graceless political rhetoric aside, we have clearly experienced a revolutionary set of international events in the last half decade. On the heels of the 1980s revival of the Cold War, the Soviet empire in Eastern Europe has collapsed, the Soviet Union itself has dissolved, Germany — long the divided heart of the Cold War — has been permitted to reunite, representative government has made a large advance throughout the region, arms control has forged ahead with (by Cold War standards) dazzling speed, and strategic tensions across the length of the European continent have eased (in some cases, only to be replaced by long-smoldering nationalist strife). Europe, historically the most divided and war torn of continents, is at one and the same time uniting and pacifying as a whole (at the international level) and dissolving and destroying in some parts (at the domestic level).

As in 1789 and 1848 and 1914, history has once again left scholars and commentators in its dust. We lack the information needed to arrive at an understanding of these momentous events; we do not know what Gorbachev, Ulbricht, or Jaruzelski were thinking. And it is simply too soon for us to get a perspective on what has happened.

In place of a general assessment, therefore, I would like to focus on how liberalism — one vision of world history — might try to account for the end of the Cold War and thus the beginning of a new era in the international system.

This involves two parts. First, I plan to account for how and why the democratic and liberalizing reforms came about. Here I shall use time and place as crucial devices with which to weed out causal claims. Can our competing explanations account for not only what occurred but also when and where the reforms took place, thus situating them in Eastern Europe in the late 1980s?[2] And, second, I plan to weigh the widely shared expectation that the consequences of these liberalizing reforms were and are connected to peace. So I explore whether liberalism and peace are part and parcel of the same transformation and together constitute the end of the Cold War.

The connection rests on the growing impression that step by step with the increase in domestic civil rights and popular self-government, the prospects for international peace improve. The spread of popular government and the growth of civil society in Eastern Europe and (with fits and starts) the Soviet Union thus seem to many not only to herald but also to cause the radical reduction of international tensions in Europe and the wider world.

In the popular press, this notion seemed so widespread that the *Economist* (ever a dasher of cold water on popular optimisms) felt the spirit of the day called for a rebuttal (September 1, 1990).[3] Prominent political leaders have clearly contributed to the perception. For example, in a speech before the British parliament in June 1982, President Reagan proclaimed that governments founded on a respect for individual liberty exercise "restraint" and "peaceful intentions" in their foreign policy. (He then announced a "crusade for freedom" and a "campaign for democratic development.")[4] Similarly, President Bush, in an address before the United Nations General Assembly on October 1, 1990, declared: "Calls for democracy and human rights are being reborn everywhere. And these calls are an expression of support for the values enshrined in the Charter. They encourage our hopes for a more stable, more peaceful, more prosperous world." In the president's next U.N. address he stated equally unequivocally: "As democracy flourishes, so does the opportunity for a third historical breakthrough: international cooperation" (the first two were individual enterprise and international trade).[5] And perhaps most consequentially, the president justified the large cuts in U.S. tactical nuclear forces as the product of the decline in hostility that stemmed from the survival of democratic forces in the USSR after the 1991 coup.

These current political perceptions find roots in classical liberal democratic theory. The American revolutionary, Thomas Paine, in 1791 proclaimed: "Monarchical sovereignty, the enemy of mankind, and the source of misery, is abolished; and sovereignty is restored to its natural and original place, the nation. . . . Were this the case throughout Europe, the cause of war would be taken away."[6] Democratic pacifism, according to Paine and other and later democrats, rests on the view that the aggressive instincts of authoritarian leaders and totalitarian ruling parties make for war. Democratic states, founded on such individual rights as equality before the law, free speech and other civil liberties, private property, and elected representation are fundamentally against war. When the citizens who bear the burdens of war elect their governments, wars become impossible. Furthermore, citizens appreciate that the benefits of trade can be enjoyed only under conditions of peace. Thus the very existence of free market democracies such as the United States, Japan, and our European allies, and now possibly Hungary, Czechoslovakia, Poland, and, perhaps, a democratic Soviet Union, makes for peace.

How might the liberals explain liberation? Is a liberated international system a peaceful one?

Democratic Liberalization

Liberalism has been identified with an essential principle: the importance of the freedom of the individual. Above all, this is a belief in the importance of moral freedom, of the right to be treated and a duty to treat others as ethical subjects, and not as objects or means only. A commitment to this principle has generated rights and institutions.

A threefold set of rights forms the foundation of liberalism. Liberalism calls for freedom from arbitrary authority, often called "negative freedom," which includes freedom of conscience, a free press and free speech, equality under the law, and the right to hold, and therefore to exchange, property without fear of arbitrary seizure. Liberalism also calls for "positive freedom" — those rights necessary to protect and promote the capacity and opportunity for freedom. Such social and economic rights as equality of opportunity in education and rights to health care and employment, necessary for effective self-expression and participation, are thus among liberal rights. A third liberal right, democratic participation or representation, is necessary to guarantee the other two. To ensure that morally autonomous individuals remain free in those areas of social action where public authority is needed, public legislation has to express the will of the citizens making laws for their own community.

Liberalism is thus marked by a shared commitment to four essential institutions. First, citizens possess juridical equality and other fundamental civic rights such as freedom of religion and the press. Second, the effective sovereigns of the state are representative legislatures deriving their authority from the consent of the electorate and exercising their authority free from all restraint apart from the requirement that basic civic rights be preserved. Most pertinently for the impact of liberalism on foreign affairs, the state is subject to neither the external authority of other states nor the internal authority of special prerogatives held, for example, by monarchs or military bureaucracies over foreign policy. Third, the economy rests on a recognition of the rights of private property, including ownership of means of production. Property is justified by individual acquisition (for example, by labor) or by social agreement or social utility. This excludes state socialism or state capitalism, but it need not exclude market socialism or various forms of the mixed economy. Fourth, economic decisions are predominantly shaped by the forces of supply and demand, domestically and internationally, and are free from strict control by bureaucracies.

These principles and institutions have shaped two high roads to liberal governance.[7] In order to protect the opportunity of the citizen to exercise freedom, laissez-faire liberalism has leaned toward a highly constrained role for the state and a much wider role for private property and the market. In order to promote the opportunity of the citizen to exercise freedom, welfare liberalism has expanded the role of the state and constricted the role of the market. Both, nevertheless, accept the four institutional requirements and contrast markedly with the colonies, monarchical regimes, military dictatorships, and communist party dictatorships with which they have shared the political governance of the modern world.

Three major strands of liberalism attempt to account for the four institutions that together establish the modern liberal regime — popular government, civic liberty, private property, and markets.

Liberal Rebellion

For Locke, rebellion is explained, as well as justified, by tyranny. "Politick Society," what we would now call civil society, precedes the existence of the state and is constituted by an explicit or implicit contract among human beings whose natural equality of passion

88

and reason makes their freely exercised choice the determinative secular source of binding authority. The legislature and executive serve to regulate the common life of the people joined together in a civil society dedicated to preservation of life, liberty, and property. Only foreign conquest dissolves a civil society. Governments, however, are dissolved by tyrannical acts: "Whenever the Legislators (or the Supreme Executor) endeavor to take away, and destroy the property of the People, or to reduce them to slavery under Arbitrary Power, they put themselves into a state of War with the People, who are thereupon absolved from any farther Obedience, and are left to the common refuge, which God hath provided for all Men, against force and violence."[8]

Considered as an explanation for rebellion, the flaw in this thesis is obvious. Tyranny may justify but hardly explains rebellion, as the longevity and prevalence of tyrannical regimes indicates. But the rebellion trope finds a constant echo in the words of those who do rebel. Rebels mix with striking regularity the rhetoric of justification and explanation. Like Locke, they too explain rebellions as responses to "Arbitrary Power." Václav Havel, for example, stresses the exceptional character of the totalitarian regime and the arbitrariness of its power when he tries to explain to Westerners the origins of the Eastern liberations in the oppressive quality of daily life: "At the mercy of the all-powerful bureaucracy, so that for every little thing they have to approach some official or other . . . the gradual destruction of the human spirit, of basic human dignity . . . lives in a state of permanent humiliation."[9]

Conditions such as these, together with Locke's faith in the equality of passion and reason, which can make people see themselves as free, explain the spirit of rebellion and the extraordinary reach of the demand for freedom through place and time, even in the least promising circumstances. For what else can unite the aspirations of Wat Tyler, the Levellers, Locke's own Glorious Revolution, the Sans Culottes, Jefferson and Paine, Lincoln and Frederick Douglass, the students of Tienanmen Square, and the desperate opposition in Burma today?

Liberal Modernization

Aspirations can help account for why citizens seek freedom (*what* a rebellion is for), but they tell us little about either where or when they are realized. A second, and economic, strand of liberalism attempts to account not merely for the aspiration for life, liberty, and property but also for where and when it succeeds and where and when it fails.

Hegel's philosophy of history may be the most important source of an idealist interpretation of liberal modernization.[10] But Joseph Schumpeter more clearly carried forward the tradition, focusing on the material interpretation of capitalist modernization in his essay "Imperialism." Capitalism produces an unwarlike disposition, he said; its populace is "democratized, individualized, rationalized." The people's (daily) energies are daily absorbed in production. The disciplines of industry and the market train people in "economic rationalism"; the instability of industrial life necessitates calculation. Capitalism also "individualizes"; "subjective opportunities" replace the "immutable factors" of traditional, hierarchical society. Rational individuals then demand democratic governance.[11]

Francis Fukuyama's striking argument about the "end of history" presents a radical restatement of the liberal modernization theme, bringing together both its materialist and idealist strains. His study envisions the failure of all forms of autocracy, whether in Eastern Europe or elsewhere, and the triumph of consumer capitalism and democracy under the irresistible onslaught of modernization. When he tells us that history (and not just wars—cold or hot) is over, he means not that life will stop and events cease but that the struggle over alternative ways of life, of identity, meaning, or purpose, will come to an end—has come to an end—because it is now clear that there are no viable alternatives to Western liberalism, no credible alternatives paths to the good life. There will be plenty of archaic illiberalism, autocracy, dictatorship, stale socialism left in what used to be the Third World (now, presumably, the Second World"). But no longer can they claim to be the wave of the future. They have given up the struggle. World politics will henceforth, with allowances for the backward areas, be a politics of boredom, of peaceful common marketization.[12]

Fukuyama tells us that this extraordinary end has come to pass for two major reasons: First, liberalism, by which he means political democracy and consumer capitalism, has resolved all the contradictions of life for which, throughout the course of history, individuals have been prepared to fight. With democracy, economic productivity, and the VCR, we have satisfied the cravings for both freedom and wealth. Liberalism has achieved a strikingly simultaneous combination of social and psycho-moral stabilization. Second, communism, and all other rival forms of political identity, are finished. They have failed to satisfy either the desire for freedom or the desire for wealth.

First let us examine his claim concerning communism. Communism may well be finished, as Fukuyama claims, and it may no longer

offer a viable alternative, and certainly Stalinism, Brezhnevism, Maoism, and their many imitators seem now to have been rejected by the
elites, and even more the masses, throughout what was once the communist Second World. Even in China after the Tienanmen crisis, and
together with reaffirmations of the supremacy of the party and a continued loyalty to Marxism and Leninism, there continue to be promises of reform, pleas for patience, and programs of partial liberal economic development. It looks like we and directly China's youth are
being asked to defer, not to abandon, the hope of freedom.[13]

But Fukuyama claims that all democratic and liberalizing reforms
that fall short of electoral multiparty democracy and the VCR — that
is, of capitalist democracy — are not stable. Communism, indeed
socialism itself, is on a slippery slope. The only really stable point is
liberalism. The police state is therefore a desperate holding measure.

He provides us with much stimulating argument for this world
historical assertion. In the process he insightfully connects and thus
accounts for the historical association between capitalism and
democracy in many of the Eastern European revolutions. But he
also leaves us with a crucial and unanswered question: Is this crisis
of established or existing communism or of all socialism? That is, is
it a crisis just of Stalinism and Maoism, or is it a crisis of the potential of a more plural but still socialist China or a democratic socialist
third way between capitalism and communism?

An insightful argument by Ellen Comisso does address the question.[14] Focusing on the work of the great Austrian libertarian economist Ludwig Von Mises, she too suggests that socialism, in all of its
forms, is doomed. Neither democratic Leninism nor democratic
socialism nor any of the historic forms of Yugoslav self-managed
socialism is a stopping point in the forced-march progress of liberal
modernization. None is an alternative to the choice between liberalism and stagnation. Socialists of all types want economic equality:
some now reject the public ownership of the means of production.
They think they can reform socialism through perestroika by having
markets for goods, recognizing that markets make for more efficiency and thereby growth.

But reforms in commodity markets, Von Mises said, were not
enough to achieve productivity. An economic system also needs real
capitalism — a market for capital. An efficient economy needs to
ensure that resources (that is, capital) will be taken away from firms
that are not profitable and given to firms that are more profitable. If
the state centralizes the ownership of capital, industrial managers
will have an incentive to mislead the state planner in order to get

more resources — more capital. After the centralized state planner invests in firms, both the state planner and the firms acquire a bureaucratic stake in the survival of the other. Since the state cannot go out of business, then neither will the industrial entrepreneurs (until they all go together). Capital will be wasted in inefficient and uncontrollable businesses, and overall national productivity will fall; as a result, Von Mises implies, socialism will not produce the VCRs for which the modern consumer hungers.

But there are good grounds for us to reject economic liberalism as a fully satisfactory explanation of the democratic liberalization of Eastern Europe.

First, we have good grounds to question the confidence in the theory of capitalism that Von Mises and other market capitalists display. On the one hand, we can envision a credible, socialist egalitarian form of the ownership of the means of production that nevertheless relies on capital markets for social efficiency. Pension funds, for example, can compete for the investments of workers and invest them in the productive enterprises of the economy. These pension funds would attempt to maximize the long-term profits of their contributors and would therefore invest in the most efficient firms, taking away funds from those less efficient. Pension funds would thus own the economy but would themselves be owned on an egalitarian basis by the workers and managers whose contributions make up their funds. The great American business guru, Peter Drucker, has described how pension funds might even bring socialism to America. But this vision is not solely American; a whole line of scientists, theorists, and promoters of industrial democracy have envisioned how workers owning (with their managers) 50 percent or so of their firms will be able to rely on external funds such as these pension funds to make up the discretionary capital they lack.[15]

Moreover, in practice, communism was not an ineffective mode of production, at least not until the 1980s. Communism, Charles Maier has noted, like other forms of central planning, was an economic success between 1930 and 1970. In an era of large productive units and heavy industry, "communism was the ideology of heavy metal."[16] Eastern and Western European growth rates in the 1950s and 1960s were comparable and both quite good by global standards as both forged ahead, rebuilding and then extending heavy and light industry destroyed by the war (see table 4.1). But in the 1980s the Eastern European economies entered a profound economic crisis (see table 4.2.) In the 1970s and 1980s communist states proved unable (unwilling) to shed industrial workers and miners when their productivity fell; capitalist states of the West were able to disemploy the workforce of heavy industry and reemploy some of them (sometimes only their wives and children) in the growing service sector. The ten-year gap in industrial technology, Maier argues, doomed communism in Eastern Europe.

TABLE 4.1: Average Annual Growth Rates
in Terms of Gross Domestic Product or Net Material Product

	GDP 1950–52 to 1967–69	GDP 1967–69 to 1979
West Germany	6.2%	3.6%
Austria	5.0	4.4
Italy	5.4	3.5
Spain	6.1	4.5
Greece	6.0	5.6
Portugal	5.1	5.0

	GDP 1950–52 to 1967–69	GDP 1967–69 to 1979
East Germany	5.7%	4.9%
Czechoslovakia	5.2	5.1
Hungary	4.8	5.4
Poland	6.1	6.3
Bulgaria	6.9	7.3
Rumania	7.2	9.3

Source: Charles Maier, Why Did Communism Collapse in 1989? Central and Eastern Europe Working Paper Series #7 (Cambridge: Minda de Gunzberg Center for European Studies, Harvard University)

TABLE 4.2: Eastern European Growth Rates: 1961–1988
(average annual growth of GNP in percentages)

	Bulgaria	Czecho-slovakia	East Germany	Hungary	Poland	Rumania
1961–70	5.8	2.9	3.1	3.4	4.2	5.2
1971–80	2.8	2.8	2.8	2.6	3.6	5.3
1981–85	0.8	1.2	1.9	0.7	0.6	-0.1
1986–88	1.9	1.5	1.7	1.5	1.0	0.1

Source: New York Times, 11 December 1989, citing CIA, Handbook of Economic Statistics.

And we have mounting evidence that free market capitalism may not even be the quintessential capitalist answer to growth under the conditions of late-late capitalism. Instead the most striking rates of growth appear to be achieved by the semiplanned capitalist economies of East Asia — Taiwan, South Korea, Singapore, and Japan. Capitalist syndicalism — indicative planning, capital rationing by parastatal development banks and ministries of finance, managed trade, incorporated unions — not capitalist libertarianism may better describe the wave of the capitalist future.[17]

If we take a more political approach to liberal modernization and examine the effects of economic development on social identities and political mobilization, a somewhat different assessment is warranted.[18] Significant (whether stabilizing or destabilizing) change in political institutions can be a product of social mobilization, itself stimulated by economic development. Political upheavals and transformations should thus tend to correlate with social mobilization, and societies that have experienced extensive economic development and social mobilization should thus either be inclusionary (democratic) or highly repressive (totalitarian, perhaps, rather than merely traditionally autocratic or authoritarian, which, in this view, should characterize less mobilized societies).

Interestingly, this is just the pattern that describes the upheavals in Eastern Europe. Czechoslovakia (together with East Germany, the most developed) was forcibly demobilized from its democratic regime in 1948. East Germany suppressed an upheaval in 1953. Hungary and Poland (the next two most economically developed) rebelled in 1956. Czechoslovakia rebelled again in 1968; Hungary began to adopt "Goulash Communism" in the 1970s; and Poland rebelled again in 1981. And Rumania and Bulgaria, the least economically developed members of the Eastern bloc, did not experience political rebellion until 1989.[19] The year 1989 appeared so striking, another 1848, in part because the earlier rebellions and upheavals were not allowed to play themselves out nationally. Communist totalitarianism appeared permanent to Jeane Kirkpatrick, and others, less because it was different from authoritarianism than because the communist states of Eastern Europe were part of a Soviet empire that controlled their political fates. What made 1989 so striking was that Gorbachev and his associates had arrived at a willingness to abandon the Soviet empire, thus allowing national development to proceed.[20]

The democratic politics of modernization, however, are not smooth. We should be concerned about the compatibility between democracy and capitalism that is assumed in much of this literature. A good case can be made that in the long run capitalism provides the dispersal of social power that effective democracy presupposes and that democracy is an especially effective mechanism with which to resolve differences within a society characterized by a pluralistic dispersal of social power. In the shorter run, a certain comfort can be drawn from the observation that the values of democratic participation and toleration of dissent are supported by majorities in some recent polls taken in the former Soviet Union. These same polls indicate that a large majority of Russians are willing to tolerate income differentials provided people are allowed to earn as much as they can."[21] (Is this enough to sustain a full-blown form of capitalist appropriation?) But in a 1989 Soviet poll concerning the future of the economy, more than 60 percent of the sample said that they preferred the rationing of basic essential commodities to relying upon market pricing. Concerning ownership, many (more than 66 percent) favored private farming, and some (more than 30 percent) would be happy to work for a multinational corporation in a joint venture in the Soviet Union. But more than half of the Soviet public rejected the private ownership of businesses, regarding private enterprise as inherently corrupt and corrupting.[22] Adam Przeworski, reflecting on the results of similar polls taken in Poland, concluded, "The one value that socialist systems have successfully inculcated is equality, and this value may undermine pro-market reforms under conditions of democracy."[23] We do not yet know whether democratic and consumer sovereignty are on the same course in the former communist economies.

Liberal developmentalism of both the economic and political variants adds a vital historical dimension to the account of democratic liberalization: First of all, it explains the overall direction of the liberal progress, the seeming long-run economic superiority of liberalism over various forms of socialism and communism. It also tells us when and where — grosso modo — liberal society found itself selected as the dominant modern type, for, employing Maier's argument, we can use industrial selection to date the collapse of communism to the 1980s. And finally it offers an explanation for the underlying pattern of political development — albeit stymied by Soviet imperialism — in Eastern Europe.

Yet the march of progress is not altogether satisfying. Consumerist modernism, we find, did not demonstrate its superiority until the 1970s, and now there are indications that East Asian capitalist syndicalism is winning the 1990s. The 1980s seem to be a thin decade on which to hang the march of world history. And dating the economic crisis of communism to the 1980s, improvement as that is, forgets that communism had already undergone political, international, and indeed imperial crises in Eastern Europe during the very height of its economic triumphs. Assume that Eastern European communism would not have survived the German rebellion of 1953, the Hungarian and Polish revolts of 1956, the Prague Spring of 1968, or the Polish Winter of 1981 if the Soviet empire had not propped up or restored its faltering communist clients; the global effect of the revolutions of 1989 might not have been so revolutionary if it had taken place piecemeal between 1953 and 1991. We should not neglect the international dimension of communism or of the Cold War between capitalism and liberalism.

Liberal Internationalism

Liberal internationalism is the third liberal vision of the end of the Cold War. It addresses the interaction of liberal with nonliberal political systems across borders. Beginning with the origins of political liberalism in the late eighteenth century, liberal states have with great success avoided getting into wars with each other. They are as warlike in their relations with nonliberals as any other state is, maybe even more so, and maybe even more prone to getting into imprudent crusades. But among themselves, liberals have established the separate peace Immanuel Kant described; since the 1790s there has been no war among these liberals.[24]

This lack of war seems to be based on the factors that Kant identified: the restraint that representative institutions impose on sometimes wayward governments, the respect that liberal societies have for the freedom that each embodies, and the transnational ties of commerce, investment, and tourism that help create mutual understandings and mutual material interests in continuing exchange. But these very same ties — representation, a concern for individual rights, and transnational ties — are the very forces that make for suspicion, a confused foreign policy, and sometimes imprudent aggression in dealing with nonliberals. In foreign relations with nonliberals, a representative state can sometimes represent the aggressions and the fears of the majority. These fears are compounded by a sense that the nonliberal opponent is oppressing its own citizens. If that government oppresses its own citizens what, liberals ask, would it be likely to do to us? Finally, those transnational ties that serve as lobbies for accommodation among liberals can serve as lobbies for strife in relations with nonliberals. Restricted by fear, those relations become vulnerable to any single flare-up of commercial or investment rivalry. The tensions can color an entire relationship.

Over the centuries, the liberal peace has expanded and contracted as liberal regimes rose and fell. Overall, it now includes the fifty to sixty states that have established governance by democratic government and a respect for individual freedom. Eventually, the theory goes, if all governments become liberal, peace will become global and, perhaps, stable and therefore perpetual — a history of peace, where the politics of force is replaced by the force of politics.

Kant expected the pacific union to expand erratically, with many setbacks. His peace train has two tracks. The first track is transnational. Commerce and other transnational ties and economic developments tend to operate on societies from below. These forces individually mobilize and pluralize the sources of power in a society and thereby put pressure on authoritarian institutions, a pressure whose release lies in political participation in liberal political institutions.[25]

The role of global civil society and international civil politics is particularly important here. Tourism, educational exchanges, scientific meetings spread tastes across borders. Contacts with the liberal world seem to have had a liberalizing effect on the many Soviets and Eastern European elites who visited the West during the Cold War, witnessing both Western material successes (where they existed) and regimes that tolerated and even encouraged dissent and popular participation (when they did).[26] The international commitment to human rights, including the Helsinki Watch process, found a reflection in Gorbachev's "universal human values." The Goddess of Liberty erected in Tienanmen Square represented another transnational expression of ideas shared on a global basis.

Trade can have even more powerful effects. In the modern economy, fostering growth has meant at least a minimal engagement with the world economy. Even the USSR in its later days traded for 5 percent of its GNP.[27] The opening of trade can distribute income to domestically abundant factors of production such as labor, capital, or land in ways that put strain on established national distributions of income and power and make it costly for states to maintain monopoly control. These effects can have political consequences that enhance democratic governance if they broaden opportunities for domestic production, as Gourevitch and Rogowski have demonstrated in their studies of the "second image reversed."[28]

Kant's second track is the international track of war. The pressure of war and military mobilization creates incentives for authoritarian rulers to grant popular participation as a way of increasing the popular contribution to the power resources of the states. Increased representation for the purpose of increasing taxation thus exerts the pressure to create republican institutions from above.

In all likelihood, the past rate of global progress in the expansion of the pacific union has been a complex and inseparable combination of the effects of both tracks. But if we imagine that progress had been achieved solely by one track or the other, we can deduce the outer limits of the underlying logics of the transnational and international progresses toward peace.

TABLE 4.3 : The Pacific Union

	1800	1800–1850	1850–1900	1900–1945	1945–[1980]
Number of liberal regimes	3	8	13	29	49
Transnational track		+5	+5	+16	+20
International track		>2X	<2X	>2X	<2X

If we rashly assume that the transnational track alone had led to the expansion of the pacific union, and if we repeated the past arithmetic rate of increase (spilling over from country to country), which tripled between the nineteenth and twentieth centuries, and if the number of states remained fixed at roughly 150 to 200, then global republicanism will be achieved in the early 2100s. On the other hand, if we assume that the future will resemble the late nineteenth century, when there were no great world wars but many small petty wars (having epidemic-like effects), and if the geometric rate of expansion, doubling the pacific union each fifty years, is thus the same, then the union will not become global before 2100 (again).

Both tracks help engender liberal regimes and thus eventually a widening of the peace, but neither the tracks nor the trips are smooth. Transnational ties create incentives for conflict as well as for cooperation, and the international track of war obviously presupposes war in the first place. Moreover, the future portrayed is only an extrapolation of the past, a past with no possibility of nuclear war, technological development that was trade and growth enhancing, and states with limited surveillance capabilities, making

98

them vulnerable to the threat and reality of popular uprisings. To put it mildly, changes in these characteristics could upset Kantian expectations.

Moreover, as social science, the liberal internationalists offer a rather uncertain set of predictions, and thus postdictions, that would allow us to account for the timing of the global transformation and of the transformation of specific countries. Kant saw history as a highly uncertain guide to human choice. All that we can say with theoretical projection (past or forward) is what table 3.3 suggests — the change was bound to have occurred sometime in the early twenty-first century. This is small help in accounting for the revolutions of 1989. Indeed, the internationalist perspective equally predicted transformation in the USSR and China. (Clearly, the liberal modernization perspective with its focus on domestic determinants — levels of economic and political development — offers necessary supplementary factors that must be taken into account to distinguish Chinese from Russian prospects.)

Two-track internationalism helps account for the international process of change, but here, too, it is far from a complete model of democratization. Its attention to transnational forces from below and international forces from above the state parallels explanations of liberalization processes that focus on splits within the governmental elite (as in Hungary 1989) as well as on collapses of the governmental elite in the face of popular mobilization (as in East Germany 1989).[29] These transnational and international forces offer important incentives for democratic liberal reform. They implicitly promise the opportunity to participate more fully in the liberal world market without security restrictions (such as those that bar the export of sensitive technology to enemy states) and with the protection of GATT standards and access to IMF programs. They also promise membership in the liberal zone of peace and the consequent reduction in insecurity and thus, possibly, in defense expenditures.

But these transnational and international forces do not capture the strategic element of either popular or governmental choice in the decisions to transform (*reforma* for Juan Linz), replace (Linz's *ruptura*), or "transplace" the existing authoritarian regime.[30] Authoritarian (and, we now know, even totalitarian) regimes can choose to lead a transformation, to collapse and suffer a replacement at the hands of a democratic opposition, or to join with a democratic opposition in a mutual transplacement toward liberalization and then democracy. Are the public, collective incentives of liberal internationalism sufficient to motivate an authoritarian elite to start a

99

transformation, to initiate a reform that carries the risk of crushed replacement, or to engage with its opponents in a transplacement?

Although it focuses on the need to account for egoistic incentives to act, the new literature on democratization also suggests that we need more focused collective incentives and perhaps what should be called "misincentives." Would Gorbachev have undertaken liberalization (glasnost and then political perestroika) had he known the outcome today (not to speak of his dangerous incarceration during the 1991 coup)? Gorbachev, it appears, sought a reformed communism — involving market socialism and a revivified (and politically rewarded) popular democratic communist party, presumably led by himself — not the collapse of the Soviet Union and the Communist Party and the current stumble toward Western-style liberal pluralism and IMF-dependent capitalism led by his rival Yeltsin.[31] The process of transformation escaped his grasp before, during, and especially after the coup.[32] A second factor affecting the risks that replacers are willing to bear is the simple concatenation of events, what has been called in other contexts the domino effect. The dominoes fell in Eastern Europe in 1989, and these had effects in the USSR, too, stimulating both the coup and some valiant Muscovites to resist it. Actions that seem imprudent from a local perspective appear reasonable when everyone else is doing the same thing. Thus what took ten years in Poland took ten months in Hungary, ten weeks in East Germany, and ten days in Czechoslovakia. Finally, simple lack of information, uncertainty, is conducive to democratic transplacements. When societies know the lines of cleavage and the distribution of social power, all the steps of transformations and transplacements must be negotiated in detail in advance, short-circuiting the open-endedness of liberal democratic contestation.[33] The very lack of knowledge of underlying social geography, after the years of straitjacketed communism, may have made for a willingness to jump into contestation in Eastern Europe and may have the same effect in Russia and Ukraine today, as elites unable to assess outcomes opt for procedures.

Nonetheless, the liberal internationalist perspective does contribute additional understanding to the transformation of the international system. It highlights possible international sources of change — commerce and war — suggesting to us that democratic liberalization was most likely where war and commerce were most intense. There was little commerce in the Soviet bloc, and none of it free. This proposition does not mean, however, that a strategy of peace through strength — military pressure and arms racing in order to force the collapse of the opposing regime — was a justified liberal strategy.[34] In the short run, outside pressure tends to strengthen regimes, especially those that hold a domestic monopoly on the means of violence. It does mean, however, that over the long run authoritarian regimes prove to be poor mobilizers of national resources, unless they call on representation as a means toward taxation, and the Cold War, together with Soviet domestic ambitions, imposed large burdens on Soviet society.[35]

Liberal internationalism also contributes a twofold perspective on change, stressing both the pressures from below mounted by trade unions such as Solidarity and intellectuals and students in Czechoslovakia and the decisions at the top made by Andropov and Gorbachev under the strain of Cold War competition. Finally, in the spread of the pacific union, it holds forth a promise of peace to all those willing to undertake the dangerous course of liberal internationalist reform.

Democratic Peace?

The issue now is whether the consequences of the spread of democracy and freedom will give rise to a secure expectation of peace. Kant's liberal internationalism furnishes good grounds to give peace the benefit of a chance. But let me suggest three reasons to regard peace and democracy as something less than necessary or guaranteed.

First, liberal internationalism offers us hope that if the next hegemonic challenger is liberal, the hegemonic transition might be peaceful, such as the one between Great Britain and the United States in the twentieth century, and we will suffer neither war nor the waste of resources in a cold war. But liberalism can also exacerbate minor differences. Already, this is at work in what we tend to call the Japan problem. Japan is quasidemocratic, like the United States, but it is less purely capitalist than the United States is. And most importantly, culturally it is not yet, and perhaps never will be, as liberal as the United States now is — Japanism always seems more important than liberalism. While the Japanese polity is representative, its economy is (we think) too closely integrated to reflect arms-length competition and a free and flat playing field. Its culture identifies community as something more important than individuality.

Like pre–World War I Germany, though for different reasons, Japan may not be fully liberal. This is partly because of Japan's particular characteristics, but more importantly it is a U.S.-Japan problem, just as the German problem was a Franco-German and Anglo-German problem. Although Wilhelm II of Germany and Bethmann-

Hollweg were sometimes idiosyncratic in the formulation of their policy, they were not noticeably more aggressive than the other statesmen of Europe at the time. The problem was that the other governments of Europe, particularly Britain and France, assumed that because Germany was not a fully representative liberal state, it was bound to be dangerous. This lack of trust then made Germany feel insecure and threatened. Naturally, it responded in ways that confirmed the expectations of Britain and France, escalated tensions, and contributed to the onslaught of World War I. Will we enter a similar spiral of escalating tension with Japan?

Second, we should be cautious about assuming that democratic rule guarantees a spirit of peace. Liberal states have frequently engaged in imprudent imperialism, as Kant himself recognized. Yet, recently, John Mueller in his *Retreat From the Doomsday* has made a serious and provocative case for seeing world politics as not merely changing but transformed before our very unseeing eyes.[36] War, Mueller argues, has become obsolescent. A durable, long peace among the developed industrial powers has changed international relations. The obsolescence of war — the transformation of great-power politics — is, Mueller argues, a function of two developments.

First, the physical costs of war, its very destructiveness, have made it intolerable since as early as the turn of the century, and clearly since World War I. War has become "rationally unthinkable." Second of all, the psychic cost of war has increased. War has become "sub-rationally unthinkable." War is simply ridiculous. Hitler and Mussolini, therefore, were ridiculous aberrations, and they caused World War II. But has war become obsolete, just as dueling did in the nineteenth century? Until the middle of the last century, dueling was very much required by honor; then, like war now, it became ridiculous. But we have to remember that dueling became a crime before it became ridiculous. At the time it was made illegal, truly harmful libels, slanders, and assaults could be addressed in the courts and punished by the law. Only petty insults and minor bumping and pushing were left to the court of public opinion. In other words, dueling was replaced not merely by a change of public opinion but by a set of effective public institutions with the capacity to enforce the prohibition against murder and manslaughter. International relations lacks such a court and such a mechanism of enforcement that could address the causes of war and thereby make war truly as unthinkable as dueling is today. The causes of war, moreover, are not just injured pride. Wars are also created by competition for scarce goods and by the very fear of war itself. Just as

Sparta decided at the origin of the Peloponnesian War to strike before it became even weaker, so other wars could be driven by a form of rationality within the wider scope of irrationality.

My final point is that not all democracies need be the same. Like Kant's constitutional democracy, intense, communal, direct democracies (such as that Rousseau envisaged) can exercise democratic caution in the interest of the majority. But unlike Rousseau's direct democracy, Kant's liberal republics are capable of acting with an appreciation of the cosmopolitan moral equality of all individuals. The Rousseauian citizen, on the other hand, cedes all rights to his or her fellow citizens, retaining only the right to equal consideration. In order to be completely self-determining, Rousseau requires that there be no limit but equality on democratic sovereignty and authority. The resulting communitarianism is intense — every aspect of culture, morality, and social life is subject to the creation and the re-creation of the nation. The tendency to enhance national consciousness through external hostility and what Rousseau calls amour propre would be correspondingly high. Just as individuality disappears into collective consciousness, so too does an appreciation for the international rights of foreign republics.[37] The international rights of republics derive from our ability to reconstruct in our imagination the act of representation of foreign individuals, who are our moral equals. Rousseau's democracy — for the sake of intensifying national identity — limits our identification to fellow citizens.

In addition, for the sake of equality and autonomy, Rousseau's democracy precludes the private ties of commerce and social interaction across borders that lead to both domestic diversity and transnational solidarity. These material ties sustain the transnational, or cosmopolitan, identity of individuals with each other that serves as the foundation of international respect, which in turn is the source of the spirit of international law that requires tolerance and peace among fellow constitutional democracies (while exacerbating conflict between constitutional democracies and all other states).

Rousseau does share with Kant democratic rationality. He excludes, however, both the moral individualism and the social pluralism that provide the foundations for Kant's international and cosmopolitan laws and thereby precludes the liberal peace.

To the extent that these theoretical distinctions tap the actual range of diversity in the development of contemporary democracies, they offer us some useful warnings about the international implications of the current trend toward democratization.[38] While majority rule may be a necessary condition of a state of peace, it is not a sufficient condition. Creative leadership will be required to moderate the autarky and nationalism that can undermine democratic peace. To establish peace among themselves, democracies must also define individual rights in such a way that the cosmopolitan rights of all humankind are entailed in the moral foundations of the rights of domestic citizens. And they must allow the material ties of transnational society to flourish among themselves.

NOTES

1   George Bush, "State of the Union Address," *New York Times*, January 29, 1992.

2   I am following the explanatory agenda suggested by Charles Maier in his provocative essay (discussed below). I am grateful for helpful comments from Thomas Risse-Kappen, Ned Lebow, and the members of seminars they organized at Cornell and Columbia universities.

3   The anonymous author of the article directed his spirited attack at what he (incorrectly) thought to be misinterpretations of the republican ideas of Immanuel Kant.

4   Ronald Reagan, "Address to Parliament," *New York Times*, June 9, 1982.

5   George Bush, "Address to the United Nations General Assembly," *New York Times*, October 2, 1990; idem, "Pax Universalis," *New York Times*, September 24, 1991. He earlier announced as a "plain truth: the day of the dictator is over. The people's right to democracy must not be denied" (*Department of State Bulletin*, June 1989).

6   Thomas Paine, *The Rights of Man*, in *Complete Writings*, ed. Eric Foner (New York: Citadel, 1945), 1:342.

7   The sources of classic laissez-faire liberalism can be found in Locke, in the *Federalist Papers*, in Kant, and in Robert Nozick's *Anarchy, State, and Utopia* (New York: Basic, 1974). Expositions of welfare liberalism are in the work of the Fabians and in John Rawls, *A Theory of Justice* (Cambridge: Harvard University Press, 1971). Amy Gutmann discusses variants of liberal thought in her book *Liberal Equality* (Cambridge: Cambridge University Press, 1980). Uncomfortably paralleling each of the high roads are low roads that, while achieving certain liberal values, fail to reconcile freedom and order. An overwhelming terror of anarchy and a desire to preserve property can drive laissez-faire liberals to support a law-and-order authoritarian rule that sacrifices democracy. Authoritarianism to preserve order is the argument of Hobbes's *Leviathan*. It also shapes the argument of right-wing liberals who seek to draw a distinction between authoritarian and totalitarian dictatorships. The justification sometimes advanced by liberals for the former is that they can be temporary and educate the population into an acceptance of property, individual rights, and, eventually, representative government. See Jeane Kirkpatrick, "Dictatorships and Double Standards," *Commentary* 68 (November 1979): 34–45. Complementarily, when social inequali-

ties are judged to be extreme, the welfare liberal can argue that establishing (or reestablishing) the foundations of liberal society requires a nonliberal method of reform, a second low road of redistributing authoritarianism. Zolberg reports a liberal left sensibility among U.S. scholars of African politics that was sympathetic to progressive autocracies; see Aristide Zolberg, *One Party Government in the Ivory Coast* (Princeton: Princeton University Press, 1969), p. vii.

8   John Locke, *Second Treatise*, ed. Peter Laslett, in *Two Treatises of Government* (Cambridge: Cambridge University Press, 1988), para. 222.

9   Quoted in Zbigniew Brzezinski, *The Grand Failure* (New York: Scribner's, 1989), p. 111. For an interesting application of Lockean ideas to Eastern Europe, see Zbigniew Rau, "Some Thoughts on Civil Society in Eastern Europe and the Lockian Contractarian Approach," *Political Studies* 35, no. 4 (1987): 573–92.

10   Francis Fukuyama, following Alexandre Kojeve, makes this controversial suggestion in *The End of History and the Last Man* (New York: Free Press, 1992), chap. 5. Although critics have challenged Hegel's liberalism, Hegel's stature as a founder of modernization theory appears to be curiously firm.

11   Joseph Schumpeter, "Imperialism," in *Imperialism and Social Classes* (Cleveland: World, 1955), p. 68.

12   Francis Fukuyama, "The End of History?" *The National Interest*, no. 16 (summer 1989): 3–18.

13   Such was the plea made by Ambassador Han Xu on August 21, 1989, in the *New York Times*, when he said, after the Tienanmen incident, that the course of progress was not over. Instead, he pleaded for American patience and in return promised progress, pluralism, and a future of cooperation with a growing People's Republic.

14   Ellen Comisso, "Crisis in Socialism or Crisis of Socialism," *World Politics* 42 (July 1990): 563–96. See also Valerie Bunce, "Rising Above the Past: The Struggle for Liberal Democracy in Eastern Europe," *World Policy Journal* 7 (summer 1990): 395–430.

15   A discussion of these issues can be found in the summer 1991 issue of *Dissent*, which is devoted to the subject of market socialism.

16   Charles Maier, *Why Did Communism Collapse in 1989?* Central and Eastern Europe Working Paper Series #7 (Cambridge: Minda de Gunzberg Center for European Studies, Harvard University, 1991).

17   Robert Wade effectively makes this case in his review essay, "East Asia's Economic Success," *World Politics* 44 (October 1992): 290–320. Interestingly, Fukuyama's book also stresses this more complicated perspective on development; his article lends itself to the more libertarian interpretation of economic development.

18   See Karl Deutsch, *Nationalism and Social Communication: An Inquiry into the Foundations of Nationality*, 2d ed. (Cambridge: MIT. Press, 1966); and Samuel Huntington, *Political Order in Changing Societies* (New Haven: Yale University Press, 1968), chaps. 5 and 6.

19 For valuable accounts of these crises, see Zbigniew Brzezinski, *The Soviet Bloc* (Cambridge: Cambridge University Press, 1965); and, for the Cold War period, Journalist M., *A Year Is Eight Months* (New York: Anchor / Doubleday, 1970). For the Polish case at the end of the Cold War, see Alain Touraine, François Dubet, Michel Wieriorka, and Jan Strzelecki, *Solidarity* (Cambridge: Cambridge University Press, 1983).

20 Jorge Dominguez, in his book *Insurrection or Loyalty: The Breakdown of the Spanish American Empire* (Cambridge: Harvard University Press, 1980) notes a similar pattern in the collapse of the Spanish empire in the Americas between 1800 and 1825. For an extension of this argument, see Michael Doyle, *Empires* (Ithaca: Cornell University Press, 1986), chap. 14.

21 ROMIR Poll, December 1991 and January 1992, reported by Ellen Mickiewicz, *Findings of Four Major Surveys in the Former Soviet Union* (Atlanta, Ga.: Carter Center, Emory University, 1992), p. 8.

22 Poll by National Opinion Research Center, directed by Valery Rutgeier, excerpted in *New York Times*, November 5, 1989.

23 Adam Przeworski, *Democracy and the Market* (New York: Cambridge University Press, 1991), p. 178.

24 The evidence for the existence and significance of a pacific union is discussed in Michael Doyle, "Kant, Liberal Legacies and Foreign Affairs, Part 1," *Philosophy and Public Affairs* 12, no. 3 (1983): 205–35. See Clarence Streit, *Union Now* (New York: Harpers, 1938), pp. 88, 90–92, who seems to have been the first to point out that in contemporary foreign relations democracies demonstrate an empirical tendency to maintain peace among themselves. He made this the foundation of his proposal for a (non-Kantian) federal union of the fifteen leading democracies of the 1930s. See D. V. Babst, "A Force for Peace," *Industrial Research* 14 (April 1972): 55–58, for a quantitative study of the phenomenon of democratic peace; and Rudolph J. Rummel, "Libertarianism and International Violence," *Journal of Conflict Resolution* 27 (June 1983): 27–71, for a similar study of libertarianism (in the sense of laissez-faire) focusing on the postwar period. See Doyle, "Kant, Liberal Legacies and Foreign Affairs," for the use of *liberal* in a wider (Kantian) sense in a discussion of this issue. In that essay, Doyle surveys the period from 1790 to the present and finds no war among liberal states. See Babst, "A Force for Peace," for a preliminary test of the significance of the distribution of alliance partners in World War I. He found that the possibility that the actual distribution of alliance partners could have occurred by chance was less than 1 percent (p. 56). But this assumes that there was an equal possibility that any two nations could have gone to war with each other; and this is a strong assumption. See Rummel, "Libertarianism and International Violence," for a further discussion of statistical significance as it applies to his libertarian thesis. Recent work has extended these arguments into considerations of strategies of international reform (e.g., see James L. Ray, "The Abolition of

Slavery and the End of International War," *International Organiza-tion* 43 [summer 1989]: 405–39), patterns of evolution in the inter-national system (see George Modelski, "Is World Politics Evolution-ary Learning," *International Organization* 44 [winter 1990]: 1–24; and Bruce Russett, *Controlling the Sword* [Cambridge: Harvard Uni-versity Press, 1990], and implications for the categorization of con-temporary international theory (see Joseph Nye, "Neorealism and Neoliberalism," *World Politics* 40 (summer 1988): 235–51).

25 See Samuel Huntington, *Political Order in Changing Societies* (New Haven: Yale University Press, 1968); and Deutsch, *Nationalism and Social Communication,* for sources of the social mobilization, politi-cal participation, institutional change hypothesis.

26 For an excellent survey of these factors, see Daniel Deudney and G. John Ikenberry, "The International Sources of Soviet Change," *Inter-national Security* 16 (winter 1991 / 92): 74–118.

27 See Timothy Colton, *Dilemmas of Soviet Reform* (New York: Coun-cil on Foreign Relations, 1992).

28 Peter Gourevitch, *Politics in Hard Times* (Ithaca: Cornell University Press, 1986); and Ronald Rogowski, *Commerce and Coalitions* (Princeton: Princeton University Press, 1989).

29 Przeworski, *Democracy and the Market,* p. 56.

30 Samuel Huntington, *The Third Wave* (Norman: University of Okla-homa Press, 1991), p. 114; and Juan Linz, "Crisis, Breakdown, and Re-Equilibration," in *The Breakdown of Democratic Regimes,* ed. Juan Linz and Alfred Stepan (Baltimore: Johns Hopkins University Press, 1978), p. 35.

31 Mikhail Gorbachev, "On Socialist Democracy," in *Socialism, Peace, and Democracy* (London: Atlantic Highlands, 1987). See also Mar-shall Goldman, *What Went Wrong with Perestroika* (New York: Norton, 1991), pp. 128–71.

32 Theodore Draper, "Who Killed Soviet Communism," *New York Review of Books,* June 1, 1992, pp. 7–14.

33 Przeworski, *Democracy and the Market,* p. 88.

34 Thomas Risse-Kappen, "Did 'Peace Through Strength' End the Cold War?" *International Security* (summer 1991): 162–88.

35 I think that this is a major assumption of George Kennan's classic strategy for eventual accommodation (not victory) in the Cold War. He relied on the "internal weakness" of Soviet power, supplemented by "international frustration," to dissolve Soviet ambitions and capac-ities (George Kennan, "Sources of Soviet Conduct," *Foreign Affairs* 25 [July 1947]: 566–82).

36 John Mueller, *Retreat from Doomsday* (New York: Basic, 1989).

37 Stephen Van Evera, "Primed for Peace: Europe after the Cold War," *International Security* 15 (winter 1990 / 91): 7–57, reaches a similar conclusion about the dangers of militaristic nationalism, drawing on historical evidence of the early twentieth century. The comparison detailed here, however, suggests an even wider indictment of the dan-ger of nationalism among democracies.

38   I have found the following especially informative: for a criticism of
liberalism, John J. Mearsheimer, "Back to the Future: Instability in
Europe After the Cold War," *International Security* 15 (summer
1990): 5–56; for a discussion of policy paths, Jack Snyder, "Averting
Anarchy in the New Europe," *International Security* 14 (spring
1990): 5–41; for advocacy of the prospects for peace, Van Evera,
"Primed for Peace"; for a discussion of the role of external pressure
in Soviet change, Risse-Kappen, "Did 'Peace Through Strength' End
the Cold War?" See also Charles and Clifford Kupchan's argument
for collective security in their work "Concerts, Collective Security,
and the Future of Europe," *International Security* 16 (summer 1991):
114–61; and Deudney and Ikenberry, "International Sources of Soviet Change."

5

Myths, Modernization, and the Post-Gorbachev World

The comparatively peaceful collapse of the Soviet empire is a virtually unprecedented event in the history of world politics. In the past, the demise of great empires has almost always been accompanied by major warfare. Either the declining power lashed out in an aggressive attempt to stem the tide, or rising powers used force to hasten the process and stake out their claims. Often the prospect even of less dramatic shifts in relative power has triggered preventive war between major powers. Decolonization has sometimes taken place without large-scale military conflict but never so close to the heart of an empire.[1]

The peacefulness of the Soviet collapse was due primarily to the fact that the strongest powers in the international system at that time were, or aspired to be, liberal democracies. As long as this remains the case, intense conflict among the great powers will be much less common than it was in the past.[2] However, since the fate of liberal democracy in Russia, China, and other potential great powers is far from certain, this outcome must remain in doubt.

To understand the future directions of world politics, therefore, international relations theorists need to study why liberal democracies are now the prevailing form of the state in the developed world, why such states pursue more moderate foreign policies, what circumstances might lead to the emergence of illiberal great powers, and how such circumstances could be averted. The concluding sections of this essay will address some of the implications of this for scholarship on international politics. First, however, I will show how my previous theoretical formulations have attempted to explain the peaceful transformation of the Soviet empire.

The Gorbachev Revolution

In *Myths of Empire* I argue that a state's foreign policy is shaped by the myths it holds about how to achieve security.[3] The foreign policy concepts of the most aggressive states have as their centerpiece the idea that security can be enhanced by aggressive expansion. This general assumption is reflected, in turn, in more specific notions like the domino theory, the image of the opponent as a paper tiger, and the belief that states jump on the bandwagon of the strongest power. These strategic myths are ideologies put forward by interest groups, bureaucracies, politicians, or domestic political coalitions that receive some parochial benefit from a policy of expansion or from a climate of impending threat. The myths help sell parochial policies in terms of a collective interest in national security.

Whether or not such myths of empire emerge, and how quickly the state learns to correct erroneous ideas, depends on the state's domestic political structure. In well-institutionalized democratic political systems, the electoral power of the average voter and open public discourse on foreign policy have tended in the long run to thwart excessively costly expansionist ideas and policies. Thus Britain and the United States successfully retrenched from their flirtations with imperial overstretch. Drawing on Alexander Gerschenkron, I argue further that the British pattern of early industrialization, which featured the gradual and decentralized accumulation of capital in the textile sector, facilitated this outcome by creating a pattern of mobile, diversified elite interests amenable to political compromise and flexible adaptation.[4]

In contrast, the pattern of capital accumulation in late industrializing states like Germany and Japan was associated with elite economic or bureaucratic cartels with relatively narrow, immobile interests. Under these conditions, politics typically took the form of logrolling among highly concentrated interest groups, some of which had parochial interests in imperial expansion. Since logrolling works by acceding to each groups' strongest parochial interest, and since the diffuse interests of average voters were insufficiently represented, imperial expansion resulted, even when its costs to the state as a whole exceeded its benefits. Strategic mythmaking ran rampant as interest groups and coalition leaders tried to justify the costly imperial policies to each other and to the broader society.

The Soviet Union was yet another type of state: a late, late industrializer.[5] In this pattern, the state developed a highly centralized set of political and economic institutions suited to the forced-draft mobilization of underutilized factors of production for the purpose of catching up militarily with more advanced powers. The tasks of what economists call extensive development led to the creation of a highly unitary political system, which hindered logrolling and mythmaking by independent interest groups. The unitary state itself mythologized foreign threats to justify political repression and economic mobilization, but the political autonomy of the state gave it more latitude to buffer actual foreign policy from threat-inflating rhetoric.

Once the revolution from above was over, however, the mobilizing institutions lived on as entrenched atavisms, bargaining with central state authorities, logrolling with each other, and using the mobilizing ideologies of the period of forced industrialization to promote their parochial interests. A number of these institutions — the combat party, the military, military-related heavy industry, and the secret police — had an interest in policies of foreign expansion or a climate of foreign threat, which were easily legitimated by the ideologies left over from the mobilization period. The resulting foreign policy was not so reckless as that of the late industrializers, however, since the comparatively stronger central state authorities in the late, late industrializer remained at least partly able to contain the logrolling and mythmaking activity when its costs mounted.

Eventually, the institutions of the late, late industrializer became increasingly dysfunctional. Though well suited for the transitory tasks of extensive development, the command economy and hyper-centralized polity were unable to provide the innovative climate and allocative mechanisms needed for the tasks of intensive development — that is, the more efficient use of already mobilized factors of production. The draining foreign and military policies demanded by atavistic interest groups exacerbated this problem.

At the same time, the partial successes of extensive development created a better-educated, urbanized, middle-class constituency for institutional change. The urban intelligentsia, in particular, was used as a spearhead by Gorbachev, a political entrepreneur who wanted to revitalize the state he commanded.[6] Domestically, the program of these reformers followed the approach to intensive development successfully adopted elsewhere: movement toward economic marketization and its necessary political concomitant, greater political pluralism. The domestic goals of the reformers required a new, more benign set of myths in foreign affairs — in particular, the belief that the advanced capitalist states were not threatening — so that military expenditures could be cut and avenues for foreign trade expanded.

This then is the main explanation for the puzzle posed at the outset: the new thinkers who controlled Soviet foreign policy in the

Gorbachev period peacefully accepted the unraveling of their empire because (1) the stage of development of the domestic political economy functionally required a foreign strategy of peace and international economic integration, (2) the previous stage of the modernization process had created a significant political constituency for that policy, and (3) proponents of the policy succeeded in developing a plausible set of strategic ideas to justify the policy to themselves and to other participants in the Soviet political arena. Put more simply, the policy had a functional requirement, a political constituency, and a legitimating concept. All these elements were rooted in Russian economic backwardness, the pattern of political modernization that flowed from it, and the ubiquitous process of using foreign policy myths to forge a consensus favoring the prevailing pattern of domestic political rule.

Admittedly, this explanation leaves out some parts of the story, which a fuller exposition should address. For example, like any macrostructural theory, it is not very helpful in explaining details of timing. More importantly, my first formulation of the argument tended to treat the creation of an urban, educated middle class as a nearly sufficient precondition for liberal democracy. This overlooked the difficulty of creating effective democratic and market institutions from scratch, even with the benefit of those social preconditions.

A final element in the explanation hinges on the cooperative behavior of the advanced capitalist states, which happily matched the ideas being advanced by Soviet new thinkers. Though Soviet opponents of the new thinking called the retreat from empire a "new Munich," the West did nothing to lend credence to that argument. As the theory put forth in *Myths of Empire* would predict, liberal democracies, moderate in their expansionist impulse, would not without concrete provocation recklessly exploit the geopolitical collapse of a nuclear-armed great power, nor would they fall to fighting among themselves over the dubious spoils. If a militarized, logrolling late industrializer like pre-1914 Germany or pre-1945 Japan had been at the doorstep of Gorbachev's Russia, however, it might have behaved much differently, and Soviet new thinking might never have emerged.

Comparisons with Realism

In *Myths of Empire* I distinguish between two kinds of realism, the aggressive and the defensive variants.[7] Both accept that security is the strongest motivation of states in anarchy, but they have opposite

views about how to achieve it. Aggressive realism holds that securi-
ty-seeking states are often compelled to adopt strategies of expansion and offensive warmaking in order to survive in the harsh environment of international anarchy. In other words, aggressive realism contends that the myths of empire are often true. In contrast,
defensive realism holds that aggression that threatens other great
powers diminishes a state's security in a balance-of-power system.
Clear-thinking states, such as the democratic early industrializers,
tend to behave in accordance with the tenets of defensive realism. In
this sense, my theory in *Myths of Empire* is fully compatible with
what I see as the true form of realism.

Realist commentary on the Gorbachev revolution has been dominated by John Mearsheimer's analysis of the likely instability that
will emerge from the increasingly multipolar international system.
Mearsheimer, arguing from what he sees as realist assumptions,
worries that "the international system creates powerful incentives
for aggression," incentives that the great powers will find hard to
ignore.[8] I generally agree with his argument that there are deductive
reasons to expect multipolarity to be less stable than bipolarity,[9] but
even in multipolarity states usually face strong incentives to avoid
overly aggressive strategies. The reason that the pre-1945 period
was more war-prone than the post-1945 era was that the late-indus-
trializing German and Japanese polities provided fertile soil for
imperial myths that left their elites and publics incapable of grasping
the true nature of the balance-of-power system. The pre-1945 system often looked like a caricature of aggressive realism, but the
engine driving this behavior was the irrational aggressiveness of
myth-ridden states, not states' rational responses to the logic of
anarchy. After 1945, these hyperaggressive states were turned into
democracies, which pursued moderate foreign policies, and so the
main source of disturbance to the international order was eliminated. The long peace occurred because no hyperaggressive great powers remained in the system.

Mearsheimer also argues that nuclear deterrence helps to explain
the long post-1945 peace. Certainly, nuclear weapons strongly reinforced the previous incentives for states to be wary about embarking
on aggression. But were those nuclear incentives so unambiguous
that even a Nazi-type state, its perceptions clouded by the myths of
empire, would have been deterred from launching a major war?
There is no clear test one way or the other of this proposition. But
even relatively prudent Soviet and American military strategists
minimized the difference between conventional and nuclear weapons

and saw benefits in first-strike strategies. Soviet war planners thought they might be able to overrun a nuclear power with conventional forces.[10] General Curtis LeMay or Marshal Andrei Grechko, who reportedly advocated a preventive strike against Chinese nuclear forces, might have caused quite a stir in a Wilhelmine-type political system, nuclear weapons notwithstanding.

Nuclear deterrence does help to explain the peacefulness of the new thinking in Soviet foreign policy, but only in conjunction with Soviet assessments of the domestic politics of their potential nuclear adversaries. For example, in the earliest authoritative article in which new thinkers made a clear case for decisively downgrading the threat from the West, Vitaly Zhurkin and his coauthors began with the argument that aggression against a nuclear-armed power would be suicide.[11] But they knew that simply reciting the facts of nuclear deterrence would not win the argument for a reduced threat assessment and a more conciliatory foreign policy. Soviet conservatives had long argued that U.S. imperialists and militarists would behave recklessly despite nuclear risks. To rebut this view, Soviet new thinkers and their precursors argued with increasing effectiveness that American public opinion, which would have no stomach for a costly war, could use the democratic processes of an increasingly autonomous state to keep aggressive circles under control.[12] Moreover, Zhurkin and his colleagues argued that Gorbachev's peace offensive was helping to accomplish this result. They acknowledged that "bourgeois democracy" did not rule out assertive U.S. behavior in instances like Grenada, Nicaragua, and Afghanistan, which involved little cost or risk for the average citizen. "Nonetheless," they insisted, "if one poses the question of large-scale aggression, a large war between two systems, whether local or global, bourgeois democracy serves as a definite barrier on the path toward the outbreak of such a war."[13] As evidence they cite the resistance of public opinion to the Vietnam War once casualties mounted.

In short, strategic factors like those considered by defensive realism may help to explain Soviet new thinking, but they should be viewed in conjunction with domestic variables. As Gorbachev recognized all along, a strategy of holding the empire by force, such as he temporarily adopted in the Baltics during the winter of 1990–91, would have ruined the political coalition behind the domestic reforms. Above all, Gorbachev's assurance that his retreats would not be exploited stemmed less from a nuclear ace in the hole than from the new thinkers' correct assessment of the relatively benign foreign policies of the democratic West.[14]

Comparison with Liberal Theories

The argument in *Myths of Empire* has some similarities with several liberal theories that offer insights on the peaceful Soviet collapse, but some differences are also pertinent to broader questions of international relations.

One hotly debated issue is how and why democratic foreign policy differs from that of other states. The currently prevailing view argues that democracies are not in general more peaceful; they just refrain from fighting each other. Quantitative studies show, for example, that democracies fight as frequently as nondemocracies, and insofar as this can be determined reliably, democracies seem to be just as likely to start wars. But mature, stable democracies, by most reasonable definitions of this term, have never fought each other. Explanations for this finding generally fall into two camps: those stressing democratic institutional constraints on war-making state leaders, and those emphasizing the prevailing norm of peaceful settlement of disputes in and between democracies. Proponents of the normative argument often point out that institutional constraints do not seem to stop democracies from attacking nondemocracies.[15]

My own view, based on the arguments in *Myths of Empire*, differs somewhat from the usual positions in the debate. I follow Michael Doyle in arguing that democracy has a moderating effect on a state's foreign policy because citizens who bear the costs of foreign adventures have power over policy. Doyle says that "the fundamental reason" why Kant thought democratic republics would have peaceful relations was, in Kant's words, that citizens "will have a great hesitation in . . . calling down on themselves all the miseries of war, such as doing the fighting themselves, supplying the costs of the war."[16] To make sense, normative explanations for the democratic peace must ultimately trace themselves back to this central insight, which is essentially an argument based on institutional constraint. Without this linchpin, there is no explanation of how the normative expectation of peaceful democratic behavior arises in the first place.

By this reasoning, democracies should avoid not only wars with each other but also recklessly aggressive policies in general. But this does not mean that democracies are predicted to be generally peaceful. Why should the self-interested average voter veto cheap, lucrative, successful, or unavoidable wars against authoritarian states whose policies threaten liberal aims? A close look at the quantitative studies reveals that most of the democracies' many wars were either cheap conflicts against weak states, which imposed few costs on the average voter, or, in the two world wars, were necessary self-defense against the authoritarian aggressors.[17]

Of course, the Soviet Union, during the loss of its empire, was less of a democracy than was Wilhelmine Germany, so democracy itself cannot explain Soviet moderation. Rather, what was important was the aspiration of Soviet new thinkers to join the peaceful Kantian league of liberal states and their expectation that the developed democracies would therefore act in security affairs as if the Soviet Union were a democracy. My theory of coalition ideology attempts to explain this, though Doyle's argument, which does more to develop the role of democratic norms, is perhaps better at explaining the overall dynamic of the Kantian league.

My argument also overlaps with Richard Rosecrance's contention that objective incentives in the contemporary international system are favoring more and more the adoption of trading-state strategies.[18] Soviet new thinkers were responding in part to this increasingly unavoidable insight. But such incentives have been present for almost all the great powers for over a hundred years. The problem is that the domestic coalitions in some great powers made them unwilling or unable to recognize these objective incentives.

Finally, there are the liberal theories that focus on the role of international institutions in fostering cooperation.[19] From this standpoint, the comparatively peaceful nature of the Soviet collapse might be explained as a consequence of international institutional structures assuring the Soviets that their concessions would not be exploited and that a strategy of international economic cooperation would be feasible. I myself wrote an article urging that international institutional arrangements in the security and economic spheres be used to create incentives for the emergence of liberal democratic coalitions in the successor states to the Soviet empire.[20] As a prescription, I think this was correct, but as an explanation of the peacefulness of the Soviet collapse, it is at best a third-order consideration. The role of international institutions and regimes in the recent transformations, whether in the area of arms control or that of economic assistance, has been quite small and lagged well behind the pace of political developments in the East.[21]

Predictions for the Future

The theory put forward in *Myths of Empire* not only advances an interpretation of the peaceful Soviet collapse but also makes contingent predictions about the future. Like Doyle's theory, it predicts that international relations will become dramatically more peaceful among the great powers if all of them become stable democracies. This is because reckless strategic ideas will not be able to survive the process of democratic scrutiny. In addition, I predict not only that democracies will not fight each other but that they will pursue reasonably prudent, cost-conscious policies toward nondemocratic states as well. (This is one area where my predictions and Doyle's partially diverge.)

The theory in *Myths of Empire* indirectly addresses the likelihood that the great powers will all become stable democracies, but it does not make an unambiguous prediction about this. The modernization theory embedded in the Soviet case implies that democratization and marketization are functional necessities for the next stage of Russian socioeconomic development. It remains to be seen whether the political constituencies and institutions needed to bring this about can emerge under present conditions. It is possible, as my colleague Seweryn Bialer once argued, that the Bolshevik attempt to skip over developmental stages not only failed but actually undid some of the preconditions for a stable, liberal, democratic society. In particular, the market institutions destroyed by Stalin's revolution from above will have to be painfully recreated. Thus Russia might have to start over again on the developmental path as one of Gerschenkron's late industrializers, as one of Huntington's praetorian societies with booming participation and weak institutions, or as a Peronist-style state oscillating between military dictatorship and populist democracy. Pernicious foreign-policy mythmaking would be expected in such states.[22]

Moreover, though mature democratic states are a moderating force in world politics, democratizing states, which combine booming mass political participation with unstable or incompletely democratic institutions, have often behaved very aggressively. Britain on the eve of the Crimean War, France under both Napoleons, Germany in the Wilhelmine and interwar periods, and Japan in the early 1930s were all great powers whose aggressive behavior in foreign affairs was exacerbated by poorly institutionalized mass political participation.[23] Today, the holding of mass elections has not made the Balkans or the Caucasus peaceful. Any predictions about the moderating effect of stable, well-institutionalized democracy on foreign policy must also take into account the contrary impact of the attempted transition to democracy.

Implications for International Relations Theory

If the argument of *Myths of Empire* is even roughly correct, the implication is that international relations theory ought to be integrated with comparative politics and an improved modernization theory. First, we need to know how different types of states behave in foreign affairs. Michael Doyle and other writers have provided a good head start on this question. Stephen Walt's work on revolutionary states will help to fill in the picture even further, while reminding us that a state's type and its international environment interact to produce an outcome.[24] Rather than scrapping international-level explanations for domestic-level ones, we should consider their interactions. This part of the task is almost at the stage of normal science.

But we also need to understand what causes the emergence of different types of states. Though this is a comparative politics topic par excellence, it is nonetheless essential for international relations scholars who hope to be at all relevant to the real questions of our day. American foreign policy debates over the past few years have hinged in large part on guesses about the likely direction of Soviet domestic reforms. Military budgets, treaties, and aid packages have been shaped by expectations about whether democrats or reactionaries could be expected to gain or retain power in Moscow. Moreover, insofar as the international setting is one of the factors that shapes domestic outcomes, we need a theory of the emergence of regime types in order to know how to exert whatever influence we may have in a responsible direction. Should one promote a liberal world order by spurring new democracies to accept economic shock therapy, or, as Karl Polanyi argued, are mass democracy and unregulated laissez-faire incompatible?[25]

Some off-the-shelf research on the impact of international forces on domestic structures will help answer these questions. Some of these works are realist, showing the effect of the security environment on the development of state institutions. Others do the same for the international economic environment. Still others explore tactical questions like the interaction of IMF conditionality and domestic regime type.[27]

Such theories will make a useful contribution. But the main tool for tracking, predicting, and influencing the emergence of regime types should be a good modernization theory, which should explain the connections among social ideologies, patterns of economic development, and the emergence of different types of polity. A gen-

eration ago, scholars like Barrington Moore and Alexander Gerschenkron were at work on theories of this type.[28] They had some
good insights, but their work was impressionistic. It remains
unclear how to apply their theories to the present day. Now, when
students of international politics really need such theories, modernization theory as a whole is derided because of the failings of a particular kind of modernization theory, which portrayed all societies
as modernizing along the same path as the West European liberal
democracies, especially England. But the most perceptive theorists
of modernization and political development — such as Moore, Gerschenkron, and Samuel Huntington — were highly attuned to the
possibility of multiple paths and culs-de-sac on the route to modernity. I made use of Gerschenkron in *Myths of Empire*, but a more
fully articulated theory is needed to carry the burden of future work
of this type.

In addition to a better theory of the evolution of domestic structures, *Myths of Empire* also suggests the need to study the role of
social myths in foreign policy. In every case I examined, strategic
myths arose from domestic politics but then took on a life of their
own. Mythmakers became trapped in their own rhetoric, in the
political arrangements their myths created, and in the internaliza-
tion of myths by second-generation elites. To understand the outcomes, it was necessary to understand the process of mythmaking,
not just the underlying structure of power and interests.

Today, the future of relations among the great powers hinges in
large part on which set of social myths prevails: those of liberalism,
aggressive nationalism, or some other ideological contender. Both
liberalism and nationalism are on the intellectual offensive, competing to occupy the void left by the collapse of Soviet-style socialism. In June 1992 Czechs voted for a Europe-oriented neoclassical
economist; Slovaks, reflecting a different economic base and an
unfulfilled national identity, voted for a protectionist nationalist. In
Russia, proponents of IMF-backed shock therapy have vied for
power against an emerging alliance of nationalists and industrial
protectionists.[29]

Which of these social programs, or what combinations of them,
will prevail in which parts of the former Soviet empire? What will be
the consequences for international politics? Once again, a modernization perspective is helpful.

Most contemporary students of politicized ethnicity argue that
nationalism, the demand of a self-defined people for its own state, is
a symptom of modernity.[30] Beginning in the late eighteenth century,

European peoples came to understand that creating a national state was a prerequisite for defending their economic and security interests in the face of the interlinked challenges of modern warfare, democratization, and industrialization. Modern warfare, argues Charles Tilly, forced states to bargain with their populations, giving them a stake in the state in exchange for taxation and conscription.[31] Increased political participation spurred nationalism, as upwardly mobile groups argued that "the people" should rule themselves and that the old elites were ineffective in advancing national interests.[32] Moreover, according to Ernest Gellner, industrialization and the expansion of market relations required a homogeneous culture, so ethnic groups were forced into a Darwinian competition to determine which would be the prevailing culture in the national market.[33] Finally, with the arrival of universal suffrage, the political backlash against unregulated markets swelled the ranks of nationalist parties, which offered a variety of projectionist, imperialist, and militarist programs that promised to subject market forces to political control.

These challenges of modernity promoted nationalism everywhere, but where ineffectual states failed to meet these challenges successfully, nationalism was especially intense.[34] States that lost wars, suffered severe economic depressions, or failed to develop legitimate democratic institutions were at high risk for what John Mearsheimer calls hypernationalism, an aggressive variant of nationalism based on fear and disdain for other peoples. Where states lacked the capacity to meet modernity's challenges, hypernationalist movements arose to demand the creation of a more effective state. As Gerschenkron argues, late developing states, fueled by nationalist ideology, often created authoritarian, hypertrophied states as a substitute for the more effective political and economic institutions that earlier-developing states developed more gradually.[35]

Impotent post-Soviet states are now navigating all the challenges of modernity simultaneously: the creation of new military and state institutions in an anarchical environment, the expansion of democratic participation, and the marketization of the economy. The literature on nationalism and modernization suggests that this situation is pregnant with the potential for the emergence of aggressive nationalism, not only in Serbia and Karabakh but also in the more consequential case of Russia. A key question is whether strong international institutions—whether the IMF or U.N. peacekeepers—can provide substitutes or supplements for underdeveloped state institutions that are struggling to meet these challenges. A better theory of modernization, nationalism, and the development of state institutions would be of great value not only in understanding but also in influencing these complex social processes.

Implications for Policy

Much depends on the outcome of the debate between realists and liberals and among the variants within each camp. Some realists, without even addressing the challenge that recent events pose to their theory, are offering policy prescriptions that could make their Hobbesian predictions a self-fulfilling prophecy. Samuel Huntington, for example, arguing that Japan now poses the greatest threat to U.S. national interests, proposes a mercantilist stance to guard America's relative power from that quarter.[36]

Liberals likewise risk doing more harm than good with their theories. Some ideologues of neoclassical economics work from the unexamined assumption that peace-loving, democratic politics cannot survive in Russia without a root-and-branch market reform, notwithstanding the ambivalence of Russian citizens about its wrenching social consequences. In their fixation on the contradictions of socialism, these laissez-faire theorists forget that classical liberalism, too, had its internal contradictions. They overlook the many historical cases when the precipitous introduction of markets into nonmarket, multiethnic societies caused hypernationalism and fascism instead of liberal democracy. Uncontrolled markets were subject to periodic, catastrophic depressions, and under the gold standard even healthy but abrupt market adjustments wreaked havoc in labor markets that was intolerable in democratic conditions. Karl Polanyi's classic book *The Great Transformation* reminds us that the rise of mass political participation coincided with rising demands for protection from the vagaries of laissez-faire.[37] A great deal of the appeal of fascism and hypernationalism was precisely that they promised protection from socially corrosive world market forces—for example, by means of protectionism inside a militarily expanded territorial base.

Liberalism mitigated this internal contradiction between democracy and market economics, however, by expanding the sphere of political control over market forces. Domestically, government intervention on Keynesian principles evened out the business cycle, and corporatist compromises spread out the costs of adjustment to shifts in world markets.[38] Internationally, the old gold standard, which necessitated draconian domestic adjustments, was supplanted by the more forgiving Bretton Woods system, which created the

International Monetary Fund, the World Bank, the General Agreement on Tariff and Trade, and other instruments to maintain an open trading system while still buffering voters from its most disruptive consequences. In short, only the political control of domestic and international markets—what John Ruggie calls the "embedded liberal compromise"—solved the contradiction between democracy and market economics and thus made liberalism fully viable under conditions of a very advanced division of labor.

A strictly rational-choice reconstruction of the embedded liberal compromise might construe it as a calculated bargain mediated by democratic politicians between owners of mobile capital, who would normally favor laissez-faire, and workers and owners of fixed capital, who would normally prefer some buffers against the unrestrained workings of the market. Ruggie, however, puts it in a cognitive and normative light. The founders of the Bretton Woods order hit upon this system because they had already internalized the concepts and norms of embedded liberalism from their domestic social orders.[39]

This has important implications for the present management of the problems of order in the former Soviet empire and of the new world order in general. Despite the practice of the embedded liberal compromise, a good deal of the ideology of contemporary American liberalism is left over from nineteenth-century laissez-faire. As a result, there remains the myth that draconian laissez-faire and strict conditionality constitute the best, indeed the only, economic basis on which democracy can survive. In this view, only if subsidies, protectionism, and other forms of political intervention in markets are swept away will a liberal political order emerge.

Naturally, no one will argue that a Peronist-style economy with heavy protectionism and grossly inefficient state-industrial subsidies provides a firm foundation for political democracy. On the other hand, all modern democratic politicians win votes and maintain social peace by buffering constituencies from the worst pain of market adjustment. In Boris Yeltsin's successful run for the Russian presidency, he promised a 50 percent increase in Russians' old-age pensions.[40] Such expedients would be severely limited under the terms of any agreement that the IMF would oversee. But if it takes populist promises and payoffs to forge a social consensus for market reform, then imposing harsh restrictions on political coalition making will only serve to undercut fragile democracies. It is therefore important to remember that even in the West it was the introduction of politically controlled markets, governed by the norms of embedded liberalism, that made democracy and economic liberalism compatible.

The peaceful collapse of the Soviet empire was the bellwether that should have alerted us to the fundamental changes in international politics that are now possible. But those changes could still be derailed if we fail to acknowledge them or if we misread the forces driving them. International relations theorists can do their part by revising the partial truths of realism and laissez-faire liberalism and exploring the connections among modernization, social myths, and international conflict.

NOTES

1   Robert Gilpin, *War and Change in World Politics* (New York and Cambridge: Cambridge University Press, 1981); Jack Levy, "Declining Power and the Preventive Motivation for War," *World Politics* 40 (October 1987): 82–107; and Miles Kahler, *Decolonization in Britain and France* (Princeton: Princeton University Press, 1984).

2   However, Robert Jervis, "The Future of World Politics: Will It Resemble the Past?" *International Security* 16 (winter 1991 / 92): 39–73, correctly argues that in the Third World "there is no reason to think that the basic contours of international politics will be unfamiliar" (61).

3   Jack Snyder, *Myths of Empire: Domestic Politics and International Ambition* (Ithaca: Cornell University Press, 1991).

4   On the political consequences of the timing of industrialization, see Alexander Gerschenkron, *Economic Backwardness in Historical Perspective* (Cambridge: Harvard University Press, 1962).

5   In addition to Snyder, *Myths of Empire*, ch. 6, see also Jack Snyder, "The Gorbachev Revolution: A Waning of Soviet Expansionism?" *International Security* 12 (winter 1987 / 88): 93–131.

6   On the intelligentsia's political role, see Sarah Mendelson, "Internal Battles and External Wars: Politics, Learning, and the Soviet Withdrawal from Afghanistan," *World Politics* 45 (April 1993): 327–60; and Mary McAuley, "Politics, Economics, and Elite Realignment in Russia: A Regional Perspective," *Soviet Economy* 8 (January–March 1992): 46–88, esp. 62.

7   Snyder, *Myths of Empire*, 11–12. On defensive realism, see also Fareed Zakaria, "Realism and Domestic Politics," *International Security* 17 (summer 1992): 177–98, esp. 190–96. Though Zakaria is critical of the notion of defensive realism, he captures the essence of the concept very astutely.

8   John J. Mearsheimer, "Back to the Future: Instability in Europe After the Cold War," *International Security* 15 (summer 1990): 5–56, at p. 12. Mearsheimer is, of course, not prescribing the adoption of aggressive strategies. He simply fears that insecure states in multipolarity will be irresistibly drawn toward bellicose policies. His policy recommendations focus on realist measures, like nuclear deterrence, that might allow the great powers to maintain their security without

resorting to aggressive means. I thank Thomas Risse-Kappen for insightful comments on this point.

9   Thomas J. Christensen and Jack Snyder, "Chain Gangs and Passed Bucks: Predicting Alliance Patterns in Multipolarity," *International Organization* 44 (spring 1990): 137–68.

10 Richard Ned Lebow, "The Soviet Offensive in Europe: The Schlieffen Plan Revisited?" *International Security* 9 (spring 1985), reprinted in *Soviet Military Policy*, ed. Sean Lynn-Jones (Cambridge: MIT Press, 1989), pp. 312–46.

11 Vitaly Zhurkin, Sergei Karaganov, and Andrei Kortunov, "Vyzovy bezopasnosti—Starye i novye," *Kommunist*, no. 1 (January 1988): 42–50. These three were prominent analysts at the USA and Canada Institute writing in what was then still the Communist Party's most authoritative journal.

12 For background, see Franklin Griffiths, "The Sources of American Conduct: Soviet Perspectives and Their Policy Implications," *International Security* 9 (fall 1984): 3–50. See also Ted Hopf, "Peripheral Visions: Brezhnev and Gorbachev Meet the 'Reagan Doctrine,'" in *Learning in U.S. and Soviet Foreign Policy*, ed. George W. Breslauer and Philip E. Tetlock (Boulder, Colo.: Westview, 1991), pp. 609–19.

13 Zhurkin, Karaganov, and Kortunov, "Vyzovy bezopasnosti," p. 45.

14 See Randall L. Schweller, "Domestic Structure and Preventive War: Are Democracies More Pacific?" *World Politics* 44 (January 1992): 235–69, for the argument that democracies virtually never fight preventive wars. More generally, see Daniel Deudney and G. John Ikenberry, "The International Sources of Soviet Change," *International Security* 16 (winter 1991/92): 74–118.

15 See, e.g., Bruce Russett, *Grasping the Democratic Peace* (Princeton: Princeton University Press, 1993).

16 Michael Doyle, "Liberalism in World Politics," *American Political Science Review* 80 (December 1986): 1160.

17 For an assessments of this evidence, see Steve Chan, "Mirror, Mirror on the Wall . . . : Are the Freer Countries More Pacific?" *Journal of Conflict Resolution* 28 (December 1984): 617–48. In general, quantitative studies must be read with a sharp eye. For example, what are we to make of the so-called fact (reported in Chan, 627) that Australia has been more war-prone than Prussia / Germany?

18 Richard Rosecrance, *The Rise of the Trading State: Commerce and Conquest in the Modern World* (New York: Basic, 1986).

19 See, e.g., Robert O. Keohane, *After Hegemony* (Princeton: Princeton University Press, 1984); Stephen Krasner, *International Regimes* (Ithaca: Cornell University Press, 1983); and, in the Gorbachev context, John Ruggie, "Multilateralism: The Anatomy of an Institution," *International Organization* 46 (summer 1992): 561–98.

20 Jack Snyder, "Averting Anarchy in the New Europe," *International Security* 14 (spring 1990): 5–41, revised and reprinted in *The Cold War and After*, ed. Sean Lynn-Jones (Cambridge: MIT Press, 1991).

21　For a more positive assessment, see Joseph Nye, Stanley Hoffmann, and Robert O. Keohane, eds., *After the Cold War: State Strategies and International Institutions in Europe* (Cambridge: Harvard University Press, 1993).

22　Snyder, "Averting Anarchy."

23　I discuss these cases, except France, in *Myths of Empire*.

24　Stephen Walt, "Revolutionary States and War," *World Politics* 44 (April 1992): 321–68.

25　Karl Polanyi, *The Great Transformation* (1944; reprint, New York: Octagon, 1975).

26　For realist views, see, e.g., Charles Tilly, *Coercion, Capital, and European States, AD 990–1990* (Cambridge, Mass.: Basil Blackwell, 1990); and Brian Downing, *The Military Revolution and Political Change: Origins of Democracy and Autocracy in Early Modern Europe* (Princeton: Princeton University Press, 1992). For works on the international economic environment, see, e.g., Peter Gourevitch, *Politics in Hard Times* (Ithaca: Cornell University Press, 1986); Ronald Rogowski, *Commerce and Coalitions* (Princeton: Princeton University Press, 1989); and Jeffry Frieden, *Debt, Development, and Democracy* (Princeton: Princeton University Press, 1991). For studies of the interaction of IMF conditionality and domestic regime type, see, e.g., Stephan Haggard, "The Politics of Adjustment: Lessons from the IMF's Extended Fund Facility," *International Organization* 39 (summer 1985): 505–34.

28　Barrington Moore, *Social Origins of Dictatorship and Democracy* (Boston: Beacon, 1966); Gerschenkron, *Economic Backwardness in Historical Perspective*.

29　See Philip Hanson and Elizabeth Teague, "The Industrialists and Russian Economic Reform," *Radio Free Europe / Radio Liberty Research Report* 1 (May 18, 1992): 1–7.

30　Good surveys include Eric J. Hobsbawm, *Nations and Nationalism since 1780* (Cambridge: Cambridge University Press, 1990); and Anthony Smith, *The Ethnic Revival* (Cambridge: Cambridge University Press, 1981).

31　Tilly, *Coercion, Capital, and European States*, ch. 4.

32　Gerald Newman, *The Rise of English Nationalism* (New York: St. Martin's, 1987); Geoff Eley, *Reshaping the German Right* (New Haven: Yale University Press, 1980).

33　Ernest Gellner, *Nations and Nationalism* (Ithaca: Cornell University Press, 1983).

34　I develop these and the following arguments in Jack Snyder, "Nationalism and the Crisis of the Post-Soviet State," *Survival* 35 (spring 1993): 5–26.

35　Gerschenkron, *Economic Backwardness*, p. 25 and passim.

36　Samuel Huntington, "America's Changing Strategic Interests," *Survival* 23 (January–February 1991): 3–17.

37　Polanyi, *The Great Transformation*, chap. 19.

38　Gourevitch, *Politics in Hard Times*, chap. 4; and Peter Katzenstein,

Small States in World Markets (Ithaca: Cornell University Press, 1985), chap. 4.

39 John Ruggie, "International Regimes, Transactions, and Change: Embedded Liberalism in the Postwar Economic Order," *International Organization* 36 (spring 1982): 379–416, esp. 393.

40 Transcript of June 6, 1991, Soviet television interview, reprinted in *Foreign Broadcast Information Service*, Soviet Union, June 7, 1991, pp. 65–66.

6

*Understanding Change in International Politics:
The Soviet Empire's Demise and the International System

This essay sets out a conceptual framework for understanding
change in international politics by analyzing the fundamental transformation of the international system occasioned by perestroika
and the revolutions in Eastern Europe. We argue that the international system was transformed by the rapid succession of mostly
nonviolent revolutions that replaced Eastern European communist
governments in 1989 and by the lack of any action by the Soviet
Union to stop these changes. The revolutions of 1989 transformed
the international system by changing the rules governing superpower conflict and thereby the norms underpinning the international
system. Practically speaking, the collapse of communism in Eastern
Europe hollowed the Warsaw Pact and led to its disintegration. Revolution also spread from Eastern Europe to the Soviet republics,
eventually tumbling the formal Soviet empire, whose demise confirmed the transformation of the international system.

At first the transformation affected only a limited area of the
international system. Given the centrality of the Cold War to the
system's bipolar configuration, however, the transformation of one
of its blocs, even if geographically circumscribed, had systemwide
implications. Hence the changes of 1989 present a crucial test case
for neorealism and its systemic approach to international politics.[1]
Since we believe the dominant school of international politics, struc-

*For reading earlier drafts and providing helpful suggestions, we
thank Daniel Deudney, Avery Goldstein, Joseph Grieco, Deborah
Larson, Richard Ned Lebow, Susan McKenney, John Odell, Kenneth
Oye, Michaela Richter, Thomas Risse-Kappen, and David Spiro. Rey
Koslowski thanks Vladimir Tismaneanu for guidance in previous
research that contributed to this project. Friedrich Kratochwil gratefully acknowledges the support of the Lawrence B. Simon Chair in
the Social Sciences.

tural neorealism, does not provide a coherent explanation for these transformations, the development of an alternative theoretical framework becomes necessary.[2]

Taking a constructivist approach, we argue that in all politics, domestic and international, actors reproduce or alter systems through their actions.[3] Any given international system does not exist because of immutable structures; rather, its structures are dependent for their reproduction on the practices of the actors. Fundamental change of the international system occurs when actors, through their practices, change the rules and norms constitutive of international interaction. Moreover, reproduction of the practice of international actors (i.e., states) depends on the reproduction of practices of domestic actors (i.e., individuals and groups); therefore, fundamental changes in international politics occur when beliefs and identities of domestic actors are altered, thereby altering the rules and norms constitutive of their political practices. To the extent that patterns emerge in this process, they can be traced and explained, but they are unlikely to exhibit predetermined trajectories that can be captured by general historical laws, be they cyclical or evolutionary.

To develop our argument further, we take the following steps. First, we criticize neorealism's theoretical treatment of change by showing that the changes of the recent past did not occur in accordance with neorealism's propositions and that its assumptions are significantly at odds with the actual practice of states. Then we develop a constructivist approach to change that emphasizes the institutional nature of social systems, domestic as well as international. Next, utilizing the constructivist approach, we analyze the transformation within the Soviet bloc and treat it as a case study of international system change. We argue that Mikhail Gorbachev's decision to end the Brezhnev Doctrine reversed the tactics of communist conquest of domestic politics. This change in the practice of one of the major actors in the international system led to the development of certain conventions similar to those of the classical European state system, which were in turn rapidly surpassed by the generation of new conventions.[4].

Neorealism and Change

Neorealist orthodoxy takes three things for granted: international politics is an autonomous realm following its own logic; the international system is only a shorthand for the organization of force; and the dynamics of the anarchical system are determined by the distribution of capabilities. Given these assumptions, neorealists believed that the world would remain bipolar by virtue of the respective capabilities of the Soviet Union and the United States, regardless of any changes in their domestic politics. Given this point of view, it is not surprising that many neorealists continued to maintain that the international system had not changed even after Gorbachev introduced perestroika and the new thinking. Focusing solely on capabilities, this argument could even be proved by pointing to the continuation of the Soviet arms buildup under Gorbachev.[5]

The end of the Cold War, however, undermined neorealist theory in two ways. First, contrary to expectations of the persistence of bipolarity, the Soviet bloc disintegrated. Second, and even more damaging, change did not follow a path derived from any of neorealism's theoretical propositions. It was not the result of a hegemonic or systemwide war. It was not due to different alliance patterns or the emergence of another superpower, such as China in the 1970s. It was not the outcome of a sudden gap in military capabilities or of U.S. compellence as envisaged by John Foster Dulles's rollback.

Gorbachev's actions confounded neorealist expectations when he discarded the Brezhnev Doctrine, allowed revolutions overthrowing Eastern European communist regimes, and accepted the demise of the Warsaw Pact. Neorealism failed to explain these unilateral concessions and conciliatory policies because it concerns itself with neither the internal structures of units nor questions of legitimacy. Below we show not only that domestic politics matters but also that Gorbachev's strategy was intended to counteract the Communist Party's loss of legitimacy in the Eastern bloc and the Soviet Union. Unlike Nikita Khrushchev, Leonid Brezhnev, and Yuri Andropov before him, Gorbachev realized that reform could only succeed if both domestic and external actors could be motivated to collaborate in the political and economic arenas without threats of repression and force. The (neo)realist tenet of force being, in Kenneth Waltz's words, the "ultima ratio" in domestic politics and "in international politics . . . the first and constant one" had lost its utility for guiding policy.[6] With the growth of civil society and organized resistance, maintaining Soviet predominance in Eastern Europe through military intervention had become exceedingly costly, threatening the very continuation of perestroika at home. Seen from this perspective, the concessions that are unexplainable or irrational within the realist framework become deliberate though risky rational policy moves, even though they ultimately failed. Once communism collapsed in Eastern Europe, it was generally accepted that the Cold

War was over, but many neorealists still denied that a fundamental transformation of the international system had occurred.

Since the end of the Cold War had the potential of representing a crucial case for the corroboration or refutation of the structural realist research program, its exponents have resorted to various gambits to shelter neorealism's theoretical core. Thus the recent transformation is treated as an anomaly, while it is suggested that the international system is, according to John Mearsheimer, on its way "back to the future."[7] Second, it is asserted that the changes are indeed the results of shifts in military capabilities.[8] Third, there remains the epistemological excuse of arguing that single cases cannot prove general theories wrong.[9] This argument is dubious, however, because it requires one implausibly to aggregate all events of a period comprising several years into one data point. A fourth fallback position is that no fundamental change has occurred given that international politics is still characterized by anarchy and bipolarity.[10] Finally, though it is theoretically inconsistent with the notion of the persistence of anarchy, there is the argument that the present system is unipolar but will inevitably evolve toward multipolarity.[11]

Such neorealist theoretical gambits have been further refuted by events since the collapse of Eastern European communism in 1989. France, Germany, the Soviet Union, and the United States behaved contrary to neorealist expectations by reaffirming the norms of multilateralism through their actions.[12] This demonstrates that the classic imagery of the international system as being characterized by poles and shifting alliances is not very useful in understanding contemporary international politics.

First of all, the Soviet Union persisted in its aberrant behavior even when viewed through the lens of neorealism. The Soviet Union, and then its successors, wished to join the "community of nations" and, more particularly, what Gorbachev termed the "common European home." The community of nations was, for him — and this is significant — not simply the sum of states recognized in accordance with international law, but a collection of states participating in the multilateral institutions of the postwar era.[13] As Coit Blacker points out,

> For Gorbachev and those closest to him, the game in world politics had changed profoundly in the four years that separated his elections as CPSU [Communist Party of the Soviet Union] general secretary and the collapse of Soviet power in Europe; if prior to 1985 the overarching object of Soviet foreign policy had been to strengthen the "positions of socialism" at the

expense of the West, by 1989 a new goal — to secure Soviet admission to the elaborate collection of institutions that constituted the Western economic and political system — had arisen to take its place.[14]

The Soviet embrace of multilateralism became most obvious in the acceptance of a multilateral framework for the solution of the German problem.[15]

Second, events since German reunification have demonstrated that the present cannot be understood in terms of a trend back to the future, as Mearsheimer has suggested. Germany has neither developed an independent nuclear force nor pursued an assertive foreign policy, and nothing indicates that these trends are about to change in the foreseeable future. Indeed, several empirical indicators suggest otherwise. Germany possesses the strongest antinuclear movement in Europe, and no significant segment of the German polity has suggested that Germany develop a nuclear capability. A similar broad consensus exists against the use of force. The established parties, as well as the public at large, have been very reluctant to deploy German troops for other than defensive purposes within the NATO, even for peacekeeping operations under UN auspices.

While Germany's stance is certainly at variance with neorealist prescriptions and historical antecedents, a policy-relevant speculation about future trends has to take note of the present political realities, irrespective of whether they are in accordance with the traditional models of politics. The fatal flaw of Mearsheimer's analogy is its systematic elimination of domestic politics that historically had led to expansionist foreign policies. Given the entirely different domestic political realities of the Federal Republic of Germany, the neorealist prediction of a resurgent Germany asserting its hegemony on the European continent is hardly plausible. A much more realistic scenario seems to be that of an internally preoccupied Germany. Unable to digest the acquisition of the former German Democratic Republic (GDR) and hampered by the structural problem of its economy, Germany is prevented from acting either as the engine of the European integration process or as an ascending hegemonic power.[16]

Finally, according to neorealist assumptions, the United States should have taken advantage of Soviet weakness with an aggressive foreign policy and efforts to compound Soviet difficulties so as to make the Soviet Union as weak as possible. Instead the United States extended to the Soviet Union an invitation to join multilateral institutions, offered large-scale financial aid for economic reform, and even supported Gorbachev's efforts to hold the Soviet Union together. It stretches the imagination to explain the supportive behavior of the United States toward the Soviet Union as "balancing" in neorealist terms.

Realists may argue that the United States' supportive behavior does not contradict their theory because great powers try both to prevent the opening of power vacuums that might lead to the emergence of small, aggressive states and to preserve essential actors in the balance of power. This line of argument, however, contradicts the neorealist postulates of power maximization and of relative gains concerns. Moreover, at what point would the United States determine that the Soviet Union was no longer a threat and was to be preserved for balance-of-power reasons? The Soviet Union was the only other country that presented a serious threat to U.S. security when the United States began its supportive moves and, with its intercontinental nuclear missiles, the Commonwealth of Independent States is still the only power that could present a threat to the United States.

Even after the Soviet Union's collapse, the United States did not deviate from its multilateral course. While the initial draft of the Defense Planning Guidance for the 1994–99 fiscal years had advocated that the United States should "prevent the emergence of a new rival" and convince "potential competitors that they need not aspire to a greater role or pursue a more aggressive posture to protect their legitimate interests," the revised draft states:

> It is not in our interest or those of the other democracies to return to earlier periods in which multiple military powers balanced one another off in what passed for security structures, while regional, or even global peace hung in the balance. . . . One of the primary tasks we face today in shaping the future is carrying long standing alliances into the new era, and turning old enmities into new cooperative relationships. If we and the other leading democracies continue to build a democratic security community, a much safer world is likely to emerge. If we act separately, many other problems could result.[17]

U.S. actions in response to Soviet collapse and declared foreign policy objectives demonstrate that even the actors with the greatest potential for relative gains in the reconstituted international system are not following neorealist logic. Rather, the United States and other actors in the international system are assessing security threats in a way that goes far beyond the distribution of capabilities and reaches deeper into the domestic politics of all the actors in the system. One thing seems to be clear: the United States is not responding to these new forms of security threats by balancing through internal arms production or by forming external alliances against potential opponents.

Indeed, the U.S. response to the collapse of Soviet communism has been motivated primarily by the potential consequences of civil war within the Soviet Union. In response to Lithuania's August 1989 declaration that Soviet annexation was illegal, the Bush administration reemphasized that the United States never recognized the incorporation of the Baltic states into the Soviet Union. Nevertheless, President Bush, National Security Adviser Brent Scowcroft, and other officials worried about civil war within the Soviet Union and its potential effect on the control of nuclear weapons. In Scowcroft's words, "It is not necessarily in the interest of the United States to encourage the breakup of the Soviet Union.... It's in our interest that the nationalist debate be tempered. Perhaps some kind of federation would be better than having all these republics arc off and go their own ways."[18] Such a civil war's perceived security threat to NATO includes political destabilization of neighboring Eastern European countries, mass migration of refugees to Western Europe, and, most dramatically, the possible loss of central control over strategic nuclear weapons.

In light of standard realist theory, these are indeed startling developments: Virtually all actors have rejected the generative logic of the system that made a balance-of-power policy with shifting alliances the paramount political maxim. Instead states, whether great, middle-sized, or small, have opted for some form of multilateralism. They also have preferred solutions predicated on integration — both in the areas of low politics (economics) and in the vital area of security — to those based on internal balancing. Finally, states have responded to nontraditional security threats arising from other states' domestic politics rather than from their foreign policies.

Whatever the merits of neorealist theory might be in illuminating the periods before World War I or during the Cold War, most of its tenets and theoretical terms do not seem to correspond to present state practice. Preoccupied with a largely misguided epistemological ideal of parsimony and elegance, structural realists have neglected to examine actual practice as well as to appraise critically the fit between their model's theoretical assumptions and the actual international game.[19] Ironically, in the attempt to meet the ideal of science, neorealists have cut themselves off from some of the important insights of George Kennan and other realist practitioners who shaped nineteenth- and twentieth-century politics.[20]

The Constructivist Approach to System Change

Instead of conceiving the international system in terms of distributions of tangible resources and invisible structures working behind the backs of the actors, constructivism views it as an artifice of manmade institutions, such as (but not limited to) states. In general, institutions are settled or routinized practices established and regulated by norms.[21]

As to the problem of change, it is useful to distinguish among different types of processes characterized as change. On the one hand, changes can occur within the framework of well-established conventions. The availability of and differential access to new resources will create new distributional patterns without necessarily changing the parameters of the system. Reproduction of systemic structures is not affected. Changes in the balance of power would be the typical example of this process. On the other hand, a more fundamental type of change takes place when the practices and constitutive conventions of a social system are altered. This second process is central to our analysis because it shows how actors can fundamentally transform the international system.

The international system is an ensemble of institutions, which are practices constituted by norms, much as a game is determined by its rules. Fundamental change in the international system occurs when some (or all) of its constitutive norms are altered. Below, we argue that the Soviet Union under Joseph Stalin changed a constitutive rule of the classical European states system and that the origins of the Cold War lie in the fact that Stalin was unwilling to accept the previous norms of great-power interaction. Similarly, U.S. universalism and its emphasis on liberal openness violated the exclusivity associated with the traditional notion of sovereignty in important respects. The result of both these changes in constitutive norms led to the emergence of the bloc politics that dominated three decades of postwar history. It was only with Gorbachev's initiatives at the end of the 1980s that the temporary détente between the blocs was overcome by a more fundamental transformation.

So far we have discussed the actors whose interactions make up the international system, that is, states. However, states are themselves institutions whose existence and characteristics are dependent on the reproduction of particular sets of practices. The state is not just a legal entity or a formal organization. Rather, it must be understood as an ensemble of normatively constituted practices by which a group of individuals forms a special type of political association.

If one understands both the international system and the state in terms of normatively constituted practices, international and domestic politics are not hermetically sealed within their own spheres. Given that political practice is divided into these two realms only by the historical fact of the state as the institutional setup that organizes politics, it becomes clear why change in domestic politics can transform the international system.

The rise of modern nationalism provides an example of a fundamental system transformation through a change in the norms of both domestic and international politics. Nationalism denotes a change in the way people thought of themselves and their relationship with existing institutions. With the emergence of nationalism, people stopped defining themselves primarily as members of a specific religious belief or of a particular family but rather as a distinctive group that spoke the same language, practiced certain customs, and possessed a history of its own. This intangible change in identification induced a shift in normative conceptions of allegiance. People no longer paid allegiance to the local noble or family elder but to an entity based on language and cultural distinctions. Such a new identity constituted and regulated very real practices, as the French Revolution and the concomitant emergence of the nation-state demonstrate. It also introduced new conventions for the legitimization of state authority.

The reconstitution of domestic politics in France radically altered practices among states. For example, with the *levée en masse*, the conventions engendered by nationalism reconstituted the practice of war. It created new conceptions of rights and duties of the population by transforming subjects into citizens. Regardless of whether other states in the international system underwent nationalist transformations of their domestic politics, the *levée en masse* immediately changed the way in which international politics was conducted. The new conception of war prompted other states to adopt the practice of conscription based on new norms of national security and citizen obligation. Thus a change in the conventions of politics within one state changed the conventions of both domestic and international politics throughout the system.

This example has several important implications for a theory of international change. First, the principles according to which units are differentiated are of extreme importance for the characterization of the system. Nationalism, for example, not only changed the tone of politics, as Fürst von Metternich and Lord Acton perceived, but also made it increasingly impossible to resort to territorial concession as a means of maintaining the balance of power. As soon as inhabitants cared whether or not they were French, German, or Austrian, their sovereigns could no longer manage the balance simply by transferring territory.[22]

Second, international change is a multilevel phenomenon in which precedence cannot be accorded a priori to either domestic or international structures. What is important instead is the way individuals adopt changed practices arising from new conceptions of identity and political community, thereby altering interactions among states, or, conversely, the way changed interactions among states alter practices among individuals. "Second image reversed" interpretations, which are often tendered against structuralist (that is, third image) approaches, point to an important failing of systemic theory.[23] But the point is not simply to assert the importance of international structures in domestic change but to examine systematically the interaction of international and domestic structures within a conceptually developed framework. The fact that causal arrows can go both ways might make for a more complicated analysis, but this is disturbing only to analysts who have already opted for the primacy of one or another level of analysis and are wedded to a particular and mostly inappropriate concept of causality. Instead of reifying one type of structure, we should be making political practice and the reproduction of the system our central focus.

Third, norms are clearly relevant to the constitution of political action and its appraisal. Constructivists and rationalists share a focus on choice. Constructivists, however, insist not only that choices must be meaningful in terms of the actors' preferences but also that intersubjective standards must provide yardsticks for the classification and appraisal of action. What qualifies as self-determination rather than sedition? What is a case of intervention rather than lawful assistance? What is a case of self-defense rather than an unauthorized resort to force? These are all highly contested issues in international and domestic politics. It is not possible to reduce this problem of appraisal to merely a question of pure description or of empirical fit between a phenomenon and a theoretical term.[24] It is equally inadvisable simply to accept actors' own characterizations (precisely because of the incentives for deception and strategic behavior). Rather, it is contested, but nevertheless partially shared, understandings that illuminate these interactions and help us in our analysis.

For some, this constructivist argument might not seem controversial. Others may contend that it cannot demonstrate what caused the constitutive rules themselves to change. Consequently, one could argue further that an adequate explanation necessitates the reduction of these rules to some incontrovertible last fundament that serves as their cause.

Before we dismiss the constructivist approach as pure idealism, we had better remember that rational choice theory and economic reasoning start precisely with the conception of the autonomous actor and his or her beliefs and / or preferences. In this way, all events can be shown to be caused by the actor even if his or her choice is made under constraints. In other words, there is no reason automatically to seek material factors that can serve as ultimate foundations for our explanations. Nevertheless, accounting for preference formation by analyzing the process of interaction in which identities are formed and interests emerge is part of the constructivist research program.[25] What constructivism, and for that matter any theory of social action, is unable to deliver is a consistent and coherent reduction of action to some ultimate foundation that supposedly causes everything else.

Attempts to demonstrate the superiority of material or structural causes result largely from clever historiography rather than from causal determinism. Of course ex post facto every action can be shown to have been determined, and the observer of complex patterns might be able to impute functional or evolutionary significance to certain events. For instance, instead of our constructivist account of systemic change concomitant with the rise of nationalism, functional and evolutionary explanations compatible with a realist perspective are usually advanced. Thus it has been argued that security imperatives caused the changes in domestic structures in the aftermath of the French Revolution.[26]

Such a functional account, however, does not explain the original shift in the self-identification of the inhabitants of France from king's subjects to citizens. It also does not tell us why this particular form of organization was adopted by other states, given that alternatives were available and citizen armies were against the interests of the military elites of absolutism, as Austria and Prussia quickly recognized after 1815. Napoleon later discovered the military potential of citizen armies for warfare, but the changes in identification of the French revolutionaries who brought down the ancien régime did not occur because of a functional imperative of security. As a matter of fact, one of the decisive repercussions of this revolution was that the concept of security itself was fundamentally altered. Instead of the security of the king and his dynasty (God save the king; the king is dead, long live the king), national security emerged. Only after we observe, historically, that nationalist politics was victorious, do functionalist arguments concerning security imperatives make sense.

Evolutionary arguments implicitly contain the belief that surviving institutions and organizational forms are successful answers to some optimization problem.[27] But institutions do not exist in fixed environments, since institutions often can change environments. Consequently, equilibrium in rational choice terms might not exist; if it does exist, it might not be achievable, or the availability of multiple equilibria makes the evolutionary path argument indeterminate.[28] Constructivism therefore focuses on practices informed by rules and norms. As James March and Johan Olsen point out:

> The advantage of treating behavior as rule driven is not that it is possible thereby to "save" a belief in historical efficiency. Rather it is that it leads more naturally than does treating behavior as optimization to an examination of the specific ways in which history is encoded into institutions . . . and more likely to generate interesting predictions about multiple equilibria or long time paths. In fact, the assumption of historical efficiency becomes mostly a matter of faith . . . if it is impossible to identify the precise mechanisms by which historical experience is transformed into current action.[29]

Thus history and political choices enter as important factors for theorizing. Neither can be understood in terms of functional necessity or instrumental relationships in an overarching system or historical whole. Precisely because political action can transcend prevailing practices and establish new beginnings, it cannot be reduced to functional logic or historical laws, as even Karl Popper has never tired of pointing out.[30]

Large-scale historical change cannot be explained in terms of one or even several causal factors but through an analysis of conjunctures. Although a covering law for this historical process is unlikely to be found, elements within it do form patterns that can be perceived and analyzed, since even largely chaotic processes are not simply random. While this last point has been made by constructivist and nonconstructivist scholars alike,[31] the constructivist research program identifies institutions as both elements of stability and strategic variables for the analysis of change. Institutional underpinnings help in the reproduction of systems (i.e., stability) and become the parameters for routine (i.e., non-system-transforming) choices. For example, markets cannot function unless property rights have been assigned and the property system remains stable during transactions. But even the scope and direction of radical change depend to a large extent on the existence of an institutional structure. Thus the classical revolutions would not have been possible without a state to be captured.[32] An explanation of change will have to blend conjunctive analysis with an understanding of rule-governed activity and the various processes by which institutions are continually reproduced and modified through the actors' practices.

In the following case study, we demonstrate how a new international system is being constituted by the changed practices of one of the major actors and their systemwide repercussions. While the relative capabilities of the European Community, the Soviet Union, and the United States did not change very much during the years leading up to 1989, international politics was fundamentally transformed in just that one year. Focusing on normative changes in the legitimacy and the constitution of international politics within the Soviet bloc, we explain why and how the conventions of international politics changed much more rapidly than did the distribution of capabilities.

The Reconstitution of the International System

Just as the Cold War began over Eastern Europe, it ended there. Stalin's rejection of free elections for Eastern European countries started the process whereby they became an informal part of the Soviet empire. Gorbachev ended this informal empire with the revocation of the Brezhnev Doctrine. Contrary to neorealist theory, this decision was not driven by systemic constraints. Rather, it was a foreign policy choice made in the context of crucial developments in the domestic politics of both Eastern Europe and the Soviet Union. The result was that Gorbachev's decision to end the Brezhnev Doctrine reconstituted the international system by changing the constitutive norms of bloc politics and thereby the rules governing superpower relations.

In this case study, we begin by sketching the constitutive norms of bloc politics that emerged in the early postwar era and underpinned superpower relations from the late 1940s to the end of the 1980s. We then analyze Gorbachev's revocation of the Brezhnev Doctrine and explain how this transformed the patterns of domestic and international political practice within the Warsaw Pact as well as relations among the superpowers. Finally, we examine the rapid and unexpected spread of revolution within Eastern Europe that led to the end of the Communist Party's monopoly on power, the dissolution of the Warsaw Pact, German reunification, and the collapse of the Soviet Union itself. These unexpected changes confirmed the transformation of the international system, since a return to bloc politics became increasingly difficult and a new set of norms governing superpower and great-power relations had emerged.

The Emergence of the Postwar International System: The Constitution of Bloc Politics

To understand the crucial nature of the Brezhnev Doctrine, it is necessary to examine the development of the constitutive norms of postwar international politics. Here, contrary to neorealist analysis, the close connection between domestic and international institutions was particularly important. This fact was recognized by Kennan in his long telegram, as it was by Stalin. Both were aware that fundamentally different conceptions of domestic politics had dramatic consequences for international politics. Stalin told Milovan Djilas in spring 1945, "This war is not as in the past; whoever occupies a territory also imposes on it his own social system. Everyone imposes his own system as far as his army can reach. It cannot be otherwise."[33]

Typically, Stalin could imagine the propagation of the socialist system only by force, opting for imperial expansion rather than hegemonic leadership or an even more limited sphere of influence. After World War II, when Britain, France, and the United States attempted to return to previous conventions of state-to-state relations and were prepared to discuss spheres of influence, they soon realized that Stalin's conceptions of such a sphere in Eastern Europe entailed total control of domestic political processes and the radical elimination of civil society. While Stalin certainly was aware of the traditional form of the sphere of influence, as the Finnish arrangement demonstrated, he did not choose that option for Eastern Europe.

In considering the imposition of the Soviet model on Eastern European societies, one has to understand the dramatic implications of this new form of domination.[34] It radically broke with the traditions of nineteenth-century European empires, including the czarist one. As John Gray noted in 1987:

> The conventional wisdom among Western scholars in seeking to explain away the horrors of the Soviet system as inheritances from a barbarous Russian political tradition, neglects the role of Marxian theory in constituting and reproducing the Soviet

system and the relentless hostility of both to the traditions and achievements of the Russian people. The so-called Russian empire of our time has, in truth, few points of similarity with the empires of nineteenth-century Europe. . . . In projecting into Soviet reality the concepts and images of the past, western observers fail to grasp the radical modernity of the Soviet totalitarian system.[35]

In contrast to the attempts of the Holy Alliance, which was designed to deny the population an influence on politics but left civil society intact, the Soviet transformation made people, willy-nilly, participants in the reproduction of the totalitarian system. Adam Michnik even noted a distinction between Nazi and Soviet occupation of Poland. The Nazi occupiers

> could not be bothered to create political organizations for the conquered people, whom they wanted to transform into a race of slaves. . . . Their execution squads were accompanied neither by dreams of a better tomorrow nor by servile declarations from Hitler's Polish fans. The Soviet conquistadores were different. They systematically destroyed all social ties, political and cultural organizations, sports associations, and professional guilds, and abrogated civil rights and confiscated private property. In contrast to the Nazis, the Soviets imposed their own organizational structures on the Poles. . . . Imitating the spirit of the Crusades, they came to spread the New Faith. They left the door open by allowing everyone — in principle — to choose to convert to the religion of the Progressive System.[36]

This form of participation, however, left the population without any influence on policy while at the same time depriving them of the protection of law.[37] Similarly, as the controversy surrounding the STASI files of the former GDR indicate, every tenth person was, in one way or the other, working for state security. This apparatus not only operated totally outside of any legal accountability, its very goal was the disruption of the trust that allows members of civil society to go on with their lives, form friendships, and engage in cooperative enterprises. The problem with the Soviet model was that — and this demonstrates the inadequacies of the realist paradigm that identifies social order with the existence of hierarchy — it produced Hobbesian "diffidence" and a state of nature among the members of society precisely because a central government existed.

Although some debate exists as to the roots of Soviet policy in the czarist imperial tradition, the analogy with previous occupied societies within the European state system quickly loses its persuasiveness. Two further examples drive this point home more clearly. While by the turn of the century the czarist secret police had some 160 full-time personnel supported by a corps of gendarmes of about 10,000 men, its successor, the Cheka, amounted in 1921 to 262,400 men, not counting the NKVD and militia.[38] Similarly, no traditional European empire found it necessary to resort to large-scale murder of an officer corps as Stalin did in the case of Poland (the Katyn massacre). It is important to realize that the radical transformation of domestic structures and the international system resulted not just from Stalin's pathologies but from the very extension of the Soviet model. Consequently, Stalin's caution vis-à-vis the West, seemingly in accordance with prudential realism, cannot be used as proof for the traditional nature of Soviet security interests.

Although attempts to exert influence beyond the generally accepted norms of the European state system were not without precedent, they had usually been checked by the other powers, if not by the limited means of coercion available to governments. Both factors fostered the pursuit of more moderate security interests and consensual procedures within a concert framework. For example, Henry Kissinger demonstrated that Metternich wanted security to include control over domestic politics but failed because Britain resisted that interpretation. Metternich relented and compromised on a more moderate version, which then allowed the Concert of Europe to function during most of the nineteenth century.[39]

However, when a similar issue arose after World War II concerning Soviet influence in Eastern Europe, particularly in Poland, Stalin did not moderate his position. Thus, irrespective of whether Stalin was reacting to Western initiatives, as revisionists have claimed, the question of legitimacy cannot be reduced to the observation of who acted first and who reacted later regardless of the quality of the acts in question.[40] The fact remains that the imposition of the Soviet model on Eastern Europe was illegitimate not only in the eyes of the Soviet Union's wartime allies but also in those of the so-called liberated Eastern European populations.[41] The Czech coup removed all doubt that Eastern Europe would become part of the Soviet informal empire. Stalin's intransigence meant that the classical state system could not be restored. Communist tactics of conquest changed the rules of the international game by subverting the European state system's conventions very much the way the *levée en masse* had changed international politics in the nineteenth century.

When the West had been convinced by Kennan's long telegram that Stalin was unlikely to play by the rules, it took countermeasures, first with the containment expressed in the Truman Doctrine and the Marshall Plan and then with the founding of NATO. As Waltz described it, this action-reaction process institutionalized the bipolar world:

> Communist guerrillas operating in Greece prompted the Truman Doctrine. The tightening of the Soviet Union's control over the states of Eastern Europe led to the Marshall Plan and the Atlantic Defense Treaty, and these in turn gave rise to the Cominform and the Warsaw Pact. The plan to form a West German government produced the Berlin blockade. And so on through the 1950s, '60s and '70s. Our responses are geared to the Soviet Union's actions, and theirs to ours, which has produced an increasingly solid bipolar balance.[42]

Ironically, Waltz's historical account challenges the logic of his argument, which holds that the bipolar world is a function of the distribution of capabilities in the international system rather than the outcome of a succession of choices by the actors. According to Waltz, the overwhelming capabilities of the superpowers entail a competitive relationship of the type that emerged in the postwar period: "In a bipolar world there are no peripheries. With only two great powers capable of acting on a world scale, anything that happens is potentially of concern to both of them. Bipolarity extends the geographic scope of both powers' concern. It broadens the range of factors included in the competition between them."[43] The problem with Waltz's conception of bipolarity is that the nature of U.S.-Soviet competition is not a general characteristic of bipolar configuration but rather the result of a certain set of practices. It was precisely Stalin's preoccupation with controlling domestic politics that "broadened the range of factors" and was later geographically expanded and projected onto global politics.

The distribution of capabilities thus seems to matter less than the incompatibility of particular conceptions of political community and their concomitant practices. Waltz treats the postwar conventions of superpower interaction as ahistorical givens. But just as these conventions developed after World War II in action-reaction cycles, they are subject to change if these incompatibilities become negotiable. Old conventions can be resurrected, and new conventions can develop. With such changes, the international system is transformed.

East-West tension decreased after Stalin's death, as first Khrushchev and then Brezhnev began to develop more extensive state-to-state relations with the United States. Stalin's subjection of Eastern Europe, however, had become institutionalized. Neither Khrushchev nor Brezhnev was prepared to relinquish the Eastern European empire Stalin had built. Essentially, a two-pronged Soviet foreign policy pairing subversion of domestic politics with state-to-state relations had become so well established that it seemed impossible to alter.

Although the Soviet policy of peaceful coexistence in the late 1950s and early 1960s ostensibly denoted a nonaggressive stance for the sake of establishing agreement on the limitation of conflict, it actually meant the avoidance of nuclear war while continuing class struggle by supporting wars of national liberation.[44] Even during détente, Brezhnev and his successors retained the two-pronged approach of pursuing state-to-state relations with the United States while maintaining the informal empire. Jack Snyder demonstrated that Brezhnev also retained a correlation-of-forces theory of détente. In a curious analogy to the Western peace-through-strength theory of change in Soviet behavior, Brezhnev's correlation-of-forces theory held that "the West would accept a relaxation of tension only when increases in Soviet power demanded it."[45]

Despite the various episodes of reduced tension, the communist tactic of conquest by subversion had become a constitutive norm of postwar bloc politics that bounded the practice of politics throughout the international system. Initiated by Stalin's insistence that countries within the Soviet sphere of influence adopt the Soviet model, the constitutive nature of this norm was reinforced by the Western response of containment and by the acceptance of the division of Europe — most notably by the lack of Western response to the Hungarian revolt in 1956. Finally, this norm was formally reconfirmed by the Brezhnev Doctrine, announced on the occasion of the Warsaw Pact invasion of Czechoslovakia in 1968. The *Pravda* article justifying that invasion argued that a threat to socialism in one country was a threat to the entire movement.[46] Given the nature of the Soviet empire, subsequent events proved this analysis correct.

The Beginning of System Transformation:
The End of the Brezhnev Doctrine

From the day in January 1989 when Gorbachev approved of General Vojciech Jaruzelski's plan to lift the ban on Solidarity and ask its leaders to participate in governing Poland to October 27, 1989, when the Soviet Union renounced the invasion of Czechoslovakia in a Warsaw Pact communiqué, the Brezhnev Doctrine was in a process of disintegration.[47] With Gorbachev's revocation of this doctrine and with his acceptance of "reasonable sufficiency" in armaments, a rather different foreign policy emerged.[48] By allowing his clients greater autonomy in the definition of domestic and eventually even foreign policy, Gorbachev relied on a substantially changed image of the adversary, a considerably narrower conception of the national interest, and a reconceptualization of security itself, which questioned the exclusive reliance on military means and stressed the link between national and mutual security.[49] The end of the Brezhnev Doctrine also indicated that Gorbachev had opted for state-to-state relations as the only acceptable mode of operation. This abandonment of the Soviet Union's traditional two-pronged approach to foreign policy meant that the emerging set of rules reconstituting the international system became more like those of the classical European state system than those of the Cold War or even of détente.

At this point, a more detailed assessment of perestroika and the new thinking in foreign policy becomes necessary. The constructivist approach analyzes the links between domestic and international change without subscribing to the idea of the historical inevitability of liberal democracy.[50] Eastern European observers such as Michnik suggested in 1987 that Gorbachev's reforms should not be interpreted as the harbingers of liberal or social democracy; rather, underlying these efforts was the agenda of socialist counter-reformation.[51] Essentially, Gorbachev attempted to retain control over Eastern European foreign policy by allowing, and then even encouraging, reform of communism domestically, with the expectation that his own model of perestroika would prevail and bring to power similarly minded leaders in the Soviet bloc. Gorbachev's counterreformation was provoked by the legitimization crisis of the Communist Party, which had an internal and bloc dimension. This crisis not only undermined Soviet claims to imperial control in Eastern Europe but also made the leading role of the Communist Party contestable at the center. Gorbachev's strategy was to encourage the reform of all communist parties in order to avert popular revolts in Eastern Europe, which would have repercussions on the Soviet Union itself. Although this was a high-risk strategy, the Soviet leadership recognized that military intervention was hardly possible in any Eastern European country without aborting reforms in the bloc and even threatening perestroika at home.[52] As we discuss in the next section, Gorbachev's expectations proved to be mistaken, and the process of change he initiated quickly went beyond his ability to control it.

Given that the Brezhnev Doctrine had been instrumental in defining the Soviet Union's Eastern European empire, an analysis of empire is useful for understanding the transformation of bloc politics.[53] Postwar Soviet control of Eastern Europe can be defined as formal as well as informal imperialism. Formal empire, in Michael Doyle's terms, is the "annexation and rule by a colonial power," often with the collaboration of local elites. Soviet Republics such as Estonia, Latvia, Lithuania, and Moldavia had been part of the Soviet empire in the formal sense. Postwar control over the rest of Eastern Europe had been informal. According to Doyle, "Informal imperialism can . . . effect the same results as formal imperialism; the difference lies in the process of control, which informal imperialism achieves through the collaboration of a legally independent (but actually subordinate) government in the periphery."[54] This characterization of Eastern Europe as part of an informal empire had been accurate since communist regimes first were installed by Stalin. Nevertheless, Soviet control over Eastern Europe underwent a rapid transformation in just a few years. This change can be conceptualized as a process involving the stages of "Ottomanization," "Finlandization," and "Austrianization."

As Timothy Garton Ash initially conceived it, Ottomanization is the slow decay of the Soviet empire enabling "an unplanned, piecemeal, and discontinuous emancipation, both of the constituent states from the imperial center, and of societies from states."[55] Ottomanization suggests a transformation from formal empire to a type of dependency that was formerly called "suzerainty." In Doyle's words, "Having already encountered the form with the reality (in formal empires) and the reality without the form (in informal empires), we should not be surprised to find the form without the reality. In suzerainty the metropole's power lacks weight in much the same way as a feudal sovereign's political power over vassals would often lack effect."[56] A trend toward suzerainty characterized imperial decomposition in the 1970s and 1980s, particularly in Hungary and Poland. There communist governments retained their form while attempting to pursue market-based economic reform and pluralist politics within the Communist Party. As this tactic failed, compromise arrangements, like those made at the Polish roundtable talks in April 1989, left the Communist Party in nominal control and kept the appearance of informal empire so as not to provoke the metropole.

Although gradual Ottomanization best described the period

146

from the late 1970s to January 1989, Gorbachev's relinquishing of the Brezhnev Doctrine made Finlandization the dominant mode of transformation through the rest of the year.[57] Gorbachev essentially chose this radical restructuring of Soviet-Eastern European relations over the slow transformation brought about by Ottomanization or military intervention.

Since the Soviet Union had its primary security interests in East Germany, it was this country that provided the hard test for the repeal of the Brezhnev Doctrine. If Gorbachev had not wanted popular pressure to be exerted against the Honecker regime, he could have intervened long before the East German government became inviable. Instead, he gave implicit approval to the Hungarian opening of the Iron Curtain that started the mass exodus from East Germany and triggered East Germany's political crisis. He also ordered Soviet troops not to intervene to save Honecker. As Michael Beschloss and Strobe Talbott note,

> The Hungarian government had obtained the Kremlin's tacit consent in advance. As the Soviet Foreign Ministry spokesman, Gennadi Gerasimov, coyly put it, Hungary's action was "very unexpected, but it does not directly affect us." ... [Gorbachev] privately told his aides that Honecker would have to go, as soon as possible: "The [East German] leadership can't stay in control." He ordered his General Staff to make sure that Soviet troops stationed in East Germany did not get involved in the strife that was sure to envelop the country.[58]

Rather than intervene with force, Gorbachev went to Finland and lauded Soviet-Finnish relations as a model for the Soviet Union's relations with its neighbors. Passing the hard test of East Germany, Finlandization seemed to have been established as the new norm of Soviet–Eastern European relations.

Finlandization entailed autonomous domestic politics in concert with a foreign policy that did not conflict with Soviet interests. It signified the transformation of an informal empire into a more conventional sphere of influence in which only the foreign policy of the subject country is regulated. Practically speaking, Finlandization as applied to the Eastern bloc meant that bloc states would have to stay in the Warsaw Pact until the Soviet leadership felt comfortable with another security arrangement. Given that Finland was not a member of the Warsaw Pact, however, and had no Soviet troops stationed on its soil, Finlandization implied eventual autonomy outside the Warsaw Pact but with Soviet consent.

REY KOSLOWSKI AND FRIEDRICH V. KRATOCHWIL

To understand the dynamics of this change, it is necessary to consider further the domestic sources of change in the Eastern bloc. Following the constructivist approach, this entails an explicit theoretical treatment of the interaction effects between internal and external conceptions of order that separate domestic and international politics. In this context, the question of the autonomy and legal nature of the state and its powers becomes crucial. Precisely because the state is the gatekeeper between domestic and international interactions, constructivist analysis stresses the importance of institutions and normative understandings for appraisal. The explanation of change must therefore focus on the state's autonomy vis-à-vis civil society, on its sovereignty vis-à-vis other powers, and on its legality in the exercise of its powers internally.

As argued above, modern nationalism was initially an intangible change in the way people thought and felt, and this in turn undermined the legitimacy of the dynastic order. This change became observable only when the practices of obedience changed. In the same way, the antitotalitarian movements in Eastern Europe changed the way people thought and felt. This new attitude undermined the legitimacy of communism, leading to the observable result of new forms of civil disobedience.[59]

Gorbachev had to contend with the antitotalitarian tactics that the opposition developed in the late 1970s. These tactics were aimed at attaining some form of suzerainty, that is, greater domestic and international autonomy but still within socialist parameters. Jacek Kuron's conception of "social self-organization," Michnik's "open but illegal activity," Václav Havel's "living within the truth," and George Konrad's "antipolitics" were all designed to develop a sphere of social existence, activity, and initiative independent of the Communist Party state—what was traditionally called "civil society."[60] The idea was to bypass communist social institutions and make them obsolete by robbing them of their functions; as Doyle put it, leave "the form without the reality."

The tactic bore its first fruit in 1980, with the rise of Solidarity and the host of independent associations that developed during the sixteen months of its legal existence. When 90 percent of Polish workers participated in a nonviolent rebellion against the workers' state, formed their own independent trade union, and began to manage production on their own, what little legitimacy communism had quickly evaporated.[61] Even though General Jaruzelski reestablished control over the country through a type of putsch in December 1981, the unprecedented necessity of calling on a military

148

leader to head the government demonstrated the collapse of the Communist Party's authority.

Even as Jaruzelski's crackdown ended the legal existence of civil society, the new tactics of civil disobedience spread first through Polish society and then were emulated throughout Eastern Europe. The spread of these tactics involved first learning about the successes and failures of opposition activities in other countries from samizdat and foreign radio broadcasts and then adopting the successful models.[62] By the late 1980s, direct international contacts between opposition groups had begun to flourish.[63]

The growth of civil society presented the Soviet Union with peculiar difficulties. In asking the rhetorical question of whether force effectively would have resolved the Soviet predicament, Eduard Shevardnadze points to the example of Poland. He came to the conclusion that imposition of martial law in 1981 did not end but rather stimulated the internal ferment, "so there is no reason to hiss at Perestroika and cheer for military force. It would not be a bad idea for us to learn the lessons of martial law in Poland ourselves." That this point of view was shared even among more conservative leaders is evidenced by Mikhail Suslov's repeated explicit declaration, "There is no way that we are going to use force in Poland."[64] Instead of dealing with these problems by using force, Gorbachev adopted the counterreformation strategy. His revocation of the Brezhnev Doctrine could be understood as a means of retaining at least minimal control over Eastern Europe through reform. By not intervening to save communism, he tried to increase his chances of saving the one structure that seemed most important to the newly circumscribed Soviet security interest: the Warsaw Pact, redefined as a classical (though hegemonic) alliance.

The policy of nonintervention, however, developed a dynamic of its own, particularly in Poland. Seven years of gradually increasing open but illegal social self-organization and a new round of strikes in 1988 finally forced the Polish communists to compromise with Solidarity in April 1989. By accepting one of Solidarity's first demands, freedom of association, the Jaruzelski regime legalized the latent civil society that had developed over the years. Jaruzelski also agreed to hold partially free elections in June. Solidarity candidates won nearly every seat open to competition. Unable to form a communist-led government, Jaruzelski asked Solidarity leaders to put together their own coalition government. Communist Party leader Mieczyslaw Rakowski refused to go along with Jaruzelski until Gorbachev telephoned him on August 22 and told him to accept the first noncommunist-led government in the Warsaw Pact.[65]

Gorbachev's toleration of this development meant that the Communist Party's leading role in society could now be challenged. Nevertheless, Solidarity accepted a silent compromise, maintaining a longstanding policy of not threatening Soviet security interests.[66] The Solidarity leadership offered reassurances that Poland would remain in the Warsaw Pact, left the Ministry of Defense under communist control, and agreed that Jaruzelski should become president and commander-in-chief of the armed forces. By retaining implicit control of Polish defense policy, Gorbachev seemingly maintained Soviet security interests. In this way, he avoided a potentially violent rebellion in the Soviet Union's client states, since popular demands could now be directed at Solidarity rather than at the Communist Party. Originally Poland's economic crisis had threatened to bring down the communist system and leave a power vacuum, forcing Gorbachev's hand. After his acquiescence, Poland's economic crisis threatened instead to bring down a Solidarity government.

Whereas the Prague Spring was considered heresy in 1968, Gorbachev welcomed the same reforms in 1989 because they reduced the chances of popular revolts. Initially Gorbachev accomplished this goal by not intervening to save communism in Poland. But by summer 1989 it became evident that, quite ironically, nonintervention now yielded the goal for which intervention in 1968 had been undertaken — the conformity of domestic systems with the Soviet model. However, the model was now one of perestroika rather than Brezhnev's orthodoxy.

Gorbachev's renunciation of the Brezhnev Doctrine changed the practices of the Warsaw Pact, which changed into an alliance more like those of the European state system. This transformation was marked by a shift in the practice of diplomacy. During the period of what Shevardnadze termed "Party diplomacy," decisions were made (or instructions given) during meetings of Communist Party General Secretaries of Warsaw Pact countries.[67] With the end of the Brezhnev Doctrine, intrabloc relations could no longer be conducted within the Communist Party because, beginning with the Mazowiecki government in Poland, noncommunists had real decision-making roles in foreign affairs as prime ministers and foreign ministers. The nominal sovereignty that Eastern European states enjoyed during the postwar era was now gradually becoming real.

As Gorbachev ended the imperial relationship with Eastern Europe, new norms of superpower relations emerged. After the Soviet leader tolerated the Hungarian communist regime's decision to allow the formation of independent political parties (February 1989) as well as the Polish roundtable agreement (April 1989) to hold elections in Poland, President Bush reciprocated in May by stating that it was "time to move beyond containment" and "seek the integration of the Soviet Union in the community of nations."[68] Bush set as a condition for this movement a "significant shift in the Soviet Union" and a "lightening-up on the control in Eastern Europe," which would allow these countries "to move down the democratic path much more." Bush also added it was "part of [his] responsibility" to make sure that the West would not threaten the Soviets.[69]

The U.S. public stance on not exploiting change in Eastern Europe emboldened the Kremlin not only to allow more such changes but also to reconceptualize the U.S.-Soviet relationship. Gorbachev and his advisers decided on "the word partnership. This suggested that the two nations were moving from 'negative peace' — that is, the effort to avoid nuclear conflagration — to joint efforts that could make the entire world more secure."[70]

It was on his trip to Hungary and Poland in July 1989 that President Bush made good on his commitment to refrain from taking advantage of the accelerating change in Eastern Europe. He even promoted continuity of leadership over rapid democratization in the wake of the Polish communists' landslide defeat in elections to freely contested parliamentary seats. Since the communists' defeat meant that Jaruzelski's election to the presidency, as agreed to by Solidarity, was no longer certain, Jaruzelski decided not to run rather than face a humiliating setback. Bush's public bestowal of respect on Jaruzelski and his private counsel to Jaruzelski that he continue to play a role in Poland's "evolution," however, helped encourage Jaruzelski to change his mind. In Hungary, Bush told Communist Party leaders, "We're with you. . . . We're not going to complicate things for you. We know that the better we get along with the Soviets, the better it is for you."[71]

The trip to Hungary and Poland convinced Bush that he should meet Gorbachev before the full-scale summit tentatively scheduled for 1990. Unbeknownst to the public, on July 18, 1989, he invited Gorbachev to meet with him at what was to become the Malta summit.[72] Setting a precedent for superpower relations, Bush envisioned a meeting with only minimal staffs and a more informal atmosphere for discussions of an open agenda. Gorbachev viewed the invitation as evidence that Bush was finally prepared to engage in serious negotiations on various Soviet arms reduction proposals. In the meantime, Gorbachev accepted the U.S. invitation to join the community of nations by sending a letter to leaders at the Group of Seven summit meeting in Paris stating that the Soviet Union was willing to increase its integration in the world economy.

Thus fairly early in the process of the Brezhnev Doctrine's demise, the changes in Eastern Europe fostered the development of new practices of superpower relations. These new practices included the support of communist leaders by the American president, an understanding of U.S.-Soviet relations in terms of partnership, and less formal and more frequent communications between the two, that is, relations more characteristic within alliances than across blocs.

The System Transformed:
The End of the Communist Party's Monopoly of Power,
German Reunification, and the Collapse of the Soviet Union

If the Hungarian and Polish revolutions proved to Bush that Gorbachev was serious about change, the Czechoslovakian, East German, and Romanian revolutions proved that the Cold War was truly over and that the international system had been transformed. The subsequent rebellions by Soviet republics confirmed this transformation by making a reimposition of external empire extremely difficult if not impossible. Moreover, the new norms of superpower relations reminiscent of those of the European state system were quickly challenged by novel situations, the most incongruous being the essentially nonviolent breakup of a superpower itself. It was clear that Gorbachev had miscalculated the breadth, depth, and speed of the changes he had initiated.

As Fyodor Burlatsky put it, Gorbachev's original hope was to have "mini-Gorbachevs" come to power.[73] As is now clear, he had overestimated the degree of legitimacy of communist reformers in Eastern Europe. His counterreformation might have worked in 1968, but communist revisionism was long dead by 1989. A civil society had developed, and with it legitimate leaders with independent political bases who could demand greater concessions from the revisionist communists espousing the perestroika line. Moreover, beyond the domestic sources of foreign policy arguments, we argue that an important contagion effect also explains the dynamics of the Eastern bloc. It is best exemplified by the formal restructuring (new constitutions!) of every political system in the area.[74]

As mentioned above, the rapid change of domestic structures through emulation changed the conventions of international politics within the Warsaw Pact, which in turn further changed the rules of the game between the superpowers. When Czechoslovakia and

Hungary eliminated the leading role of the Communist Party from their constitutions in the fall of 1989, they quickly went beyond the accepted boundaries of perestroika.[75] When Czechoslovakia began to assert an independent foreign policy, Finlandization rapidly disappeared from the Soviet foreign policy agenda. The Polish formula of opposition-led government deferring to Soviet security interests was overtaken by Jiri Dienstbier's announcement on December 14, 1989, that the agreement with the Soviet Union on stationing its troops was invalid.

The accelerating development of civil society across Eastern Europe and the Czechoslovak moves beyond Finlandization both had implications for Gorbachev's reforms. Czechoslovak demands occasioned a new round of debates about Soviet security interests. Here Gorbachev himself opened the discussion of what constituted Soviet security when he agreed to begin negotiations on Soviet troop withdrawal within a week of the Czechoslovak demand. He agreed five weeks later to a withdrawal within the context of overall conventional force reductions in Europe. By allowing the eclipse of the leading role of the Communist Party within the bloc and then at home, Gorbachev, probably unwittingly, not only gave up one of its most powerful means of control but also destroyed the rationale for the very existence of the bloc and its domestic institutions. When socialism was not automatically accorded a privileged position in the constitutions of every bloc state, the Warsaw Pact lost one of its fundamental reasons for existence, making its continuation as an effective alliance less likely.

Also, the contagion of civil society, which spread through the informal empire of Eastern Europe in 1989, repeated itself within the boundaries of the formal empire, the Soviet Union itself, the next year. As Andrei Sahkarov's call for an end to the Communist Party's leading role in Soviet society indicated, Soviet dissenters were inspired by Eastern European examples.[76] Since it had been the party and not strong autonomous state institutions that had served as the empire's integrative force, the demise of the Soviet Communist Party had two repercussions.[77]

First, Soviet citizens' lack of loyalty to the federation became obvious, bringing to the fore more nationalist identifications. The long-suppressed national identities of the constituent republics quickly emerged among the population as well as in the communist elite and the military. Politics in the Baltics, in which communists aided and even joined national fronts, suggested that such abrupt turns were not just a function of individual opportunism.[78] In a way, these events showed the same dynamics of national communism observed earlier in Eastern Europe with cases ranging from Władysław Gomułka to János Kádár, Alexander Dubchek, and Jaruzelski. Similarly, just as in Hungary, Czechoslovakia, and East Germany, where nationalist communists espousing the perestroika line became transitional figures, so communist leaders like Algirdas Brazauskas of Lithuania were bypassed by noncommunists who emerged from civil society.

As self-identification along national lines fundamentally altered practices in postrevolutionary France, so national self-identification among young men in the Soviet Union affected conscription in the Soviet Army. While conscripts were ready to fight for the independence of their republic, they were increasingly unwilling to serve in the Soviet armed forces. This was made clear by large-scale non-compliance with the 1990 draft.[79] Republics enhanced their legitimacy by appealing to their citizens, assuring them that troops would not be used to suppress national movements. This contest for legitimate authority began with Boris Yeltsin's instructions to Russian soldiers not to use force during the Lithuanian crackdown and the movement to establish a Ukrainian army in February 1991.[80]

The second repercussion of the Communist Party's demise also arose out of the issue of self-identification. Given the lack of individual and group rights, serious minority problems emerged within the republics, such as the Gagauz independence movement within Moldavia, the South Ossetians in Georgia, the Tartars in Russia, and, perhaps most critically, the twenty-five million Russians outside Russia. These tensions are probably manageable only within a complex federal constitutional arrangement. However, such an arrangement presupposes strong state institutions and, above all, the acceptance of a rule of law that would limit the excesses of Communist Party rule as well as those of popular sovereignty. Here the importance of the state as a protector of rights becomes clearly visible.

The end of the Communist Party's monopoly on power in Eastern Europe and then in the Soviet Union rapidly changed the practice of international politics, continuing the transformation of the international system that had begun in the spring of 1989. For example, the Bush administration responded to East German, Lithuanian, and Romanian revolutions with further steps to reassure the Soviets. Secretary of State Baker set a precedent by traveling to East Germany to meet with Premier Modrow and offering economic assistance to the GDR. In response to the violence in Romania, Baker went beyond respect for Soviet security interests by saying that the United States would not oppose Soviet intervention.[81] (Only two years before, Romania had enjoyed preferential U.S. treatment because of its independence from Moscow.) In response to the Lithuanian declaration of independence, the U.S. administration refrained from recognizing the new government, even though it had never recognized the Soviet annexation under Stalin. Bush implored Gorbachev not to use force and made it clear that doing so would set back U.S.-Soviet relations. At the same time, he reassured Gorbachev that the United States would not press the issue of Baltic independence.[82]

The acceleration of revolutions across Eastern Europe during the winter of 1989 ushered in Austrianization as a possible mode of transforming the Soviet empire in Eastern Europe.[83] Austrianization originally meant neutrality through great-power agreement as exemplified by the 1955 Austrian settlement. Unlike Finlandization, Austrianization could not be unilateral: it required agreement with the West. Hence a more complicated transformation toward some form of multilateral arrangement began. This was evidenced by the February 1990 agreement to begin the two-plus-four talks on the status of Germany. The introduction of multilateral concerns would have been minimal had the German problem been solved by Austrianization of East Germany. The collapse of East German communism and the March 18, 1990, victory of the electoral coalition Alliance for Germany, however, prompted the acceleration of German reunification. This raised the possibility of Austrianization of all of Germany and, in the absence of that option, made it necessary to confront Germany's alignment.

Although the Soviets initially rejected the unified Germany's membership in NATO, NATO's declaration at the London summit that the Soviet Union was no longer an enemy, and Secretary Baker's proposal to transform NATO from a primarily military to a primarily political institution prompted the Soviets to change their position.[84] Eventually, in July 1990, Gorbachev officially agreed to Germany remaining within NATO, thereby moving beyond a neutrality analogous to Austria's and further establishing Soviet acceptance of the web of Western multilateral institutions. The evolution of the Soviet position on multilateral arrangements as a solution to the German problem and to Soviet security interests in Europe has been detailed in the day-by-day account of Chancellor Kohl's foreign policy adviser Horst Teltschik,[85] and consequently only its implications need some further discussion.

By accepting reunified Germany's integration within NATO, the

Soviet Union abandoned its old dream of separating America from its allies and eliminating the United States as a political and military force from the Continent. The Soviets also abandoned their policy of limiting the Germans to a choice between national independence and neutrality on the one hand and division and Western integration on the other.

Having failed to create within their sphere of influence a viable political order that could instill loyalty and weather changes, Soviet policy makers were not blind to the fact that the political and military integration of Western Europe had successfully dealt with important problems of European politics that previously had eluded adherents of realpolitik and peacemakers alike. It had solved the Franco-German problem by making both states part of the Western alliance. (It is often forgotten that American troops were stationed on the European continent largely to reassure the French — and possibly other Europeans — that a rearmed Germany was not going to be a renewed security threat.) Gorbachev expressed his desire to see U.S. forces stay in Europe at the May 30–June 2, 1990, Washington summit, saying to Bush, "I want you to know that I regard this as in your interest and in our interest." By the end of the summit, the Soviets offered no objections to an American statement that both leaders were " 'in full agreement' that alliance membership was a 'matter for the Germans to decide.' "[86]

The Soviet leadership opted for a united Germany within Western European structures because it had decided that this solution was likely to serve Soviet security interests better than would a neutral Germany. Obviously, such a policy was not unopposed, as the debate within the Soviet leadership indicated.[87] But Gorbachev and Shevardnadze made their definition of Soviet interests stick, thereby contravening the traditional realist positions espoused by their opponents.

Western multilateral institutions also had solved the problem of prosperity for which only insufficient provisions had been made at Versailles. This lesson was not lost on Soviet leaders as they actively sought Soviet membership in the very multilateral institutions the Soviet Union had once opposed, not only for ideological reasons but on the realist basis of preserving autonomy and sovereignty. Soviet foreign policy makers' expressed desire to become part of Europe and, in particular, to profit from the emergence of a single European market suggests that they considered maintaining and developing European multilateral institutions preferable to weakening them.[88]

The importance of the existing multilateral institutions in Western Europe not only affected Soviet decision making; it also provided Western leaders with a framework within which a reunited Germany could be accepted. This enabled European states to avoid a return to balance-of-power politics, which had served neither their security nor their welfare interests in the interwar period.

French policy planners briefly considered such a return to a balance-of-power policy after both François Mitterand and Margaret Thatcher had privately shared their misgivings about German reunification in December 1989. Despite Thatcher's suggestion of an Anglo-French axis and renewed efforts at reducing Germany's influence in Eastern Europe, France had rejected such a course of action by the end of January 1990.[89] This choice was publicly enunciated in March by Foreign Minister Dumas, who advocated the deepening of European integration in order to restructure relations with Germany. He even suggested on that occasion a continentwide "European confederation."[90]

Similarly, Germany once more opted against neutralization and against becoming a wanderer between East and West, a role played with bravado by Bismarck but ultimately ending in disaster. This concern was particularly well conceptualized in the Genscher plan announced in January 1990, which tried to assuage Soviet fears of a resurgent Germany by accepting limitations on German forces and by attempting to persuade the Kremlin that a neutral Germany was not in Soviet security interests. At the end of April 1990, East German Prime Minister Lothar de Maizières echoed Genscher's argument against neutralization.[91]

After Eastern European countries also attempted diplomatic forays toward NATO, the wider implications of going beyond Austrianization became apparent.[92] Justifying its stance in terms of maintaining stability, the West initially rebuffed these advances in deference to the Soviet Union, insisting that transformation outside of East Germany should be limited to Austrianization. In the wake of the failed Soviet coup, however, Germany and the United States proposed in October 1991 that NATO organize the North Atlantic Cooperation Council as a forum for airing security issues among officials from Eastern Europe, the Soviet Union, and the West. The council first met on the day the Soviet Union dissolved and soon included all the Soviet successor states except Georgia.

The rapid transition from Ottomanization to Finlandization to Austrianization and then even beyond Austrianization showed that the process of reform had escaped efforts to control its scope, speed, and direction. The consequences of this increasingly broad-based transformation can best be appreciated by its impact on the Soviet political system itself, which made a return to Finlandization or even Austrianization of the Eastern bloc all but impossible. In July 1990 Ukraine declared the supremacy of the republic's law over Soviet law, that is, it declared sovereignty. As Moscow contended with maintaining the integrity of the Soviet Union itself, the reimposition of Soviet control over the informal empire in Eastern Europe became increasingly improbable, especially since once the movement for an independent Ukrainian army began, Moscow could no longer count on participation of Soviet armed forces.

In this essay, we have sought to offer a new approach to analyzing fundamental changes in world politics and outlined an alternative to neorealism for the conceptualization of system-transforming changes. For these purposes, the revocation of the Brezhnev Doctrine and perestroika's domestic and international implications served as a case study. By examining the importance of civil society, nationalism, and self-identification within the processes of glasnost and perestroika, we showed that international politics is not an autonomous sphere but always part of the larger endeavor of institutionalizing both identities and political communities as well as their interactions.

We argued that the rapid and fundamental change of the international system from 1989 to 1991 demonstrated the inadequacy of analyzing present international politics in terms of its anarchical structure and its distribution of capabilities. The recent changes that reconstituted the international system were not the result of a shift in capabilities, though they have led to such a shift. Roughly speaking, the total number of Warsaw Pact weapons and forces did not change much between February 1989 and February 1991; the political context of their potential use did. It was this political change that resulted in the deterioration of Soviet capabilities. To that extent, systemic theories that use balancing as an explanation do not explain change; at best, they only describe its outcome.

Rather than viewing political practice as being derived from military capabilities, we must understand military capabilities in terms of political practices and their underlying conventions. In this sense, changes in conventions eventually are reflected in changed capabilities. This has been demonstrated by the rise of nationalism and the *levée en masse* after the French Revolution, by the delegitimization of Eastern European communism in 1989 and the hollowing of the Warsaw Pact, by the subsequent delegitimization of Soviet communism and imperialism, and finally by the rebirth of nationalism and movements of self-determination in the Soviet Union.

NOTES

1   See John Lewis Gaddis, "International Relations Theory and the End of the Cold War," *International Security* 17 (winter 1992 / 93): 5–58.
2   On structural neorealism, see Kenneth N. Waltz, *Theory of International Politics* (Reading, Mass.: Addison-Wesley, 1979); and Robert Gilpin, *War and Change in World Politics* (New York and Cambridge: Cambridge University Press, 1981). For a good review of the problems realism encounters when explaining change, see R. B. J. Walker, "Realism, Change, and International Political Theory," *International Studies Quarterly* 31 (March 1987): 65–86.
3   We use the term *constructivist* in the sense elaborated by Nicholas Onuf, *World of Our Making* (Columbia: University of South Carolina Press, 1989), esp. part 1. See also Alexander Wendt, "Anarchy Is What States Make of It: The Social Construction of Power Politics," *International Organization* 46 (spring 1992): 391–425. For a further discussion, see Alexander Wendt, "The Agent-Structure Problem in International Relations Theory," *International Organization* 41 (summer 1987): 335–70; and David Dessler, "What's at Stake in the Agent-Structure Debate?" *International Organization* 43 (summer 1989): 441–73.
4   By *conventions*, we mean all types of norms and rules that constitute and regulate practices, not just those norms that alleviate problems of coordination. For an extensive discussion, see Friedrich Kratochwil, *Rules, Norms, and Decisions: On the Conditions of Practical and Legal Reasoning in International Relations and Domestic Affairs* (Cambridge: Cambridge University Press, 1989).
5   Until 1988 the conceptualization of perestroika as *peredyshka* (a breathing spell) in which to recharge before resuming the same competition with the United States was very popular in the USA. See Ernest W. Lefever and Robert D. Vander Lugt, eds., *Perestroika: How New Is Gorbachev's New Thinking* (Washington, D.C.: Ethics and Public Policy Center, 1989), especially Richard Nixon, "Challenge and Response," Henry Kissinger, "A Threat to Global Balance," and Jeane Kirkpatrick, "A Return to Leninist Orthodoxy." Also see Simon Serfaty, ed., "Symposium: Old Adversaries, New Ground," *SAIS Review* 8 (summer–fall 1988): 1–40, especially the contributions by Zbigniew Brzezinski and William Hyland, pp. 10–11 and 20–22, respectively.
6   Waltz, *Theory of International Politics*, p. 113.
7   See John J. Mearsheimer, "Back to the Future: Instability in Europe After the Cold War," *International Security* 15 (summer 1990): 5–56.
8   For a critical discussion of this argument and a statistical analysis demonstrating that Soviet behavior was unaffected by increased U.S. spending, see Fred Chernoff, "Ending the Cold War: The Soviet

Retreat and the U.S. Military Buildup," *International Affairs* 67 (January 1991): 111–26. For an argument that increased U.S. arms spending did not lead to major concessions in the periphery, see Richard K. Herrmann, "Soviet Behavior in Regional Conflicts: Old Questions, New Strategies, and Important Lessons," *World Politics* 44 (April 1992): 432–65. Similarly, Garthoff credits a new generation of Soviet leaders rather than the Reagan military buildup with the end of the Cold War. See Raymond L. Garthoff, "Why Did the Cold War Arise, and Why Did It End?" in *The End of the Cold War: Its Meaning and Implications*, ed. Michael J. Hogan (Cambridge: Cambridge University Press, 1992), chap. 11.

9   This was the argument made by Robert Keohane at a conference on multilateralism in La Jolla, California, December 6, 1990. The same point was reiterated by Steve Walt and Kenneth Waltz, among others, at a conference at Cornell University, Ithaca, New York, in October 1991.

10   Kenneth N. Waltz, "The Emerging Structure of International Politics," *International Security* 18 (fall 1993): 44–79.

11   Christopher Layne, "The Unipolar Illusion: Why New Great Powers Will Rise," *International Security* 17 (spring 1993): 6–51.

12   For a discussion and conceptual clarification of multilateralism as an organizational form, see John Ruggie, ed., *Multilateralism Matters* (New York: Columbia University Press, 1993).

13   Robert Legvold was one of the first to argue that Gorbachev's commitment to multilateralism was genuine and should not be dismissed by the West. See "The Revolution in Soviet Foreign Policy," *Foreign Affairs* (special issue) 68 (1988 / 89): 82–98, and particularly pp. 97–98.

14   Coit D. Blacker, *Hostage to Revolution: Gorbachev and Soviet Security Policy, 1985–1991* (New York: Council on Foreign Relations, 1993), p. 188.

15   A Bush administration analyst with major responsibility for U.S. policy on German unification, Condoleezza Rice, has come to a similar conclusion in an unpublished work entitled "Soviet Policy Toward German Unification: Implications for Theories of International Negotiation." See Blacker, *Hostage to Revolution*, p. 188 n. 3.

16   For an early recognition of these facts, see Eckart Arnold, "German Foreign Policy and Unification," *International Affairs* 67 (July 1991): 453–71.

17   This document is quoted in Patrick E. Tyler, "Pentagon Drops Goal of Blocking New Superpowers: Policy Document Revised," *New York Times*, May 24, 1992, p. A14.

18   Michael R. Beschloss and Strobe Talbott, *At the Highest Levels: The Inside Story of the End of the Cold War* (Boston: Little, Brown, 1993), pp. 102 and 109.

19   See Dessler, "What's at Stake in the Agent-Structure Debate?"

20   For a further elaboration on this point, see Friedrich Kratochwil, "The Embarrassment of Changes: Neo-Realism as the Science of

Realpolitik Without Politics," *Review of International Studies* 19 (1993): 63–80.

21   For a further discussion of institutions and the importance of the norms constituting them, see Kratochwil, *Rules, Norms, and Decisions*, chaps. 3 and 4.

22   See Friedrich Kratochwil, "On the Notion of Interest," *International Organization* 36 (winter 1982): 1–30.

23   On "second image reversed" interpretations, see Peter Gourevitch, "The Second Image Reversed: The International Sources of Domestic Politics," *International Organization* 32 (autumn 1978): 881–911. For an example of such an analysis, see Daniel Deudney and G. John Ikenberry, "The International Sources of Soviet Change," *International Security* 16 (winter 1991 / 92): 74–118.

24   For a further explanation of essentially contested concepts, see William E. Connolly, *The Terms of Political Discourse* (Lexington, Mass.: Heath, 1974).

25   See Wendt, "Anarchy Is What States Make of It."

26   See Otto Hintze, "The Formation of States and Constitutional Development: A Study in History and Politics," and Otto Hintze, "Military Organization and the Organization of the State"; both in *The Historical Essays of Otto Hintze*, ed. Felix Gilbert (New York: Oxford University Press, 1975).

27   See, for example, Robert Axelrod, *The Evolution of Cooperation* (New York: Basic, 1984).

28   This point is eloquently made by Jon Elster in *Ulysses and the Sirens* (Cambridge: Cambridge University Press, 1979), part 1.

29   James G. March and Johan P. Olsen, *Rediscovering Institutions: The Organizational Basis of Politics* (New York: Free Press, 1989), p. 56.

30   Karl Popper, *The Poverty of Historicism* (London: Routledge and Kegan Paul, 1957).

31   See for example, Gabriel Almond and Stephen J. Genco, "Clouds, Clocks, and the Study of Politics," *World Politics* 20 (July 1977): 489–522.

32   J. P. Nettl, "The State as a Conceptual Variable," *World Politics* 20 (July 1968): 559–92.

33   Quoted in Alvin Z. Rubinstein, *Soviet Foreign Policy Since World War II: Imperial and Global*, 3d ed. (Glenview, Ill.: Scott, Foresman, 1989), p. 73.

34   This point was eloquently made by Hannah Arendt in *Origins of Totalitarianism* (New York: Harcourt, Brace, Jovanovich, 1973). A similar distinction is drawn between traditional dictatorship and the Soviet case in Václav Havel, "The Power of the Powerless," in *The Power of the Powerless: Citizens Against the State in Central-Eastern Europe*, ed. John Keane (London: Hutchison, 1985).

35   John Gray, "The Politics of Cultural Diversity," *Postliberalism* (New York: Routledge, 1993), p. 257.

36   Adam Michnik, "On Resistance," in *Letters from Prison and Other*

Essays, trans. Maya Liatynski (Berkeley: University of California Press, 1985), pp. 43–44.

37   For a depiction of the perversion of law in totalitarian systems, see the Experience and the Future Discussion Group, *Poland Today: The State of the Republic* (Armonk, N.Y.: Sharpe, 1981), pp. 18–43. This report was based on an independent survey of prominent professionals, scholars, and writers of a broad range of political views conducted to make policy recommendations to the Polish communist government in 1979 and 1980.

38   On the czarist secret police, see Richard Pipes, *Russia Under the Old Regime* (London: Weidenfeld and Nicolson, 1974), p. 301. On the Checka, see John J. Dziak, *Chekisty: A History of the* KGB (Lexington, Mass.: Lexington, 1988).

39   Henry Kissinger, *A World Restored* (New York: Grosset and Dunlap, 1964), chap. 5.

40   For a good review of more recent (revisionist) Cold War history, see Lynn Eden, "The End of U.S. Cold War History? A Review Essay," *International Security* 18 (summer 1993): 174–207.

41   For an elaboration on this point, see John Lewis Gaddis, "The Cold War, the Long Peace, and the Future," in *The End of the Cold War: Its Meaning and Implications*, ed. Michael J. Hogan (Cambridge: Cambridge University Press, 1992), pp. 21–38.

42   Waltz, *Theory of International Politics*, p. 171.

43   Ibid.

44   Adam Ulam, *Expansion and Coexistence: The History of Soviet Foreign Policy, 1917–1967* (New York: Praeger, 1968), p. 448.

45   Jack Snyder, "International Leverage on Soviet Domestic Change," *World Politics* 42 (October 1989): 15.

46   See Rubinstein, *Soviet Foreign Policy*, p. 119.

47   The Polish communist government, the Catholic church, and Solidarity announced the beginning of roundtable discussions to negotiate political reform on January 27, 1989. "Jaruzelski told the U.S. ambassador in Warsaw, John Davies, that he was consulting frequently with Gorbachev, who fully supported his policies of conciliation" (Beschloss and Talbott, *At the Highest Levels*, p. 53).

48   On the importance of reasonable sufficiency, see Thomas Risse-Kappen, "Ideas Do Not Float Freely: Transnational Coalitions, Domestic Structures, and the End of the Cold War," the eighth essay in this book.

49   For an explanation of Gorbachev's changed image of the adversary in terms of learning theory and cognitive attribution theory, see Ted Hopf, "Peripheral Visions: Brezhnev and Gorbachev Meet the 'Reagan Doctrine,' " in *Learning in U.S. and Soviet Foreign Policy*, ed. George W. Breslauer and Philip E. Tetlock (Boulder, Colo.: Westview, 1991), pp. 586–629. For a more organization-based model stressing the impact of academics and policy research institutions, see Jeff Checkel, "Ideas, Institutions, and the Gorbachev Foreign Policy Revolution, *World Politics* 45 (January 1993): 271–300. For an infor-

mative discussion of the national interest, see Stephen Sestanovich, "Inventing the Soviet National Interest," *The National Interest*, no. 20 (summer 1990): 3–16. On the reconceptualization of security, see Legvold, "The Revolution in Soviet Foreign Policy," pp. 84–87.

50 Francis Fukuyama, "The End of History?" *The National Interest*, no. 16 (summer 1989): 3–18.

51 Counterreformation, for Michnik, characterized glasnost and perestroika as a response to delegitimization of Soviet communism and as an attempt to retain control through reform: "[Counterreformation] is a self-critical show of strength with the aim of incorporating those values created against the will of [the established orthodoxy], and outside the social institutions in order to stop them [from] becoming antagonistic and subversive"("The Great Counter-reformer," *Labor Focus on Eastern Europe* 9 [July–October 1987]: 23).

52 In resisting military intervention in Eastern Europe, Eduard Shevardnadze explicitly rejected the scenarios of 1956 and 1968 by arguing that, "leaving aside the impossibility of operating in the new conditions with the old methods, we could not sacrifice our own principles regarding the right of peoples to freedom of choice, noninterference in internal affairs, and the common European home" (*The Future Belongs to Freedom*, trans. Catherine A. Fitzpatrick [New York: Free Press, 1991], p. 120). Similarly, when referring to the Baltics, Gorbachev stated that the use of force "would be the end of Perestroika" (quoted in Beschloss and Talbott, *At the Highest Levels*, p. 164).

53 Michael Doyle defines empires as "relationships of political control imposed by some political societies over the effective sovereignty of other political societies. They include more than just formally annexed territories, but they encompass less than the sum of all forms of international inequality" (*Empires* [Ithaca: Cornell University Press, 1986], p. 19).

54 Ibid., p. 130, table 3; p. 38.

55 Timothy Garton Ash, "The Empire in Decay," *New York Review of Books*, September 29, 1988, p. 56.

56 Doyle, *Empires*, p. 42.

57 *Finlandization* originated in Jacek Kuron's 1976 essay, which outlined a program for the newly formed democratic opposition in Poland. He borrowed the term of Western analysts for Soviet objectives in Western Europe and postulated it as an objective for Poland. See "Reflections on a Program of Action," *The Polish Review* 22, no. 3 (1977):. 51–69.

58 Beschloss and Talbott, *At the Highest Levels*, pp. 132–33.

59 For discussions of the collapse of legitimacy, see George Schoepflin, "The End of Communism in Eastern Europe," *International Affairs* (London) 66 (January 1990): 3–16, esp. pp. 5–7; and Giuseppe Di Palma, "Legitimation from the Top to Civil Society: Politico-Cultural Change in Eastern Europe," *World Politics* 44 (October 1991): 49–80.

60 See Kuron, "Reflections on a Program of Action"; Michnik, "On

Resistance"; Havel, "The Power of the Powerless"; and George Konrad, *Antipolitics* (New York: Harcourt, Brace, Jovanovich, 1984), respectively. On civil society, see Jacques Rupnik, "Dissent in Poland, 1968–1978: The End of Revisionism and the Rebirth of the Civil Society," in *Opposition in Eastern Europe*, ed. Rudolf Tokes (Baltimore: Johns Hopkins University Press, 1979), pp. 60–112; and Andrew Arato, "Civil Society Against the State: Poland 1980–81," *Telos* 47 (spring 1981): 23–48.

61 Jadwiga Staniszkis, *The Self-Limiting Revolution* (Princeton: Princeton University Press, 1984).

62 Hungarian dissident George Konrad made this point in an interview with Rey Koslowski, October 14, 1988, Colorado Springs.

63 See "Joint East European Statement to Commemorate the Twentieth Anniversary of the Warsaw Pact Invasion of Czechoslovakia on August 21, 1968," and the "Border Declaration" issued on July 10, 1988, by members of Polish-Czechoslovak Solidarity after a clandestine meeting on the border between the two countries, both in the *East European Reporter* 3 (autumn 1988): 59–62.

64 Shevardnadze, *The Future Belongs to Freedom*, pp. 120–21.

65 Beschloss and Talbott, *At the Highest Levels*, p. 102.

66 On the opposition's tactics and Soviet security interests, see Adam Michnik, "A New Evolutionism" (originally written in 1976), in *Letters from Prison and Other Essays*, trans. Maya Latynski (Berkeley: University of California Press, 1985), pp. 143–44.

67 Shevardnadze, *The Future Belongs to Freedom*, p. 114.

68 Peter Hayes, ed., "Chronology 1989," *Foreign Affairs* (special issue) 69 (1989 / 1990): 231.

69 Beschloss and Talbott, *At the Highest Levels*, pp. 82–83.

70 Ibid., p. 82.

71 Ibid., p. 90. For Bush and Jaruzelski, see ibid., pp. 88–89.

72 Ibid., pp. 93–94, 126–31.

73 Fyodor Burlatsky, speech at the University of Pennsylvania, Philadelphia, January 28, 1991.

74 For a discussion of emulation among bloc members, see Schoepflin, "The End of Communism in Eastern Europe," p. 9; and Adam Przeworski, "The East Becomes the South? The Autumn of the People and the Future of Eastern Europe," *PS* 25 (March 1991): 20–24.

75 The Hungarian National Assembly voted to delete from the constitution mention of the party's leading role on October 18, 1989. The Czechoslovak parliament followed suit on November 11, 1989.

76 See the discussion of repealing article 6 of the Soviet constitution that appeared in *Pravda*, December 8, 1989, p. 1.

77 On the weakness of state institutions relative to the Communist Party, see Don Van Atta, "The U.S.S.R. as a Weak State: Agrarian Origins of Resistance to Perestroika," *World Politics* 41 (October 1989): 129–49; and Rey Koslowski, "Market Institutions, East European Reforms, and Economic Theory," *Journal of Economic Issues* 26 (September 1992): 673–705. For an argument that the

Communist Party was the force that held the republics together, see Jerry Hough, "Gorbachev's Politics," *Foreign Affairs* 68 (winter 1989 / 90): 26–41.

78   Philip Roeder, "Soviet Federalism and Ethnic Mobilization," *World Politics* 43 (January 1991): 320–22.

79   On the spring draft, see Andrei Krivov, "Many Young Soviets Bid Earnest Farewell to Arms," *Russian Thought*, July 27, 1990, reprinted in *Glasnost News and Review* (October–December 1990): 14–19. In the fall draft, only 78.8 percent of those conscripted reported for service. See Stephen Foye, "Crackdown Ordered to Enforce Military Draft," *Report on the U.S.S.R.* 3 (January 18, 1991).

80   Kathleen Mihalisko, "Ukrainians Ponder Creation of a National Army," *Report on the U.S.S.R.* 3 (February 22, 1991).

81   Interview with James Baker on NBC's *Meet the Press*, December 24, 1989.

82   Beschloss and Talbott, *At the Highest Levels*, p. 164.

83   Austrianization was advocated in the early 1960s by the editors and contributors of the emigré journal *Studies for a New Central Europe* and developed by Hungarian dissident George Konrad in *Antipolitics*.

84   Shevardnadze, *The Future Belongs to Freedom*, pp. 138–41.

85   Horst Telschik, *329 Tage: Innenansichten der Einigung* (329 days: Participatory observations on unification) (Berlin: Goldmann, 1993).

86   Beschloss and Talbott, *At the Highest Levels*, pp. 220, 227.

87   Ibid., p. 239.

88   See "General Secretary Mikhail Gorbachev's Address to the Council of Europe," July 6, 1989, in *Europe Transformed: Documents on the End of the Cold War*, ed. Lawrence Freedman (New York: St. Martin's, 1990), pp. 322–32 and especially p. 327ff. Also see "Eduard Shevardnadze Speaks to the European Parliament Committee," *The Current Digest of the Soviet Press* 41, no. 51 (1989): 11f.

89   Margaret Thatcher, *The Downing Street Years* (New York: Harper Collins, 1993), pp. 796–99.

90   See article by Roland Dumas published in the *New York Times*, March 13, 1990, reprinted in *Europe Transformed: Documents on the End of the Cold War*, ed. Lawrence Freedman (New York: St. Martin's, 1990), pp. 508–9.

91   Beschloss and Talbott, *At the Highest Levels*, p. 207.

92   An example of such a foray was Poland's establishment of a liaison office in Brussels in 1990. See Jan B. de Weydenthal, "Rapprochement with the West Continues," *Report on Eastern Europe*, December 20, 1991, p. 23.

7

The Search for Accommodation:
Gorbachev in Comparative Perspective

The reorientation of Soviet foreign policy under Mikhail S. Gorbachev and the East-West reconciliation it brought about constitute a formidable challenge to theories of international relations. These theories did not recognize the possibility of such change and have been hard put in retrospect to find convincing explanations.[1] Our collective failure, while embarrassing, represents an opportunity. Theory progresses by acknowledging its failures and reformulating its assumptions. With this end in mind, I will offer a critical review of my theory of need-driven aggression and reformulate it on the basis of recent events.

The Theory

Between Peace and War, published in 1981, analyzed why states challenged critical adversarial commitments.[2] In contrast to theories of deterrence that identify opportunity as the catalyst for such challenges, my explanation was rooted in need. I hypothesized that leaders are most likely to resort to force or challenge important adversarial commitments when they confront serious foreign or domestic threats or, more often, a combination of the two. Case studies of acute international crises indicate that the most frequent objective of such behavior is to prevent or compensate for an adverse shift in the balance of power brought about by military deployments or changing international alignments. Examples include the 1905–6 Moroccan crisis, which was triggered by the Anglo-French entente and the fear of encirclement it aroused in Germany, and the Cuban missile deployment of 1962, which followed in part from Soviet concerns that the United States had achieved a first-strike capability.[3]

Resorts to force and other foreign policy challenges can also be a response to internal threats to the state, its regime, or its leadership. Leaders are most likely to adopt aggressive foreign policies to cope with domestic problems when these pose immediate threats and are beyond the power of leaders to address directly but can be alleviated in part—or so leaders believe—by means of a forceful foreign policy. Such a calculus lay behind Austria's decision to wage war on Serbia in 1914 and the Argentine junta's decision in 1982 to invade the Islas Malvinas (Falkland Islands).[4]

Domestic problems and foreign insecurities prompt aggressive foreign policies for a second, related reason: leaders of states who confront domestic or foreign threats worry that weakness—real or perceived—will encourage challenges by adversaries or defections by allies. Concern for their country's reputations prompts leaders to look for ways to demonstrate resolve and makes them loath to back down in international confrontations. Austria-Hungary and Russia behaved this way in the years before 1914. Their attempts to cope with mounting domestic challenges by expansionist foreign policies were a fundamental cause of the First World War. During the Cold War, the superpowers attempted to bolster their military capabilities and reputations for resolve, especially in the aftermath of foreign policy setbacks.[5] These superpower confrontations did not lead to war but provoked war-threatening crises and costly military interventions in the Third World.

The Prediction

In 1980 I speculated about the structural problems that would confront the superpowers in the course of the coming decade. Drawing on the propositions of *Between Peace and War*, I predicted how the superpowers would respond if these conditions were realized and suggested that both would suffer a series of foreign and domestic setbacks that would prompt more aggressive foreign policies.[6]

The Soviet Union confronted two major adversaries: the United States and the People's Republic of China. I predicted that during the eighties both would grow relatively more powerful and more coordinated in their opposition to Moscow. Like German leaders in the early years of the century, Soviet leaders had a long-standing fear of encirclement. To the extent that they expected "opportunistic collusion" between China and the United States to develop into a full-blown anti-Soviet alliance, linked perhaps to Japan and NATO, they might feel compelled to try to prevent this coalition from congealing. In 1905, 1909, and 1911 Germany brought Europe to the brink of war in three unsuccessful attempts to break out of its encirclement.

Moscow would also face a growing direct threat in Eastern

Europe. The growing disparity between Eastern living standards and those of the West, a decline in upward mobility, discouraging prospects for economic growth, and the emergence of human rights groups in Poland, Hungary, Czechoslovakia, and East Germany would subject pro-Soviet regimes to increasing pressure from dissident workers and intellectuals. By the end of the decade, I argued, Moscow would have to accept much greater diversity and autonomy among its Eastern European satellites or use force on a large scale to maintain its authority.[7]

I thought that the most serious long-term threat to the Soviet Union would be internal. In the Caucasus and Central Asia, Soviet-sponsored economic and educational development had promoted the emergence of new classes of indigenous intelligentsia and workers who enjoyed a degree of prosperity. This elite had resisted Russification and showed increasing signs of resenting Russian domination. If the Soviet economy stagnated — as many economists predicted — and if military involvement in Afghanistan further alienated Soviet Muslims, demands for autonomy or independence might erupt in Central Asia and the Caucasus. Widespread alienation among young Russians, also a reaction to economic stagnation, corruption, and Afghanistan, could pose an even greater challenge to the survival of Soviet-style communism.

I did not expect the United States to experience threats of the same magnitude. The United States would confront more independent allies, especially in Europe, where opposition to the deployment of new nuclear delivery systems could become pronounced. In the Third World, terrorism and revolutions against American client regimes would continue to be a source of mounting frustration. The biggest threat to America's world position would be economic. The United States' economy would decline relative to Japan and Western Europe but not the Soviet Union. The threatened loss of industrial primacy would not immediately degrade the country's standard of living — it would be maintained through borrowing and a growing trade deficit — but would be a blow to national self-esteem and make Americans susceptible to appeals for a more assertive foreign policy.

Drawing on the propositions of *Between Peace and War*, I predicted that the relative decline of the superpowers would make them more insecure and intent on demonstrating resolve to adversaries and allies alike. Their rivalry, in the Third World and in space, would become sharper and could result in the kinds of acute crises that had characterized the tensest years of the Cold War. The most serious of these confrontations — Berlin 1948–49, 1959–62, and

Cuba 1962 — had been provoked by leaders who felt cornered. In their concern to prevent loss, the superpowers had been willing to accept the risks of confrontation, or, worse still, to delude themselves that the actions they considered essential to national security would not unduly provoke their adversary.[8]

The Reality

My expectation of structural decline was accurate, although not derived from any theory. By March 1985, when Mikhail Gorbachev came to power, the Soviet Union had experienced major foreign and domestic setbacks. These included a costly and still unresolved war in Afghanistan, the failure to prevent NATO's deployment of a new generation of highly accurate nuclear delivery systems in Europe, and a stagnating economy that ultimately threatened to make it impossible for the Soviet Union to play the role of a global power. By 1992 the combined effects of political liberalization and unexpectedly rapid economic decline had brought about the demise of the Soviet Union.

The decline of the United States was not nearly so severe. Tensions within NATO mounted, American primacy in Latin America was challenged by the electoral and military success of left-wing movements, and the American economy suffered a series of shocks that threatened to make it the sick man of the First World. Public opinion polls revealed that Americans felt increasingly frustrated by their country's relative decline as a world power and uncertain about what could be done to regain economic and political primacy.

The American response was generally consonant with the expectations of my theory. Democrats and Republicans alike showed a heightened concern for the country's credibility and supported a more forceful foreign policy. Beginning in the mid-1970s influential members of the American national security establishment began to voice concern about their country's putative military decline and the consequent erosion of its credibility. They interpreted the Soviet Union's more active policy in Africa and its intervention in Afghanistan as evidence of Moscow's belief that the correlation of forces had swung in its favor.[9] They advocated a major military buildup to restore the status quo. Begun in the last two years of the Carter administration and accelerated by Ronald Reagan, the buildup of American conventional and strategic forces was the largest carried out in peacetime.

The buildup was accompanied by a crescendo of anti-Soviet rhetoric and threatening weapons deployments. The Carter and

Reagan administrations considered installation of Pershing IIs and cruise missiles in Europe essential to preserving NATO's credibility in the face of the ongoing Soviet nuclear buildup there. Concern for its credibility also prompted the Reagan administration to dispatch marines to Lebanon, invade Grenada, threaten Nicaragua, and provide military aid to the contras in Nicaragua and the mujahideen in Afghanistan. During Reagan's first term, Soviet-American relations reached a level of tension not witnessed since the height of the Cold War. To many observers, Reagan's support of Star Wars and militant opposition to pro-Soviet governments in the Third World put the superpowers on a collision course.

My theory predicted that the relatively greater decline in Soviet power and the rising threats to its primacy in Eastern Europe would lead to an even more assertive foreign policy. This prediction was utterly confounded by the conciliatory policy of Gorbachev and his foreign minister, Eduard Shevardnadze. They withdrew Soviet forces from Afghanistan, agreed to theater arms control that was advantageous to the West, allowed anticommunist revolutions in Eastern Europe, and, to everyone's surprise, agreed to the unification of Germany within NATO. By 1992 the Cold War was over, and the Soviet Union had ceased to exist.

The Reasons

The fundamental premise of need-driven theories of foreign policy is that serious domestic and foreign threats prompt proportionally dramatic responses. However, Soviet foreign policy between 1986 and 1992 represented a response to foreign and domestic threats that this theory does not envisage: accommodation with erstwhile adversaries. The Soviet experience is not unique. France's reconciliation with Britain in the years after Fashoda and Anwar el-Sadat's overtures to Israel after the 1973 Middle East War also were attempts by leaders to cope with domestic and foreign threats by extending the olive branch to their adversaries. Need-driven theories of foreign policy must be reformulated to take this response into account and to specify the conditions under which it is likely to occur. The French, Egyptian, and Soviet cases indicate three conditions associated with conciliatory responses: (1) commitments by leaders to domestic political and economic reforms; (2) the prior failure of confrontation; and (3) the expectation that conciliatory policies will be reciprocated.

The first of these conditions relates to the domestic agenda of leaders. I hypothesize that leaders are likely to pursue conciliatory foreign policies when they are committed to domestic programs that will directly benefit from accommodation with foreign adversaries. For Britain and France, the entente cordiale of 1904 paved the way for a lasting accommodation. Only five years before the agreement, the two rivals had been at the brink of war as a result of their dispute on the Upper Nile. In September 1898, as the Fashoda crisis neared its dénouement, the Dreyfus affair also entered its most acute phase following the revelation of the "faux Henri" on August 31. The humiliation of Fashoda and the exposure of the conspiracy against Captain Dreyfus facilitated a fundamental shift in French politics, pitting conservative, proclerical, anti-Dreyfusard colonialists against liberal, anticlerical, pro-Dreyfusard continentalists. At issue were competing visions of France; the one authoritarian, anti-British, and expansionist; the other republican, anti-German, and more conscious of the limits of French power.

In 1899 a government of republican solidarity came to power and then gave way in June 1902 to a government of the Dreyfusard left. Finding itself defending the Republic against a possible coup by authoritarian, nationalist, and anti-Semitic opponents, the Dreyfusard coalition — led by René Waldeck-Rousseau and his successor, Emile Combes — set out to weaken the church and the army, the principal institutional bases of the anti-Republican forces. Many clerical organizations were outlawed, the church's role in education was limited, the navy budget was sharply reduced, and national service in the army was reduced from three to two years. Broad measures were introduced to regulate working hours and conditions in order to maintain the support of the working class. When a military tribunal convicted Alfred Dreyfus a second time, the government had President Emile Loubet pardon him.[10]

Beyond its instrumental interests in accommodation with Britain — prompted by France's diplomatic isolation and the growing power of Germany — the Dreyfusard left wanted to strengthen the hold of republicanism by aligning France with Europe's greatest liberal democracy. The coalition and its foreign minister, Théophile Delcassé, had strong domestic incentives for seeking accommodations with both Italy and Britain. Improved relations with these countries would justify the coalition's assault on the military budget and shortening of the period of national service. An understanding with Britain could also facilitate French colonial goals; Delcassé offered to renounce all claims on Egypt in return for British support for France's effort to establish a protectorate over Morocco. French success in Morocco would co-opt the colonial agenda of the right and broaden support for the coalition. Lord Lansdowne and the British government were equally keen to encourage democratic forces in France and responded positively to this proposition. Negotiations began in the spring of 1903 and quickly led to the Anglo-French entente of 1904.

President Anwar el-Sadat was equally driven by domestic considerations to seek an accommodation with Israel. Egypt faced an acute economic crisis in the early 1970s. Socialism from above had failed, and Sadat, in a sharp break with the past, sought to liberalize the Egyptian economy and attract the foreign investment necessary to stimulate development. Sadat was convinced that foreign investors would not come to Egypt unless the Arab-Israel conflict was removed as a source of instability. After the war in 1973 had failed to end that conflict, Sadat pinned his hopes on a diplomatic solution, anticipating that a peace agreement with Israel brokered by the United States would create the conditions for the successful liberalization of the Egyptian economy. In a more secure and stable environment, foreign investment from the capitalist countries would flow into Egypt, accelerating economic growth. The United States, he hoped, would provide extensive economic aid and technical assistance to jump-start the Egyptian economy. Only if its economy grew could Egypt begin to address the fundamental infrastructural and social problems that it faced. Thus peace with Israel was important not primarily because of the direct benefits that it would bring—the return of the Sinai oil fields and an end to humiliation—but because of the opportunity it provided to open Egypt to the West and particularly to the United States.[11]

Mikhail S. Gorbachev's attempt to transform East-West relations was motivated in large part by his commitment to domestic reform. Perestroika required accommodation with the West. This would permit the Soviet Union to shift scarce resources from the military to production and investment and to attract credits, investment, and technology from the West. According to Foreign Minister Shevardnadze, the chief objective of foreign policy was "to create the maximum favorable external conditions needed in order to conduct internal reform."[12]

In the view of Perestroichiks, the conflict with the West had been kept alive and exploited by the Communist Party to justify its monopoly on power and suppression of dissent.[13] New thinking in foreign affairs was designed to break the hold of the party and the influence of the military-industrial complex allied to it.[14] It sought to replace the long-standing fixation on national security with the concept of "common, indivisible security, the same for all." Gorbachev proclaimed that the goal of the Soviet Union was to join a "common European house" that would foster security and prosperity through "a policy of cooperation based on mutual trust."[15]

The promotion of change in Eastern Europe was another means of fostering and protecting change at home. Perestroika had provoked a conservative backlash among the party elites of the region, who attempted to forge an anti-Gorbachev coalition with their Soviet counterparts. "Here," Shevardnadze observed, "the socialist 'community' showed its true face, and we saw what it had always been: a fraternal alliance of Party-state elites."[16] Gorbachev expected socialist reformers to come to power in Eastern Europe and become his natural allies in the common struggle against the forces of reaction.

For committed democrats like Shevardnadze, perestroika and glasnost were more than mechanisms intended to reform and revitalize the Soviet economy. For the Soviet Union to join the Western family of nations, it had to become a democratic society with a demonstrable respect for the individual and collective rights of its citizens and allies. Granting independence to the countries of Eastern Europe was the international analog to emptying the gulags, ending censorship in the media, and choosing members of the Supreme Soviet through free elections. Perestroika, Shevardnadze explained, "was understood to be universally applicable and could not be guided by a double standard. If you start democratizing your own country, you no longer have the right to thwart that same process in other countries."[17]

The second mediating condition of a conciliatory response concerns leaders' understandings of the consequences of confrontation. Leaders are more likely to pursue conciliatory foreign policies when they believe confrontation has failed. In all three cases discussed above, leaders recognized that confrontation had failed, had been extraordinarily costly, and was unlikely to succeed in the future.

Fin de siècle France had pursued the ambitions of a first-rank power although it no longer possessed the required capabilities. The gap between French ambitions and French power was most apparent in colonial policy and in the challenge to Britain's primacy in Egypt. France's ill-conceived attempt to establish a military presence on the Upper Nile provoked a British military expedition to the Sudan and an ultimatum to the small French force to withdraw. Outgunned on the Nile, at the mercy of the British fleet in the Mediterranean and Atlantic, and divided at home, France capitulated.[18]

The humiliation of Fashoda did much to disabuse French leaders of their grandiose colonial illusions and encouraged serious rethinking of the premises that had guided French foreign policy during the previous decades. The view was increasingly expressed in the press and *bureaux* that opposition to Britain was pointless because it could not be effective. The crisis also dramatized the full extent of France's isolation. For months after France's capitulation in the Sudan, leaders on both sides of the channel continued to think that war could break out. Russia, France's only ally, was unprepared for war, and Muraviev, its foreign minister, urged caution on Paris. French leaders confronted a hostile Germany on their eastern border. Throughout the crisis, the kaiser tried to goad Britain into attacking by promising neutrality and military support if Russia intervened on the side of France. Fashoda encouraged thoughtful Frenchmen, alarmed by their isolation, to seek an accommodation with Britain, an objective made possible by a shift of power within France.

The Fashoda crisis had been an expression of the conflict between the Colonial Ministry and the Foreign Ministry. The Colonial Ministry regarded Britain as the major obstacle to the fulfillment of its colonial ambitions. The Foreign Ministry was primarily concerned with the military threat Germany posed to France and saw Britain as a natural ally. Fashoda discredited the Anglophobes within the Colonial Ministry and paved the way for the Ministry of Foreign Affairs to seek rapprochement with Britain.

President Sadat's peace initiative took place in the aftermath of military failure, a costly war during which Egypt's battlefield goals were frustrated. Egyptian officials recognized that military conditions in 1973 had been optimal — Egyptian and Syrian armies armed with the latest weapons mounted a joint attack and achieved surprise — yet the war ended with Egyptian armies on the verge of a catastrophic military defeat. It was clear to Sadat and his generals that even under the best possible conditions, Egypt could not hope to defeat Israel. President Sadat accordingly began to search for a diplomatic solution that would return the Suez Canal to Egypt. To this end, he sought to involve the United States as mediator, broker, and guarantor of any peace settlement that ensued.

Mikhail Gorbachev's search for accommodation was also a reaction to the failure and costs of confrontation. Under Leonid Brezhnev, the Soviet Union had steadily built up its conventional and nuclear arsenals in a bid for military superiority. Brezhnev and many of his colleagues, as well as the Soviet military establishment, were convinced that a shift in the correlation of forces in favor of the socialist camp would compel the West to treat the Soviet Union as an equal superpower. Nixon and Kissinger's interest in détente, which came at a time when the Soviet Union was drawing abreast of the United States in strategic nuclear capability, confirmed the Soviets' view of the political value of military forces.[19]

Reasoning that additional forces would further improve their position vis-à-vis the West, Soviet leaders continued their buildup into the 1980s. The policy had the opposite effect. Moscow's seeming pursuit of strategic superiority coupled with its more assertive policy in the Third World handed American militants a powerful weapon to use against détente. The Carter administration was forced to begin its own strategic buildup and then to withdraw the proposed SALT II treaty from the Senate. The apparent upsurge in Soviet aggressiveness and Carter's seeming inability to confront it contributed to Reagan's electoral landslide and support for his more extensive military buildup and anti-Soviet foreign policy.

Soviet foreign policy analysts in the institutes were sensitive to the ways in which Brezhnev's crude military and foreign policies had provoked a pernicious American reaction. Their critiques of Soviet policy circulated widely among the Soviet elite. These analyses were especially critical of the increasingly costly intervention in Afghanistan. They also took Brezhnev and the military to task for their deployment of SS-20s in Eastern Europe and the western military districts of the Soviet Union. They maintained that NATO's commitment to deploy Pershing IIs and the ground launched cruise missiles (GLCMs) that Moscow found so threatening was a predictable response to Moscow's provocative and unnecessary deployment of highly accurate short- and intermediate-range nuclear systems.[20]

The overarching theme of these analyses was that the Brezhnev buildup had provoked the same kind of dangerous overreaction in the United States that the Kennedy-McNamara buildup of the 1960s had spurred in the Soviet Union. Soviet attempts to intimidate China with a massive buildup along its border were said to have had the same effect. A different and more cooperative approach to security was necessary.

Soviet failures in Afghanistan and in managing relations with the United States and Western Europe prompted a fundamental reassessment of foreign policy on the part of intellectuals and politicians not associated with the policies. Gorbachev and Shevardnadze maintain that their foreign policy views were formed in reaction to Brezhnev's failures and were significantly shaped by the analyses of Soviet critics in the Foreign Ministry and institutes. Both men had long conversations with analysts and Foreign Ministry critics of Brezhnev's policies before they decided to withdraw from Afghanistan. Such individuals were also instrumental in Gorbachev's and the Politburo's decision to accept on-site inspection, which helped break the logjam in arms control.[21]

The Gorbachev revolution in foreign policy is reminiscent of the French experience in a second important way. The humiliation of Fashoda was the catalyst for a major shift of power within France that facilitated the emergence of a new foreign policy line. Soviet officials agree that economic stagnation and the running sore of Afghanistan paved the way to power for a reform-oriented leader. Once in the Kremlin, Gorbachev exploited Afghanistan and NATO's deployment of Pershing IIs and GLCMs in Western Europe to discredit the militants and gain the political freedom to pursue a more conciliatory policy toward the West.[22]

The third condition facilitating accommodation is the expectation of reciprocity. Leaders will be more likely to initiate conciliatory policies when they believe that their adversaries are more likely to reply in kind than to exploit their overtures for unilateral advantage. In many, if not most adversarial relationships, leaders fear that any interest they express in accommodation, or any concessions they make, will communicate weakness and so prompt more aggressive policies rather than concessions in kind. Given the serious foreign and domestic costs of failed attempts at accommodation, leaders are only likely to pursue conciliatory policies when they expect them to be reciprocated. In two of the three cases analyzed in this essay, leaders had clear indications beforehand that their adversaries were also interested in more accommodative relationships. During the Fashoda crisis, Lord Salisbury had expressed his country's willingness to consider French claims in Africa after France agreed to withdraw from the Sudan, and British leaders reaffirmed their interest after the crisis. Only after a series of private conversations about the possible form an agreement might take did the two countries enter into negotiations in 1903.

Anwar el-Sadat, too, had reason to suppose that Israel might respond positively to an offer of a peace treaty. He made extensive private inquiries about Prime Minister Menachem Begin. He asked Nicolae Ceauşescu of Romania, who had met Begin several times, whether the prime minister was sincere in his interest in peace and if he could fulfill any commitment that he made. Reassured by the Romanian leader, Sadat sent his deputy premier, Hassan Tuhami, to meet secretly in Morocco with Israeli foreign minister Moshe Dayan to explore the outlines of an agreement. Dayan assured Tuhami that Israel would consider returning the Sinai to Egypt in exchange for a full peace. In other words, President Sadat waited for his expectations of reciprocity to be confirmed before he undertook his public and dramatic visit to Jerusalem.

In the third case, the importance of the expectation of reciprocity is best illustrated by the different policies of Nikita Khrushchev and Mikhail Gorbachev, the two Soviet leaders most interested in accommodation with the West. Gorbachev was able to pursue—and to persevere with—his search for accommodation because of the positive evolution of superpower relations since the height of the Cold War in the early 1960s. He had no explicit promise from the United States but had reason to hope that conciliatory actions might elicit a positive response. Khrushchev, on the other hand, was convinced that the United States and its allies would exploit any Soviet concession, and this intense mistrust severely constrained his search for accommodation. He was unprepared to gamble, as Gorbachev did, that conciliatory words and deeds would generate sufficient public pressure on Western governments to reciprocate. Khrushchev did make some unilateral concessions—he reduced the size of the armed forces and proclaimed a short-lived moratorium on nuclear testing—but when his actions were not reciprocated, he felt the need to demonstrate firmness to buttress his position at home and abroad. His inflammatory rhetoric then strengthened the position of militants in the West who all along had been opposed to accommodation with the Soviet Union.[23]

Gorbachev succeeded in transforming East-West relations and ending the Cold War because the West became his willing partner. Unlike Khrushchev's quest for a German peace treaty, which frightened France and West Germany, Gorbachev's attempt to end the division of Europe met a receptive audience, especially in Germany and Western Europe. Disenchantment with the Cold War, opposition to the deployment of new weapons systems, and a widespread desire to end the division of Europe created a groundswell of support for exploring the possibilities of accommodation with the Soviet Union. Western public opinion, given voice by well-organized peace movements, was a critical factor in encouraging Gorbachev and his colleagues in their attempts at conciliation.

Gorbachev was intent on liberalizing the political process at home and improving relations with the West. Within a month of assuming office, he made his first unilateral concession—a temporary freeze on the deployment of Soviet intermediate-range missiles in Europe. This was followed by a unilateral moratorium on nuclear tests and acceptance of the Western "double zero" proposal for reducing intermediate-range nuclear forces (INF) in Europe. In subsequent speeches and proposals, he tried to demonstrate his support for sweeping arms control and a fundamental restructuring of superpower relations. President Reagan, however, continued to describe the Soviet Union as an evil empire and remained committed to his quest for a near-perfect ballistic missile defense.

To break this impasse, Gorbachev pursued a two-pronged strategy. In successive summits, he tried and finally convinced Reagan of his genuine interest in ending the arms race and restructuring East-West relations on a collaborative basis. When Reagan changed his opinion of Gorbachev, he also modified his view of the Soviet Union and quickly became the leading dove of his administration. Gorbachev worked hard to convince Western publics that his policies represented a radical departure from past Soviet policies. The withdrawal from Afghanistan, freeing of political prisoners, and liberalization of the political system eventually evoked widespread sympathy and support in the West and generated strong public pressures on NATO governments to respond in kind to Gorbachev's initiatives.

Gorbachev's political persistence succeeded in breaching Reagan's wall of mistrust. At their Reykjavik summit in October 1986, the two leaders talked seriously about eliminating all their ballistic missiles within ten years and making deep cuts in their nuclear arsenals. No agreement was reached because Reagan was unwilling to accept any restraints on his Strategic Defense Initiative. Even so, the summit, as Gorbachev had hoped, began a process of mutual reciprocation, reassurance, and accommodation between the superpowers. That process continued after an initially hesitant George Bush became Gorbachev's full-fledged partner in eliminating the vestiges of forty years of Cold War.

In our analysis of need-driven aggression, Janice Stein and I argued that leaders who feel compelled to challenge adversaries to cope with serious foreign and domestic problems become motivated to believe that their challenges will succeed. We have documented how motivated bias of this kind encouraged unrealistic assessments of adversarial responses and was an important contributing cause of many acute crises and wars.[24] Leaders pressed to seek accommodation may be similarly biased in their assessment. Certainly, Gorbachev appears to have been unreasonably confident of his ability to end the Cold War and reform Soviet society. For him to have made unilateral or one-sided concessions in the face of Reagan's initial hostility was an extraordinary gamble. Neither Delcassé nor Sadat publicly offered concessions until after they were assured of reciprocation.

When accommodation is the goal, motivated bias can play a constructive role. Gorbachev's perseverance may have helped to make some of his foreign policy expectations self-fulfilling. Reagan was ultimately convinced of his sincerity and responded in a more positive way than any of his foreign policy advisers thought judicious.[25] Gorbachev and his advisers were equally insensitive to the dangers of success in encouraging reform in Eastern Europe and improved relations with the West. None of them foresaw that their policies would lead to the rapid demise of the Warsaw Pact and the reunification of Germany within NATO or that the end of the Cold War would lead to the breakup of the Soviet Union.

The same air of unrealism characterized Gorbachev's domestic program. Gorbachev convinced himself that the Communist Party could be revitalized and transformed into an agent of progressive change and that freedom of expression and limited democracy could be introduced in the Soviet Union without undermining its Leninist political system. Interviews with Gorbachev advisers in the Kremlin in the spring of 1989 indicated that they also greatly exaggerated their ability to cope with national unrest. Vadim Zagladin insisted that the leaders of the Baltic states, and of their national movements, "were intelligent, cautious men who know just how far they could go without causing serious problems for themselves or their countries."[26]

These miscalculations derived in part from political inexperience. Gorbachev and his advisers had little understanding of the nature of public institutions, the difficulty of reforming them and of overcoming vested interests. They also had at best a textbook understanding of democracy. Having grown up in an extraordinarily rigid and authoritarian political system, they overestimated the ability of leaders to control public opinion. They failed to realize that popular passions, once aroused, feed on themselves and that leaders who do not follow the crowd are likely to be shunted aside in favor of those who do. In domestic policy—and probably also in foreign policy—ignorance of public opinion and its potential power allowed motivated bias to flourish. Gorbachev knew how essential it was to revitalize the Soviet economy and convinced himself that he could bring about the foreign and domestic changes necessary to achieve this goal. A more insightful analysis of the likely consequences of liberalization at home and accommodation abroad might have made Gorbachev much more cautious in his foreign and domestic policies. Much the same could be said about Sadat, who had entirely unreasonable expectations about resolving the Palestinian-Israeli conflict and the beneficial consequences of foreign investment and aid for the Egyptian economy. The Soviet and Egyptian cases suggest the proposition that wishful thinking may play as powerful a role in bringing about accommodation as it does in confrontation.

The French, Egyptian, and Soviet cases indicate that my theory of foreign policy aggression was underspecified. Threats can prompt conciliatory as well as aggressive responses and do so under different conditions. I hypothesize that conciliatory responses are most likely when leaders (1) are committed to internal reforms that require or are expected to benefit from improved relations with an adversary; (2) recognize that confrontation has been counterproductive in the past; and (3) expect their adversaries to respond positively to conciliatory overtures.

The first two conditions were present in the three cases discussed above. Political logic suggests that they are essential. The commitment to domestic reform provides a much needed incentive to attempt the difficult and risky task of restructuring relations with an adversary. Equally important is the recognition that confrontation has failed in the past and is unlikely to succeed in the future. Without that awareness, leaders might be tempted to use threats or force to accomplish their foreign policy objectives, as Sadat did in 1973.

Condition three may be more important in influencing the scope and outcome of accommodation than in bringing it about. Not knowing if an adversary will respond positively to a conciliatory gesture, leaders are likely to proceed more cautiously so as to minimize the consequences of rejection. Yet dramatic gestures may be necessary or at least very helpful in overcoming adversarial distrust. Such initiatives carry great risks and are rarely undertaken. Leaders are more likely to take risks if they have reason to expect positive responses.

My propositions about accommodation need to be tested. One way to do this would be to search the same cases for other times when any of the three conditions was present. Evidence that other attempts at conciliation were made under similar conditions would strengthen my propositions' claim to validity. A finding that the three conditions were present on one or more occasions and no attempt at conciliation was made would indicate that they are insufficient, requiring a search for additional conditions and evidence that they were also present in the three attempts at conciliation investigated in this essay. The finding that additional attempts at conciliation were made under different conditions would point to the existence of different pathways to accommodation.

My propositions also need to be tested in other cases. To do this, I need to construct an appropriate data set. Ideally, it should include the universe of twentieth-century cases of attempted conciliation. This would allow the testing of propositions about the conditions under which conciliation is attempted and the conditions under which it succeeds. Once again, the next step would be to see if the conditions associated with conciliation were present on occasions when conciliation was not attempted.

This essay examined only one pathway to accommodation. In all three cases, leaders sought to resolve long-standing international conflicts because they regarded it as essential or extremely beneficial to the success of their domestic reforms. I fully expect that a search of other cases would reveal other incentives and pathways to accommodation. One alternative incentive is mutual fear of a third party, which played a role in Anglo-French relations in the years between 1905 and 1914 and was probably central to the Sino-American rapprochement of the 1970s. And economic incentives may have been critical in the partial accommodations between the two Germanies during the era of *Ostpolitik* and the two Chinas today.

A data set of the kind I have described could be used to make judgments about the relative frequency and importance of different pathways to accommodation and the conditions associated with them. It would also tell us if all roads lead to Rome or if some pathways are more successful than others in bringing about accommodation. Research into the causes of successful accommodation would have to specify its dependent variables as precisely as possible. It would need to distinguish between the limited accommodations of the kind sought by Soviet and American leaders in the early 1970s and the more far-reaching attempts described in this study. With respect to the latter, it must recognize the possibilities of failure, success, and partial success like the Egyptian-Israeli peace, which removed the threat of war between the two countries without leading to the closer political, economic, and social ties that one expects between friendly neighbors.

The research program I have outlined addresses only one-half of the accommodation problematique. For conciliatory overtures to lead to accommodation, they must be reciprocated. If they are spurned, they are unlikely to prompt further attempts at conciliation and may provoke more aggressive behavior on the part of the would-be conciliator. Soviet-American relations provide examples of both responses.

In 1953, following Stalin's death, the *troika* of Bulganin, Khrushchev, and Malenkov came to power and signaled its interest in ending the Cold War. President Dwight D. Eisenhower and his secretary of state, John Foster Dulles, recognized the *troika*'s intent but spurned most of their overtures. More, they interpreted the overtures as signs of weakness and decided to push harder in the hope of further weakening the Soviet Union and its hold over the countries of Eastern Europe.[27]

In 1959–60 Khrushchev made another attempt at accommodation. Eisenhower was initially receptive and invited Khrushchev to visit the United States. Their summit raised the prospect of some kind of accord on Germany and led to the short-lived "Spirit of Camp David." Under pressure from Konrad Adenauer, however, Eisenhower became more recalcitrant. This about-face exposed Khrushchev to blistering criticism at home from powerful hardliners, leading him to protect himself by intensifying confrontation with the West.[28]

A third unsuccessful attempt at conciliation was made by Jimmy Carter in the late 1970s. Brezhnev and the Soviet leadership had already soured on détente, and from their perspective the Carter administration was sending mixed messages at best. Like Khrushchev before him, Carter suffered severe political embarrassment as a result of his adversary's failure to reciprocate. The Soviets' intervention by proxy in Africa and invasion of Afghanistan exposed Carter to further serious criticism, compelling him to pursue a harder line and begin a major military buildup.[29]

Conciliation was not reciprocated until the secretary generalship of Mikhail Gorbachev and the presidency of Ronald Reagan. The reasons for these different responses are beyond the scope of this essay. But the importance of reciprocation is undeniable. In all three of the cases I have discussed here, other attempts at conciliation had not been reciprocated. In all three cases, reciprocation was necessary to transform initial attempts at conciliation into full-fledged processes of accommodation. It is just as important to discover why leaders reciprocate as it is to find out why they initiate conciliatory gestures.

NOTES

1   On realism's failure, see Richard Ned Lebow "The Long Peace, the End of the Cold War, and the Failure of Realism," the second essay in this book.

2 Richard Ned Lebow, *Between Peace and War: The Nature of International Crisis* (Baltimore: Johns Hopkins University Press, 1981).

3 For an analysis of the origins of the Cuban missile crisis, see Lebow, *Between Peace and War*; and Richard Ned Lebow and Janice Gross Stein, *We All Lost the Cold War* (Princeton: Princeton University Press, 1994), chap. 2.

4 See Lebow, *Between Peace and War*, chap. 4; and Richard Ned Lebow, "Miscalculation in the South Atlantic: The Origins of the Falklands War," in Robert Jervis, Richard Ned Lebow, and Janice Gross Stein, *Psychology and Deterrence* (Baltimore: Johns Hopkins University Press, 1985), pp. 89–124.

5 Lebow and Stein, *We All Lost the Cold War*, passim.

6 Richard Ned Lebow, "Clear and Future Danger: Managing Relations with the Soviet Union in the 1980s," in *New Directions in Strategic Thinking*, ed. Robert O'Neill and D. M. Horner (London: Allen and Unwin, 1981), pp. 221–45; and Richard Ned Lebow, "The Deterrence Deadlock: Is There a Way Out?" in Robert Jervis, Richard Ned Lebow, and Janice Gross Stein, *Psychology and Deterrence* (Baltimore: Johns Hopkins University Press, 1985), pp. 180–202, which offered a substantially revised and updated version of the argument.

7 Richard Ned Lebow, "Superpower Management of Security Alliances: The Soviet Union and the Warsaw Pact," in *The Future of European Alliance Systems*, ed. Arlene Idol Broadhurst (Boulder, Colo.: Westview, 1982), pp. 185–236.

8 For a bibliography and discussion of the Berlin crises of 1948–49 and 1959–62, see Richard Ned Lebow and Janice Gross Stein, "The Huth and Russett Data Collection Reevaluated," in *Specifying and Testing Theories of Deterrence*, ed. Kenneth A. Oye (Ann Arbor: University of Michigan Press, forthcoming).

9 For a critical review of this literature and the policy debates it spawned, see Richard Ned Lebow, "Western Images of Soviet Strategy," *International Journal* 44 (winter 1988 / 89): 1–40.

10 On French politics between 1899 and 1904 and on the negotiations leading to the entente, see Jacques Chastenet, *La République triumphante, 1893–1906* (Paris: Hachette, 1955); Christopher Andrew, *Théophile Delcassé and the Making of the Entente Cordiale* (London: Macmillan, 1968), pp. 201–15; Jack D. Ellis, *The French Socialists and the Problem of Peace, 1904–1914* (Chicago: Loyola University Press, 1967); Leslie Derfler, *Alexandre Millerand: The Socialist Years* (The Hague: Mouton, 1977); Keith Eubank, *Paul Cambon: Master Diplomatist* (Norman: University of Oklahoma Press, 1960); Pierre Guillen, "Les accords coloniaux franco-anglais de 1904 et la naissance de l'entente cordiale," *Revue d'histoire diplomatique* 82 (October–December 1968): 315–57; George Monger, *The End of Isolation: British Foreign Policy, 1900–1907* (London: Thomas Nelson, 1963); Pierre Renouvin, *La politique extérieure de Th. Delcassé, 1898–1905* (Paris: Institut d'Etudes Politiques, Univer-

sité de Paris, 1962); P. J. V. Rolo, *Entente Cordiale: The Origins and Negotiation of the Anglo-French Agreements of 8 April 1904* (London: Macmillan, 1969).

11 See Janice Gross Stein, "The Political Economy of Security Agreements: The Linked Costs of Failure at Camp David," in *Double-Edged Diplomacy: International Bargaining and Domestic Politics*, ed. Peter Evans, Harold Jacobson, and Robert Putnam (Berkeley: University of California Press, 1993), pp. 77–103.

12 Eduard Shevardnadze, *The Future Belongs to Freedom*, trans. Catherine A. Fitzpatrick (New York: Free Press, 1991), p. xi.

13 Interviews with Fedor Burlatsky, Cambridge, Mass., October 12, 1987; Vadim Zagladin, Moscow, May 18, 1989; Oleg Grinevsky, Vienna and New York, October 11 and November 10, 1991; Georgi Arbatov, Ithaca, New York, November 15, 1991; and Anatoliy Dobrynin, Moscow, December 17, 1991.

14 For a good Western discussion of new thinking in foreign policy, see David Holloway, "Gorbachev's New Thinking," *Foreign Affairs* 68 (winter 1988/89): 66–81.

15 Mikhail S. Gorbachev, "Speech to the United Nations," December 9, 1988, *Novosti*, no. 97 (December 9, 1988): 13; Gorbachev, *Perestroika*, p. 187. See Holloway, "Gorbachev's New Thinking."

16 Shevardnadze, *The Future Belongs to Freedom*, pp. 115–16.

17 Ibid., p. xii.

18 On Fashoda, see Roger Glenn Brown, *Fashoda Reconsidered: The Impact of Domestic Politics on French Policy in Africa* (Baltimore: Johns Hopkins University Press, 1970); E. Malcolm Carrol, *French Public Opinion and Foreign Affairs, 1870–1914* (New York: Century, 1931); William Langer, *The Diplomacy of Imperialism, 1890–1902* (New York: Knopf, 1960); J. A. S. Grenville, *Lord Salisbury and Foreign Policy* (New York: Oxford University Press, 1964); C. J. Lowe, *The Reluctant Imperialists: British Foreign Policy, 1878–1902* (London: Routledge and Kegan Paul, 1967); G. N. Sanderson, *England, Europe, and the Upper Nile* (Edinburgh: Edinburgh University Press, 1965); Philip Williams, "Crisis in France: A Political Institution," *Cambridge Journal* 35 (October 1963): 36–50; Christopher M. Andrew, "The French Colonialist Movement During the Third Republic: The Unofficial Mind of Imperialism," *Transactions of the Royal Society*, 5th series, 26 (1976): 143–66; Christopher M. Andrew, "Gabriel Hanotaux, the Colonial Party, and the Fashoda Strategy," in *European Imperialism and the Partition of Africa*, ed. E. F. Penrose (London: Cass, 1975), pp. 55–104; Lebow, *Between Peace and War*, chaps. 4 and 9; and Stephen R. Rock, *Why Peace Breaks Out: Great Power Rapprochement in Historical Perspective* (Chapel Hill: University of North Carolina Press, 1989), pp. 91–122.

19 Lebow and Stein, *We All Lost the Cold War*, chap. 8.

20 Interviews with Oleg Grinevsky, Vienna, October 11, 1991, New York, November 10, 1991, and Stockholm, April 25, 1992; with Leonid Zamyatin, Moscow, December 16, 1991; and with Anatoliy

Dobrynin, Moscow, December 17, 1991. See also Sarah E. Mendelson, "Explaining Change in Foreign Policy: The Soviet Withdrawal from Afghanistan" (Ph.D. diss., Columbia University, 1993); and Robert Herman, "Ideas, Institutions and the Reconceptualization of Interests: The Political and Intellectual Origins of New Thinking in Soviet Foreign Policy" (Ph.D. diss., Cornell University, 1995).

21   Ibid. See also Shevardnadze, *The Future Belongs to Freedom*, passim.

22   Shevardnadze, *The Future Belongs to Freedom*, passim; and interviews with Oleg Grinevsky, Vadim Zagladin, Leonid Zamyatin, and Anatoliy Dobrynin.

23   For Khrushchev's strategy, see Lebow and Stein, *We All Lost the Cold War*, chap. 3.

24   See Lebow, *Between Peace and War*, passim; Robert Jervis, Richard Ned Lebow, and Janice Gross Stein, *Psychology and Deterrence* (Baltimore: Johns Hopkins University Press, 1985); and Richard Ned Lebow and Janice Gross Stein, "Beyond Deterrence," *Journal of Social Issues* 43 (winter 1987): 5–72.

25   Don Oberdorfer, *The Turn from the Cold War to a New Era: The United States and the Soviet Union, 1983–1990* (New York: Poseidon, 1991), chaps. 5–7.

26   Interview with Vadim Zagladin, Moscow, May 18, 1989.

27   The best source on this is Matthew A. Evangelista, "Cooperation Theory and Disarmament Negotiations in the 1950s," *World Politics* 41 (July 1990): 502–28.

28   Lebow and Stein, *We All Lost the Cold War*, chap. 3.

29   Raymond L. Garthoff, *Détente and Confrontation: American-Soviet Relations from Nixon to Reagan* (Washington, D.C.: Brookings, 1985), pp. 563–1009.

8

*Ideas Do Not Float Freely:
Transnational Coalitions, Domestic Structures,
and the End of the Cold War

Efforts to explain the end of the Cold War — that is, the systemic transformation of world politics that started with the turnaround in Soviet foreign policy in the late 1980s — have to find answers to at least two sets of questions. First, why did Soviet foreign policy change as it did rather than in other conceivable ways?, Why did this great power dramatically shift its course toward accommodationist policies, withdraw from its (informal) empire, and then collapse in a comparatively peaceful way? Why did the Soviet Union in retreat never try to reverse its course forcefully? Second, why did the Western powers — the alleged winners of the Cold War — never attempt to exploit the situation in order to accelerate their opponent's collapse? What accounts for the specific Western response to the changes in the Soviet Union? Why did both the United States

*This essay also appeared in *International Organization* 48 (spring 1994): 185–214. It draws on insights from another collaborative project — Thomas Risse-Kappen, ed., *Bringing Transnational Relations Back In: Non-State Actors, Domestic Structures and International Institutions* (Cambridge: Cambridge University Press, forthcoming) — whose contributors I thank for helping to clarify my thoughts on the subject. I am also very grateful to Ned Lebow, John Odell, Steve Ropp, Jack Snyder, and several anonymous reviewers for helpful comments on this article. Since I cannot claim to be an expert on the former Soviet Union, I owe a lot to the work of Matthew Evangelista, in particular, *Taming the Bear: Transnational Relations and the Demise of the Soviet Threat*, forthcoming, and of Robert Herman, especially his "Ideas, Institutions and the Reconceptualization of Interests: The Political and Intellectual Origins of New Thinking in Soviet Foreign Policy" (Ph.D. diss., Cornell University, 1994). Finally, I thank Janice Stein for this article's title. I would also like to acknowledge the support of Cornell University's Peace Studies Program, Yale University's International Security Program, and the International Studies Program at the University of Wyoming.

and its Western European allies help end the Cold War in a comparatively smooth way?

I argue in this essay that structural or functional explanations for the end of the Cold War — whether realist or liberal — are underdetermining and cannot account for either the specific content of the change in Soviet foreign policy or the Western response to it. Existing theories need to be complemented by approaches that emphasize the interaction of international and domestic influences on state behavior and take seriously the role of ideas — knowledge, values, and strategic concepts. Ideas intervene between material, power-related factors, on the one hand, and state interests and preferences, on the other.[1]

Some of the ideas informing the reconceptualization of Soviet security interests that centered around the notions of common security and reasonable sufficiency originated in the Western liberal internationalist community.[2] This community, comprising arms control supporters in the United States and peace researchers and left-of-center political parties in Western Europe, formed transnational networks with new thinkers in the foreign policy institutes and elsewhere in the former Soviet Union. Mikhail Gorbachev, as a domestic reformer and uncommitted thinker in foreign policy, was open to these ideas because they satisfied his needs for coherent and consistent policy concepts. As a result, the new ideas became causally consequential for the turnaround in Soviet foreign policy. At the same time, they influenced the Western reactions to the new Soviet policies, albeit to different degrees (consider, for example, the cautious American and the enthusiastic [West] German responses to the revolution in Soviet foreign policy).

Ideas, however, do not float freely. Decision makers are always exposed to several, often contradictory policy concepts. Research on transnational relations and, most recently, on epistemic communities of knowledge-based transnational networks has failed so far to specify the conditions under which specific ideas are selected while others fall by the wayside.[3] Transnational promoters of foreign policy change must align with domestic coalitions supporting their cause to make an impact. I argue that the domestic structure of the target state — that is, the nature of its political institutions, state-society relations, and the values and norms embedded in its political culture — determines both access to the political system and the ability to build winning coalitions.

In the former Soviet Union, with its state-controlled structure, the transnational actors needed to gain access to the very top of the decision-making hierarchy to have an impact. Their specific ideas and concepts also had to be compatible with the beliefs and goals of the top decision makers. On the other hand, access to the U.S. political system, with its society-dominated structure, is comparatively easy, but the requirements for building winning coalitions are profound. Moreover, concepts such as common security were rather alien to a political culture emphasizing pluralist individualism at home and sharp zero-sum conflicts with ideological opponents abroad. As a result, the liberal arms controllers and their societal supporters, together with their European allies, succeeded in moving the Reagan and Bush administrations toward cautious support for Gorbachev's policies, but not much further. In the German democratic corporatist structure, however, access to political institutions is more difficult than it is in the United States, but strong policy networks such as the party system ensure profound influence once access is achieved. The notion of common security resonated well with this political culture emphasizing consensus building and compromise among competing interests at home and abroad. Indeed, it was embedded in the German foreign policy consensus long before Gorbachev embraced it, which explains the enthusiastic German response to the new Soviet foreign policy years before the Berlin Wall came down.

Deficiencies of Prevailing Theories

Arguments about domestic-international linkages and the transnational diffusion of ideas would be unnecessary if more parsimonious theories could account for the dramatic turnaround in Soviet foreign policy and the accommodating Western response. But the prevailing structural approaches in international relations theory are mostly indeterminate and thus cannot adequately answer the two sets of questions raised above. They are not wrong, but more complex approaches are also required to explain the dramatic changes in world politics.[4]

Sophisticated realism goes a long way toward showing how the interaction between international systemic and domestic economic factors created a set of conditions that permitted the accommodationist foreign policies pursued by the Gorbachev coalition. Kenneth Oye, for example, argues that the long-term decline of the Soviet economy and the decreasing growth rates of the Eastern European states led to a growing burden on the Soviet Union during the early 1980s that required a fundamental policy change.[5] At the same time, nuclear deterrence as a systemic condition in East-West relations precluded the adventurous foreign policies that might otherwise have been the response of a declining great power.[6] The nuclear deterrence system might also explain the cautious U.S. response to the change in Soviet foreign policy. Bullying Gorbachev into speeding up the retrenchment from Third World conflicts and Eastern Europe was too risky, given that even a Soviet Union in retreat possessed enough nuclear missiles to annihilate the United States.

One can agree with this analysis and still remain puzzled by the Gorbachev revolution and by at least part of the Western response. The Soviet economic crisis and the nuclear deterrence system permitted a variety of responses of which the new Soviet foreign policy was only one. Why did the reformers in the Politburo embark on perestroika and glasnost instead of technocratic economic reforms that would have kept the repressive state apparatus intact? After all, the Chinese leadership pursued just such a path under roughly similar domestic conditions. With regard to foreign policy, Gorbachev could have continued or rather returned to the détente and arms control of the 1970s, which would have allowed him a similar international breathing space during which to promote internal reforms. Instead, he radically changed the Soviet foreign policy outlook by embracing common security and reasonable sufficiency for military means. Moreover, he matched words with deeds by embarking on unilateral initiatives in the nuclear and conventional arms fields that seemed to come right out of the textbooks for "strategies of reassurance."[7] He accepted the zero option for intermediate-range nuclear forces (INF), together with intrusive on-site inspections, unilateral troop withdrawals, and asymmetrical cuts in Soviet conventional forces. These moves took place even before the Soviet leadership decided to let Eastern Europe go. In other words, Gorbachev went far beyond what one can reasonably expect from a prudent realist perspective. Even sophisticated realism could not tell us which of the Soviet Union's possible choices was to be expected.

Realist bargaining theory, however, can be used to make an additional point. Some argue that Ronald Reagan's coercive strategy with regard to the Soviet Union and his massive arms buildup during the early 1980s finally drove Moscow's leadership over the edge.[8] Cornered by the West and faced with an economic crisis at home, Gorbachev had virtually no choice but to cut losses in military and foreign policy, since striking back at the United States was precluded by the nuclear deterrence system. In short, according to this view, it was the combination of structural international and domestic conditions with Western "peace through strength" that led to the turnaround in Soviet foreign policy.

Evidence suggests that the new thinkers perceived the Western reaction to Brezhnev's foreign policy as a further incentive to change Soviet foreign policy. But to argue that "peace through strength" and structural conditions left no choice to the Soviet Union seems to miss the mark.[9] First, the initial Soviet response to the Western buildup was to continue arms racing as usual. Under Andropov and Chernenko, who faced economic conditions as gloomy as those confronting Gorbachev, Moscow not only left the negotiating table in 1983 but also accelerated the production and deployment of new nuclear weapons. Second, some new thinkers argue that Reagan's buildup actually made it harder for them to push for changes in the Soviet security outlook.[10] The transformation of Moscow's foreign policy was contested all along; the reaction of conservatives in the military and other institutions to the Reagan buildup was the opposite of the Gorbachev coalition's. That the latter prevailed must be explained by the dynamics of Soviet domestic politics rather than assumed away theoretically.

As to the Western response to the Gorbachev revolution, the American caution may be roughly accounted for by a sophisticated realist argument. It is the German "Gorbimania" that should pose a puzzle to realists.[11] On the one hand, as a divided frontline state on the East-West border, the Germans had a lot to gain from the success of Gorbachev's reforms; indeed, the rapidly decreasing Soviet threat alone could have induced the enthusiasm with which Bonn supported the new Soviet foreign policy. On the other hand, the risks involved in a premature and overly accommodative reaction to Gorbachev could just as easily have led the Germans to adopt a cautious policy similar to that of the United States. Realism could not predict which of the two lines of reasoning the West Germans would follow. Ultimately, then, although sophisticated realism can explain how structural conditions and Western policies created a window of opportunity and thus a demand for new ideas in foreign policy, the theory fails to show why particular ideas were selected over equally possible alternatives that would have led to different foreign policies.[12] Thus the end of the Cold War serves to confirm the indeterminate nature of the realist approach.[13]

Liberal theory, a major competitor of realism in international relations theory, does not score much better in explaining the momentous changes in world politics.[14] Liberal accounts take the role of ideas in foreign policy seriously and emphasize that perceptions, knowledge, and values shape the state actors' responses to changing material conditions in the domestic and international environments. Several liberal "second image reversed" arguments have been made to explain the end of the Cold War. Daniel Deudney and G. John Ikenberry suggested, for example, that the Soviet Union was faced with an international environment in which liberal ideas about democracy, human rights, and market economy not only dominated but also proved successful in serving human needs.[15] As a result, Moscow found itself more and more isolated and, finally, was unable to escape the influence of these long-term liberal trends. In short, Soviet-type communism lost the competition over the organization of political, social, and economic life.[16]

This analysis suffers from three problems. First, even large-scale failure does not necessarily result in the adoption of the competitor's solution. Here again the Chinese attempt to embark on economic reforms while maintaining the repressive political system is a case in point. Second, the analysis cannot explain the timing of the Soviet foreign policy change. Why did the Soviet leadership acknowledge the victory of liberalism in the mid-1980s and not, say, ten or twenty years earlier? Third, the argument that the Soviet leadership essentially adopted Western ideas about domestic and foreign policies ignores the fact that Moscow was confronted with more than one Western concept. In the foreign policy area, for example, one approach that dominated U.S. foreign policy during Reagan's first term (peace through strength) was alien to a liberal conceptualization of world politics. It was rooted in a Hobbesian understanding of international relations and in realist bargaining theory. A second approach — deterrence plus détente — was adopted by the North Atlantic Treaty Organization's Harmel report in 1967 and dominated the foreign policies of most Western European countries during the 1970s and early 1980s. It combined liberal and realist ideas and claimed that limited cooperation under anarchy was possible across the East-West divide.[17] Finally, a genuine liberal internationalist — or, by European standards, Social Democratic — vision of common security held that a "security partnership" (in the words of Helmut Schmidt) through multilateral institutions could transform the East-West conflict and the nuclear deterrence system and that far-reaching peace and cooperative arrangements were possible among opponents.[18]

A liberal account emphasizing the international sources of the Soviet change cannot explain why the new leadership under Gorbachev discarded the first two concepts and subscribed to the third.

One might argue, though, that Gorbachev could safely embark on liberal internationalist foreign policies because he knew that the Western democracies would not exploit the Soviet pullback. Democracies not only rarely fight each other, it is claimed, but also tend toward moderation in their relations with nondemocracies.[19] Once the Soviet Union embraced détente and arms control, it could count on an equally accommodative Western response. This argument not only asserts that the Soviet leadership believed in liberal theory but also offers an explanation for the Western reaction to the change in Soviet foreign policy.

Unfortunately, the claim is based on a misreading of the democratic peace argument.[20] While it is conceptually and empirically well established that democracies rarely fight each other, there is not much evidence that liberal democracies pursue moderate foreign policies toward nondemocracies or even political systems in transition to democracy.[21] Immanuel Kant never argued that democracies are peaceful in general.[22] Rather, they engage in as many militarized disputes and wars with autocracies or partially authoritarian states (such as the former Soviet Union under Gorbachev) as these pursue among themselves. This is not to suggest that the West could have waged war against a Soviet Union in retreat. But liberal theory is indeterminate with regard to a democratic state's reaction to a retreating authoritarian state; Reagan's earlier "peace through strength," Bush's caution, and Genscher's enthusiasm are all compatible with the approach.

To understand the revolution in Soviet foreign policy and the various Western responses to it that together brought the Cold War to an end, one cannot ignore domestic politics and leadership beliefs. Thus Matthew Evangelista and Sarah Mendelson emphasize that Gorbachev had first to consolidate his domestic power base in the Politburo and the Central Committee before the turnaround in foreign policy was possible. Richard N. Lebow argues that leaders committed to broad economic and political reforms tend to be motivationally biased toward accommodative foreign policies under certain conditions. Janice Stein maintains that Gorbachev was predisposed toward new thinking in foreign policy and embarked on "learning by doing."[23]

Domestic politics accounts and learning theories offer significant insights into why particular ideas carry the day in specific policy choices; however, they do not tell much about the origins of those ideas. Three possibilities come to mind regarding the case under discussion here. First, Gorbachev himself might have developed the new foreign policy beliefs earlier and then put them into practice after he had assumed power. The facts do not indicate, however, that Gorbachev held firm foreign policy convictions before entering office, particularly in comparison to the clarity of his domestic reform ideas. His few foreign policy speeches during the early 1980s do not reveal much more than a general open-mindedness about East-West cooperation. Even the first major attempt to outline the new foreign policy concept, Gorbachev's report to the Twenty-seventh Communist Party Congress in early 1986, represents a strange mix of old and new thinking.[24] Eduard Shevardnadze has suggested that Gorbachev knew all along that he was opposed to Brezhnev's foreign policies but had no consistent framework and a coherent concept of international politics before he entered office.[25] It is clear, though, that he learned extremely quickly.

Second, the ideas and foreign policy concepts might have originated in domestic intellectual communities that then gained access to the leadership.[26] Jeff Checkel has convincingly shown that *institutchiks* at the Institute of the World Economy and International Relations (IMEMO) were able to convince Gorbachev, through advisers such as Aleksandr Yakovlev and Yevgeniy Primakov, that world politics had to be analyzed in terms of nonclass categories such as "interdependence" and that his enemy image of American capitalism had to change. Of course, these analysts might have read Robert Keohane and Joseph Nye's *Power and Interdependence*, but little evidence suggests that transnational contacts were important to them (with the possible exception of Yakovlev's time as the Soviet ambassador to Canada). Sarah Mendelson has similarly demonstrated that the decision to withdraw from Afghanistan was influenced by a domestic epistemic community.[27]

Analyzing world politics in other than Marxist-Leninist categories—a change in worldviews, according to Judith Goldstein and Robert Keohane—was certainly a precondition for the foreign policy revolution.[28] But it is unlikely that worldviews determine the transformation of specific policies. Rather, changes in basic assumptions about the world open up an intellectual space for changes in principled or causal beliefs that—in the words of Goldstein and Keohane—"provide road maps that increase actors' clarity about goals or ends-means relationships" and thus affect policies.[29] Strategic prescriptions such as common security, reasonable sufficiency, or nonoffensive defense combine principled and causal beliefs—values and knowledge—and are then operationalized into specific policies.[30]

But strategic prescriptions centering around common security were new to the Soviet security debate, so their intellectual origins must be found outside the country and its foreign policy institutes.[31] Indeed, Checkel argues that the epistemic community at IMEMO was less influential regarding the new approach to military security than were, for example, natural scientists at the Academy of Sciences technical divisions (such as Yevgeny Velikhov and Roald Sagdeev) and *institutchiks* at the USA and Canada Institute (ISKAN) who regularly participated in exchanges and meetings with Western security analysts and scholars.[32] Complementing Checkel's analysis, I argue below that transnational networks between those in the West who supported common security and nonoffensive defense, on the one hand, and natural scientists and *institutchiks* at ISKAN, on the other, were crucial in promoting the new Soviet approach to security. The foreign policy ideas of these transnational exchanges translated a somewhat diffuse new thinking about foreign policy into a coherent security policy. When Gorbachev adopted these concepts and then went on to act on them, he could count on the support of the very groups in the West that had provided the ideas in the first place. It is no coincidence that Gorbachev's new foreign policy drew the most immediate and positive response from Germany, where common security had gradually become ingrained in the foreign policy consensus of the society. It is also not surprising that a positive response to Gorbachev's overtures took longest in the United States, where liberal internationalist and Social Democratic ideas about foreign policy were not part of mainstream thinking. Thus an emphasis on transnational networks not only sheds additional light on the origins of the new thinking in Soviet foreign policy, but, in conjunction with the dynamics of domestic politics, also helps to explain the variation in Western responses to the Gorbachev revolution.

Transnational Relations and the End of the Cold War

In the following section, I first identify the actors who developed the new strategic prescriptions about security and the transnational networks through which these concepts were promoted. I then look at the different impact of these ideas on the Gorbachev revolution in foreign policy and the American and German responses to it.

Transnational Actors and Their Ideas:
The Liberal Internationalist Community

Four intellectual communities together form a liberal internationalist community sharing political values and policy concepts. First, the liberal arms control community in the United States traces its origins to the late 1950s, when it was among the first to promote the idea of arms control to stabilize the deterrence system.[33] This community is an alliance of natural scientists organized in such groups as the Union of Concerned Scientists (UCS) and the Federation of American Scientists (FAS), policy analysts at various think tanks such as the Brookings Institution, scholars at academic institutions, public interest groups such as the Natural Resources Defense Council (NRDC), and policy makers in the U.S. Congress, mostly liberal Democrats.

This group's contribution to the broader liberal internationalist agenda during the late 1970s and early 1980s consisted primarily of specific proposals in the nuclear arms control area. The main focus during that time was to oppose the Reagan administration's efforts to do away with nuclear arms control. In particular, the community concentrated on promoting a comprehensive nuclear test ban and on preserving the 1972 Anti-Ballistic Missile (ABM) treaty threatened by Reagan's Strategic Defense Initiative (SDI).[34]

The second subgroup of the liberal internationalist community consists of mostly Western European peace researchers based at various institutes such as the Stockholm International Peace Research Institute, the Peace Research Institute Oslo, the Institute for Peace Research and Security Policy Hamburg, the Peace Research Institute Frankfurt, and various universities.

The third group includes European policy makers in Social Democratic and Labour parties and their transnational organization, the Socialist International. Security specialists in the German Social Democratic Party (SPD) as well as the British and Dutch Labour parties were particularly influential in the liberal internationalist debate during the period under consideration.[35]

The two European components of the liberal internationalist community shared their U.S. counterparts' concerns about the future of arms control. But their main contribution to the transnational liberal agenda consisted of developing the concepts of common security and nonoffensive defense (or, to use the German misnomer, *strukturelle Angriffsunfähigkeit*, that is, "structural inability for offensive operations").

Common security transformed the original arms control idea of stabilizing strategic deterrence through cooperative measures into a concept transcending the notion of national security. Its proponents claimed that the security dilemma in international relations could be overcome through stable cooperative arrangements and peace orders that excluded the risk of war among states. Security in the nuclear age could no longer be achieved through unilateral measures;

no one in the East-West relationship could feel secure unless every-one did. As Egon Bahr, the leading SPD promoter of the idea, put it: "[Security partnership] starts with the insight that war can no longer be won and that destruction cannot be restricted to one side. . . . The consequence of this insight is that there is no reliable security *against* an opponent, but only *with* an opponent. There is only common security, and everybody is partner in it, not despite potential enmity, but *because* of it."[36]

Common security was widely discussed among peace researchers as well as mainstream and center-left parties in the Benelux coun-tries, Great Britain, Scandinavia, and West Germany during the late 1970s and early 1980s. In West Germany, for example, then-chan-cellor Helmut Schmidt introduced the idea of a security partnership between East and West in 1978, although he conceptualized it main-ly as complementing nuclear deterrence. In 1979 the SPD adopted the concept and eventually transformed it into the notion of com-mon security meant gradually to overcome deterrence.[37] By the time Gorbachev came into power, common security was one of the main-stream foreign policy concepts in Europe.

The European peace research community also developed propos-als to restructure the Western conventional force posture in such a way that offensive operations would become virtually impossible — nonoffensive defense — thereby overcoming the security dilemma by reconciling peaceful intentions with purely defensive capabilities.[38] By the mid-1980s, various European Social Democratic and Labour parties had incorporated nonoffensive defense into their policy plat-forms.

The fourth component of the transnational community provides the link with the former Soviet Union. It consists of natural scientists and policy analysts in various institutes, primarily at the Academy of Science (for example, the Kurchatov Institute of Atomic Energy headed by Velikhov, the Space Research Institute headed by Sagdeev, and the foreign policy institutes IMEMO and ISKAN). The Soviet new thinkers were mainly on the receiving end of ideas promoted by their European and American counterparts.

These four groups not only shared values and policy concepts but also frequently exchanged their views. Since the connections between the United States and the European arms control communities are well documented, I concentrate on the East-West exchanges.

First, specific nuclear arms control proposals were the subject of increasingly institutionalized contacts between the U.S. arms con-trol community, particularly natural scientists working for the UCS, the FAS, and the NRDC, and Soviet experts such as Velikhov and Sagdeev. Evangelista has documented these exchanges and shown in detail how these interactions influenced Soviet arms control decisions. His analysis provides further empirical evidence for the argument developed in this essay.[39]

Second, the concept of common security was introduced to Soviet *institutchiks* and foreign policy experts by the Independent Commission for Disarmament and Security, (known as the Palme commission, in honor of former Swedish Prime Minister and Social Democrat Olof Palme).[40] Founded in September 1980, the commission brought together mostly elder statesmen and -women from around the world to study East-West security issues. Academician Georgi Arbatov, the head of ISKAN, served as the Soviet member, while retired general Mikhail Milshtein of the same institute was one of the principal advisers.[41] Common security was introduced into the commission's deliberations by the German Social Democrat Bahr, who had been one of the architects of German *Ostpolitik*. In 1982 the Palme commission issued a report entitled *Common Security* that defined the principles of a cooperative East-West security regime and spelled them out with regard to arms control, confidence-building measures, and economic cooperation.

Third, regular exchanges took place between various Western European Social Democratic and Labour parties — particularly the German SPD — and Communist parties in Eastern Europe and the Soviet Union. These relations had begun during the détente period of the 1970s and continued throughout the 1980s. The SPD, for example, conducted regular meetings on security policy issues with the East German, Polish, Soviet, and other Communist parties. Agreements were worked out on principles of common security, on nuclear and chemical weapon free zones in Central Europe, and on nonoffensive defense.[42] The Social Democrats tried to gain Eastern European and Soviet support for the recommendations achieved in the Palme commission. Given the reality of East-West relations in the pre-Gorbachev era, Western participants in these contacts had to walk a thin line. As a result, on the one hand, the contacts legitimized official Eastern European and Soviet policy proposals by promoting nuclear weapon free zones and the like, while, on the other hand, they served to make acceptable in the East the concept of common security and notions that later became known as military glasnost (on-site inspections, for example).

Fourth, the Soviet *institutchiks* and even Soviet military academies frequently consulted Western experts of the nonoffensive defense community.[43] This is all the more significant because nonoffensive defense was alien to traditional Soviet military thinking. In fact, the initial reaction of even civilian experts in the Soviet Union to the alternative defense debate in Western Europe had been quite hostile and turned more sympathetic in their publications only after Gorbachev had come into power.[44]

Some of the transnational contacts were initiated through well-known frameworks such as the Pugwash conferences. In 1984, for example, Pugwash established a working group on conventional forces that became a major East-West forum on these issues; it included most of the European peace researchers, such as Anders Boserup, Horst Afheldt, and Albrecht von Müller, specializing in alternative defense models. Andrei Kokoshin, deputy director of ISKAN and one of the most prominent new thinkers in Soviet foreign policy, also participated and eventually became a leading proponent of a defensive restructuring of the Soviet armed forces. The annual Pugwash conferences regularly dealt with issues of defensive restructuring, particularly the 1988 meeting in the Soviet Union.[45]

Transnational Exchanges and the Turnaround in Soviet Security Policy

In February 1986 Gorbachev made the following remarks about his vision of security:

> Security cannot be built endlessly on fear of retaliation, in other words, on the doctrines of "containment" or "deterrence." . . . In the context of the relations between the USSR and the USA, security can only be mutual, and if we take international relations as a whole it can only be universal. The highest wisdom is not in caring exclusively for oneself, especially to the detriment of the other side. It is vital that all should feel equally secure. . . . In the military sphere we intend to act in such a way as to give nobody grounds for fear, even imagined ones, about their security.[46]

These remarks from Gorbachev's report to the Twenty-seventh Party Congress closely resemble comments in the Palme commission's report on common security, as well as the statement by Bahr quoted above.[47] They represent the first instance of the Soviet leader identifying himself with this new concept of security so alien to traditional Soviet thinking. Yet, although liberal internationalist ideas about common security and nonoffensive defense unquestionably reached new thinkers in several Soviet institutes through a variety of transnational exchanges with like-minded groups in the West, can Gorbachev's change of heart be attributed to these transnational exchanges?[48] Was there a causal link beyond a mere correlation?

Various facts suggest that ideas about common security developed by European peace researchers and Social Democrats indeed influenced Gorbachev's thinking. First, the Soviet leader himself acknowledged that his views about international security and disarmament were "close or identical" to those of European Social Democrats such as Willy Brandt, Bahr, and the Palme commission.[49] In a meeting with Brandt, he argued that the new thinking combined traditions going back to Lenin with insights from socialist friends and "proposals reflected in such documents as reports by the commissions of Palme, Brandt, and Brundtland."[50] Gorbachev made a deliberate effort to develop closer contacts with the Socialist International and its chairman, Brandt. At the same time, European Social Democrats were eager to promote their security policy ideas directly to the Soviet leader.

One could argue, of course, that Gorbachev's references to Western thinking were self-serving, meant to legitimize his own views. Even if this is true, the similarities between his arguments and those of European analysts and policy makers are still striking, and the Soviet leader recognized these affinities. Moreover, as mentioned above, Gorbachev did not hold firm convictions on foreign policy before he entered office. Finally, he was not paying mere lip service to these notions; his policy proposals and actions on nuclear and conventional weapons in Europe directly followed from the newly developed strategic prescriptions on enhancing international security.

Second, the transnational links between European institutes and policy makers, on the one hand, and *institutchiks* at ISKAN and other Soviet institutes, on the other, became increasingly important in the reconceptualization of the Soviet approach to security. ISKAN's head, Georgi Arbatov—a member of the Palme commission—while certainly not among the most radical new thinkers, belonged to the inner circle of Gorbachev's foreign policy advisers during the early years of perestroika. Arbatov was extremely impressed by Bahr—"one of the outstanding political minds of our time"—and considered him a friend.[51] The Palme report, with its international clout, became a major tool with which liberal *institutchiks* influenced both Foreign Minister Shevardnadze and Gorbachev. According to Arbatov, it had a significant effect on political thinking in the Soviet Union and introduced the concept of common security to officials. Its publication in Moscow also confronted the Soviets with Western estimates of the conventional forces (im)balance in Europe.[52]

Proposals to restructure the Soviet conventional forces from an offensive posture toward nonoffensive defense seem similarly to have influenced the leadership. The report to the Twenty-seventh Party Congress had mentioned the defensive orientation of the Soviet military doctrine and the concept of reasonable sufficiency without being specific. One year later, Gorbachev referred to doctrines of defense "connected with such new or comparatively new notions as the reasonable sufficiency of armaments, non-aggressive defense, elimination of disbalance and asymmetries in various types of armed forces, separation of the offensive forces of the two blocs, and so on and so forth."[53]

His statement led to an intensive debate among civilian and military analysts in the Soviet Union about its implications for the conventional force posture. The military in particular claimed that nonoffensive defense related to the overall goals of Soviet military doctrine rather than to its implementation. The *institutchiks* argued that reasonable sufficiency should lead to a restructuring of Soviet military forces that precluded the ability to conduct (counter)offensive operations.[54] Analysts at ISKAN such as Vitaly Zhurkin, Sergei Karaganov, and Andrei Kortunov as well as its deputy head Kokoshin became leading advocates of the concept, embraced Western ideas of nonoffensive defense, and translated them into the Soviet context. Kokoshin, with Major General Valentin Larionov of the General Staff Academy, published various articles on the subject.[55] As mentioned above, Kokoshin was involved in transnational exchanges at Pugwash and had frequent contacts with European peace researchers such as Boserup and Lutz Unterseher, who were also in touch with Alexei Arbatov — who headed the new Department of Disarmament and International Security at IMEMO and was far more radical than his father — Karganov, and the bureaucracy of the Soviet Foreign Ministry.[56]

In December 1988 Gorbachev showed that he sided with the *institutchiks* and the new thinkers in Shevardnadze's Foreign Ministry when he announced large-scale unilateral troop reductions. Shortly afterward, the Soviet Union accepted the core of Western proposals at the Conventional Forces in Europe negotiations to establish conventional parity in Central Europe. Two years later, the Soviet Defense Ministry published a draft statement on military doctrine that explicitly defined *sufficiency* as the inability "for conducting large-scale offensive operations."[57] New thinking had reached the defense bureaucracy.

These two examples suggest that important parts of the reorientation of Soviet security policy were indeed influenced by strategic prescriptions transmitted to the leadership through transnational interactions.[58] Once the foreign policy experts and their transnational contacts had aligned with the domestic reform coalition in the Soviet Union, the transnational exchanges influenced the very content of the new Soviet security policy and thus the scope of the change. The new leadership needed independent expertise outside the military, which opened a window of opportunity for the *institutchiks*.[59] The new ideas about common security and reasonable sufficiency transformed a general uneasiness with the state of Soviet international affairs into a coherent foreign policy concept. The *institutchiks* and their transnational networks persuaded the Gorbachev coalition of necessary and bold steps to change Soviet foreign policy toward the West. At the same time, their ideas rationalized and legitimized the need for a turnaround in foreign policy. It is impossible to separate these two aspects of how ideas influence policy decisions.

The contribution of the *institutchiks* and their transnational contacts to the change in Soviet foreign policy was not trivial. By helping Gorbachev match words and deeds, they were crucial in targeting his message to a receptive Western audience, particularly in Europe. Transforming Western attitudes toward the Soviet Union, however, was itself critical, not just to end the Cold War but to create the benign international environment that Gorbachev needed to pursue perestroika and glasnost domestically.

Liberal Internationalists and the Western Responses to Gorbachev: The U.S. and German Cases

Most peace researchers and liberal arms controllers in Western Europe and the United States were primarily concerned about Western policies and did not expect the Soviet Union to be receptive to their proposals. Nevertheless, their impact varied from country to country. I illustrate this in the following sections through the examples of the United States and West Germany.

THE UNITED STATES: PRESERVATION OF ARMS CONTROL AND CAUTIOUS RESPONSE TO GORBACHEV. In the U.S. case, the liberal arms control community pursued three main objectives during the 1980s: (1) restoring the Reagan administration to the arms control track and preserving the nuclear arms control agreements of the 1970s, such as the ABM treaty; (2) convincing the administration of the necessity to launch rigorous arms control efforts in the areas of test ban negotiations and nuclear reductions; and (3) ensuring a positive American response to the Gorbachev revolution in foreign policy. The first goal was achieved, the second was not, and the third met with mixed results, and it is by no means clear that the successes were due primarily to the efforts of the members of the arms control community.[60]

When the Reagan administration brought hard-liners into power, the U.S. arms control community was removed from policy influence. It was the American peace movement and what became known as the freeze campaign, together with pressure from the European allies, that revived the arms control process.[61] Then, empowered by social movement and allied pressure, the expert community reentered the policy-making process, particularly in Congress. At the same time, there developed a transnational coalition between the arms control community and the European allies that succeeded in moving the Reagan administration away from its early militaristic rhetoric toward the resumption of arms control talks. The main impact was to shift the bureaucratic balance of power from conservative hard-liners such as Caspar Weinberger and Richard Perle to moderate conservatives such as George Shultz and Paul Nitze. The policy impact of this shift first became visible in early 1984 when Reagan gave several moderate foreign policy speeches that later led to the Shultz-Gromyko agreement to resume arms control talks in January 1985 — before Gorbachev came into office.

The single most important success of the liberal arms control community in the United States was probably the preservation of the ABM treaty despite Reagan's SDI.[62] In this case, a powerful coalition emerged, including liberal internationalists, Congress (particularly Senator Nunn, who became chairman of the Senate Armed Services Committee in 1986), and the European allies. The arms control community was less successful, however, in the absence of a winning domestic coalition. In 1986–87, for example, a transnational coalition between the NRDC and the Soviet Academy of Science tried to influence U.S. testing policy. In an attempt at private diplomacy, they established seismic verification stations close to the two principal nuclear testing sites in the United States and the Soviet Union. The stations demonstrated publicly that a comprehensive test ban was verifiable and thus discredited a major U.S. objection to a test stop.[63] The transnational alliance quickly gained access to Congress. In the autumn of 1986 the House of Representatives passed an amendment to the defense budget bill calling for a one-year moratorium on nuclear tests, but a countercoalition including the Reagan administration, Republicans in Congress, and leading Democrats such as Senator Nunn defeated the House resolution.

The efforts of the liberal internationalist community did not have a long-term impact on attitudes toward the Soviet Union and the Cold War in general. Liberal arms controllers failed to build a stable policy consensus around their strategic prescriptions. Common security, for example, remained a minority position in the United States. As a result, the Reagan administration reacted rather cautiously to the changes in Moscow, even though Reagan developed a friendly personal relationship with Gorbachev. As late as early 1989, half a year before the Berlin Wall came down, the new Bush administration advocated status quo plus as its response to the Gorbachev revolution.[64]

GERMANY: "SECURITY PARTNERSHIP" AND "GORBIMANIA." The reluctant U.S. response to the revolution in Soviet foreign policy contrasts strongly with the West German answer.[65] As I mentioned earlier, ideas about common security and nonoffensive defense originated in the European peace research community as well as in Social Democratic and Labour parties during the late 1970s. The SPD was crucial in promoting these ideas domestically and in Europe. By the mid-1980s, before Gorbachev assumed power, a stable German public and elite consensus on common security emerged, ranging from the center-left to the center-right and comprising both the SPD and the two governing parties, the Christian Democrats and the Free Democrats. However, ideas about a defensive restructuring of the German armed forces were still contested. The attitude of the Bonn government under Chancellor Kohl toward nonoffensive defense began to change only after the Soviet Union had embraced the concept.

The liberal internationalist community of peace researchers and Social Democrats did not somehow manipulate the German public into believing these ideas, as some have suggested.[66] Just as the freeze campaign cleared the way for the arms control community in the United States, the German peace movements opened a window of opportunity for common security to gain widespread acceptance. The movements emerged in reaction to the confrontational U.S.-Soviet relationship of the early 1980s and the planned deployment of new medium-range missiles on German soil; their majority advocated unilateral disarmament — a more radical idea than common security. German social organizations such as churches and trade unions quickly supported the ideas promoted by peace researchers and the SPD. By about 1982 / 83 the notion of common security had strong support, well documented in public opinion polls.[67]

Shortly afterward, Christian Democrat leaders such as Chancellor Kohl and Richard von Weizsäcker, the federal president, increasingly used common security language in their speeches, possibly in order to preserve their constituency. Eschewing the Social Democratic slogan of "security partnership," they referred instead to a "community of responsibility" (*Verantwortungsgemeinschaft*). Common security became the center of a new German security policy consensus after the mid-1980s, after the peace movements had vanished but before Gorbachev initiated his foreign policy change.

German enthusiasm for Gorbachev and the revolution in Soviet foreign policy is easy to explain, given these domestic developments. Tapping into the German domestic consensus on security policy, Gorbachev's overtures met an almost immediate welcome in Bonn. His acceptance of the INF zero option in 1986 became the defining moment for the Germans to embrace his policies. (One has to bear in mind in this context the divisiveness of the German INF debate in the early 1980s, as well as the fact that in 1979 the SPD and then-chancellor Schmidt had promoted the zero option that became Reagan's INF negotiating position in 1981.)[68] Popular support for the Soviet leader skyrocketed, and the center-right Kohl government, in particular Free Democrat Foreign Minister Genscher, became the first in the West to appreciate the changes in Soviet foreign policies. From about mid-1986 on, while most of its allies were still skeptical, the German government promoted a positive Western response to the new Soviet foreign policy ("Genscherism" quickly became the word for this attitude). Germany became the first and only Western state to commit substantial amounts of financial assistance to the Soviet economic reform process. In effect, the Cold War ended for the Germans about two years before the Berlin Wall came down.

The Limits of Transnationalism: Domestic Structures as Intervening Variables

I have tried to document above that a liberal internationalist and transnational community of scholars, policy analysts, and center-left political parties promoted new strategic prescriptions such as common security, nonoffensive defense, and far-reaching arms control agreements during the late 1970s and early 1980s. New thinkers in the Soviet Union picked up these ideas and influenced the views of the Soviet leadership. The particular content of Gorbachev's foreign policy revolution cannot be understood unless one acknowledges the input of this community. The transnational community also influenced Western responses to Gorbachev, albeit to different degrees. It was less successful in the United States but very effective in West Germany, where it contributed to the creation of a new foreign policy consensus around common security.

I suggest that the end of the Cold War — both in the East and the West — cannot be adequately understood without taking the role of these transnationally transmitted ideas into account. The impact of these ideas, however, varied considerably. Only the Soviet Union under Gorbachev reconceptualized its security policy toward both common security and nonoffensive defense. The German polity achieved a domestic consensus on the former but remained reluctant on the latter, while the American public and elite opinion failed to agree on either of the two concepts. Moreover, the interval between the initial promotion of these ideas in the target countries and their acceptance by the political leaderships varies considerably. If the Palme Commission report represented the first exposure of Soviet *institutchiks* to common security, it took less than four years for the ideas to have a policy impact. It took about ten years to accomplish the same result in Germany — from the mid-1970s, when peace researchers and Social Democrats started promoting the strategic prescriptions, to the mid-1980s. In Washington, common security never became as politically relevant as it did in Moscow and Bonn.

How is this considerable variation in policy impact to be explained? To influence policies, transnational actors need, first, channels into the political system of the target state and, second, domestic partners with the ability to form winning coalitions. Ideas promoted by transnational alliances or epistemic communities do not matter much unless those two conditions are met. Answering the question, then, requires looking at intervening variables between transnational alliances and policy change. I suggest that differences in the three countries' domestic structures largely account for the variation in the policy impact of transnationally circulated ideas.

Originally developed in the field of comparative foreign economic policy, domestic structure approaches have generated empirical research across issue areas to explain variation in state responses to international pressures, constraints, and opportunities.[69] The concept refers to the structure of the political system, of society, and of the policy networks linking the two. Domestic structures encompass the organizational apparatus of political and societal institutions, their routines, the decision-making rules and procedures as incorporated in law and custom, as well as the values and norms prescribing appropriate behavior embedded in the political culture.

This last point marks a departure from earlier conceptualizations

of domestic structures, which emphasized organizational characteristics of state and society but neglected political culture and thus
insights from the new institutionalism, particularly the focus on
communicative action, duties, social obligations, and norms.[70] Political culture refers to those worldviews and principled ideas — values
and norms — that are stable over long periods of time and taken for
granted by the vast majority of the population. Thus the political
culture as part of the domestic structure contains only those ideas that
do not change often and about which there is a societal consensus.[71]

Until about 1988–89, the former Soviet Union represented an
extremely state-controlled domestic structure with a highly centralized decision-making apparatus.[72] Such structures lead to top-down
policy-making processes, leaving little room for policy innovations
unless they are promoted by the top leadership. It follows that leadership beliefs are expected to matter more than attitudes of the
wider population.[73]

Centralized and state-dominated domestic structures provide
transnational coalitions with comparatively few access points into
the political system, in that they must reach the top echelon of the
decision-making structure directly rather than build winning coalitions in civil society. Prior to Gorbachev's gaining power, the transnational exchanges between Western liberal internationalists and
Soviet *institutchiks* had almost no impact on Soviet foreign policy. A
reform-oriented leadership had to gain power first. It needed to be
open-minded, and its worldviews needed to be predisposed toward
the strategic prescriptions promoted by the transnational actors.

Beyond his general inclination to change foreign policy, Gorbachev seems to have been attracted to common security for a more
specific reason.[74] His domestic reform ideas closely resembled policy concepts promoted by democratic socialism and the Socialist
International, which emphasized political democracy and a market
economy with a heavy dose of state interventionism. Gorbachev,
who made a strong, successful effort to gain the support of the European Social Democrats, might have been attracted to their foreign
policy ideas because they were promoted by groups that to an extent
shared his beliefs about domestic politics.

The combination of a centralized decision-making structure with
a reform-oriented leadership explains why the strategic prescriptions promoted by the transnational coalition had such a strong
impact on Gorbachev's foreign policy revolution in a comparatively
short period of time. Once a channel to the top decision-making circle was open, the transnational coalition profoundly influenced

policies. Given the absence of a strong civil society backing the ideas, the impact depended almost entirely on the leadership's willingness to listen.

In contrast to the Soviet Union, the United States represents, of course, a more society-dominated domestic structure, with a strong organization of interest groups, in which societal demands can be mobilized rather easily. At the same time, it lacks effective intermediate organizations such as a strong party system, and its political system is comparatively fragmented and decentralized, without a powerful center (Congress versus Executive, Pentagon versus State Department, etc.).[75] Moreover, and throughout the Cold War, the American national security culture incorporated rather strong and consensual enemy images of the Soviet Union and defined national security mainly in military terms.[76]

Society-dominated structures are expected to mediate the impact of transnational coalitions in almost the opposite way as state-controlled structures do. Transnational actors should have few problems in finding access into a decentralized political system. Yet, while this initial hurdle is comparatively low, the task of building a winning coalition is expected to be more complex than in state-dominated systems. Since society-dominated structures are characterized by frequently shifting coalitions, transnational alliances may successfully influence policies in the short run, but their long-term impact is probably rather limited. Thus the liberal arms control community had virtually no problems finding channels into the political system but failed to form stable winning coalitions with a lasting policy impact. The group was successful only to the extent that its demands were compatible with either a public opinion consensus — as in the case of Reagan's return to the arms control table — or the views of powerful players in Congress — as in the case of the preservation of the ABM treaty. The more far-reaching goals of the community required a change in basic attitudes toward the Soviet Union and a mellowing of the U.S. Cold War consensus as a precondition to forming a domestic winning coalition.

Germany represents a third type of domestic structure, the democratic corporatist model.[77] It is characterized by comparatively centralized societal organizations, strong and effective political parties, and a federal government that normally depends on a coalition of at least two parties. As a result, and supported by cultural norms emphasizing social partnership between ideological and class opponents, the system is geared toward compromise-oriented consensus building in its policy networks.

Democratic corporatist structures tend to provide societal and transnational forces with fewer access points to political institutions than do society-dominated systems. The policy impact of these forces should also be more incremental because of the slow and compromise-oriented nature of the decision-making processes. Any impact they do make, however, is expected to last longer because corporatist structures are geared toward institutionalizing consensus on policies.

As argued above, ideas about common security were gradually picked up, first by the SPD as one of the two leading mass integration parties and second by societal organizations, thereby reaching the constituency of the conservative Christian Democrats. In the end, the polarized debate about détente during the 1970s and about nuclear weapons during the early 1980s evolved into a new consensus centered around common security that explains the German enthusiasm for the Gorbachev revolution. The structure of German political institutions and policy networks explains why it took much longer for the new ideas to influence policies than in the Soviet case. The German political culture was geared toward class and ideological compromise, and past experiences with *Ostpolitik* explain why common security or security partnership became a consensual belief as the foreign policy equivalent of the domestic social partnership.

In sum, a domestic structure approach that incorporates political culture can account for the different foreign policy impacts of ideas promoted by transnational communities. The channels by which these ideas enter the policy-making process and become incorporated into national foreign policies seem to be determined by the nature of the political institutions. At the same time, strategic prescriptions need to be compatible with the worldviews embedded in the political culture or held by those powerful enough to build winning coalitions. In the case of the former Soviet Union and its centralized decision-making structure, the transnational coalition's policy ideas required both incorporation into Gorbachev's basic beliefs and his determination to implement reforms in order to have an impact. In the German case, a political culture geared toward compromise and consensus enabled elite and public opinion to accept the strategic prescription of common security. In the United States, however, a decentralized and fragmented policy-making structure together with a deeply rooted Cold War consensus made it much harder for the ideas to have a policy impact.

The prevailing realist and liberal theories of international relations account for underlying structural changes opening a window of opportunity for the end of the Cold War. Understanding its immediate causes, however, requires an explanation of the specific content of Gorbachev's foreign policy revolution as well as the Western responses to it. Structural explanations are insufficient for this task, which instead demands an account that integrates international and domestic politics.

The content of the Soviet foreign policy change and the Western reactions that together brought the Cold War to an end were informed by specific principled and causal beliefs — values and strategic prescriptions. Some of these ideas originated independently in various domestic intellectual communities. Others, particularly those informing the reconceptualization of Soviet security interests, emanated from a transnational liberal internationalist community comprising the U.S. arms control community, Western European scholars and center-left policy makers, and Soviet *institutchiks*. These ideas were causally consequential for the end of the Cold War; however, they had different impacts in the former Soviet Union, the United States, and Germany. The difference can be explained by a revised domestic structure approach that incorporates political culture. The differences between the Soviet, U.S., and German domestic structures explain to a large degree the variation in policy impact of the transnational networks and their strategic prescriptions.

I conclude, therefore, that structural theories of international relations need to be complemented by approaches that integrate domestic politics, transnational relations, and the role of ideas if we are to understand the recent sea change in world politics. The approach presented here does not pretend to offer a general theory of international relations. It is more limited and focuses instead on comparative foreign policy — a neglected and undertheorized field. As a result, the main competitors are not realism or liberalism but behavioral decision-making analysis as well as rational choice and assumptions about the state as unitary actor. Bureaucratic politics and cognitive psychological accounts offer complementary rather than alternative explanations.

The approach presented here promises insights with regard to two questions in the study of comparative foreign policy. First, the argument I have developed could prove helpful in analyzing the policy impact of transnational actors and coalitions. Reviving this subject is long overdue, to move it beyond the earlier sterile debate between society-dominated and state-centered approaches to world politics. Focusing on domestic structures as intervening variables between transnational coalitions and the foreign policy of states appears to offer a way of theorizing systematically about the inter-actions between states and transnational relations.[78]

Second, this essay attempts to contribute to the study of how ideas matter in foreign policy. Many scholars recently have drawn attention to the institutional conditions under which new values and policy strategies become politically relevant.[79] A modified domestic structure approach incorporating long-held worldviews embedded in the political culture appears to account for varied impact of transnationally diffused principled and causal beliefs across different countries.

But the argument developed in this article differs in one impor-tant aspect from the approach adopted by Goldstein and Keohane, who argue that "the materialistically egocentric maximizer of mod-ern economic theory" allows us to "formulate the null hypothesis" against which the role and impact of ideas can be measured.[80] The problem is that both the reconceptualization of Soviet security inter-ests and the German enthusiasm for Gorbachev are perfectly consis-tent with such a null hypothesis — after the event. I have tried to argue that the issue is not whether the end of the Cold War can be explained in terms of power relationships. Rather, a power-based analysis using the model of egoistic utility maximizers is underdeter-mining in the sense that it leaves various options as to how actors may define their interests in response to underlying structural condi-tions. The role and impact of ideas must be conceptualized as inter-vening variables between structural conditions and the definition of actors' interests and preferences. In other words, ideas determine which material international and domestic conditions matter and how they lead to outcomes.

NOTES

1   This essay is part of a growing body of literature on the role of ideas in foreign policy. With regard to the former Soviet Union, see in par-ticular George W. Breslauer and Philip E. Tetlock, eds., *Learning in U.S. and Soviet Foreign Policy* (Boulder, Colo.: Westview, 1991); Jef-frey Checkel, "Ideas, Institutions, and the Gorbachev Foreign Poli-cy Revolution," *World Politics* 45 (January 1993), pp. 271–300; Matthew Evangelista, "Sources of Moderation in Soviet Security Pol-icy," in *Behavior, Society, and Nuclear War*, ed. Philip Tetlock, Jo L. Husbands, Robert Jervis, Paul C. Stern, and Charles Tilly (New York: Oxford University Press, 1991), vol. 2; Matthew Evangelista, *Tam-ing the Bear: Transnational Relations and the Demise of the Soviet Threat*, forthcoming; Robert Herman, "Ideas, Institutions and the Reconceptualization of Interests: The Political and Intellectual Ori-gins of New Thinking in Soviet Foreign Policy" (Ph.D. diss., Cornell

University, 1994); Sarah E. Mendelson, "Internal Battles and External Wars: Politics, Learning, and the Soviet Withdrawal from Afghanistan," *World Politics* 45 (April 1993), pp. 327–60; Rey Koslowski and Friedrich Kratochwil, "Understanding Change in International Politics: The Soviet Empire's Demise and the International System," the sixth essay in this book; Richard Ned Lebow, "The Search for Accommodation: Gorbachev in Comparative Perspective," the seventh essay in this book; and Janice Gross Stein, "Political Learning by Doing: Gorbachev as Uncommitted Thinker and Motivated Learner," the ninth essay in this book. On ideas and foreign policy in general, see Emanuel Adler, *The Power of Ideology: The Quest for Technological Autonomy in Argentina and Brazil* (Berkeley: University of California Press, 1987); Judith Goldstein, "Ideas, Institutions, and American Trade Policy," *International Organization* 42 (winter 1988): 179–217; Judith Goldstein and Robert O. Keohane, eds., *Ideas and Foreign Policy* (Ithaca: Cornell University Press, 1993); Ernst Haas, *When Knowledge Is Power* (Berkeley: University of California Press, 1990); Peter Haas, ed., *Knowledge, Power, and International Policy Coordination, International Organization* (special issue) 46 (winter 1992); John Odell, *U.S. International Monetary Policy: Markets, Power, and Ideas as Sources of Change* (Princeton: Princeton University Press, 1982); and Kathryn Sikkink, *Ideas and Institutions: Developmentalism in Brazil and Argentina* (Ithaca: Cornell University Press, 1991).

2   I use the term *common security* (in Russian, *vseobshaia bezopasnost'*) throughout the article, even though Soviet / Russian and American authors frequently speak of mutual security (*vzaimnaia bezopasnost'*) or equal security (*bezopasnost' dlia vsekh*). I do this because, though all the terms refer to the same concept, *common security* is the generic term that was originally used in the German security debate (*gemeinsame Sicherheit*) and later in the Palme commission's report. See Independent Commission on Disarmament and Security Issues, *Common Security: A Blueprint for Survival* (New York: Simon and Schuster, 1982). On the various Russian terms, see Georgi Arbatov, *Zatianuvsheesia vysdorovlenie (1953–1988 gg.), Svidetel'stvo sovremennika* (Moscow: Mezhdunarodnye otnosheniia, 1991), pp. 240–41; published in English as *The System: An Insider's Life in Soviet Politics* (New York: Random House, 1992). I thank Matthew Evangelista for clarifying the Russian terms for me and for alerting me to Arbatov's book.

3   On epistemic communities, see P. Haas, *Knowledge, Power, and International Policy Coordination*; and E. Haas, *When Knowledge Is Power*. On transnational relations, see Robert O. Keohane and Joseph Nye, Jr., eds., *Transnational Relations and World Politics* (Cambridge: Harvard University Press, 1971).

4   The following discussion is based on Isabelle Grunberg and Thomas Risse-Kappen, "A Time of Reckoning? Theories of International Relations and the End of the Cold War," in *The End of the Cold War:*

Evaluating Theories of International Relations, ed. Pierre Allan and Kjell Goldmann (Dordrecht, Holland: Martinus Nijhoff, 1992), pp. 104–46.

5 See Kenneth Oye, "Explaining the End of the Cold War: Morphological and Behavioral Adaptations to the Nuclear Peace?" the third essay in this book. For a critical discussion of this argument, see Matthew Evangelista, "Internal and External Constraints on Grand Strategy: The Soviet Case," in *The Domestic Book of Grand Strategy*, ed. Richard Rosecrance and Arthur Stein (Ithaca: Cornell University Press, 1993), pp. 154–78.

6 Robert Gilpin, *War and Change in World Politics* (New York and Cambridge: Cambridge University Press, 1981).

7 For excellent surveys of strategies of reassurance see Alexander George, "Strategies for Facilitating Cooperation," in *U.S.-Soviet Security Cooperation*, ed. Alexander L. George, Philip J. Farley, and Alexander Dallin (New York: Oxford University Press, 1988), pp. 692–711; Richard Ned Lebow and Janice Gross Stein, "Beyond Deterrence," *Journal of Social Issues* 43 (winter 1987): 5–72; and Janice Gross Stein, "Reassurance in International Conflict Management," *Political Science Quarterly* 106 (fall 1991): 431–51.

8 See, for example, John Lewis Gaddis, "Hanging Tough Paid Off," *Bulletin of Atomic Scientists* 45 (January 1989): 11–14; and Valéry Giscard d'Estaing, Henry Kissinger, and Yasuhiro Nakasone, "East-West Relations," *Foreign Affairs* 68 (summer 1989): 1–21, esp. pp. 8–9. See also Robert Einhorn, *Negotiating from Strength: Leverage in U.S.-Soviet Arms Control* (New York: Praeger, 1985).

9 For empirical evidence, see Fred Chernoff, "Ending the Cold War: The Soviet Retreat and the U.S. Military Buildup," *International Affairs* 67 (January 1991): 111–26; Ted Hopf, "Peripheral Visions: Brezhnev and Gorbachev Meet the 'Reagan Doctrine,'" in *Learning in U.S. and Soviet Foreign Policy*, ed. Breslauer and Tetlock, pp. 586–629; Sarah Mendelson, "Internal Battles and External Wars: Politics, Learning, and the Soviet Withdrawal from Afghanistan," *World Politics* 45 (April 1993): 327–60; and Thomas Risse-Kappen, "Did 'Peace Through Strength' End the Cold War," *International Security* 16 (summer 1991): 162–88. For a general discussion of the effects of Western leverage on the Soviet Union, see Jack Snyder, "International Leverage on Soviet Domestic Change," *World Politics* 42 (October 1989): 1–30.

10 For evidence, see Mendelson, "Internal Battles and External Wars," p. 334.

11 I am referring to West German enthusiasm for Gorbachev in 1987 and 1988 — two years before the Soviet leadership consented to German reunification.

12 For a similar point, see Checkel, "Ideas, Institutions, and the Gorbachev Foreign Policy Revolution," pp. 274 and 279–80.

13 See Kenneth N. Waltz, "Reflections on *Theory of International Politics*: A Response to My Critics," in *Neorealism and Its Critics*, ed.

Robert O. Keohane (New York: Columbia University Press, 1986), pp. 322–45. Waltz seems to acknowledge this point when he writes that "any theory of international politics requires also a theory of domestic politics" (331). On the indeterminate nature of realism, see Robert O. Keohane, "Realism, Neorealism, and the Study of World Politics," in *Neorealism and Its Critics*, ed. Robert O. Keohane (New York: Columbia University Press, 1986), pp. 1–26; Stephen Haggard, "Structuralism and Its Critics: Recent Progress in International Relations Theory," in *Progress in Postwar International Relations*, ed. Emanuel Adler and Beverly Crawford (New York: Columbia University Press, 1991); and Richard N. Lebow and Thomas Risse-Kappen, "Introduction: International Relations Theory and the End of the Cold War," the first essay in this book.

14   For examples of efforts at systematizing liberal thinking in international relations, see Ernst-Otto Czempiel, *Friedensstrategien* (Strategies for peace) (Paderborn, Germany: Schöningh, 1986); Robert O. Keohane, "International Liberalism Reconsidered," in *The Economic Limits to Modern Politics*, ed. John Dunn (Cambridge: Cambridge University Press, 1990), pp. 165–94; Andrew Moravcsik, "Liberalism and International Relations Theory," working paper no. 92–6, Center for International Affairs, Harvard University, Cambridge, Mass., 1992; and Bruce Russett, *Grasping the Democratic Peace* (Princeton: Princeton University Press, 1993).

15   See Daniel Deudney and G. John Ikenberry, "The International Sources of Soviet Change," *International Security* 16 (winter 1991 / 92): 74–118; and Daniel Deudney and G. John Ikenberry, "Soviet Reform and the End of the Cold War: Explaining Large-Scale Historical Change," *Review of International Studies* 17 (summer 1991): 225–50. For a critique of the argument, see Mendelson, "Internal Wars and External Battles," pp. 330–31.

16   For an extreme version of this argument, see Francis Fukuyama, *The End of History and the Last Man* (New York: Free Press, 1992).

17   Grieco calls this perspective *neoliberal institutionalism*, while Jack Snyder uses the term *defensive realism*. See Joseph M. Grieco, "Anarchy and the Limits of Cooperation: A Realist Critique of the Newest Liberal Institutionalism," *International Organization* 42 (summer 1988): 485–507; and Jack Snyder, "Myths, Modernization, and the Post-Gorbachev World," the fifth essay in this book. See also Kenneth A. Oye, ed., *Cooperation Under Anarchy* (Princeton: Princeton University Press, 1986). This approach also influenced the original arms control literature. See, for example, Thomas Schelling and Morton Halperin, *Strategy and Arms Control* 2 (New York: Pergamon and Brassey, 1961); and Hedley Bull, *The Control of the Arms Race* (London: Weidenfeld and Nicolson, 1961).

18   The bible of that approach is Independent Commission on Disarmament and Security Issues, *Common Security*. See also Egon Bahr, *Was wird aus den Deutschen?* (What will happen to the Germans?) (Reinbek, Germany: Rowohlt, 1982); Dieter S. Lutz, ed., *Gemeinsame*

Sicherheit (Common security), 2 vols. (Baden-Baden, Germany: Nomos, 1986).

19 For this argument, see Snyder, "Myths, Modernization, and the Post-Gorbachev World."

20 See Michael Doyle, "Liberalism and the End of the Cold War," the fourth essay in this book; Michael Doyle, "Liberalism and World Politics," *American Political Science Review* 80 (December 1986): 1151–69; and Russett, *Grasping the Democratic Peace.*

21 For the most recent data on the democratic peace, see Russett, *Grasping the Democratic Peace.* See also *Journal of Conflict Resolution* 35 (June 1991) and *International Interactions* 18 (February 1993), both special issues; and Zeev Maoz and Bruce Russett, "Alliances, Contiguity, Wealth, and Political Stability: Is the Lack of Conflict Among Democracies a Statistical Artifact?" *International Interactions* 17 (February 1992): 245–267.

22 Immanuel Kant, "Zum Ewigen Frieden: Ein philosophischer Entwurf" (Perpetual peace: A philosophical sketch, 1795), in *Immanuel Kant: Werke in sechs Bänden* (Immanuel Kant: Works in six volumes), ed. Wilhelm Weischedel (Frankfurt: Insel, 1964), 6:193–251.

23 See Evangelista, "Sources of Moderation"; Mendelson, "Internal Battles and External Wars"; Lebow, "The Search for Accommodation"; and Stein, "Political Learning by Doing." See also Robert Legvold, "Soviet Learning in the 1980s," in Breslauer and Tetlock, *Learning in U.S. and Soviet Foreign Policy*, pp. 684–732; and Jack Snyder, "The Gorbachev Revolution: A Waning of Soviet Expansionism?" *International Security* 12 (winter 1987/88): 93–131.

24 See M. S. Gorbachev's speech before the British Parliament, December 18, 1984, reprinted in M. S. Gorbachev, *Speeches and Writings* (Oxford: Pergamon, 1986), pp. 123–30; and M. S. Gorbachev, "Report to the Twenty-Seventh Congress of the Communist Party of the Soviet Union," February 25, 1986, also reprinted in Gorbachev, *Speeches and Writings*, pp. 1–109, 5–21. In particular, see pp. 5–21 of the latter for an example of old thinking, which emphasized the world class struggle, and pp. 70–85 for a mix of old and new thinking.

25 Shevardnadze is quoted in Checkel, "Ideas, Institutions, and the Gorbachev Foreign Policy Revolution," p. 294, esp. n. 78.

26 I hesitate to use the term *epistemic communities* because Peter Haas's definition emphasizes policy-relevant knowledge and shared causal beliefs as their primary source of authority. While the intellectual community in the former Soviet Union shared certain knowledge claims about international politics, their internal consensus derived mostly from shared principled beliefs or values. To put it differently, their knowledge claims made sense only if one shared their values. Moreover, their expertise and competence in a particular domain was only recognized (another part of Haas's definition) when Gorbachev came into power and increasingly relied on their ideas. Finally, their competence remained contested in the Soviet domestic debate. For the definition of epistemic communities, see Peter Haas, "Introduc-

tion: Epistemic Communities and International Policy Coordination," in *Knowledge, Power, and International Policy Coordination*,
pp. 1–35, esp. p. 3. For a discussion, see Margaret Keck and Kathryn
Sikkink, "International Issue Networks in the Environment and
Human Rights," paper prepared for the International Congress of
the Latin American Studies Association, September 24–27, 1992, Los
Angeles.

27 Checkel, "Ideas, Institutions, and the Gorbachev Foreign Policy Revolution"; Robert O. Keohane and Joseph Nye, *Power and Interdependence* (Boston: Little, Brown, 1977); Mendelson, "Internal Battles and External Wars."

28 See Judith Goldstein and Robert O. Keohane, "Ideas and Foreign
Policy: An Analytical Framework," in Judith Goldstein and Robert
O. Keohane, eds., *Ideas and Foreign Policy* (Ithaca: Cornell Universi-
ty Press, 1993), pp. 3–30.

29 Ibid., p. 3.

30 On the term *strategic prescription*, see Checkel, "Ideas, Institutions,
and the Gorbachev Foreign Policy Revolution," p. 281. Strategic prescriptions contain both values (such as peace and security) and
assumptions about causal relationships between ends and means.
Thus they do not fall neatly into either of the two categories of principled and causal beliefs identified by Goldstein and Keohane.

31 For the evolution of Soviet security thinking, see Stephen Kull, *Bury-
ing Lenin: The Revolution in Soviet Ideology and Foreign Policy*
(Boulder, Colo.: Westview, 1992); and Allen Lynch, *Gorbachev's
International Outlook: Intellectual Origins and Political Conse-
quences*, Institute for East-West Security Studies Occasional Paper
No. 9 (Boulder, Colo.: Westview, 1989).

32 Checkel, "Ideas, Institutions, and the Gorbachev Foreign Policy Revolution," pp. 291–94.

33 For overviews, see Emanuel Adler, "The Emergence of Cooperation:
National Epistemic Communities and the International Evolution of
the Idea of Nuclear Arms Control," *International Organization* (special issue) 46 (winter 1992): 101–45; Gert Krell, "The Problems and
Achievements of Arms Control," *Arms Control* 2 (December 1981):
247–86.

34 On the domestic arms control debate during the Reagan administration, see Dan Caldwell, *The Dynamics of Domestic Politics and
Arms Control: The SALT II Treaty Debate* (Columbia: University of
South Carolina Press, 1991); Michael Krepon, *Arms Control in the
Reagan Administration* (Washington, D.C.: University Press of
America, 1989); Bernd W. Kubbig, *Amerikanische Rüstungskon-
trollpolitik: Die innergesellschaftlichen Auseinandersetzungen in der
ersten Amtszeit Ronald Reagan* (U.S. arms control policy: The
domestic debates during Reagan's first term) (Frankfurt: Campus,
1988); David Meyer, *A Winter of Discontent: The Freeze and American Politics* (New York: Praeger, 1990); and Philip G. Schrag, *Listen-*

ing for the Bomb: A Study in Nuclear Arms Control Verification (Boulder, Colo.: Westview, 1989).

35 On the German debate, see Jeffrey Boutwell, *The German Nuclear Dilemma* (Ithaca: Cornell University Press, 1990); and Thomas Risse-Kappen, *Die Krise der Sicherheitspolitik: Neuorientierungen und Entscheidungsprozesse im politischen System der Bundesrepublik Deutschland 1977–1984* (The crisis of security policy: New orientations and decision-making processes in the political system of the Federal Republic of Germany, 1977–1984) (Mainz-Munich: Grünewald-Kaiser, 1988).

36 Egon Bahr, "Sozialdemokratische Sicherheitspolitik" [Social Democratic security policy], *Die Neue Gesellschaft*, no. 2 (1983): 108 (my translation and emphasis). See also Bahr, *Was wird aus den Deutschen?*; Egon Bahr, "Gemeinsame Sicherheit: Gedanken zur Entschärfung der nuklearen Konfrontation in Europa," (Common security: Thoughts on the deescalation of the nuclear confrontation in Europe), *Europa-Archiv* 37, no. 14 (1982): 421–30; and Lutz, *Gemeinsame Sicherheit*. See also Richard Smoke and Andrei Kortunov, eds., *Mutual Security: A New Approach to Soviet-American Relations* (New York: St. Martin's, 1991).

37 For details, see Risse-Kappen, *Die Krise der Sicherheitspolitik*, pp. 110–18, 152–71.

38 See, for example, Horst Afheldt, *Defensive Verteidigung* (Defensive defense) (Reinbek, Germany: Rowohlt, 1983); Anders Boserup and Andrew Mack, *Krieg ohne Waffen* (War without weapons) (Reinbek, Germany: Rowohlt, 1974); Anders Boserup, *Foundations of Defensive Defense* (New York: Macmillan, 1990); Bjorn Moller, *Non-Offensive Defense: A Bibliography* (Copenhagen: Center for Peace and Conflict Research, 1987); Bjorn Moller, *Common Security and Non-Offensive Defense: A Neorealist Perspective* (Boulder, Colo.: Rienner, 1992); Studiengruppe Alternative Sicherheitspolitik, *Strukturwandel der Verteidigung* (Structural change of defense) (Opladen, Germany: Westdeutscher, 1984); and Albrecht A. C. von Müller, "Integrated Forward Defense," unpublished manuscript, Starnberg, Germany, 1985. On the security dilemma, see Robert Jervis, "Cooperation Under the Security Dilemma," *World Politics* 30 (January 1978): 186–214.

39 Evangelista, *Taming the Bear*; and Matthew Evangelista, "Transnational Relations, Domestic Structures, and Security Policy in the U.S.S.R. and Russia," in *Bringing Transnational Relations Back In: Non-State Actors, Domestic Structures and International Institutions*, ed. Thomas Risse-Kappen (Cambridge: Cambridge University Press, forthcoming).

40 See Independent Commission on Disarmament and Security Issues, *Common Security*. In the late 1980s, there was also a transnational U.S.-Soviet effort to discuss common security. See Smoke and Kortunov, *Mutual Security*.

41   See Georgi Arbatov, *The System*, pp. 341–43. Milshtein frequently published in Western journals. See, for example, Mikhail Milshtein, "Problems of the Inadmissibility of Nuclear Conflict," *International Studies Quarterly* 20 (March 1976): 87–103.

42   The most far-reaching agreement was the SPD–Polish Communist Party declaration entitled "Criteria and Measures for Establishing Confidence-Building Security Structures in Europe," released in Warsaw on February 2, 1988. For details, see Stephan Kux, "Western Peace Research and Soviet Military Thought," unpublished manuscript, Columbia University, New York, April 20, 1989.

43   For details, see Kux, "Western Peace Research and Soviet Military Thought"; and Matthew Evangelista, "Transnational Alliances and Soviet Demilitarization," paper prepared for the Council on Economic Priorities, October 1990, pp. 33–41. See also Anders Boserup, "A Way to Undermine Hostility," *Bulletin of the Atomic Scientists* 44 (September 1988): 16–19.

44   For the initial Soviet reactions, see Stephan Tiedtke, *Abschreckung und ihre Alternativen: Die sowjetische Sicht einer westlichen Debatte* [Deterrence and its alternatives: The Soviet view of a Western debate] (Heidelberg, Germany: Forschungsstätte der Evangelischen Studiengemeinschaft, 1986).

45   On the history of Pugwash, see Joseph Rotblat, *Scientists in the Quest for Peace: A History of the Pugwash Conference* (Cambridge, Mass.: MIT Press, 1972). On the various Pugwash meetings, see Joseph Rotblat and Laszlo Valki, eds., *Coexistence, Cooperation, and Common Security: Annals of Pugwash 1986* (New York: St. Martin's, 1988); and Joseph Rotblat and V. I. Goldanskii, eds., *Global Problems and Common Security: Annals of Pugwash 1988* (Berlin: Springer, 1989).

46   Gorbachev, "Report to the Twenty-Seventh Congress," pp. 71, 74. For a more coherent and less ambiguous argument about common security, see Mikhail S. Gorbachev, *Perestroika: New Thinking for Our Country and the World* (New York: Harper and Row, 1987), pp. 140–44. For comprehensive analyses of the new Soviet thinking about security, see Kull, *Burying Lenin*; Raymond Garthoff, *Deterrence and the Revolution in Soviet Military Doctrine* (Washington, D.C.: Brookings, 1990); and Klaus Segbers, *Der sowjetische Systemwandel* (The Soviet system change) (Frankfurt: Suhrkamp, 1989), pp. 299–330.

47   See, for example, Independent Commission on Disarmament and Security Issues, *Common Security*, pp. 6–11.

48   Tracing the policy impact of transnational coalitions requires extensive data on decision-making processes in order to allow for causal inferences. The evidence I present is not sufficient to meet these requirements. For more detailed studies, see Evangelista, *Taming the Bear*; Evangelista, "Transnational Relations"; and Herman, "Ideas, Institutions and the Reconceptualization of Interests."

49   Gorbachev, *Perestroika*, pp. 206–7. See also ibid., p. 196, regarding the Brandt commission on North-South issues.

50 *Pravda*, April 6, 1988, as quoted in Kux, "Western Peace Research and Soviet Military Thought," p. 13. See also Evangelista, "Transnational Alliances and Soviet Demilitarization," pp. 29–31. As Georgi Arbatov put it: "We do not claim to have invented all the ideas of the new thinking. Some of them originated outside the Soviet Union with people such as Albert Einstein, Bertrand Russell, and Olof Palme. We are developing them, along with our own ideas, into a full program for international conduct" (quoted in Stephen F. Cohen and Katrina Vanden Heuvel, eds., *Voices of Glasnost* [New York: Norton, 1989], p. 315).

51 Arbatov, *The System*, p. 171.

52 See ibid., pp. 311–12; Checkel, "Ideas, Institutions, and the Gorbachev Foreign Policy Revolution," pp. 291–94; Mendelson, "Internal Battles and External Wars," p. 340; Lynch, *Gorbachev's International Outlook*, pp. 56–58; and Pat Litherland, "Gorbachev and Arms Control: Civilian Experts and Soviet Policy," Peace Research Report No. 12, University of Bradford, November 1986.

53 Gorbachev, *Perestroika*, pp. 142–43. See also his "Report to the Twenty-Seventh Congress," p. 74.

54 For details of these arguments, see Garthoff, *Deterrence and the Revolution in Soviet Military Doctrine*, pp. 149–85; Stephen M. Meyer, "The Sources and Prospects of Gorbachev's New Political Thinking on Security," *International Security* 13 (fall 1988): 124–63; R. Hyland Phillips and Jeffrey I. Sands, "Reasonable Sufficiency and Soviet Conventional Defense," *International Security* 13 (fall 1988): 164–78; and Willard C. Frank and Philip S. Gillette, eds., *Soviet Military Doctrine from Lenin to Gorbachev, 1915–1991* (Westport, Conn.: Greenwood, 1992).

55 See, for example, Andrei Kokoshin and Valentin Larionov, "Confrontation of Conventional Forces in the Context of Ensuring Strategic Stability," in *Alternative Conventional Defense Postures in the European Theater*, ed. Hans Günter Brauch and Robert Kennedy (New York: Crane Russak, 1992), 2:71–82. The Russian original of this article first appeared in 1988. See also Andrei Kokoshin, "Restructure Forces, Enhance Security," *Bulletin of the Atomic Scientists* 44 (September 1988): 35–38, and Valentin Larionov, *Prevention of War: Doctrines, Concepts, Prospects* (Moscow: Progress, 1991); and Valentin Larionov, "Soviet Military Doctrine: Past and Present," in Frank and Gillette, *Soviet Military Doctrine*, pp. 301–19.

56 For details of these exchanges, see Evangelista, "Transnational Alliances and Soviet Demilitarization," pp. 31–37. For Alexei Arbatov, see his book *Lethal Frontiers: A Soviet View of Nuclear Strategy, Weapons, and Negotiations* (New York: Praeger, 1988), which first appeared in Russian in 1984 and shows a superb knowledge of the American strategic debate.

57 Frank and Gillette, *Soviet Military Doctrine*, p. 397.

58 Other examples include arms control proposals on test ban negotiations and the ABM treaty (see Evangelista, "Transnational Rela-

tions") and ideas about the "common European home" and the Conference for Security and Cooperation in Europe. See Gorbachev, *Perestroika*, pp. 194–98.

59   See Litherland, "Gorbachev and Arms Control"; Lynch, *Gorbachev's International Outlook*; and Kimberley Martin Zisk, "Soviet Academic Theories on International Conflict and Negotiation: A Research Note," *Journal of Conflict Resolution* 34 (December 1990): 678–93.

60   The details in the remainder of this section are rather sketchy. However, enough empirical analyses are available to support the argument. See, for example, the literature cited in note 35 above. See also Bernd W. Kubbig, *Die militärische Eroberung des Weltraums* (The military conquering of space), vol. 1 (Frankfurt: Campus, 1990). The best narratives of arms control under the Reagan and Bush administrations are Strobe Talbott, *Deadly Gambits* (New York: Knopf, 1984); Strobe Talbott, *The Master of the Game* (New York: Knopf, 1988); and Michael R. Beschloss and Strobe Talbott, *At the Highest Levels: The Inside Story of the End of the Cold War* (Boston: Little, Brown, 1993). See also George Shultz's memoirs, *Turmoil and Triumph* (New York: Scribner's, 1993).

61   The best analysis of the freeze campaign is Meyer, *A Winter of Discontent*.

62   See Kubbig, *Die militärische Eroberung des Weltraums*; and Raymond Garthoff, *Policy Versus the Law: The Reinterpretation of the ABM Treaty* (Washington, D.C.: Brookings, 1987).

63   For details on this case, see Michèle Flournoy, "The NRDC / SAS Test Ban Verification Project: A Controversial Excursion in Private Diplomacy," unpublished manuscript, Washington, D.C., 1989; and Schrag, *Listening for the Bomb*. For a discussion of the Soviet involvement in these activities, see Evangelista, "Transnational Relations."

64   The cautious and reactive U.S. approach to the revolutionary changes in the Soviet Union and Eastern Europe is well documented in Beschloss and Talbott, *At the Highest Levels*.

65   This discussion builds on my earlier work, in particular *Die Krise der Sicherheitspolitik*. See also Boutwell, *The German Nuclear Dilemma*; and Barry Blechman and Cathleen Fisher, *The Silent Partner: West Germany and Arms Control* (Cambridge, Mass.: Ballinger, 1988). On the evolution of European public opinion on security policy, see Richard Eichenberg, *Public Opinion and National Security in Western Europe* (Ithaca: Cornell University Press, 1989).

66   See, for example, Jeffrey Herf, "War, Peace, and the Intellectuals: The Long March to the West German Peace Movement," *International Security* 10 (spring 1986): 172–200.

67   Details in Risse-Kappen, *Die Krise der Sicherheitspolitik*, pp. 43–89.

68   See Thomas Risse-Kappen, *The Zero Option: INF, West Germany, and Arms Control* (Boulder, Colo.: Westview, 1988); and Talbott, *Deadly Gambits*.

69   See, for example, Peter Katzenstein, ed., *Between Power and Plenty*

(Madison: University of Wisconsin Press, 1978); Peter Katzenstein, *Small States in World Markets* (Ithaca: Cornell University Press, 1985); Peter Gourevitch, *Politics in Hard Times* (Ithaca: Cornell University Press, 1986); G. John Ikenberry, *Reasons of State: Oil Politics and the Capacities of the American Government* (Ithaca: Cornell University Press, 1988); and G. John Ikenberry, David Lake, and Michael Mastanduno, eds., *The State and American Foreign Economic Policy* (Ithaca: Cornell University Press, 1988). For examples of attempts to apply the approach to other issue areas, see Michael Barnett, "High Politics Is Low Politics: The Domestic and Systemic Sources of Israeli Security Policy, 1967–1977," *World Politics* 42 (July 1990): 529–62; Matthew Evangelista, *Innovation and the Arms Race* (Ithaca: Cornell University Press, 1988); idem, "Domestic Structures and International Change," in *New Thinking in International Relations Theory*, ed. Michael Doyle and G. John Ikenberry (forthcoming); and Thomas Risse-Kappen, "Public Opinion, Domestic Structure, and Foreign Policy in Liberal Democracies," *World Politics* 43 (July 1991): 479–512. See also my introduction in *Bringing Transnational Relations Back In.*

70 See, for example, James G. March and Johan P. Olsen, *Rediscovering Institutions: The Organizational Basis of Politics* (New York: Free Press, 1989); G. John Ikenberry, "Conclusion: An Institutional Approach to American Foreign Economic Policy," in Ikenberry, Lake, and Mastanduno, *The State and American Foreign Economic Policy*, pp. 219–43; and Friedrich Kratochwil, *Rules, Norms, and Decisions: On the Conditions of Practical and Legal Reasoning in International Relations and Domestic Affairs* (Cambridge: Cambridge University Press, 1989). For various applications, see Peter Katzenstein and Nobuo Okawara, "Japan's National Security: Structures, Norms, and Politics," *International Security* 17 (spring 1993): 84–118; Peter Katzenstein and Nobuo Okawara, *Japan's National Security: Structures, Norms, and Policy Responses in a Changing World* (Ithaca: Cornell University Press, 1993); and Thomas Berger, "From Sword to Chrysanthemum: Japan's Culture of Anti-militarism," *International Security* 17 (spring 1993): 119–50.

71 Clearly, it is important to distinguish between consensual ideas that are stable over time and those that are altered frequently and promoted by specific groups. The strategic prescriptions discussed in this article are examples of the latter type of ideas. I thank John Odell and an anonymous reviewer for alerting me to this point.

72 See Evangelista, *Innovation and the Arms Race*; and idem, "Transnational Relations."

73 A domestic structure approach explains why cognitive and learning theories are so widely used to explain the Gorbachev revolution. See Breslauer and Tetlock, *Learning in U.S. and Soviet Foreign Policy*; and Stein, "Political Learning by Doing." For a similar point, see Sue Peterson, "Strategy and State Structure: The Domestic Politics of Crisis Bargaining" (Ph.D. diss., Columbia University, New York, 1993).

74 I owe the following argument to Steve Ropp.

75 Of course, U.S. autonomy is greater in national security affairs than in other issue areas. But compared with the former Soviet state, the difference is still striking.

76 On the Cold War consensus in the United States and its limits, see Bruce Russett, *Controlling the Sword* (Cambridge: Harvard University Press, 1990), chap. 3; and Eugene Wittkopf, *Faces of Internationalism: Public Opinion and American Foreign Policy* (Durham, N.C.: Duke University Press, 1990).

77 See Peter Katzenstein, *Corporatism and Change* (Ithaca: Cornell University Press, 1984); idem, *Policy and Politics in West Germany* (Philadelphia: Temple University Press, 1989).

78 For a further evaluation of this approach, see Risse-Kappen, *Bringing Transnational Relations Back In*. See also Kathryn Sikkink, "Human Rights, Principled Issue-Networks, and Sovereignty in Latin America," *International Organization* 47 (summer 1993): 411–41.

79 See, for example, Checkel, "Ideas, Institutions, and the Gorbachev Foreign Policy Revolution"; Goldstein, "Ideas, Institutions, and American Trade Policy"; Goldstein and Keohane, *Ideas and Foreign Policy*; Odell, *U.S. International Monetary Policy*; and Sikkink, *Ideas and Institutions*.

80 Goldstein and Keohane, "Ideas and Foreign Policy," p. 26.

9

*Political Learning by Doing:
Gorbachev as Uncommitted Thinker
and Motivated Learner

*At a moment when history has turned, experience is not necessarily
the first qualification. There are differences between being locked
into foreign policies that reflect the thinking of the last decade and
promoting foreign policies designed for the next decade.*
— Anthony Lake

The dramatic changes in Soviet foreign policy initiated by Mikhail
Gorbachev marked the beginning of the end of the Cold War. Some
analysts look largely to changes in the international distribution of
power to explain the transformation of Soviet foreign policy, while
others give primacy to domestic politics. I argue that both these
explanations are underdetermined and that a satisfactory explanation of the change in Soviet foreign policy must include individual as
well as international and domestic variables.[1] Although most Soviet
leaders recognized the need for change by the mid-1980s, the direction and scope of the change that took place cannot be explained
without reference to the impact of Gorbachev and his representation of the Soviet security problem.

There is no obvious explanation of how and why Gorbachev
developed his representation of the issues that were central to the
Cold War. Several different hypotheses are plausible. Gorbachev's
cognitive constructs, different from those of his predecessors, may

*I would like to acknowledge the helpful comments of Richard Ned
Lebow, Jack Levy, Thomas Risse-Kappen, Jack Snyder, Yaacov Y. I.
Vertzberger, and David Welch. I am grateful to the United States
Institute of Peace, the Connaught Committee of the University of
Toronto, and the Social Science and Humanities Research Council of
Canada for their generous support of this research. The Lake state-
ment used in the epigraph is quoted from Adam Clymer, "Bush and
Clinton Open Fire on the Foreign Policy Front," *New York Times*,
August 2, 1992, p. E3.

have been embedded in his cognitive structure for a considerable time. Those cognitive constructs did not change, but the man came to power. Under these conditions, a political explanation of generational change and new elites would capture most of what is important.

Two other related but distinct explanations are also possible. First, Gorbachev may have changed his cognitive constructs as he approached the senior leadership position in the Soviet Union. Cognitive concepts of schemata change are then an obvious candidate to explain the change. Theories of cognitive change, however, are insufficiently specified to predict the conditions and processes that would provoke the change in Gorbachev's representation of the security dilemma. In this sense, they share the limitations of structural explanations of political change.

A second possibility is that Gorbachev did not have well-developed cognitive constructs about security and international relations until fairly late in his career. As he approached the leadership, he developed new constructs. Theories of learning may provide a more satisfactory explanation of the development of Gorbachev's cognitive constructs. Here too the analyst encounters difficulties. No unified theory of learning exists, and concepts are open to multiple interpretations and measures. Any attempt to explain the development of Gorbachev's cognitive constructs confronts underspecified theories and very limited empirical evidence. For the moment, we can at best choose the explanation that most plausibly interprets the available data. I argue that through inductive trial-and-error learning stimulated by failure, Gorbachev developed a new representation of the ill-structured Soviet security problem. Learning by doing must be embedded within the broader social and political context to provide a convincing explanation of how and why Gorbachev was able to learn.

This explanation of the development of Gorbachev's cognitive constructs is only one piece, albeit an important one, of the larger puzzle of the changes in Soviet foreign policy. I conclude this essay with some observations about the importance of political learning as a component of a broader explanation of the changes in Soviet foreign policy that ended the Cold War and sketch the outlines of the rich research agenda that grows out of the analysis of learning and policy change.

International and Domestic Explanations of Change

Shortly after Gorbachev became general secretary of the Communist Party of the Soviet Union in March 1985, he began to emphasize the importance of new thinking that challenged long-standing Soviet concepts of security.[2] Over the next few years, Gorbachev, some of his colleagues, and their advisers reformulated the basic axioms and strategic principles of Soviet security and defense.[3] Change was disorderly and ad hoc but encompassed the fundamentals of Soviet concepts of security.

By the end of 1988 Gorbachev's thinking had led him to a far-reaching and fundamental assault on established Soviet concepts of security. He repudiated the class basis of international relations that had dominated Soviet thinking since its inception, asserting that "all human values" had to take precedence over the narrower interests of the class struggle in the nuclear age.[4] This rejection of class-based competition within coexistence was heresy to any Marxist-Leninist and a sharp departure from thinking about security under Nikita Khrushchev and Leonid Brezhnev. Gorbachev emphasized the interdependence of capitalism and socialism in a common human civilization. National and international security, he insisted, were inextricably linked. Security was mutual, and political solutions, rather than military technology, should be at the forefront of policy.[5]

One obvious explanation of these changes in Gorbachev's cognitive constructs is the unfavorable shift in the international distribution of capabilities. Yet Soviet military capability, the focus of realist theories, did not decline. On the contrary, many Western analysts worried about a relative improvement in Soviet nuclear capability and power to project conventional forces abroad at the beginning of the 1980s.[6] The Soviet economy, however, which had grown at rates of 5 percent or more until the early 1970s, was growing at a rate of only 2.5 percent in 1984. When the world economy began to shift away from the traditional heavy industries toward high value-added and knowledge-based manufacturing, the Soviet economy seemed increasingly less able to compete.[7]

If the changes in Gorbachev's concepts that spilled over into Soviet doctrine and behavior were a straightforward response to relative economic decline, then new thinking is an epiphenomenal and unnecessary component of an explanation of the change in Soviet foreign policy. The data, however, do not sustain this interpretation in the way realist theories expect. The decline in growth rates during the 1970s and 1980s was not unique to the Soviet Union. Growth in the United States, the obvious point of reference, also slowed. The U.S. economy grew at an average rate of 4 percent throughout the 1960s, but the rate of growth declined to about 2.7 percent in the 1970s and 1980s.[8]

The data do not show the relative decline in Soviet economic capabilities that is the focus of realist explanations. Evidence suggests, however, that Gorbachev was concerned about the absolute economic decline and stagnation of the Soviet Union. Even before his election as general secretary, Gorbachev warned, "Only an intensive, fast-developing economy can ensure the strengthening of the country's position in the international arena, enabling it to enter the new millennium appropriately, as a great and prosperous power."[9] When asked directly whether he knew before he became general secretary that the economic status quo was untenable and that radical change would be required, Gorbachev replied: "Like many others, I had known that our society needed radical change. That really was not some kind of revelation for me because after the death of Stalin, there were many attempts to do it. Khrushchev tried it. Kosygin tried it. Some agricultural reformers tried it, and some other reformers. . . . If I had not understood that, I would not have accepted the position of general secretary."[10]

Although the leadership shared widespread concern about Soviet economic performance and a general recognition that change was required, possible responses to economic decline varied widely. Robert Gilpin argues that in periods of uneven shifts in relative power, either rising challengers or status quo great powers go to war to establish a new equilibrium.[11] A second possible response to economic stagnation was a neo-Stalinist retrenchment, with economic change directed from above. A third option was an accommodation with the West to free resources for investment in the Soviet economy. Since the variation across these responses is fairly wide, the structural explanation of the shift in Soviet foreign policy toward accommodation is underdetermined.[12]

The limits of a structural explanation become clear when one looks at the response of Yuri Andropov and Konstantin Chernenko, Gorbachev's immediate predecessors, to fundamentally the same set of international conditions. Their initial response to the increased hostility of the United States in the early 1980s, under similar conditions of economic stringency, was to reiterate traditional Soviet concepts of security and to adopt a more confrontational policy.[13] Andropov withdrew from the intermediate-range nuclear forces (INF) talks after NATO began its deployment of Pershing II missiles, and Chernenko agreed to return to the table only in January 1985, two months before Gorbachev succeeded to the leadership. Little had changed in the distribution of economic and military capabilities in those three years. Under Gorbachev, both concepts and policy were very different.

The serious division within the Soviet leadership as new thinking began to develop is further evidence of the indeterminacy of structural explanations. This intense debate could have reflected decision making in an environment of imperfect or incomplete information. Politicians can disagree over the likely consequences of policy options and debate alternatives to clarify uncertainty. Undoubtedly, the kinds of ill-structured problems Soviet leaders confronted involved high levels of uncertainty that led to different representations of the dilemmas of security in a changing environment. The debate was about problem representation, not simply about the uncertain consequences of options.

Analysts of Soviet politics, writing in late 1989, argued that new thinking was limited to a few central Soviet leaders and advisers.[14] Almost all its fundamental components were politically contested; prevention of war and protection against accidental war were the least controversial. Long before Gorbachev became general secretary in 1985, the Soviet military had instituted procedures to reduce the risk of accidents.[15] Brezhnev had insisted that it would be suicidal to start a nuclear war. Even so, the Soviet military, in its doctrine and in its journals, continued to emphasize the importance of preparing to fight and win a war. This discontinuity had perpetuated Western suspicion of Soviet intentions.

Gorbachev rejected out of hand any military planning based on the assumption that either the United States or the Soviet Union would deliberately attack the other. He did not believe that intentional nuclear war was possible. He told his senior military officials to stop bringing him any plans that presumed a war with the United States. "Don't put any such programs on my desk," he ordered.[16] Influential figures in the defense establishment such as Minister of Defense Dmitri Yazov and Dmitri Volkogonov, director of the Military Historical Institute in the Ministry of Defense, nevertheless continued to insist that the threat of an intentional attack against the Soviet Union was real, citing as evidence ongoing Western development and deployment of strategic weapons. They and others also challenged the heavy emphasis on political solutions to security problems, arguing that the United States remained committed to achieving military superiority.[17] Evidence of U.S. intentions was the failure of the United States to join the unilateral Soviet moratorium on nuclear testing and past duplicity on arms control.

Critics also challenged the fundamental political logic that under-pinned new thinking on security. In August 1988, for example, three years after Gorbachev had come to power, Yegor Ligachev reiterat-ed the importance of the international class struggle and argued that there was not and could not be any contradiction between peace and socialism. "Active involvement in the solution of general human problems," he insisted, "by no means signifies any artificial 'brak-ing' of the social and national liberation struggle."[18]

Given that senior Soviet leaders, officials, and policy analysts in the Gorbachev era disagreed fundamentally about the appropriate direction of Soviet foreign and defense policy, changes in interna-tional structures could not be determining of the change in concepts of security. It is thus unsatisfying to explain the changes in Soviet thinking about security as a rational adaptation to unambiguous feedback from the environment.[19]

Cognitive variables are epiphenomenal in realist models that assume that changes in international capabilities are obviously and easily read by rational leaders, who then adapt to changing struc-tures. The evidence suggests that in the Soviet case feedback was not obvious, that it was open to radically different interpretations, and that its meaning was construed very differently by Soviet leaders within a short period of time. Insofar as this is the case, the construc-tion of meaning becomes a critical rather than epiphenomenal fac-tor in any explanation of the end of the Cold War.

A second candidate explanation for the change in Soviet foreign policy is domestic politics. The strong version holds that leaders are put in place by powerful constituencies because of their commitment to change. Gorbachev would have had to have been chosen by the Politburo primarily because of his commitment to a new approach to Soviet defense and security. His new thinking could then be under-stood as a calculated response to the demands of his constituency and could be nicely explained as a rational response to interest politics.

Historically, periods of succession in the Soviet Union have pro-moted logrolling and political trade-offs in policy until the new leader consolidates his authority.[20] Andropov succeeded Brezhnev in November 1982 but became ill in the summer of 1983 and died in February 1984. Chernenko, also in failing health, was chosen as the new general secretary, but with the tacit understanding that Gor-bachev would be considered the heir apparent.[21] In this long period of succession after Brezhnev, a coalition in favor of radical change in Soviet foreign policy could have formed behind Gorbachev as the successor.

The evidence does not suggest that Gorbachev was chosen because of his commitment to change Soviet foreign policy. Rather, he was acknowledged as one of the leading proponents of domestic reform. The limited evidence that is available suggests that he was chosen to end the period of stagnation at home and begin the revitalization of Soviet society. Domestic politics and political succession do explain why Gorbachev came to power. They are also important in explaining why his thinking on security mattered once he had become general secretary.[22] In a state-centered society, the influence of even a new general secretary was considerable. Domestic politics cannot adequately explain, however, why Gorbachev changed or developed new representations of the Soviet Union's security problem.

A weaker variant of a domestic politics explanation does provide important pieces of the puzzle. The configuration of domestic politics can help to explain the direction and scope of change once Gorbachev began to think differently about and to reorient Soviet foreign policy. Some of Gorbachev's actions were specifically designed to fracture alliances among those opposed to the new direction in policy. For example, he was reluctant to extend support to repressive leaders in Eastern Europe in part because they were allies of those in the Soviet Union who opposed reform both at home and abroad.[23] In this sense, domestic politics helped to accelerate rather than to initiate change.

Domestic politics is also helpful in explaining how Gorbachev deepened his commitment to policy change. The strands of domestic politics were woven in complex ways. I argue that Gorbachev drew on institutional expertise within the political system to develop and refine ideas and policy. He also crafted a political coalition in an effort to build political support for new policies that threatened established interests. In both these ways, domestic politics was an important component of foreign policy change. Domestic politics, however, cannot address the important questions of why Gorbachev began to think differently about security, why he rejected the conventional wisdom of the time, and how and why he developed new concepts to organize his thinking about foreign and defense policy.

Neither international nor domestic variables provide satisfactory answers to these questions. The Soviet leadership's recognition of the need for change permitted a wide variation in response, and domestic politics did not determine the vector of policy that emerged. To explain the shift in Soviet foreign policy, one must look to the role of individuals within the parameters set by an environment that pressed the Soviet leadership.

Generational Succession and Foreign Policy Change

Generational change provides a more convincing explanation of the change in Soviet foreign policy. It incorporates political and cognitive variables to suggest that cohorts learn collectively from shared formative experiences. Leaders do not change their concepts; rather, as one generation of leaders succeeds another, it brings with it different experiences and therefore different conceptions of policy. At first glance, this explanation provides a plausible interpretation of new thinking.

Gorbachev was a generation younger than Brezhnev and his colleagues. He was nineteen years younger than Chernenko and thirteen years younger than the average age of the ten surviving full voting members of the Politburo. Most members of Brezhnev's Politburo were born around 1910 and so lived through the early revolutionary years. They were young adults during the forced collectivization under Stalin and fully responsible adults during World War II. Their formative experiences were the creation of the Soviet Union, the surprise attack by Hitler's Germany, and the trauma of the "Great Patriotic War."

Many members of the Politburo under Gorbachev were born around 1930, and their formative political experience was Khrushchev's denunciation of Stalin in 1956. Those who came of political age during this period were heavily influenced by Khrushchev's attempt to liberalize the political process, to free Soviet society of the Stalinist legacy, and to reform Soviet politics. They described themselves as children of the Twentieth Party Congress, and many emerged as colleagues or advisers to Gorbachev in the first few years of his administration.[24] Some of Gorbachev's advisers lived through the years of stagnation in frustrated isolation and were receptive to reform and change.

Yet generational change is not an entirely satisfactory explanation. Many in Gorbachev's cohort did not change their fundamental constructs. New thinking was contested not only by those of Brezhnev's generation entrenched within the institutional network but also by members of Gorbachev's cohort, who challenged both its validity and its consequences. The predisposition to reform of Soviet society was a powerful incentive to change among Gorbachev's generation, but not all the leaders of this generation drew the same conclusions from Soviet history; nor did they agree on the representation of the problem of Soviet security or the direction of change. Insofar as Soviet history could be and was read differently by members of Gorbachev's generation, generational change is an insufficient explanation of new thinking. In the end, the individual interpretation by the senior leader in a highly centralized political system becomes the starting point in any explanation of the change in the Soviet concept of security. In the Soviet political system from 1985 to 1989, Gorbachev's political thinking mattered.

Cognitive Change

Cognitive psychologists suggest that stability is the default position and change the exception. People use schemata — cognitive structures that represent knowledge about a concept, person, role, group, or event — to organize their interpretations of their environments and develop scripts for action. Theories of schemata explore the impact of these cognitive constructions on problem representation, memory, and information processing. They postulate that schemata are generally resistant to change once they are established.[25] The well-established tendency to discount information that is discrepant with existing schemata contributes significantly to cognitive stability.[26] The cognitive economy of schemata precludes their reevaluation in the face of small amounts of discrepant information.

Conservatism does not hold unconditionally. Generally, schemata change gradually over time rather than undergoing quick and far-reaching conversion. Change is also most likely to occur at the periphery and incrementally. Thus people tend to make the smallest possible changes, allow a large number of exceptions and special cases, and make superficial alterations rather than rejecting existing schemata.

Schema theory has not yet developed an integrated set of propositions about why schemata change.[27] The centrality of schemata, their refutability, the diagnosticity of discrepant information, the pattern of attribution, and cognitive complexity all have been identified as predictors of the likelihood of change.

Change is in part a function of the rate at which discrepant information occurs and its diagnosticity. Contradictory evidence dispersed across many instances should have a greater impact on schemata than would a few isolated examples.[28] As people consider information inconsistent with previous knowledge, they incorporate into their schema the conditions under which the schema does not hold; this kind of process permits gradual change and adjustment.[29] Important schemata are challenged only when they cannot account for contradictory data that people consider diagnostic. Even the strongest schema cannot withstand the challenge of strongly incongruent information or a competing schema that fits the data better.[30] Cognitive psychologists have not, however, established thresholds for strongly incongruent and diagnostic information.

Significant change in a person's schema about another also occurs when a subject is exposed to incongruent information and persuaded that the behavior is not arbitrary but reflects the nature of the target. Change occurs when inconsistent information is attributed to dispositional rather than situational factors.[31] The general tendency to prefer situational rather than dispositional attributions for incongruent behavior explains why change occurs so infrequently.[32] It is not clear, however, when and why people make uncharacteristic attributions of inconsistent information to dispositional factors.

Change is also a function of cognitive complexity — the complexity of the cognitive rules used to process information about objects and situations. Cognitive complexity refers to the structure or the organization of cognition rather than to the content of thought. Complexity has a somewhat contradictory impact on schema change. The more complex the cognitive system, the more capable the decision maker of making new or subtle distinctions when confronted with new information.[33] Experts with highly complex cognitive schemata are more sensitive to new information than are novices with low cognitive complexity whose schemata are likely to be fixed.[34] On the other hand, because experts have more relevant information, they can more easily incorporate inconsistent information as exceptions and special cases. Incongruent data therefore have less impact on their schemata than they would have on those of novices.[35] A person's level of cognitive complexity is not unchanging but responds to situational, socializing, and role factors. Crisis-induced stress decreases cognitive complexity, while pluralistic values and political responsibility socialize people to the need to balance competing goals.[36]

Cognitive Explanations of New Thinking

How helpful are these sets of propositions drawn from cognitive psychology in explaining Gorbachev's new thinking? A fair test would require that Gorbachev's schemata before he became general secretary in 1985 be compared with his schemata some time after he took office. Only then could the extent of change be assessed and the likely impact of the different conditions that stimulated change be estimated. No such reconstruction of Gorbachev's schemata exists, and it could not be done validly after the fact. Indeed, whether and when Gorbachev's schemata changed are still empirical questions.

Reliable and valid evidence to test these propositions with regard to the schema change of a leader in a closed political system is at present not available; a fair evaluation must await the opening of the records of party and leadership deliberations.[37] Nevertheless, the logic of elimination, and some currently available evidence allow some preliminary assessment of their utility.

The volume, rate, and diagnosticity of discrepant information that Gorbachev received are not very helpful in explaining the emergence of new thinking. Information about the economic performance of the Soviet Union, the difficulties in Afghanistan, the impasse in arms control, and the heightened tension with the United States was available to Andropov and Chernenko as well as to members of Gorbachev's Politburo, yet it led to no significant change in their cognitive constructs.[38] Neither qualitative nor quantitative changes in discrepant information can help to explain why Gorbachev but not Andropov, Chernenko, or Ligachev developed new representations of the Soviet security problem. Even though individual receptivity to discrepant information differs significantly, schema theory suggests that change occurs in the face of unambiguously incongruent information. In foreign policy making, information is frequently ambiguous, and problems are ill structured. Even were adequate longitudinal evidence available about Gorbachev's schemata, the volume, rate, and diagnosticity of discrepant information do not provide a satisfactory explanation.

The complexity of Gorbachev's thinking is somewhat more helpful in explaining the development of new thinking. Complexity can be assessed along two dimensions — differentiation, or the number of logically distinct arguments considered, and integration among the idea elements within a schema, or the development of principles for coping with trade-offs.[39] One way to assess the relationship between complexity and schema change is to compare Gorbachev's thinking about peaceful coexistence, a central concept in Soviet thinking about security, to that of a predecessor who exhibited little propensity for cognitive change. Brezhnev's peace platform speech to the Twenty-Fourth Party Congress in March 1971 and Gorbachev's Political Report of the Central Committee to the Twenty-Seventh Party Congress in February 1986 were content-analyzed. These two speeches were selected because they signaled new initiatives by each of the leaders, and the initiatives were announced before the concepts and programs that followed were fully developed. Both, however, as with almost all major speeches, went through many drafts and therefore are not completely valid indicators of the thinking of the two general secretaries. Coders were instructed to map the logical arguments connected with peaceful coexistence and to search for any discussion of trade-offs connected with the issue.

Differences in the number of logical arguments connected to peaceful coexistence are apparent. Brezhnev made only two arguments about the destructiveness of nuclear weapons and the impossibility of nuclear war as imperatives for peaceful coexistence. Gorbachev's thinking about peaceful coexistence demonstrated significantly greater complexity in the number of logically distinct arguments he considered.

Gorbachev repeatedly referred to the "hegemonic-seeking aspirations" of the United States. He did not reject the earlier Soviet concept of the "imperialist ambitions" of the United States. Rather, he located the concept of the United States as an imperial enemy within a more complex cognitive structure that included an analysis of the situation and integrated the concept within his schema of peaceful coexistence. Gorbachev considered many more elaborate dimensions than did Brezhnev, who focused almost exclusively on the nuclear threat to survival. Gorbachev spoke of global threats to survival that emanated not only from nuclear weapons and the arms race but also from the fragility of the ecosystem, the widening gap between the rich and the poor, and the tight linkages across those dimensions. The urgency of the situation, Gorbachev concluded, overwhelmed the narrowly defined interests of nation-states and required a different kind of peaceful coexistence appropriate for an "interdependent" and "integral" world.[40]

The two scripts for action differed even more dramatically in their recognition of trade-offs. Brezhnev argued that peaceful coexistence would require no compromise in Soviet support of revolutionary movements and progressive forces in the Third World. His schema did not include any recognition of trade-offs. Gorbachev, on the other hand, acknowledged trade-offs and the necessity for compromise. The fundamental question, Gorbachev argued, was "To be or not to be?" The answer was not the competitive coexistence of the Brezhnev years but cooperative coexistence in which states accommodated each other's needs and interests.[41]

Cognitive psychologists who work with the affective concept of attitude rather than the concept of schema have noted that turning-point decisions, or decisions that deviate significantly from the pattern of prior decisions, depend on resolving the contradiction between the attitude toward an object and the attitude toward a situation in favor of the situation.[42] Gorbachev integrated his attitude toward the United States within a structurally more complex schema of an interdependent global system.

Gorbachev's higher level of cognitive complexity certainly is consistent with the changes subsequently embodied in new thinking. It is difficult, however, to disentangle the causal dynamics of cognitive change inherent in the levels of development of causal schemata, or their cognitive complexity.[43] Tautological inference is a serious risk: evidence of Gorbachev's higher level of cognitive complexity comes from analysis of his new thinking and therefore cannot be used to explain his new representation of the Soviet security problem.[44] The content of schemata can change without structural change, cognitive structure and content can change simultaneously, or changes in cognitive structure can lead to changes in cognitive content. At best, the evidence suggests that increased cognitive complexity is associated with change in the content of schema; it does not explain the change in that content.[45]

Not only "cold" cognition but also "hot" emotions affect the likelihood of schema change. Not all schemata are equivalent; people vary in their commitment to different schemata.[46] The greater the emotional commitment to a schema, the more resistant it is to change by disconfirming evidence.[47] Intensity of commitment, however, does not offer much help with the puzzle of the change in Gorbachev's constructs.

Gorbachev was a committed socialist who reaffirmed his commitment to the validity of the socialist experiment and its goals even as he began to articulate a new concept of peaceful coexistence. "We are looking within socialism," Gorbachev argued, "rather than outside it, for the answers to all the questions that arise."[48] In his commitment to socialism, Gorbachev did not differ significantly from his predecessors. Yet, while his commitment to the most fundamental concepts at the core of his cognitive constructs did not change, this was not the case in more peripheral areas. It is surprising that his intense commitment to core concepts did not preclude change in closely related schemata. Gorbachev was able to reconstruct his cognitive system so that his core concepts were not inconsistent with his new concept of peaceful coexistence.[49]

Theories of social cognition also do not specify the external conditions or mediating causes of change, and critics rightly contend that the neglect of context is disturbing. The social dimension of social cognition research is largely absent.[50] Theories do not model explicitly the processes that link environmental stimuli to cognitive constructs and explain how these constructs change. Until they do, social cognition will remain incomplete as a theoretical tool in the analysis of change in political schemata. To extend the analysis, I build on propositions from social cognition and organizational psychology to develop a concept of trial-and-error learning from failure that examines why and how Gorbachev changed his concepts.

Learning in Context

The concept of learning may be more helpful than others in explaining the emergence of Gorbachev's new thinking. Learning is a subset of cognitive change: not all change is learning, but all learning is change. Theories of learning, unlike schema theory, are inherently dynamic. Learning is also an explicitly normative concept. It measures cognitive change against some set of explicit criteria.

There is as yet no unified theory of learning, and psychology has not identified the conditions or thresholds that predict when different forms of learning are likely to occur. Most psychological theories of learning are not very useful in specifying the dynamics of learning, in large part because they analyze learning within highly structured environments. Learning theorists in educational and experimental psychology are associationist. They treat learning as a change in the probability of a specified response in the face of changing reward contingencies.[51] This concept of learning is not helpful in an environment where appropriate responses are unknown or disputed.

Political psychologists distinguish between simple and complex learning. Learning is simple when means are better adjusted to ends. Complex learning occurs when a person develops a more differentiated schema that is integrated into a higher order structure highlighting difficult trade-offs.[52] Learning can be causal, an analysis of causal paths, and / or diagnostic — an examination of the conditions under which causal generalizations apply.[53] Complex learning, at its highest level, may lead to a reordering or redefinition of goals. From this perspective, learning must include the development of more complex structures as well as changes in content.[54]

These concepts of learning are a useful first cut at explaining changes in a leader's schema that then shape new directions in policy, but they fail to distinguish change from learning. Without some evaluative criteria, any cognitive change can be considered learning, and the concept of learning becomes redundant. Change in cognitive content or structure does not always constitute learning. Saddam Hussein, for example, in the year preceding his decision to invade Kuwait, extended his schema and developed a differentiated analysis of a changing international system. He then concluded that the United States, the sole remaining superpower, was engaged in a conspiracy to undermine his regime, when the United States not only had no such intention but was attempting to reinforce its relationship with Iraq. These changes in Saddam's schema provide a powerful explanation of his foreign policy behavior.[55] They must, however, be characterized as pathological thinking, not learning.[56] Inescapably built into the concept of political learning is an evaluation of the structure and content of cognitive change.[57] These kinds of evaluative judgments inevitably are and will be essentially contested.[58]

More helpful are several strands of theory and research about solving ill-structured problems and learning from failure. A problem is well structured when it has a well-established goal, known constraints, and identified possible solutions. Sometimes even the solution to the problem is established. Generally, problems in foreign policy are ill structured. Goals are often multiple and vaguely defined, one or more constraints are open, information is ambiguous and incomplete, and little may be known about the solution to the problem. Learning is the construction of new representations of the problem, the development of causal relations among the factors, the identification of constraints, and the organization of relevant knowledge.[59] Initially ill-structured problems become well structured during this representation process, which largely determines the solution. Learning is considered successful when the solution can be explained so that it is largely acceptable to the relevant community of problem solvers.[60]

A second strand of research examines the liabilities of success and the benefits of failure in promoting organizational learning.[61] When failure challenges the status quo, it can draw attention to problems and stimulate the search for solutions. Only certain kinds of failures promote learning: highly predictable failures provide no new information, whereas unanticipated failures that challenge old ways of representing problems are more likely to stimulate new formulations. Responding to failure, leaders can learn through experimentation rather than through more traditional patterns of avoidance.[62]

Learning through failure can provoke a series of sequential experiments that generate quick feedback and allow for a new round of trial-and-error experimentation.[63] This kind of trial-and-error model of learning captures the dynamics of social cognition far more effectively than do the statics of schema theory, in which the perceiver is a "passive onlooker, who . . . doesn't *do* anything — doesn't mix it up with the folks he's watching, never tests his judgments in action or interaction."[64] It does not represent learning as a neat linear process with clear causal antecedents but as a messy, dynamic, interactive process.

Drawing on models of the solution of ill-structured problems and learning through failure, I argue that Gorbachev, stimulated by failure, learned through trial-and-error experimentation and constructed a new representation of the ill-structured Soviet security problem. From 1986 to 1988 Gorbachev and some of his colleagues acknowledged the mutuality of security in the nuclear age, the interdependence of states in an integrated system, the danger of inadvertent war, the risks inherent in the security dilemma, the importance of "defensive defense" in ameliorating the security dilemma, and some of the difficult trade-offs inherent in this representation of the problem of security. These changes reflected to a far greater degree the consensus of experts, within the Soviet Union and abroad, on the representation of the problem of security in the nuclear age than did earlier Soviet concepts. Once the changes in Gorbachev's representation of the Soviet security problem are designated as learning, the important analytic questions are why and how he learned.

Why Gorbachev Learned

Political psychology offers some suggestive hypotheses about why Gorbachev learned. Evidence suggests that Gorbachev may have been a relatively uncommitted thinker on security issues. Born in 1931, his early years were spent in Stavropol. He received his degree in law from Moscow State University and traveled in the West during the 1970s. In 1978 he was elected secretary of the Central Committee, and in 1980 he became the youngest voting member of the Politburo. Until he joined the Politburo, his exposure to issues of security was limited. Only in 1982, after Brezhnev died, did he become a member of the inner circle. He then chaired the Foreign Affairs Commission of the Politburo, and by mid-1984 he frequently chaired meetings of the Politburo itself.

Gorbachev's primary interest and responsibility before he became general secretary were in the domestic economy. He was in contact with many of the scholars and directors of the principal economic institutes for several years, and his commitment to economic reform grew out of his study of local, not international, policy.[65] Unlike Andropov, who dealt largely with security issues long before he became general secretary, Gorbachev quite probably joined the Politburo less deeply interested in issues of security than some of his predecessors were.

Eduard Shevardnadze asserts that during the early 1980s Gorbachev knew the kind of foreign policy that he did not want but had few clear ideas about what he did want. In 1979, Shevardnadze noted, Gorbachev's ideas on foreign policy had not crystallized.[66] Aleksandr Yakovlev recalled that he first talked openly with Gorbachev about security in 1983, when he was ambassador to Ottawa, and Gorbachev was on a visit to Canada. In the few hours they had alone together, Yakovlev recounted, "We began to talk openly. We were surprised by how much we agreed. We agreed that it was necessary to do something. Mikhail Sergeievich [Gorbachev] did not know what he wanted to do, but our idea was to stop the Cold War before it led to catastrophe. We had to do something."[67] Valentin Falin, who subsequently became chief of the International Department of the Central Committee, described Gorbachev as "not an expert in foreign policy at all" but unusually willing to listen to what others had to say.[68] If Gorbachev was dissatisfied with existing policy and struggling to redefine the problem, he would be a prime candidate for learning. The absence of well-developed schemata and deep commitments would make learning easier.

The proposition that Gorbachev was a largely uncommitted thinker on security gets some support from his heavy emphasis on domestic restructuring in the early months of his administration. In a speech to the French parliament in October 1985, Gorbachev explained that the highest Soviet priority was economic reform and renewal. Soviet foreign policy, he observed, "like the foreign policy of any government, is determined first of all by internal demands."[69]

Some analysts of Soviet politics under Gorbachev have speculated that his initial interest in security was largely instrumental, that he was attempting above all to seize control of the Soviet defense agenda in order to rebuild the Soviet economic-industrial base. Gorbachev quickly learned at the tactical level that the commitment of resources implicit in the threat assessments of traditional thinkers would seriously constrain economic restructuring. His interest in new thinking about security grew out of his strong commitment to perestroika at home.[70]

The argument that new thinking was more a product of "instrumental necessity than of military-strategic enlightenment" is a false dichotomy.[71] Learning is the product of cognitive processes and emotional factors. Learning theorists in educational and behavioral psychology model enlightenment as a response to incentives. Gorbachev's commitment to fundamental change at home, along with an absence of deeply embedded constructs about security, both motivated and permitted him to learn about security.

Motivated and relatively free to learn, Gorbachev was far more receptive to new representations of the security problem in the face of common evidence of blockage and failure than were many of his cohort. Evidence of his unusual interest in acquiring relevant knowledge is very strong. Anatoliy Dobrynin, then the Soviet ambassador to Washington, recalled a visit to Moscow shortly after President Reagan was elected: "I walked around to meet the leaders of the Politburo, and almost no one asked me any questions. They said, 'How is life?' I said, 'Well, it's okay,' and that was it. There was one man, just one man, who asked me twenty, thirty questions. His name was Gorbachev. He was so interested. And what's surprising, he had read so many books about the United States. Gorbachev took all the books he could find about the United States and read them all."[72]

Gorbachev began by asking new questions and was open to a broader range of answers than were his predecessors and many of his cohort. He was also motivated to search actively for new ideas and new representations of an ill-structured problem. Andrei Aleksandrov-Agentov, adviser to Brezhnev, Chernenko, and Gorbachev on security issues, observed that Gorbachev felt that Soviet foreign policy had become rigid and difficult to change.[73] The failure in Afghanistan was an especially powerful incentive to learn. With no personal responsibility for the war, Gorbachev concluded as soon as he heard about the invasion that it was a costly error.[74] Even before he became general secretary, he invited specialists for private discussions about Afghanistan. Convinced of the need for change and motivated to learn, Gorbachev began to search for new representations of the problem of Soviet security.

Learning by Doing

If the proposition that Gorbachev was highly motivated to learn but a largely uncommitted thinker about security is correct, the obvious question is, how did he learn? How did he acquire the schema that were at the core of new thinking about security? The evidence suggests that beginning in the early 1980s, several years before he became general secretary, Gorbachev began to look for ideas from civilian and academic specialists inside and outside the government.[75] After he became a full member of the Politburo, he began to consult with members of the specialist community on issues of foreign as well as domestic policy.[76]

Immediately after he became general secretary, Gorbachev ordered a series of critical examinations of security issues. His predecessor had commissioned hundreds of studies of economic and social problems but almost none of foreign policy and security issues other than Afghanistan. Gorbachev requested studies from the Foreign Ministry, the Defense Ministry, and the State Security Committee (KGB). He had arranged for Yakovlev to be brought back from Canada to head the Institute of World Economy and International Relations; Yakovlev drew on specialists there to provide a flow of expert advice directly to the general secretary.[77] Gorbachev also asked Georgi Arbatov, the director of the USA and Canada Institute, for papers and advice.[78] Oleg Grinevsky, the chief Soviet negotiator at the Conference on Confidence and Security Building Measures, was invited to Gorbachev's office for confidential discussions.[79]

Many of those Gorbachev consulted worked in the policy institutes of the Soviet Academy of Sciences in Moscow and in journalism and had long been critical of established Soviet concepts of defense.[80] Partially sheltered in the institutes from broader political repercussions, these policy intellectuals, in a slow, cumulative process, had for years critically examined the failure of Soviet concepts of security to realize Soviet goals. Much of the analysis and commentary referred to the failures of policy under Brezhnev.[81] Long before Gorbachev became general secretary, analysts had written about the irrelevance of superiority and victory in nuclear war, the growing risk of inadvertent war, the dangers of the security dilemma, and the importance of transcending the class factor in the search for security.[82]

Policy scientists working in the institutes had access to Western journals and scholarly articles that critically analyzed both Soviet and American concepts of security. From the late 1960s, academic specialists and journalists had come to know specialists in the Western European and U.S. arms control community, both through their work and personally. They met at Pugwash meetings, at seminars organized by the American Academy of Arts and Sciences with the Soviet Academy of Sciences, at international scientific conferences, and through exchange programs.[83] These international contacts facilitated the exchange of ideas between transnational communities and the development of mutually understandable vocabularies and concepts. In the Gorbachev years, some senior Soviet military officers acknowledged that their supposedly new idea of unacceptable damage in nuclear war could be traced to the thinking of U.S. Secretary of Defense Robert McNamara.[84]

Expert learning was a long, slow process but particularly important were the acknowledgment of the growing costs of the Soviet intervention in Afghanistan and the recognition that Afghanistan was the Soviet Vietnam.[85] Yakovlev and Arbatov agreed in early 1985 that the Soviet Union had to withdraw from Afghanistan.[86] They also, along with other analysts, argued that NATO's deployment of Pershing II missiles was provoked by Moscow's deployment of highly accurate intermediate-range nuclear systems.[87] Yakovlev termed the deployment a "stupid and strange" policy.[88] These were the kinds of unexpected policy failures that stimulated learning.

Others have studied extensively the size and strength of the policy community that promoted new thinking on security.[89] What is important for purposes of this argument is that a community of policy intellectuals deeply critical of past failures of policy under Brezhnev and aware of analyses by Western colleagues was prepared and accessible to Gorbachev when he began to look for new ideas about security. This community proposed new ways of representing the problem of security, identified new causal relationships, and made some of the difficult trade-offs explicit. These policy entrepreneurs were ready to teach when Gorbachev, anxious to learn, gave them a policy window.[90]

The evidence suggests that Gorbachev did not learn in an orderly linear fashion or through deductive reasoning. Rather, the development and articulation of Gorbachev's new thinking imply a complex interactive relationship between political learning and action that provided quick feedback. Through a process of trial and error, Gorbachev learned through experimentation.[91]

Experimentation began long before new thinking was wholly in place. On April 7, 1985, barely a month after Gorbachev became general secretary, he announced the suspension of Soviet countermeasures in response to INF deployments by NATO and a moratorium on further deployments of ss-20s. In August of the same year, he proclaimed a unilateral moratorium on nuclear testing. The Soviet Union also paid its back dues to the United Nations for peacekeeping, began to cooperate with the International Atomic Energy Agency, and reworked its position in the Strategic Arms Reduction Talks (START) in October 1985. In January 1986 Gorbachev urged a program of complete nuclear disarmament to be achieved in three stages by the year 2000. Committed to change yet frustrated by the initially slow U.S. response, Gorbachev gradually expanded his schema and his scripts for action.

At the same time, he was learning from his meetings with U.S.

officials, particularly Secretary of State George Shultz. He considered Shultz an important "interlocutor" in discussions of "big philosophical questions" about the world and its future in the next century. "He helped me a great deal," Gorbachev said, "in developing my policies."[92] Ideas and action were synergistically related, as new thinking began first tentatively to encourage unilateral action and the response to Soviet behavior then fed and expanded Gorbachev's new thinking.

One final factor is worth noting. When Gorbachev first recognized the need for new thinking about security, his motives were largely instrumental; his interest was focused on the restructuring of the domestic economy. As he learned, however, the importance and autonomy of new thinking about security grew. By 1987 Gorbachev insisted that the unforgiving realities of the nuclear age demanded new concepts and new policies, independent of perestroika at home:

> Some people say that the ambitious goals set forth by the policy of perestroika in our country have prompted the peace proposals we have lately made in the international arena. This is an oversimplification. . . . True, we need normal international conditions for our internal progress. But we want a world free of war, without arms races, nuclear weapons, and violence; not only because this is an optimal condition for our internal development. It is an objective global requirement that stems from the realities of the present day.[93]

Gorbachev's commitment to his representation of the problem of security intensified as he learned.

The answer to the question of how Gorbachev learned is that he learned in part from those in the Soviet Union who had been thinking about security for a long time, in part from the meetings he held with senior officials abroad, and in part through the trial-and-error experimentation that he and his colleagues initiated. As he began to learn, he replaced older colleagues with new people committed to the ideas and problem representations he wanted to promote and began to build the political coalition that would make change politically possible. Shevardnadze replaced Andrei Gromyko as foreign minister, and Gorbachev ensured the election of a substantial number of new members to the Central Committee.[94] Learning promoted both personnel shifts and political support that, in turn, pushed new thinking even further.[95] Over time, learning from others and from behavior became self-reinforcing and self-amplifying.

Individual Learning and Foreign Policy Change

No explanation of individual learning, even by a senior leader in a hierarchical system, can explain foreign policy change. Institutional and political processes must intervene to build the political support necessary to transform individual learning into changes in foreign policy behavior. To speak of state learning is to anthropomorphize these processes in ways that leave out the critical political and organizational variables. I have examined whether Gorbachev learned, but I have not explored how his learning shaped the changes in Soviet foreign policy — a far more complex problem that requires systematic analysis of political and institutional variables. The analysis of how Gorbachev learned is suggestive, however, of some preliminary observations about the importance of individual learning in policy change.

Analysts of learning have identified several conditions that are necessary if individual learning is to be translated into policy change. At a minimum, learning must be institutionalized in the central political agencies, a dominant political coalition must be committed to the new representations of problems, and new policies must be created. Institutions with a stake in the old order must be restaffed, reorganized, given new missions, or marginalized. Institutionalized changes are most effective when policy experts first agree on the need for change.[96]

Only some of these conditions were present in the Soviet Union from 1985 to 1989. Gorbachev changed the top leadership in the Foreign Ministry and the International Department of the Central Committee, put civilians with defense expertise on the staff of the Central Committee, and named policy intellectuals to his personal staff. Large-scale restaffing of the foreign and defense policy-making apparatus took place.[97] Despite these changes, however, no broad-based consensus in favor of new thinking existed. As I have shown, almost all the fundamental concepts of new thinking about security were politically contested.

Yet even though traditional thinkers powerfully placed within the Soviet general staff challenged the new concepts of security with increasing vigor from mid-1987, policy change proceeded and indeed gathered momentum. The evidence suggests that a broad-based expert consensus and institutionalized change in the Soviet general staff were not necessary conditions of policy change. Some institutionalization to translate individual learning into policy change was clearly necessary, as was a new political coalition, but both were smaller in scope than many analysts expected.

This observation is open to challenge. A counterfactual argument can be made that the forces opposed to new thinking about security that gathered momentum and organized politically in 1990–91 could have compelled a retreat. In his last year in office, Gorbachev was forced to give greater political weight to traditional thinkers and to slow somewhat the pace of policy change. The proposition that limited institutionalization would have impeded further change or even partially reversed policy cannot be put to the test because Gorbachev resigned in December 1991, as the Soviet Union disintegrated in the wake of the failed coup attempt the previous August.

The evidence from this case suggests that the relationship among individual learning, political institutionalization, and foreign policy change was not linear but highly interactive. Individual learning provoked initial tentative changes in policy that in turn led to more learning, co-optation of intellectual and political entrepreneurs, coalition building and some institutionalization, and further policy change. The social cognition of learning by doing captures these dynamics. It suggests an incremental process whereby new representations were reinforced by experimentation abroad and politics at home as the process escalated. Gorbachev was an inductive, or data-driven, learner – not the kind of deductive thinker assumed by rational models.

Although individual learning by doing was a necessary condition of foreign policy change, it is not a sufficient explanation. It does not adequately capture the politics of doing as Gorbachev developed a new representation of the problem of Soviet security. Gorbachev's new thinking activated the engine of policy change, but politics determined whether, when, how far, and in what ways change occurred.

Political learning is not a necessary condition of policy change. Policy can change as the result of shifting domestic coalitions or new patterns of institutionalization in the face of changing international conditions, and it does so routinely in large numbers of cases. That individual learning is neither necessary nor sufficient across all cases of policy change should not be disturbing. It is unlikely that there is a single path to policy change. Multiple paths to single outcomes are part of the larger problem of equifinality, in which similar outcomes are explained by the interaction of different factors under different conditions. Only the outlines of the rich research agenda that arises from the conditionality of political learning in foreign policy change can be drawn.

Analysis of the individual leader is the critical starting point. Social learning is created only by individuals; organizations learn only by institutionalizing individual learning. Openness to new ideas and the capacity to create new representations of ill-defined problems are in part functions of personality. Research on the personalities of political leaders suggests, for example, that low cognitive complexity and intolerance of ambiguity are associated with an aggressive political style. Creativity, however, is inversely related to openness to the ideas of others.[98] We need much better developed theories of personality that explore openness and creativity as traits influencing individual capacity for political learning.

Political learning by individuals occurs in context. Evidence suggests that some leaders have learned from unexpected policy failures and from crisis, while others have abstracted from past policy successes. We know little about the political conditions, at home and abroad, that motivate learning. Theories of social cognition have to identify the linkages between different kinds of political contexts and political learning.

Finally, the interaction between learning and politics must be systematically examined to explain policy change. Gorbachev learned through trial-and-error experimentation and initiated an incremental process of policy change. Other analyses have found that policy learning is a spasmodic process catalyzed by the creation of new intellectual constructs, the establishment of new organizations, or a major failure of past policy. In evolutionary models, political learning is occasional and erratic.[99] These different representations of the interaction between policy learning and change may be a function partly of differences in policy arenas but, more importantly, of different units — individuals or collectives — that learn and of the kind of learning they do.

Just beneath the surface of the controversies about the kinds of interaction between learning and politics that produce policy change lies an important debate about the attributes of knowledge. Broadly speaking, for those who consider that knowledge is socially constructed, politics determines knowledge and learning.[100] For those who conceive of knowledge as reasoned truth, learning shapes politics. The analysis of the interaction among learning, politics, and foreign policy change is inextricably joined to a deep debate about the construction of knowledge in political life. It is a debate worth having.

NOTES

I   Explanations of foreign policy change are less extensive than explanations of stability and obstacles to change. Most analyses of change are focused at the system level. See, for example, R. J. Barry Jones, "Concepts and Models of Change in International Relations," in *Change and the Study of International Relations: The Evaded Dimension*, ed. Barry Buzan and Barry Jones (New York: St. Martin's, 1981), pp. 11–29; Robert Gilpin, *War and Change in World Politics* (New York and Cambridge: Cambridge University Press, 1981); John Lewis Gaddis, "Tectonics, History, and the End of the Cold War," in *The United States and the End of the Cold War: Implications, Reconsiderations, Provocations*, ed. John Lewis Gaddis (New York: Oxford University Press, 1992), pp. 155–67; and John Gerard Ruggie, "Continuity and Transformation in the World Polity: Toward a Neorealist Synthesis," in *Neorealism and Its Critics*, ed. Robert O. Keohane (New York: Columbia University Press, 1986), pp. 131–57. Hermann focuses most explicitly on directed foreign policy change and argues for a multilevel, multivariate explanation. See Charles F. Hermann, "Changing Course: When Governments Choose to Redirect Foreign Policy," *International Studies Quarterly* 34 (March 1990): 3–21.

2   The phrase *new thinking* was first used by foreign policy specialists Anatoliy Gromyko and Vladimir Lomeiko. See R. Craig Nation, *Black Earth, Red Star: A History of Soviet Security Policy, 1917–1991* (Ithaca: Cornell University Press, 1992), p. 288.

3   Bruce Parrott, "Soviet National Security Under Gorbachev," *Problems of Communism* 6 (November–December 1988): 1–36.

4   See *Pravda*, October 21, 1986; and Gorbachev's speech to the United Nations General Assembly, December 7, 1988, as quoted in *Pravda*, December 8, 1988.

5   Vitaly Zhurkin, Sergei Karaganov, and Andrei Kortunov argued that relying exclusively on military-technical instruments was to set Soviet security against the security of others ("Reasonable Sufficiency—Or, How to Break the Vicious Circle," *New Times* 40 [October 12, 1987]: 13–15).

6   A recently declassified CIA National Intelligence Estimate of Soviet military capability in 1983 highlighted the extensive modernization and deployment of Soviet strategic forces. It emphasized the growing capability of a force of land-based intercontinental ballistic missiles (ICBMs), intermediate-range SS-20s, submarine-launched ballistic missiles (SLBMs), long-range cruise missiles, and strategic bombers. The CIA estimated that there was significant potential for an increase in the size and capability of the forces and that political and economic factors would not play much of a role in restraining the expansion of Soviet forces.

7   Paul Kennedy, *Preparing for the Twenty-First Century* (New York: HarperCollins, 1993), p. 231.

8   Ibid., p. 295.

9   Quoted in Robert G. Kaiser, *Why Gorbachev Happened: His Triumph and His Failure* (New York: Simon and Schuster, 1991), p. 76.

10   Interview with Mikhail Gorbachev, Toronto, April 1, 1993.

11 Gilpin, *War and Change in World Politics*, pp. 15, 33, 42–43, 187, and 197–201.

12 For an examination of the limits of structural explanations for the end of the Cold War, see Richard Ned Lebow, "The Long Peace, The End of the Cold War, and the Failure of Realism," the second essay in this book.

13 Parrott, "Soviet National Security Under Gorbachev," p. 35.

14 See, e.g., Allen Lynch, *Gorbachev's International Outlook: Intellectual Origins and Political Consequences*, Institute for East-West Security Studies Occasional Paper No. 9 (Boulder, Colo.: Westview, 1989), p. 53.

15 These included mechanical and electronic control systems, personnel reliability programs, and changes in methods of deployment. See Stephen M. Meyer, "The Sources and Prospects of Gorbachev's New Political Thinking on Security," *International Security* 13 (fall 1988): 124–63, and note 33, p. 137 in particular.

16 Interview with Gorbachev.

17 Meyer, "Sources and Prospects of Gorbachev's New Political Thinking on Security," pp. 135–38.

18 *Pravda*, August 6, 1988.

19 Steven Weber argues this point cogently in "Interactive Learning in U.S.-Soviet Arms Control," in *Learning in U.S. and Soviet Foreign Policy*, ed. George W. Breslauer and Philip E. Tetlock (Boulder, Colo.: Westview, 1991), pp. 784–824.

20 See George W. Breslauer, *Khrushchev and Brezhnev as Leaders: Building Authority in Soviet Politics* (London: Allen and Unwin, 1982); and Richard D. Anderson, Jr., "Why Competitive Politics Inhibits Learning in Soviet Foreign Policy," in *Learning in U.S. and Soviet Foreign Policy*, ed. George W. Breslauer and Philip E. Tetlock (Boulder, Colo.: Westview), pp. 100–31.

21 Nation, *Black Earth, Red Star*, p. 286.

22 Shifts in social structure and political power determine whose learning matters. See Joseph S. Nye, Jr., "Nuclear Learning and U.S.-Soviet Security Regimes," *International Organization* 41 (summer 1987): 371–402, esp. p. 381.

23 Interview with Gorbachev.

24 Jerry F. Hough, *Russia and the West: Gorbachev and the Politics of Reform* (New York: Simon and Schuster, 1988), pp. 18–32.

25 For a definition of *schemata*, see Susan Fiske and Shelley Taylor, *Social Cognition* (New York: Random House, 1984), p. 140. For arguments about cognitive stability, see Robert Jervis, *Perception and Misperception in International Relations* (Princeton: Princeton University Press, 1976); Yaacov Y. I. Vertzberger, *The World in Their Minds: Information Processing, Cognition, and Perception in Foreign Policy Decisionmaking* (Stanford: Stanford University Press, 1990); and Richard R. Lau and David O. Sears, "Social Cognition and Political Cognition: The Past, the Present, and the Future," in *Political Cognition*, ed. Richard R. Lau and David O. Sears (Hills-

dale, N.J.: Lawrence Erlbaum, 1986), pp. 347–66. For a discussion of cognitive psychology and foreign policy change, see Richard Ned Lebow and Janice Gross Stein, "Afghanistan, Carter, and Foreign Policy Change: The Limits of Cognitive Models," in *Diplomacy, Force, and Leadership: Essays in Honor of Alexander L. George*, ed. Dan Caldwell and Timothy J. McKeown (Boulder, Colo.: Westview, 1993), pp. 95–128.

26   Lee Ross, Mark R. Lepper, and Michael Hubbard, "Perseverance in Self Perception and Social Perception: Biased Attributional Processes in the Debriefing Paradigm," *Journal of Personality and Social Psychology* 32 (November 1975): 880–92. The postulate that schemata are resistant to change can be interpreted as consistent with statistical logic if people assign a low variance estimate to their expectations. Psychological research contradicts this interpretation through repeated observations that exposure to discrepant information strengthens rather than undermines existing schemata. See Craig A. Anderson, Mark R. Lepper, and Lee Ross, "Perseverance of Social Theories: The Role of Explanation in the Persistence of Discredited Information," *Journal of Personality and Social Psychology* 39 (December 1980): 1037–49; Craig A. Anderson, "Abstract and Concrete Data in the Perseverance of Social Theories: When Weak Data Lead to Unshakable Beliefs," *Journal of Experimental and Social Psychology* 19 (March 1983): 93–108; and Edward R. Hirt and Steven J. Sherman, "The Role of Prior Knowledge in Explaining Hypothetical Events," *Journal of Experimental and Social Psychology* 21 (November 1985): 519–43. The strengthening of schemata after exposure to contradictory information results from the processes of reasoning people use to explain apparent inconsistencies. Reasoning may transform inconsistent information to make it consistent with the schema. See Jennifer Crocker, "Judgment of Covariation by Social Perceivers," *Psychological Bulletin* 90 (March 1981): 272–92; James A. Kulik, "Confirmatory Attribution and the Perpetuation of Social Beliefs," *Journal of Personality and Social Psychology* 44 (June 1983): 1171–81; Thomas K. Srull, "Person Memory: Some Tests of Associative Storage and Retrieval Models," *Journal of Experimental Psychology* 7 (November 1981): 440–63; Robert S. Wyer, Jr., and Sallie E. Gordon, "The Recall of Information about Persons and Groups," *Journal of Experimental Social Psychology* 18 (March 1982): 128–64; and Chris S. O'Sullivan and Francis T. Durso, "Effect of Schema-Incongruent Information on Memory for Stereotypical Attributes," *Journal of Personality and Social Psychology* 47 (July 1984): 55–70.

27   In large part because schema theories focus on whole schemata, they are relatively static. For a critical review of the static quality of schema theory, see James H. Kuklinski, Robert C. Luskin, and John Bolland, "Where Is the Schema: Going Beyond the 'S' Word in Political Psychology," *American Political Science Review* 85 (December 1991): 1341–56.

28   Jennifer Crocker, Darlene B. Hannah, and Renee Weber, "Person Memory and Causal Attributions," *Journal of Personality and Social Psychology* 44 (January 1983): 55–66.

29   E. Tory Higgins and John A. Bargh, "Social Cognition and Social Perception," in *Annual Review of Psychology*, vol. 38, ed. Mark R. Rosenzweig and Larry W. Porter (Palo Alto, Calif.: Annual Reviews, 1987), pp. 369–425, esp. p. 386.

30   Hazel Markus and Robert B. Zajonc, "The Cognitive Perspective in Social Psychology," in *Handbook of Social Psychology*, ed. Gardner Lindzey and Elliot Aronson, 3d ed. (New York: Random House, 1985). Cognitive psychologists who study processes of attribution are less explicit in modeling processes of change. They note only that individuals may vary in their propensity to acquire schemata and in their tendency to use them to process information when they do have them. See Susan Fiske, "Schema-Based Versus Piecemeal Politics: A Patchwork Quilt, but Not a Blanket," in Fiske and Taylor, *Social Cognition*, pp. 154–81.

31   Crocker, Hannah, and Weber, "Person Memory and Causal Attributions," p. 65.

32   See Edward E. Jones and Richard E. Nisbett, "The Actor and Observer: Divergent Perceptions of the Causes of Behavior," in *Attribution: Perceiving the Causes of Behavior*, ed. Edward E. Jones, David E. Kanouse, Harold H. Kelley, Richard E. Nisbett, Stuart Valins, and Bernard Weiner (Morristown, N.J.: General Learning Press, 1971), pp. 79–94; H. H. Kelley, "Attribution Theory in Social Psychology," in *Nebraska Symposium on Motivation*, ed. D. Levine (Lincoln: University of Nebraska Press, 1967), pp. 192–240; Lee Ross, "The Intuitive Psychologist and His Shortcomings: Distortions in the Attribution Process," in *Advances in Experimental and Social Psychology*, ed. Leonard Berkowitz (New York: Academic, 1977), 10:174–77; and Lee Ross and Craig A. Anderson, "Shortcomings in the Attribution Process: On the Origins and Maintenance of Erroneous Social Assessments," in *Judgment Under Uncertainty: Heuristics and Biases*, ed. Daniel Kahneman, Paul Slovic, and Amos Tversky (New York: Cambridge University Press, 1986), pp. 129–52.

33   See Peter Suedfeld and A. Dennis Rank, "Revolutionary Leaders: Long-Term Success as a Function of Changes in Conceptual Complexity," *Journal of Personality and Social Psychology* 34 (August 1976): 169–78; Peter Suedfeld and Philip Tetlock, "Integrative Complexity of Communication in International Crisis," *Journal of Conflict Resolution* 21 (March 1977): 168–84; and Philip Tetlock, "Integrative Complexity of American and Soviet Foreign Policy Rhetorics: A Time-Series Analysis," *Journal of Personality and Social Psychology* 49 (December 1985): 1565–85.

34   Pamela J. Conover and Stanley Feldman, "How People Organize the Political World: A Schematic Model," *American Journal of Political Science* 28 (February 1984): 95–126. Those who possess multiple judgment dimensions also tend to possess rules of abstraction that

facilitate the integration and comparison of information. They tend to produce alternative interpretations of new information but, by using their capacity for abstraction and integration, are able to resolve these ambiguities. People with low cognitive complexity tend to produce absolute, fixed judgments. See William L. Bennett, *The Political Mind and the Political Environment* (Lexington, Mass.: Lexington, 1975), pp. 33–35; and Vertzberger, *The World in Their Minds*, pp. 134–37.

35 Higgins and Bargh, "Social Cognition and Social Perception."

36 See Ariel Levi and Philip Tetlock, "A Cognitive Analysis of Japan's 1941 Decision for War," *Journal of Conflict Resolution* 24 (June 1980): 195–211; Philip Tetlock, "Cognitive Style and Political Ideology," *Journal of Personality and Social Psychology* 45 (July 1983): 118–26; Philip Tetlock, "Content and Structure in Political Belief Systems," in *Foreign Policy Decision Making: Perception, Cognition, and Artificial Intelligence*, ed. Donald Sylvan and Steve Chan (New York: Praeger, 1984), pp. 107–28; and Philip Tetlock and Richard Boettger, "Cognitive and Rhetorical Styles of Traditionalist and Reformist Soviet Politicians: A Content Analysis Study," *Political Psychology* 10 (June 1989): 209–32.

37 Richard Herrmann, "The Empirical Challenge of the Cognitive Revolution," *International Studies Quarterly* 32 (June 1988): 175–204.

38 It is difficult to draw definitive conclusions about Andropov, given his short tenure as general secretary. In his fifteen months in office, Andropov withdrew from the INF talks after NATO began its deployment of Pershing IIs. He was also the patron of many of the young reformers during the Brezhnev years and was well placed to tap new ideas. A policy review of the war in Afghanistan was conducted while he was general secretary, and Arbatov, the director of the USA and Canada Institute, suggests that Andropov concluded that no military solution was possible in Afghanistan. However, Arbatov maintains that the review did not touch more fundamental aspects of Soviet security. (This information is from an interview with Georgi Arbatov, Moscow, May 19, 1989).

39 Tetlock identifies four structural dimensions of complexity: cognitive complexity; evaluative complexity, or the degree of inconsistency, tension, or dissonance existing among the various cognitions; cognitive interaction; and metacognition. Tetlock argues that increasing cognitive complexity increases the likelihood both of pursuing policies that lead to important goals and of setting realistic goals, especially when the environment is highly complex and rapidly changing. See Philip Tetlock, "Learning in U.S. and Soviet Foreign Policy: In Search of an Elusive Concept," in *Learning in U.S. and Soviet Foreign Policy*, ed. George W. Breslauer and Philip E. Tetlock (Boulder, Colo.: Westview, 1991), pp. 20–61, esp. pp. 32–35 and 40; and Tetlock and Boettger, "Cognitive and Rhetorical Styles."

40 *Izbrannye rechi i stat'i.* Gorbachev developed these arguments in more detail later in his career: "This can only be achieved by learning

251

to live together, to cohabit side by side on this small planet threatened by ecological and environmental degradation, mastering the difficult art of taking into account each other's mutual interests. This is what we mean by peaceful coexistence" (Mikhail S. Gorbachev, *Izbrannye rechi i stat'i* (Selected speeches and articles) (Moscow: 1987–90), 2:461.

41   In related research, Tetlock and Boettger find significant differences in complexity between Soviet traditionalists and reformers. See "Cognitive and Rhetorical Styles." Other scholars have compared Gorbachev with previous Soviet leaders and find that he scored higher on conceptual complexity. He was able to differentiate among alternative principles and policies and then integrate disparate elements into complex higher-order generalizations. See David G. Winter, Margaret G. Hermann, Walter Weintraub, and Stephen G. Walker, "Theory and Predictions in Political Psychology: The Personalities of Bush and Gorbachev Measured at a Distance: Procedures, Portraits, and Policy," *Political Psychology* 12 (June 1991): 215–46.

42   Yudit Auerbach, "Turning-Point Decisions: A Cognitive-Dissonance Analysis of Conflict Resolution in Israel–West German Relations," *Political Psychology* 7 (September 1986): 533–50.

43   See Kuklinski, Luskin, and Bolland, "Where Is the Schema," p. 1345, for the essential equivalence between levels of development of cognitive schema and cognitive complexity.

44   An analysis of Gorbachev's speeches before and after he became general secretary classifies Gorbachev as a traditionalist until March 1985 and an ardent reformer thereafter. See Tetlock and Boettger, "Cognitive and Rhetorical Styles." The speeches Gorbachev delivered before he became general secretary do not provide valid data to assess his cognitive complexity because of the constraints on Soviet leaders.

45   Tetlock argues that whereas beliefs (or content) can shift without entailing structural change, a change in structure necessarily leads to a change in beliefs. See Tetlock, "Learning in U.S. and Soviet Foreign Policy." Tetlock and Boettger argue that integrative complexity is in part a function of role and ideology; see their "Cognitive and Rhetorical Styles." Liberals are far more likely than conservatives to become integratively complex when they assume office.

46   Cognitive psychologists identify a variety of different types of expectancies or schemas. See Edward E. Jones and Daniel McGillis, "Correspondent Inferences and the Attribution Cube: A Comparative Reappraisal," in *New Directions in Attribution Research*, ed. John H. Harvey, William J. Ickes, and Robert F. Kidd (Hillsdale, N.J.: Lawrence Erlbaum, 1976), 1:389–420; John M. Darley and Russell H. Fazio, "Expectancy Confirmation Processes Arising in the Social Interaction Sequence," *American Psychologist* 35 (October 1980): 867–81; E. Tory Higgins and Gillian King, "Accessibility of Social Constructs: Information-Processing Consequences of Individual and Contextual Variability," in *Personality, Cognition, and Social Inter-*

action, ed. Nancy Cantor and John F. Kihlstrom (Hillsdale, N.J.: Lawrence Erlbaum, 1981), pp. 69–121; Jeffrey S. Berman, Stephen J. Read, and David A. Kenny, "Processing Inconsistent Social Information," *Journal of Personality and Social Psychology* 45 (December 1983): 1211–24; and John A. Bargh and Roman D. Thein, "Individual Construct Accessibility, Person Memory, and the Recall-Judgment Link: The Case of Information Overload," *Journal of Personality and Social Psychology* 49 (November 1985): 1129–43.

47 Vertzberger, *The World in Their Minds*, p. 136.

48 Mikhail S. Gorbachev, *Perestroika: New Thinking for Our Country and the World* (New York: Harper and Row, 1987), p. 10.

49 See Vertzberger, *The World in Their Minds*, pp. 123–25, for a discussion of relative value stability in the face of belief change.

50 For the absence of the social dimension in social cognition research, see Kuklinski, Luskin, and Bolland, "Where Is the Schema?" p. 1346. Exceptions are Tetlock and Boettger, "Cognitive and Rhetorical Styles"; and Ralph Erber and Susan T. Fiske, "Outcome Dependency and Attention to Inconsistent Information," *Journal of Personality and Social Psychology* 47 (October 1984): 709–26. Erber and Fiske find that outcome dependency increases people's attention to inconsistent information. They hypothesize that when the perceiver's outcomes depend on another person, the perceiver may be more motivated to have a sense of prediction and control, rather than simply to maintain an expectation.

51 Thomas L. Good and Jere E. Brophy, *Educational Psychology: A Realistic Approach* (New York: Longman, 1990). Developmental psychology is more helpful, but it too works largely with known responses.

52 Haas describes this dimension of political learning as "nested problem sets." See Ernst Haas, *When Knowledge Is Power* (Berkeley: University of California Press, 1990), p. 84.

53 Jack Levy, "Learning and Foreign Policy: Sweeping a Conceptual Minefield," *International Organization* 48 (spring 1994): 279–312.

54 See Tetlock, "Learning in U.S. and Soviet Foreign Policy," p. 40. E. Haas, *When Knowledge Is Power*; and George W. Breslauer and Philip E. Tetlock, eds., *Learning in U.S. and Soviet Foreign Policy* (Boulder, Colo.: Westview, 1991). An early study of Soviet and American learning on security issues is Alexander L. George, Philip J. Farley, and Alexander Dallin, *U.S.-Soviet Security Cooperation* (New York: Oxford University Press, 1988).

55 See Janice Gross Stein, "Deterrence and Compellence in the Gulf: A Failed or Impossible Task?" *International Security* 17 (autumn 1992): 147–79.

56 In an effort to deal with the problem of evaluation, analysts refer to *pathological learning*, or changes that impede future cognitive growth. See James Clay Moltz, "Divergent Learning and the Failed Politics of Soviet Economic Reform," *World Politics* 45 (January 1993): 301–25, esp. p. 303.

57 For a similar argument, see George W. Breslauer, "What Have We Learned About Learning?" in *Learning in U.S. and Soviet Foreign Policy*, ed. Breslauer and Tetlock, pp. 825–56.

58 Levy argues that an efficiency concept of learning—one that emphasizes the matching of means to ends—can be assessed only against empirically confirmed laws of social behavior. In their absence, he concludes, it is preferable to exclude efficiency from concepts of learning and include only changes in beliefs. See Levy, "Learning and Foreign Policy."

59 See Walter R. Reitman, *Cognition and Thought* (New York: Wiley, 1965); Allan Newell and Herbert A. Simon, *Human Problem Solving* (Englewood Cliffs, N.J.: Prentice-Hall, 1972); Herbert A. Simon, "The Structure of Ill-Structured Problems," *Artificial Intelligence* 4 (October 1973): 181–201; James F. Voss, Terry R. Greene, Timothy A. Post, and Barbara C. Penner, "Problem-Solving Skill in the Social Sciences," in *The Psychology of Learning and Motivation: Advances in Research and Theory*, ed. Gordon H. Bower (New York: Academic, 1983), pp. 165–215; James F. Voss and Timothy A. Post, "On the Solving of Ill-Structured Problems," in *The Nature of Expertise*, ed. Michelene H. Chi, Robert Glaser, and Marshall J. Farr (Hillsdale, N.J.: Lawrence Erlbaum, 1988), pp. 261–85; and James F. Voss, Christopher R. Wolfe, Jeanette A. Lawrence, and Randi A. Engle, "From Representation to Decision: An Analysis of Problem Solving in International Relations," in *Complex Problem Solving: Principles and Mechanisms*, ed. Robert J. Sternberg and Peter A. Frensch (Hillsdale, N.J.: Lawrence Erlbaum, 1991), pp. 119–58.

60 Voss and Post, "On the Solving of Ill-Structured Problems," pp. 281–82.

61 Sim B. Sitkin, "Learning Through Failure: The Strategy of Small Losses," in *Research in Organizational Behavior*, ed. Larry L. Cummings and Barry H. Staw (New York: JAI, 1992), 14:231–66.

62 See Donald T. Campbell, "Reform as Experiments," *American Psychologist* 24 (January 1969): 409–29; B. Hedberg, "How Organizations Learn and Unlearn," in *Handbook of Organizational Design*, ed. Paul C. Nystrom and William H. Starbuck (New York: Oxford University Press, 1981), 1:3–27.

63 See Chris Argyris and Donald A. Schon, *Organizational Learning* (Reading, Mass.: Addison-Wesley, 1978) for a discussion of the importance of theory in action; and Thomas Peters and Robert H. Waterman, *In Search of Excellence* (New York: Harper and Row, 1982) for an analysis of action bias.

64 Ulric Neisser, "On 'Social Knowing,' " *Personality and Social Psychology Bulletin* 6 (December 1980): 603–4, cited in Kuklinski, Luskin, and Bolland, "Where Is the Schema," p. 1346.

65 Sarah Mendelson, "Internal Battles and External Wars: Politics, Learning, and the Soviet Withdrawal from Afghanistan," *World Politics* 45 (April 1993): 327–60, esp. p. 344. In *Pravda*, January 7, 1989, Gorbachev referred to a broad-based canvas of reports from

specialists on the need for change in the Soviet Union that he conducted with the assistance of Nikolai Ryzhkov, then the head of the Economic Department of the Central Committee, before he became general secretary.

66   Eduard Shevardnadze, *The Future Belongs to Freedom*, trans.
Catherine A. Fitzpatrick (New York: Free Press, 1991), p. 26.

67   Interview with Aleksandr Yakovlev, Toronto, September 27, 1993.

68   Falin is quoted in Don Oberdorfer, *The Turn from the Cold War to a
New Era: The United States and the Soviet Union, 1983–1990* (New
York: Poseidon, 1991), p. 113.

69   Gorbachev, *Izbrannye rechi i stat*, 2:459–60.

70   Meyer, "Sources and Prospects of Gorbachev's New Political Thinking on Security," p. 125–29, which cites interviews with senior Gorbachev advisers. Shevardnadze observed that the most important
purpose of foreign policy was "to create the maximum favorable
external conditions needed in order to conduct internal reform" (*The
Future Belongs to Freedom*, p. xi).

71   Meyer, "Sources and Prospects of Gorbachev's New Political Thinking on Security," p. 129, makes this argument.

72   Interview with Anatoliy Dobrynin, Moscow, December 17, 1992.

73   Interview with Andrei Aleksandrov-Agentov, Moscow, August 12,
1993.

74   Shevardnadze, *The Future Belongs to Freedom*, p. 26.

75   An analysis of Gorbachev's personality scored him low on creativity
and predicted that he would be especially receptive to others' ideas
and to solutions suggested by his advisers. See Winter et al., "Theory
and Predictions in Political Psychology," p. 235.

76   Mendelson, "Internal Battles and External Wars," p. 344.

77   Interview with Yakovlev. Also see Jeff Checkel, "Ideas, Institutions,
and the Gorbachev Foreign Policy Revolution," *World Politics* 45
(January 1993): 271–300.

78   Interview with Georgi Arbatov, Moscow, May 19, 1991.

79   See Oberdorfer, *The Turn*, p. 113; and interview with Oleg Grinevsky,
Stockholm, October 16, 1992. Gorbachev also institutionalized an
informal advisory system that provided a wider flow of ideas and critical advice on security issues. Although Andropov, and at times
Brezhnev, had occasionally engaged in private discussions with institute officials, Gorbachev created bodies of experts from the institutes, the press, and the ministries and met frequently to ask their
advice and opinions. He made almost no major decision without
expert advice. Based on interview with Pavel Palazchenko, Gorbachev's long-standing interpreter, Toronto, April 1, 1993.

80   See Thomas Risse-Kappen, "Ideas Do Not Float Freely: Transnational Coalitions, Domestic Structures, and the End of the Cold War," the
eighth essay in this book; and Mendelson, "Internal Battles and
External Wars."

81   Yevgenii Primakov, "Novaia filosofiia vneshnei politiki" (New
philosophies of foreign policy), *Pravda*, July 11, 1987.

82 See, for example, Olegovich Bogomolov, "Afghanistan as Seen in 1980," *Moscow News* 30 (July 30–August 6, 1988). For a detailed examination of the impact of policy scientists as an epistemic community, see Stephen Shenfield, *The Nuclear Predicament: Explorations in Soviet Ideology* (London: Routledge and Kegan Paul, 1987); Allen Lynch, *The Soviet Study of International Relations* (Cambridge: Cambridge University Press, 1987); Parrott, "Soviet National Security Under Gorbachev"; and Robert Herman, "Ideas, Institutions and the Reconceptualization of Interests: The Political and Intellectual Origins of New Thinking in Soviet Foreign Policy" (Ph.D. diss., Cornell University, 1995).

83 See Emanuel Adler, "The Emergence of Cooperation: National Epistemic Communities and the International Evolution of the Idea of Nuclear Arms Control," *International Organization* (special issue) 46 (winter 1992): 101–45, esp. pp. 137–40; Michael Mandelbaum, "Western Influence on the Soviet Union," in *Gorbachev's Russia and American Foreign Policy*, ed. Seweryn Bialer and Michael Mandelbaum (Boulder, Colo.: Westview, 1988); and Mendelson, "Internal Battles and External Wars."

84 Edward L. Warner III, "New Political Thinking and Old Realities in Soviet Defence Policy," *Survival* 31 (January–February 1989): 18–20.

85 Interview with Vadim Zagladin, formerly head of the Department of International Relations of the Central Committee and subsequently a policy adviser to Gorbachev, Moscow, May 18, 1989.

86 Interviews with Yakovlev and Arbatov, May 19, 1991.

87 Interviews with Ambassador Leonid Zamyatin, who subsequently headed TASS, Moscow, December 16, 1991, and with Dobrynin. See also Herman, "Ideas, Institutions, and the Reconceptualization of Interests."

88 Interview with Yakovlev.

89 See Herman, "Ideas, Institutions, and the Reconceptualization of Interests"; Mendelson, "Internal Battles and External Wars"; and Checkel, "Ideas, Institutions, and the Gorbachev Foreign Policy Revolution." For a broader study of epistemic communities, or networks of knowledge-based experts, see the collection of essays in Peter M. Haas, ed., *Knowledge, Power, and International Policy Coordination*, *International Organization* (special issue) 46 (winter 1992).

90 On the concept of *policy entrepreneur*, see Matthew A. Evangelista, "Sources of Moderation in Soviet Security Policy," in *Behavior, Society, and Nuclear War*, ed. Philip E. Tetlock, Jo L. Husbands, Robert Jervis, Paul C. Stern, and Charles Tilly (New York: Oxford University Press, 1991), 2:254–355, esp. pp. 275–77. On the concept of a *policy window*, see John W. Kingdon, *Agendas, Alternatives, and Public Policies* (Boston: Little, Brown, 1984).

91 In a complementary stream of evidence, research in cognitive psychology suggests that at times behavior leads to changes in schema as people make inferences from their behavior about their convictions.

See Gerald R. Salanick and Mary Conway, "Attitude Inference from Salient and Relevant Cognitive Content About Behavior," *Journal of Personality and Social Psychology* 32 (November 1975): 829–40; and Mark P. Zanna, James M. Olson, and Ralph H. Fazio, "Attitude-Behavior Consistency: An Individual Difference Perspective," *Journal of Personality and Social Psychology* 38 (March 1980): 432–40. Once people are convinced that their behavior has been shaped by their prior beliefs, those beliefs become even more important in shaping future behavior. Inference from behavior is a dominant cognitive mechanism in the early stages of development of beliefs and attitudes. See J. Daryl Bem, "Self-Perception Theory," in *Advances in Experimental and Social Psychology*, ed. Leonard Berkowitz (New York: Academic, 1972), 6:1–61; Ralph H. Fazio, Mark P. Zanna, and Joel Cooper, "Dissonance and Self-Perception: An Integrative View of Each Theory's Proper Domain of Application," *Journal of Experimental Social Psychology* 13 (September 1977): 464–79; Richard E. Nisbett and Stuart Valins, "Perceiving the Causes of One's Own Behavior," in *Attribution: Perceiving the Causes of Behavior*, ed. Edward E. Jones, David E. Knouse, Harold H. Kelley, Richard E. Nisbett, Stuart Valins, and Bernard Weiner (Morristown, N.J.: General Learning, 1971), pp. 63–78; and Vertzberger, *The World in Their Minds*, p. 169. Decision makers who have little prior experience develop their beliefs while on the job; their beliefs and attitudes can change as a result of the inferences they draw from their behavior.

92   Interview with Gorbachev.

93   Gorbachev, *Perestroika*, p. 11.

94   See Thane Gustafson and Dawn Mann, "Gorbachev's First Year: Building Power and Authority," *Problems of Communism* 35 (May–June 1986): 1–19, and Jerry F. Hough, "Gorbachev Consolidating Power," *Problems of Communism* 36 (July–August 1987): 169–70.

95   Andrew Owen Bennett, "Patterns of Soviet Military Interventionism 1975–1990: Alternative Explanations and Their Implications," in *Beyond the Soviet Threat: American Security Policy in a New Era*, ed. William Zimmerman (Ann Arbor: University of Michigan Press, 1992), pp. 105–27.

96   See E. Haas, *When Knowledge Is Power*: and Ernest Haas, "Collective Learning: Some Theoretical Speculations," in *Learning in U.S. and Soviet Foreign Policy*, ed. Breslauer and Tetlock, pp. 62–99. See also Lloyd Etheredge, *Can Governments Learn?* (New York: Pergamon, 1985); and James G. March and Johan P. Olsen, "The Uncertainty of the Past: Organizational Learning Under Ambiguity," in *Decisions and Organizations*, ed. James G. March (New York: Basil Blackwell, 1988), pp. 335–58.

97   Parrott, "Soviet National Security Under Gorbachev."

98   Winter et al., "Theory and Predictions in Political Psychology."

99   See John Odell, *U.S. International Monetary Policy: Markets, Power, and Ideas as Sources of Change* (Princeton: Princeton University

Press, 1982), pp. 367–76; and Peter Haas, "Towards an Evolutionary Model of Institutional Learning: Ideas and Structuration," paper presented at the annual meeting of the American Political Science Association, Washington, D.C., September 1–4, 1993.

100 For an analysis of part of this debate, see Rey Koslowski and Friedrich Kratochwil, "Understanding Change in International Politics: The Soviet Empire's Demise and the International System," the sixth essay in this book.

10

Conclusions: The End of the Cold War —
What Have We Learned?

Did the end of the Cold War undermine or confirm basic theories of
international relations? Does the failure of most theories to predict
this event demonstrate the weakness of their insight into international affairs? These are complicated questions, and it is not surprising that the authors in this book answer them differently. The questions raise subsidiary prior questions about what constitutes international relations theory, what the Cold War was, when it ended,
and what the proper role of prediction is in evaluating theory. All
these prior questions remain intensely controversial, and any simple
and definitive answer to the larger question of how the end of the
Cold War affects international relations theory would only mask the
real issues being debated. Fortunately, the essays in this book do not
avoid controversy and take us directly into both the debate about
theory and the debate about the Cold War.

Rather than summarize the arguments in the previous essays, I
plan to organize this essay around three questions. First, what have
we learned about structural realism, and how does this relate to
what we already knew? Second, what was the Cold War, and when
did it end? Third, did the end of the Cold War settle the long-standing debate about Soviet foreign policy that centered on the interpretation of Soviet motivation? I intend to devote a section of this paper
to each question and then to end with some brief comments on how
we might proceed from here. My theme throughout is that structural theory has important insights but they are commonplace at the
level of foreign policy analysis, which is the level where most interpretations of the Cold War rest. At the foreign policy level, motivation — the key concept for interpretation — remains a variable we
identify as much by assertion as by careful empirical defense. The
end of the Cold War provides new information and access to more
old information, but it will not solve the analytical challenge of

259

interpretation. That challenge requires examining the political process that defines national interests in a way that leads to testable propositions. Rather than jumping to this conclusion, however, I will first look at the utility of structural theory.

Structural Theory

In 1957 and again in 1975 the former president of the American Psychological Association wrote about the two disciplines of psychology.[1] One discipline explained human action with personality theory and the features of individuals; the other explained action in terms of the environment and its effect on people. This structure-agent problem is not unique to psychology; it permeates international relations theory as well.[2] It is unlikely that the end of the Cold War is going to move this debate much past the interactionist position that Cronbach argued for in psychology.

The search for a system construct that integrates the actor and the environment is hardly new in international relations theory.[3] It requires combining two levels of systems thinking usually kept separate — that is, the international system, defined as the relationships among the great powers in the world, and the national system in which foreign policy is made. Because the focus of this book is on the end of a particular conflict and a specific set of actors, most of the essays struggle with the integration of these two levels of analysis. Along the way, structural theory is criticized heavily because it fails to provide the cross-level integration that advocates of interactionism want. The end of the Cold War has raised doubts about neorealist assumptions, predictions, and operationalizations. More needs to be said on all of these points.

Assumptions

Classic realism assumed that all states would define their interests in terms of power. This was not an empirical judgment but an axiom. For Morgenthau, it grew out of a conclusion that state motivations would be too many and too difficult to identify in any convincing manner.[4] Consequently, he assumed that whatever ends states wanted, they needed power to achieve them. This simplifying assumption allowed realists to hold the motive forces driving state behavior constant and to concentrate on variations in the distribution of power in the international system. Neorealists substituted a universal desire for security for the traditional focus on power, but within a self-help system that they assumed was anarchic, security typically depended on the acquisition of power, whether military or alliance based.[5] World system theorists, a perspective missing from this book, made a comparable simplifying assumption, treating economic gain, instead of power, as the universal motive driving state behavior.[6]

If world politics worked as if all great states pursued power until they were constrained by other great states, then, as Morton Kaplan did, one could designate a series of possible power distributions and derive the dynamics for each international system.[7] But these abstract worlds would explain events only to the degree that the simplifying assumption about motivation was reasonable. How to judge this was never clear. Predictive accuracy alone was not enough. After all, people can predict consequences without understanding causes. Anyone who drives a car or operates a computer without really knowing how the machinery works can attest to this. In any case, realists did not claim that their simplifying assumption regarding motivation was an adequate description at the foreign policy level.[8] Consequently, simply demonstrating that not all states behave as if this motive were driving them or that more complex compounds of interests including many domestic as well as international concerns affect policy would not topple the theory.

Although classic realism rested fundamentally on power determinism, even as distinguished an advocate as Hans Morgenthau wrote at length about the importance of distinguishing status quo–oriented states from those that were imperialist or prestige driven.[9] Jack Snyder in this book speaks of two types of realism, aggressive and defensive, reintroducing the unit-level variation that realism was designed to avoid. Once the monocausal assumption at the foreign policy level is relaxed, however, the ability to deduce behavioral predictions at the international system level is seriously complicated, and data demands increase exponentially. To talk about the specific case of the Cold War and the Soviet Union, however, one has little choice but to cross this analytical divide.

A number of essays in this book question the monocausal assumption at the root of most structural theory. Koslowski and Kratochwil go even further and challenge assumptions about actors. At a simple level, realism can be criticized for concentrating on states. Other actors affect world affairs, and arguments for transnational players by this time are commonplace.[10] Adding international organizations, nongovernmental transnational organizations, and multinational corporations, however, does not seriously undermine the core ideas of realism. Morgenthau presented the theory of causation at a general level that could apply to most actors. What Koslowski and Kratochwil concentrate on, however, is critical. They are not simply arguing for the inclusion of other actors; they are calling into question the intellectual and political processes that affect the construction of aggregate concepts in international relations theory.

Nations are not natural categories.[11] They are not primordial entities waiting to be awakened.[12] Nor are they material categories determined in any regular way by race, religion, or ethnicity.[13] They are constructed communities shaped by leaders and politicians who often look to scholars for help in mobilization, socialization, and legitimation.[14] Academic recognition that a community is a nation thus has political implications in an era in which national self-determination commands substantial normative appeal and typically means statehood. Reexamining the political origins of what realists take to be actors not only reveals implicit assumptions about power and legitimacy but draws attention to nonmilitary conceptions of power and to causes of the Cold War's demise that are not immediately evident in the bilateral Soviet-American relationship.

For instance, an era of mass politics in the former colonial worlds of Asia and Africa empowered a series of nationalist movements in the 1950s that gave strength to the nonaligned movement in the 1960s.[15] These developments did not end the Soviet-American contest, but they did reduce its systemic effects. No longer did the East-West conflict define the agenda for the entire international system. Growing mass participation in politics, economic development, and nationalist mobilization made it increasingly costly for the superpowers to sustain control in places they felt were important to their Cold War strategies.[16] The American setbacks in Vietnam and Iran and the Soviet setbacks in Afghanistan and Eastern Europe provided dramatic evidence of this. They also highlighted the importance of regime legitimacy in power calculations.

Nationalism played a role in these cases, as did the norm of self-determination. In the case of Vietnam, however, the issue was not simply the realization of independence free of foreign influence — which, after all, is impossible in a highly interdependent world. What was at stake was the very definition of the state and what nation it represented. The Cold War constrained the process of decolonization, often resting statehood and self-determination on principles of territoriality and stability as much as on political identity. Nations could be built within the states, or so the assumption went.

If states are taken as the analytical unit, the end of the Cold War unleashed a new period in which the principle of national identity can compete successfully with territoriality as a basis for statehood.

No doubt this will be associated with horrible bloodshed and human dislocations, as in the Caucasus, Yugoslavia, and Kashmir. If instead the focus is on the political processes that lead to national identity and state legitimacy, then the pressures for legitimate government — however violently expressed — and shifting international norms may be seen as important causes leading to the end of the Cold War, not simply as consequences resulting from it. Moreover, the focus should broaden to include cases in which these processes strengthened states or led to peaceful unification (e.g., in Germany and for a while in Yemen) or peaceful separation (e.g., in Ukraine and Slovakia). Along the way, analysis of the violence, its causes and cures, will also be affected, highlighting the political significance of the theoretical assumptions.

Besides power and states, a third assumption important in neorealism is the lack of system governance, that is, the condition of anarchy.[17] In a self-help world, in which actors are motivated by desires for survival, neorealists claim that a security dilemma among the great powers is likely and that cooperation will be difficult to achieve.[18] Although critics of neorealism challenge the strict logical character of this deduction and argue for a more complex conceptualization, most realist-based analyses accept it as a working assumption.[19] Of course, within this realist framework, should a third party emerge as a new challenger to both bipolar great powers, then a modus vivendi or superpower condominium could easily be anticipated and cooperation achieved. More difficult to deduce from the anarchy assumption, however, is the possibility that the security dilemma could be overcome by the great powers redefining the threat they posed to each other with little change evident in their material abilities to threaten one another. As in the case of motivation, the complexity of the Cold War case once again highlights the costs associated with accepting the simplifying assumptions of structural realism — in this case, the assumption about the environment.

Predictions

Abstract models of the international system are not true or false. They are merely more or less accurate representations of some part of world politics.[20] Hedley Bull argued that none of the most common models was sufficient by itself because parts of world politics reflected all three elements represented by Hobbesian, Kantian, and Grotian perspectives.[21] For Bull, it was not so much that structural realism was wrong; the problem was that during the Cold War the reality of Soviet-American relations was much more complicated and simple realist perspectives did not capture nearly enough to be very useful. Soviet-American relations, even in the toughest days, included elements of transnational and cooperative behavior that were not captured in the stark assumptions of anarchy and self-help.[22] If the test of a model's utility and importance as a scientific (as distinct from mathematical) representation rests on measures of its empirical accuracy, then one typical way to determine this is by its predictive power.

While philosophers of science disagree about the exact relationship between prediction and theory testing,[23] fairness demands examination of a theory's predictive power with regard to the phenomenon it claims to explain. For example, although the Cold War affected international relations theory in the United States in many ways and may have even promoted the popularity of realist simplifications, it is not fair to dismiss realism because it failed to predict a change in Soviet foreign policy. It is not a theory of foreign policy. On the other hand, realism should be expected to predict the systemic effects of the change in the great-power relationship. This, after all, was the subject realists discussed at length. Some, like Morton Kaplan, even worked out specific transformation rules to describe the change likely in each system.[24]

Previous scholarship testing realism typically began with the balance — or concentration — of power, polarity, or perhaps great-power alliances and from these independent variables predicted peace, war, the likelihood of war, types of war, stability in alliances, or the likelihood that regional wars would escalate to great-power war.[25] At times, intervening variables such as abundance of resources in the system are added to modify the prediction of polarity alone.[26]

The diversity in independent and dependent variables and the differences in the way they are operationalized make the large literature on structural factors and war difficult to summarize in a brief article. What is important to note here is that this research relates systemic characteristics like polarity to peace, war, and stability among great powers. The theory does not question where polarity comes from but aims to explain what its consequences are. It could not predict the end of the Cold War, understood as loose bipolarity,[27] but it may be able to predict the systemic consequences of this transformation in great-power relations. The period of change in great-power relationships is too close — if not still in progress — for us to know whether the realist predictions in this regard will hold or not.[28]

When the Cold War is seen as a case of great-power rivalry, comparable to other historical cases that have frequently been used in the examination of realist theory, it also is not fair to concentrate only on the beginning and end of the contest. The appropriate test of realism may not be the end of the Cold War but rather the "long peace," as John Gaddis calls the nearly forty years of stalemate between the United States and the Soviet Union.[29] Still, this stability is overdetermined, and with so little variation in Soviet-American relations, it is difficult to identify the effects of various plausible causal factors. Lebow, however, raises important questions about the relationship between polarity and stability in the Cold War.[30] He does so not by challenging the stalemate from the 1950s to 1980s but by arguing that essential stability also prevailed in the 1940s before bipolarity, as he measures it, was established. The argument will gain strength, if the post–Cold War world evolves into a clearly multipolar world, and stability among the great powers persists.

Operational Indicators

For the past twenty years, scholars and politicians alike have been anticipating the advent of a multipolar world.[31] Many considered that the Cold War international system evolved into loose bipolarity in the 1960s and showed signs of multipolarity in the 1970s. Of course, consensus never existed on this point, not even among American scholars, much less among observers from around the world. Different conceptions and operational measures of power greatly complicate efforts to evaluate the predictive utility of structural theories. It is difficult to decide when to attribute error to measurement problems, when to theoretical shortcomings. Several essays in this book address the problems of an underspecified theory but only begin to wrestle with the task of operationally measuring relative power.

Hans Morgenthau, like most realists, described in some detail the various components of national power. His picture was multidimensional and complicated, including material, psychological, and social aspects of power.[32] As Morgenthau conceives it, power is more than simply the military and financial instruments of influence; it also involves the government's ability to mobilize support and sustain morale. Moreover, power includes the leverage derived from intelligent diplomacy and covert information gathered about the objectives and calculations of other players in the bargaining context. Few scholars have tried to measure all these aspects of power.[33] Some concentrate on the material resource base and parts of the military instrument base.[34] A few have tried to factor in a general notion of domestic support and strategic leverage that might accrue from the type of decision-making process or the wisdom of the military planning.[35] These efforts are less likely to include as many countries in the sample and have a far more difficult time defending the validity of their measures. Constructing a formula for aggregating across the various dimensions and sources of power and arriving at a composite relative score is more difficult still.

All these problems inherent in measuring power have received a great deal of attention (with no terrific solutions forthcoming as yet). A more complicated and theoretically troublesome dilemma, however, has received less attention than it deserves. It derives from the relationship between power and motivation. One cannot test how powerful a state is unless one knows how hard it is trying to exert influence. Hedley Bull described the problem this way:

> The idea that if one state challenges the balance of power, other states are bound to seek to prevent it, assumes that all states seek to maximize their relative power position. This is not the case. States are constantly in the position of having to choose between devoting their resources and energies to maintaining or extending their international power position, and devoting these resources and energies to other ends. . . . Some states which have the potential for playing a major role . . . prefer to play a relatively minor one.[36]

If the exertion of power is a variable, then measuring power requires a prior assumption about exertion, which involves returning to the domain of motivation. James March recognized this problem in structural power theories and suggested that "force activation" models were necessary to make power analysis a more useful enterprise.[37] Unfortunately, he did not explain how to determine the level of exertion or motivational intensity. At times of total war, it may be reasonable to make the assumption of maximum exertion that realist theory is based on. At other moments, however, that assumption is misleading and interferes with the accurate measurement of power. During the Cold War, for instance, neither superpower ever used all the instruments it had available to compete in projecting influence, and assumptions that they did inject political, almost ideological, assumptions into the empirical evaluation of relative capability. A brief look at the Persian Gulf illustrates the point.

The importance of oil to the Western world and the Persian Gulf's role in supplying this oil make the Gulf a key strategic zone in the international system. If the Cold War can be represented as a loose bipolar system operating on anything like the rules spelled out by Kaplan and Waltz, then both the Soviet Union and the United

States should have competed actively for control over this area.[38] In fact, the United States did devote substantial effort to this task.[39] Soviet behavior, however, is more puzzling. Why, for instance, did it remain so passive in 1953 when the United States participated in a coup in Iran? The United States would not have behaved similarly had Moscow been implicated in such activities in Mexico — or Iran, for that matter. Yet, far from interfering, Moscow developed a reasonably positive relationship with the Shah and did very little to actively assert its influence in the Gulf, despite the close U.S.-Iranian relationship in the 1960s and 1970s.[40]

Many Americans may object to this description of Soviet behavior in the Gulf. They remember a Soviet Union that was aggressively trying to court Iraq, interfere in Dohfar, and promote the Tudeh party in Iran.[41] They may also see the U.S. nuclear deterrent as relevant and conclude that Moscow was doing everything it could to compete in the Gulf; it simply was weaker than the United States in this theater.[42] The problem is that this interpretation rests as much on assumptions about Soviet motives as it does on Soviet capabilities. After all, Iran shares a sixteen hundred mile border with the USSR. Moscow had twenty-five divisions north of Iran that could have been fleshed out to combat ready strength. It had sixty more divisions in the European areas of the USSR and thousands of combat aircraft nearby or easy to mobilize into the theater.[43] To respond to any Soviet movement, the United States would need to project force halfway around the world, since it had little conventional capability in place.[44] The Shah, of course, did have a large military force, but much of it was deployed to the south of Iran, and the Shah developed quite good relations with Moscow, giving little indication that he intended to fight the Soviet Union.

My point here is not to rewrite the history of the Cold War in the Gulf but rather to highlight the interdependent nature of estimates of power and assumptions about motivations. Americans who assume that Moscow was highly expansionist and opportunistic would attribute Soviet passivity in the Gulf to its lack of capability and to successful American deterrence. They might not look as hard at the empirical evidence concerning Soviet capability. After all, if Moscow was seen to have the capability to do more and was not actively doing it, then this would challenge the basic perception of an expansionist and opportunistic adversary. Important psychological processes protect and inhibit change in people's fundamental perceptions of adversaries.[45] In this case, the central beliefs are not just related to assumptions about a structural theory of world politics but to fundamental political disputes over what the Cold War was.

What Was the Cold War?

Ironically, Hans Morgenthau did not see the Cold War in terms of a bipolar balance of power; rather, he saw it as proof that a balance-of-power system was no longer possible.[46] The rise of mass politics and democracy had swept away the transnational aristocracy that had provided the common norms necessary for a balance-of-power system to work.[47] Morgenthau concluded that in the modern era a balance of power was uncertain, unreal, and inadequate, more often a part of a state's ideological justification of aggression than a serious characteristic of the system. For Morgenthau, the Cold War was explained in terms of nationalistic universalism — perhaps the most interesting idea in his most famous work and one that has attracted surprisingly little attention.[48]

The Cold War, according to Morgenthau, was a crusade. Two states, each promoting its own national ideological moral code as universally valid for the world, were locked in a battle to the death. Almost everything about the struggle violated the principles of a balance-of-power system. The great states were willing to invest heavily in geostrategically insignificant theaters in the name of the ideological crusade. Realpolitik considerations were set aside, and the struggle pursued at high costs in Third World areas that, because of the psychological basis of the crusade, had symbolic value, though marginal intrinsic strategic importance.[49] The battle for a way of life also meant that compromise and a modus vivendi were unlikely until one of the two major players was eliminated from the system. Kenneth Oye, in this book, returns to the ideological factor as a key cause driving the Cold War but tries to preserve a realist perspective just the same.

It is interesting that for the most part the controversy over what the Cold War was is not central to this book. A bipolar security dilemma and balance of power seem to be assumed by most authors. Yet Morgenthau was not alone in proposing an alternative conception of the Cold War. Some historians, for instance, emphasized the U.S. role in Europe, the containment of Germany and Japan, the extension of Western commercial influence into the Third World periphery, and Washington's domestic transformation into an outward-looking global military power as just as central to the Cold War as the bilateral Soviet-American relationship.[50] In these other conceptions, it was not simply a struggle for relative power or ideology that sustained the set of conflicts that we call the Cold War; material economic interests and domestic vested interests played an important role as well. The United States was not seen as consistently promoting a democratic way of life, particularly in the Third World. Nor was the Soviet Union seen as spreading socialism in any pure way. More often, the superpowers were described as making alliances for economic and material gain, putting whatever ideological face on it that made sense for domestic consumption and international propaganda.

In the power transition theory of A. F. K. Organski, the international system was not assumed to be anarchical; rather, it was described as hierarchical.[51] Rules similar to those constraining domestic politics were assumed also to constrain international politics, and nations were thought to pursue net gain, not power. In this theory, the Cold War was a struggle between a dominant power, allied to other satiated states, and an unsatisfied nation (i.e., the Soviet Union) that challenged the existing hierarchy. The relative power of the actors was not an independent variable; it was an intervening variable dependent on domestic development processes. Organski's central theoretical focus was on the level and types of production, fertility and mortality rates, political mobilization by the government, and social mobilization of populations.[52]

World systems theory provided yet another conception of the Cold War. Here, as in power transition theory, system hierarchy not anarchy was assumed, and attention focused primarily on the political economy of production and economic growth.[53] The Cold War in this scheme could be seen as a struggle between a hegemonic country (i.e., the United States) expanding the reach of world capitalism and an economic revolutionary Soviet Union. For many in this tradition, the revolutionary nature of the Soviet Union was somewhat in doubt. Immanuel Wallerstein, for instance, described it as a supermercantilist country as much as a revolutionary force challenging the essential logic of capital accumulation and production.[54] He, and Christopher Chase-Dunn, would cite what most authors in this book take to be the end of the Cold War as evidence of continuity, not change, in the system.[55] The hegemony of the dominant mode of production was reaffirmed, and the socialist mercantilists persuaded to accept assimilation, an outcome to which they had been resigning themselves for some time.

Recognizing that the Cold War is not an event with obvious characteristics but rather a historical representation constructed by scholars draws attention not only to the question of what it was but also to the question of when it ended. It is odd that while the debate over when the Cold War started and who started it still rages, the collective judgment evident in this book is that when it ended is obvious. If the Cold War was the ideological struggle that Morgenthau and Oye describe, then perhaps it did end with the renunciation of communism in the Soviet Union and the USSR's collapse. But one wonders then what to make of Malenkov and Khrushchev and the important ideological revisions of the late 1950s.[56] Was Moscow really crusading for communist ideology during the Brezhnev years of stagnation? Was this why it aligned with Nasser in the 1960s, Saddam Hussein in the 1970s, and broke with China?[57]

Perhaps the ideological zeal of the Cold War did decline with the death of Stalin. After that, more dogmatic leaders on both sides kept up some of the rhetoric, but the language of peaceful coexistence gained ground, as did a policy of stalemate and stabilized deterrence.[58] Maybe after the mid-1950s the Cold War was more clearly a struggle for power between a status quo–oriented United States and the revisionist-minded Soviet Union.[59] In this conception, however, it is not entirely clear just how revisionist the Soviet Union was and when it stopped being so. After all, the modus vivendi worked out with Willy Brandt in the early 1970s and codified in the Helsinki Final Act established a political-territorial status quo that Moscow seemed to accept and in fact, demanded and protected with vigor.

Moscow's efforts in Vietnam also gave way to its interest in détente. Both Richard Nixon and Henry Kissinger expected a much more vigorous Russian response to U.S. policy in Vietnam in the spring and fall of 1972.[60] Certainly, Moscow's exit from Egypt in the same year hardly seemed like committed revisionist behavior. Perhaps the Cold War, in terms of a revisionist Soviet Union, ended in the late 1960s, only to be revived by a series of regional conflicts in the late 1970s that Americans read, often wrongly, as Soviet inspired. Despite another decade of competition in places like Angola and Cambodia, in the 1990s the United States agreed to deal and work with previously unacceptable Soviet allies like the Popular Movement for the Liberation of Angola (MPLA) and Hun Sen. In Iran, meanwhile, the Islamic revolutionaries, who have said all along that they are a third force and not agents of the bipolar system, still reign, and revolutionary Iran never fell under Soviet control as Cold War–minded Americans feared it might.

The purpose here is not to suggest that the events of 1989–1990 were not dramatic; without question, they were more dramatic than the history of previous decades. The point is that these events were part of a process of change that already boasted many important benchmarks. Détente did not die in Europe, even if it did take a nosedive in the United States during the late 1970s and throughout the 1980s. Cautious and sometimes cooperative behavior in the Third World was not unheard of before Gorbachev.[61] And Gorbachev did not follow Stalin in Moscow, but Brezhnev. It is understandable why Gorbachev presented his reforms in contrast to Stalinism, maximizing the distinctions, but the comparison greatly oversimplifies the history of the 1960s, 1970s, and 1980s. More care in reconstructing the history, and the debates about it, is necessary before recent events can serve as convincing evidence in a consideration of international relations theory.

Was the Cold War a struggle between two active, ideologically messianic states, as Morgenthau described? Was it a period of active American expansion and Soviet response, or, on the other hand, Soviet challenge and American defense? And what were the protagonists defending? Their security, economic self-interest, and mode of production? Their sense of grandeur? Or all three and more? These are the kinds of questions that have fueled the debate over the Cold War for nearly fifty years. They have not been solved in this book, and, at root, they turn on the question of national motivation. The structural realist effort to avoid the question by assumption simply pushed the issue into the realm of ideology and assertion. How far we have come in addressing the question theoretically and empirically is the next subject to explore.

What Were Soviet Motives?

Traditional realists did not avoid the motivational question because they thought it was unimportant; they tried to sidestep it because they thought it was impossible to answer. In foreign affairs, a particular motive may produce many different types of behavior, depending on the circumstances, just as the same action can be caused by various motives. Many of the essays in this book have pointed out the limitations of structural realism, but few have showed how to move to the next level of causal regression with empirical rigor. It is easier to recognize the need to understand domestic processes and the political construction of national interest than it is to figure out how to study them. The Cold War, of course, involved assumptions about both Soviet and American motives; for the sake of brevity, I will look only at the debate over Soviet motives here. Unfortunately, despite the labor-intensive efforts of many scholars, little consensus was ever achieved on the subject, and not much more is likely in the post–Cold War period.

Over twenty years ago, William Gamson and Andre Modigliani tried to devise a strategy for testing rival theories of the Cold War.[62] They identified six major interpretations, all of which included a central judgment about Soviet intentions. Moscow was either destructionist, interested in destroying the values and social system embodied in the United States and Western Europe; expansionist, seeking to expand its control through the achievement of specific political goals; or consolidationist, interested in maintaining the status quo. William Welch, at roughly the same time, examined the competing American academic views of Soviet foreign policy and developed a comparable scale on which to portray the very diverse set of American opinions.[63] Whether the Soviet Union was seen as revisionist or as defending the status quo became a central divide in American strategic analysis and sat at the bedrock of competing policy advice. Some scholars, frustrated by the inability to settle the dispute, tried to get around it by concentrating on Soviet behavior instead, simply trying to decide if Soviet behavior was confrontational, competitive, opportunistic, or cooperative.[64] Unfortunately, this sort of description only begged the strategic question of why the Soviet Union behaved as it did, which remained the critical question underpinning advice on what Washington should do to affect Moscow's behavior.

Robert Jervis reached the sobering conclusion that despite the mountains of literature written on the Soviet Union, few analysts were persuaded by anyone else's arguments about Soviet motives. Alexander George concluded that helping to adjudicate between these different descriptions of the adversary's intentions was the most pressing task of policy relevant foreign policy level theory. Unfortunately, he did not tell us how to do this and the obstacles to it were substantial.[65]

For instance, many of the claims were nonfalsifiable.[66] If one was convinced that Nathan Leites was right and the Bolshevik operational code included a notion of pressing ahead until encountering solid resistance, then Moscow's aggressive behavior would confirm expectations, and its restraint would be attributed to American strength.[67] Typically, as was the case in the Persian Gulf example discussed earlier, the empirical situation was sufficiently unclear that some argument for American strength was possible even if complicated. Defensive interpretations were equally invulnerable, rarely spelling out what sort of behavior could not be attributed to some sort of perceived provocation. In the Cold War, after all, the whole world was seen as part of the competitive theater, and Moscow may have believed that actions possibly entirely independent of U.S. decision making were orchestrated in Washington. Certainly, many Americans attributed regional events beyond Moscow's control to Soviet foreign policy.

Furthermore, many of the motives that scholars ascribed to Moscow as causal factors were not mutually exclusive. The Soviet Union could have maintained the Warsaw Pact for ideological, defensive, and expansionist reasons all at once. Moreover, the maintenance of the alliance could have served the vested interests of the military and the party bureaucracy and even the domestic coalitional needs and intra-Politburo bargaining of individual leaders. It is difficult to imagine controlling in a rigorous research design the many degrees of freedom introduced by so many possible causal motives. Perhaps if scholars could have penetrated the decision-making process more adequately, convincing differentiations of the relative importance of one motive over others could have been established. Most efforts to penetrate the process, however, involved so much conjecture and controversial Kremlinology that the prior theory about what was motivating Moscow may have guided the description of the decision-making process more than did any objective examination of the competing propositions about Soviet motivation.[68]

Because the various interpretations of Soviet policy were typically nonfalsifiable, they can easily explain the end of the Cold War, although they could never have predicted its timing. Theories that emphasized the expansionist interests of Moscow argued that vigilant containment would eventually force Soviet leaders to face their overextension, give up their practice of securing domestic legitimacy from foreign adventure, and attend to domestic demands and inward-looking priorities.[69] Scholars that described Soviet policy as opportunistic and theoretically attributed its behavior to bureaucratic, party, and military vested interests also can explain the change. Since the early 1970s this perspective had argued that Moscow faced the choice of petrification or pluralism.[70] Economic modernization would force change as the realities of production in an advanced industrial high-technology system produced not only new technical pressures but also a new elite that over time would represent new vested interests.[71] Defensive and status quo theories of Soviet foreign policy can explain the change, too. They attributed past Soviet policy to the excessive security fears of Soviet leaders and to the geopolitical pressures these leaders rightly or wrongly felt.[72] If new Soviet leaders did not share these fundamental assumptions about the nature of the external threat, profound change would follow.

While any of the competing perspectives can explain the change, none anticipated that Gorbachev would unleash dramatic change in the late 1980s. However, scholars can look backward and find antecedent causes and confirmatory evidence to bolster their prior interpretations. Hawks can point to Reagan's foreign policy and conclude that it tipped the scales in Moscow and forced a reconsideration of power. They are likely to downplay or ignore the effects of détente in Europe, which never really waned despite the American policy of the 1980s. They also may overlook the security-minded elite in Moscow that never agreed with Gorbachev's policy, describing it as a foolish and unnecessary retreat. Modernization theorists, meanwhile, can describe the emergence of a new elite and the pressures of the technical age but pay less attention to the Chinese experience and that of the Asian tigers, where economic and political change were not so deterministically connected. Moreover, in Iran, a profoundly different value system came to prevail — as it could have in Russia — setting aside the drive to economic growth. Finally, the doves can concentrate on Gorbachev's new thinking and show that it represented a recognition of the security dilemma, a sense that past Soviet leaders were too preoccupied with security, and a test of a disengagement strategy. As Ned Lebow points out, however, they did not expect a leader to emerge in Moscow who was more confident of Soviet security and more willing to test American intentions while the United States was developing SDI, accelerating the arms race, and through the Reagan Doctrine arming anti-Soviet insurgencies in the Third World.

The critical theoretical problem with all the motivational theories is that they cannot specify the relative effect of various motives that are not mutually exclusive, and thus they cannot make a concrete prediction. They can explain post hoc, but in doing so, they eliminate the contingencies that actually confront their predictions. In other words, a hawk, after the fact, can know that a U.S. policy of strength had more effect in convincing Soviet leaders of their overextension than the European détente policy did in undermining the credibility of the American policy and convincing Soviet leaders that they should persevere. Before the fact, however, they could not tell which trend would prevail. The deterministic-sounding modernization theories also hide the real level of contingency in their predictions. After the fact, it is possible to conclude that the new vested interests of the technical elite overtook elements in the older ruling coalition, but before the fact, it was hard to forecast what form the new demands would take, or whether those demands would prevail, produce more efficient corporatism, or simply be defeated domestically. Looking at the uncertainty surrounding the survival and success of Yeltsin's policies in Russia reinforces the point. We recognize contingency in the future but forget that it also existed in the past. The result is that our reconstruction of the past often leaves contingency out; we simply search for the likely antecedent causes that correlate with what happened, not with what might have happened and even seemed likely at one time.[73]

Not only do the motivational theories confront problems of non-falsifiability, the difficulty of specifying what actions motives will and will not produce, and the understandable psychological biases involved in reading the past, they also must deal with the implications of the cognitive revolution in the social sciences. The key point here is to recognize that the perception of the situation that the subjects — in this case, Soviet leaders — have may not be the same as that of the scholar doing the analysis.[74] Both Lebow and Stein in this book, for instance, feel that the learning they ascribe to Soviet leaders was motivated by domestic priorities and needs more than by external stimuli. Yet this depends critically on what external stimuli they think the Soviet elite saw. Perhaps the Soviet decision to withdraw from Afghanistan will make the point concrete.

For Americans operating in a strictly bipolar mind-set, the only stimulus Soviet leaders could have picked up from U.S. diplomacy in the early 1980s was increased hostility.[75] The Reagan administration was not pursuing détente but revived containment. For scholars looking at potential stimuli in the regional context, the situation was different. Moscow had intervened in Afghanistan to ensure that a pro-Soviet government would rule in Kabul.[76] In Cold War terms, it feared that Washington would make a comeback after the fall of the Shah and move through Pakistan into Afghanistan. Motivated by this East-West simplification and misled by imperial images of a backward Afghanistan that would be easy to subdue, Brezhnev intervened.[77]

Nothing went as planned. Babrak Karmal did not gain legitimacy; instead, by the way he had come to power, he lost it forever. The mujahideen resistance increased as did Soviet casualties. Washington did not make a comeback in Iran; to the contrary, the Islamic Republic remained intensely hostile. American efforts to court Iran in the mid-1980s seemed more comical than truly threatening. As the costs escalated, the perceived threat of an American presence in the area looked ever more remote, not because of Reagan but because of the rise of regional powers and especially because of the rise of political Islam.

Just as the war in Vietnam convinced many Americans that the Soviet threat was exaggerated, the war in Afghanistan seemed to have a comparable effect in Moscow.[78] This happened not because it demonstrated a lack of American, competitiveness but because it brought to light regional realities and high costs that shattered the simple metaphors of the Cold War and undermined the domestic willingness to defend symbolic, as distinct from intrinsic, interests. The idea that the Americans would encircle the Soviet Union by controlling Kabul seemed increasingly fanciful as the realities of the Afghan scene sunk in. Moreover, as the political power of populist Islam grew, killing Muslims by the thousands in Afghanistan was hardly the way to close off Washington's options in the area. Not surprisingly, in February 1989, as the last Soviet soldier left Afghanistan, Soviet foreign minister Shevardnadze launched a major tour of the Middle East, courting Arab and Islamic favor and finally arriving in Tehran, where he was the first foreign minister ever received by the Ayatollah Khomeini.

The learning in Soviet foreign policy may not only be attributed to stimuli Americans miss, but it may also be the result of the reformulation of the problem. In the 1960s, William Fulbright and George Kennan, both hawks in the late 1940s and early 1950s, had changed their minds about the Soviet Union. They did not argue that Moscow was a passive and idealistically motivated state; no, they continued to argue that it was highly aggressive and capable of brutal action. What had changed dramatically in their thinking was their explanation for Moscow's aggressiveness. Abandoning the notion that Moscow was primarily driven by messianic revisionist interests, they argued instead that it was motivated by defensive concerns about its security. With this reformulation of what was causing the problem, fundamentally different strategic opinions appeared sensible to them.[79]

A similar transformation could have occurred in the Soviet Union. Gorbachev and the advisers he empowered may have still read the United States as highly aggressive and dangerous but concluded that the reason for this aggressiveness was a deep-seated American fear of communism and the Soviet Union. They could have come to this view, or at least to the view that the proposition ought to be tested, over a long period, as did the Americans who came to doubt the expansionist interpretation of Soviet behavior. The shift may have had little to do with the foreign policy behavior of the United States but a lot to do with a better understanding of domestic American politics. In this regard, the academic experts that Risse-Kappen discusses in this book may have played a role. Just how important a role, however, is difficult to determine.

While communication between Soviet and American academics increased in the 1970s and 1980s, so did many other potential causal variables. Moreover, many of the ideas exchanged on arms control and confidence building came as much from Moscow as they did from Washington. In fact, for most of the Cold War, leading politicians in Washington assumed that the notion of peaceful coexistence and many of the ideas discussed in the European-led forums Risse-Kappen mentions originated in Moscow and were part of a propaganda strategy designed to subvert Western resolve. Maybe the importance of these meetings lay less in establishing channels through which technical ideas could flow than in providing forums in which those involved could get a better understanding of the motive forces and domestic constraints facing leaders on the other side. Unfortunately, without better information about the decision-making process in Moscow, it will remain hard to defend the causal claim or weigh its relative impact.

International Relations Theory After the Cold War

In some ways the traditional dilemma in international relations research persists, and looking at the end of the Cold War only illustrates the problem. Analysis at the structural level is underspecified and relies too heavily on auxiliary assumptions that are not empirically defended.[80] Meanwhile, analysis at the foreign policy level, facing vexing problems of inference with regard to motivation and contingency, retreats to a study of the decision-making process that is nearly impossible to do with convincing evidence. Largely, there still remain two disciplines of international relations, to use Cronbach's concept. We have not succeeded in constructing interactionist theories, nor have we overcome the difficult data demands. More attention to both objectives is needed now.

For neorealists, the gravitation toward a balance-of-threat theory as distinct from a balance-of-power theory leads into the realm of foreign policy analysis.[81] As soon as the interest in relative, rather than absolute, gains is treated as a variable, realists introduce the motivational distinction with which foreign policy analysts begin.[82]

But where should the causal regression end? Should we try to unpack the decisional process and decipher the psychological roots of perception and the socioeconomic-political determinants of the perceptions that prevail?

Surely these questions are important, but are they manageable, and do we need to answer them as part of the analysis of international relations? At this point, a middle ground may be more practical. After all, the cognitive revolution in psychology has been driven by the difficulty of predicting how a subject will see and interpret a stimulus. If the causal problem is too tough to crack in the controlled environment of the laboratory, can we really hope to deal with it in the natural setting? And if we cannot know with confidence how specific officials in the United States government feel about particular policies and interact with one another inside an administration, can we really hope to penetrate the decision-making processes of other states?

What does seem possible is the identification of important elites and their perceptions of the world. We can speculate about why they hold various views but leave that question somewhat open. How these elites interact with each other inside the decision-making process of the government may be impossible to track with confidence, but with the help of area experts, international relations scholars can identify the constellation of elites in a country and which ones prevail. This would take the identification of key leaders, their perceptions, and their relative influence as variables requiring empirical evidence. Rather than trying to predict these factors from modernization theories or the like or defining them by assumption, we could try to operationalize them and with a reintegration of the area specialist into international relations theory begin our studies with a concrete evidential foundation.

If we began with elite perceptions and the constellation of elite views in a country, we would then have a basis for making inferences about the interests in that society that foreign policy is likely to reflect. A rank ordering of these interests could guide our judgments about motivation at the state level of analysis. If this sort of analysis were done for two or three states simultaneously, we could speculate on the interaction patterns among them. The international system would thus be operationally defined not only by the distribution of material power bases among the great powers but also by the distribution of interests and aims. This, of course, would plunge theorists back into the interpretative debates that were at the heart of the Cold War but do so in a way that required them to address issues directly rather than implicitly.

Predicting the end of the Cold War is not a fair test of international relations theory. Neither international relations theory nor the Cold War is easy to define as a single entity. Moreover, much of the theorizing about international affairs tried to avoid the main controversies that were in dispute with regard to the Cold War. Questions about polarity and war took precedence over the questions about Soviet and American motives. Perhaps the most troubling shortcoming of international relations theory is not its failure to predict system change but rather its irrelevance to the interpretative controversies that drove strategic choices. Hans Morgenthau left his realist theory behind as he analyzed the Cold War. Many others did likewise, simply asserting what the motives of the actors were and then operating as if their theory rather than their motivational assumptions led to strategic implications. If science is an enterprise driven by problem solving, then addressing this shortcoming is the task we need to attend to now.

NOTES

1   See L. J. Cronbach, "The Two Disciplines of Scientific Psychology," *American Psychologist* 12 (November 1957): 671–84, and idem, "Beyond the Two Disciplines of Scientific Psychology," *American Psychologist* 30 (February 1975): 116–27.

2   See Alexander Wendt, "Anarchy Is What States Make of It: The Social Construction of Power Politics," *International Organization* 46 (spring 1992): 391–425, and Walter Carlsnaes, "The Agency-Structure Problem in Foreign Policy Analysis," *International Studies Quarterly* 36 (September 1992): 245–70.

3   See Morton Kaplan, *System and Process in International Relations* (Huntington, N.Y.: Krieger, 1975); Richard Mansbach and John Vasquez, *In Search of Theory: A New Paradigm for Global Politics* (New York: Columbia University Press, 1981); and James Rosenau, *Turbulence in World Politics: A Theory of Change and Continuity* (Princeton: Princeton University Press, 1990).

4   Hans Morgenthau, *Politics Among Nations*, 5th ed. (New York: Knopf, 1973), pp. 5–10.

5   See Kenneth N. Waltz, *Theory of International Politics* (Reading, Mass.: Addison-Wesley, 1979); and Stephen Walt, *The Origins of Alliances* (New York: Cornell University Press, 1985).

6   See Immanuel Wallerstein, *The Politics of the World-Economy* (New York: Cambridge University Press, 1984); and Christopher Chase-Dunn, *Global Formations: Structures of the World-Economy* (Cambridge: Basil Blackwell, 1989).

7   See Kaplan, *System and Process in International Politics*, pp. 21–53.

8   See Waltz, *Theory of International Politics*, pp. 71–73.

9   See Morgenthau, *Politics Among Nations*, pp. 64–72.

10   See Robert O. Keohane and Joseph Nye, Jr., eds., *Transnational Rela-*

tions and World Politics (Cambridge: Harvard University Press, 1971); and Robert O. Keohane and Joseph Nye, *Power and Interdependence* (Boston: Little, Brown, 1977).

11 See Benedict Anderson, *Imagined Communities: Reflections on the Origin and Spread of Nationalism*, rev. ed. (New York: Routledge, Chapman, and Hall, 1991); John Breuilly, *Nationalism and the State* (Chicago: University of Chicago, 1982); and Anthony Smith, *Theories of Nationalism* (New York: Harper and Row, 1972).

12 See Anderson, *Imagined Communities*; and Ernst Gellner, *Nations and Nationalism* (Ithaca: Cornell University Press, 1983).

13 See Ernst Haas, "What Is Nationalism and Why Should We Study It?" *International Organization* 40 (summer 1986): 707–44; Gellner, *Nations and Nationalism*; and Breuilly, *Nationalism and the State*.

14 See Breuilly, *Nationalism and the State*. See also Karl Deutsch, *Nationalism and Social Communication: An Inquiry into the Foundations of Nationality*, 2d ed. (Cambridge: MIT Press, 1966).

15 See Rupert Emerson, *From Empire to Nation* (Boston: Beacon, 1960).

16 For more on this argument, see Richard Cottam, *Iran and the United States: A Cold War Case Study* (Pittsburgh: University of Pittsburgh, 1988).

17 See Waltz, *Theory of International Politics*, pp. 88–93.

18 Ibid., pp. 186–87.

19 Two such critical views are Robert Jervis, "Cooperation Under the Security Dilemma," *World Politics* 30 (January 1978): 167–214; and Wendt, "Anarchy Is What States Make of It."

20 See F. S. C. Northrop, *The Logic of the Sciences and Humanities* (New York: World, 1959).

21 Hedley Bull, *The Anarchical Society: A Study of Order in World Politics* (New York: Columbia University, 1977), p. 41.

22 Ibid., p. 43.

23 See S. Toulmin, *Foresight and Understanding: An Enquiry into the Aims of Science* (New York: Harper, 1961).

24 Kaplan, *System and Process in International Politics*, p. 9. For an example of the transformation rules in bipolar systems, see ibid., pp. 27–36, and 39–43.

25 For testing focusing on the balance of power, see, e.g., Edward D. Mansfield, "The Concentration of Capabilities and the Onset of War," *Journal of Conflict Resolution* 36 (March 1992): 3–24; and J. D. Singer, S. Bremer, and J. Stucky, "Capability Distribution, Uncertainty, and Major Power Wars, 1920–1965," in *Peace, War, and Numbers*, ed. B. Russett (Beverly Hills, Calif.: Sage, 1972), pp. 19–48. For testing focusing on polarity, see Waltz, *Theory of International Politics*; Richard N. Rosecrance, "Bipolarity, Multipolarity, and the Future," *Journal of Conflict Resolution* 10 (September 1966): 314–27; and Manus Midlarsky, *The Onset of World War* (Boston: Unwin Hyman, 1988). Also see B. Most and H. Starr, "Polarity, Preponderance, and Power Parity, in the Generation of International Conflict," *International Interactions* 13 (May 1987): 225–62. For testing focusing on

great-power alliances, see Jack Levy, "Alliance Formation and War Behavior," *Journal of Conflict Resolution* 25 (1981): 581–614; and idem, *War in the Modern Great Power System, 1495–1975* (Lexington: University Press of Kentucky, 1983). For predictions of peace, war, the likelihood of war, and types of war, see J. A. Vasquez, "Capability, Types of War, Peace," *Western Political Quarterly* 39 (June 1987): 313–27. For a good summary, see Jack Levy, "The Causes of War: A Review of Theories and Evidence," in *Behavior, Society, and Nuclear War*, ed. Philip E. Tetlock, Jo L. Husbands, Robert Jervis, Paul C. Stern, and Charles Tilly (New York: Oxford University Press, 1989), 1:209–333.

26 See Manus Midlarsky, "Polarity and International Stability," *American Political Science Review* 87 (March 1993): 173–77.

27 See Kaplan, *System and Process in International Politics*, pp. 36–43.

28 See John J. Mearsheimer, "Back to the Future: Instability in Europe After the Cold War," *International Security* 15 (summer 1990): 5–56.

29 John Gaddis, "The Long Peace: Elements of Stability in the Postwar International System," *International Security* 10 (spring 1986): 99–142.

30 Others have noted the lack of this relationship in other eras as well. See, e.g., Ted Hopf, "Polarity, the Offense-Defense Balance, and War," *American Political Science Review* 85 (June 1991): 475–93.

31 See, e.g., Richard Nixon, *United States Foreign Policy for the 1970's: Building for Peace* (New York: Harper and Row, 1971).

32 Morgenthau, *Politics Among Nations*, pp. 103–64.

33 One effort is Richard Cottam and Gerald Gallucci, *The Rehabilitation of Power in International Relations* (Pittsburgh: University Center for International Studies, 1978).

34 Klaus Knorr, *The Power of Nations: The Political Economy of International Relations* (New York: Basic, 1975); J. D. Singer, *The Correlates of War, II: Testing Some Realpolitik Models* (New York: Free Press, 1980).

35 Ray Cline, *World Power Assessment* (Washington, D.C.: CSIS, 1975); and Cottam and Gallucci, *The Rehabilitation of Power in International Relations*.

36 Bull, *Anarchical Society*, pp. 111–12.

37 James March, "The Power of Power," in *Varieties of Political Theory*, ed. David Easton (Englewood Cliffs, N.J.: Prentice-Hall, 1966), pp. 39–70.

38 See Kaplan, *System and Process in International Relations*, pp. 36–43; and Waltz, *Theory of International Politics*, pp. 161–93.

39 See James Bill, *The Eagle and the Lion* (New Haven: Yale University Press, 1988); and Mark Gasiorowski, *U.S. Foreign Policy and the Shah: Building a Client State in Iran* (Ithaca: Cornell University Press, 1991).

40 See Richard K. Herrmann, "The Role of Iran in Soviet Perceptions and Policy, 1946–1988," in *Neither East Nor West*, ed. Nikki Keddie

and Mark Gasiorowski (New Haven: Yale University Press, 1990), pp. 63–99.

41   Robert Freeman, "Gorbachev, Iran and the Iran-Iraq War," in *Neither East Nor West*, ed. Nikki Keddie and Mark Gasiorowski (New Haven: Yale University Press, 1990), pp. 115–44.

42   Dennis Ross, "The Soviet Union and the Persian Gulf," in *Soviet International Behavior and U.S. Policy Options*, ed. Dan Caldwell (Lexington, Mass.: Heath, 1985), pp. 159–86; and Joshua Epstein, *Strategy and Force Planning: The Case of the Persian Gulf* (Washington, D.C.: Brookings, 1987).

43   International Institute for Strategic Studies, *The Military Balance, 1983–1984* (London: Brassey, 1983).

44   Thomas McNaughter, *Arms and Oil: U.S. Military Strategy and the Persian Gulf* (Washington, D.C.: Brookings, 1985).

45   Robert Jervis, *Perception and Misperception in International Politics* (Princeton: Princeton University Press, 1976), pp. 117–318; and Susan Fiske and Shelley Taylor, *Social Cognition* (Reading, Mass.: Addison-Wesley, 1984), pp. 139–83.

46   Morgenthau, *Politics Among Nations*, pp. 202–21.

47   Ibid., pp. 241–56.

48   Ibid., pp. 349–59.

49   Robert Jervis, *The Meaning of the Nuclear Revolution: Statecraft and the Prospect of Armageddon* (Ithaca: Cornell University Press, 1989), pp. 174–225; Bruce Cummings, "The Wicked Witch of the West Is Dead; Long Live the Wicked Witch of the East," in *The End of the Cold War: Its Meaning and Implications*, ed. Michael Hogan (Cambridge: Cambridge University Press, 1992), pp. 87–102, esp. p. 98.

50   Walter LaFeber, "An End to *Which* Cold War?" in *The End of the Cold War: Its Meaning and Implications*, ed. Michael Hogan (Cambridge: Cambridge University Press, 1992), pp. 13–20; Cummings, "The Wicked Witch of the West Is Dead"; Melvin Leffler, *A Preponderance of Power: National Security, the Truman Administration, and the Cold War* (Stanford: Stanford University Press, 1992); and Daniel Yergen, *Shattered Peace: The Origins of the Cold War and the National Security State* (Boston: Houghton Mifflin, 1977).

51   A. F. K. Organski, *World Politics*, 2d ed. (New York: Knopf, 1967); A. F. K. Organski and Jacek Kugler, *The War Ledger* (Chicago: University of Chicago Press, 1980); idem, "The Power Transition: A Retrospective and Prospective Evaluation," in *Handbook of War Studies*, ed. Manus Midlarsky (Boston: Unwin Hyman, 1989), pp. 171–94.

52   Organski and Kugler, *The War Ledger*.

53   Wallerstein, *The Politics of the World-Economy*.

54   Ibid., pp. 86–96.

55   Christopher Chase-Dunn, *Global Formation: Structures of the World-Economy* (Cambridge: Basil Blackwell, 1989).

56   William Zimmerman, *Soviet Perspectives on International Relations, 1956–1967* (Princeton: Princeton University Press, 1969).

57   For a view of Soviet foreign policy that does not stress ideology, see

Raymond L. Garthoff, *Détente and Confrontation: American-Soviet Relations from Nixon to Reagan* (Washington, D.C.: Brookings, 1985).

58 Ibid.

59 Adam Ulam, *Dangerous Relations: The Soviet Union in World Politics, 1970–1982* (New York: Oxford University Press, 1983).

60 Henry Kissinger, *The White House Years* (Boston: Little, Brown, 1979), pp. 1117–20, 1144–45, 1151–56.

61 See Richard K. Herrmann, "Soviet Behavior in Regional Conflicts," *World Politics* 44 (April 1992): 432–65.

62 William Gamson and Andre Modigliani, *Untangling the Cold War: A Strategy for Testing Rival Theories* (Boston: Little, Brown, 1971).

63 William Welch, *American Images of Soviet Foreign Policy: An Inquiry into Recent Appraisals from the Academic Community* (New Haven: Yale University Press, 1970).

64 See, e.g., Joshua Goldstein and John Freeman, *Three-Way Street: Strategic Reciprocity in World Politics* (Chicago: University of Chicago Press, 1990); and George Breslauer, "Soviet Policy in the Middle East, 1967–1972: Unalterable Antagonism or Collaborative Cooperation?" in *Managing U.S.-Soviet Rivalry: Problems of Crisis Prevention*, ed. Alexander George (Boulder, Colo.: Westview, 1983), pp. 65–106.

65 Robert Jervis, "Beliefs About Soviet Behavior," in *Containment, Soviet Behavior, and Grand Strategy*, ed. R. Osgood (Berkeley: University of California Institute of International Studies, 1981), pp. 56–59; and Alexander George, *Presidential Decision-Making in Foreign Policy* (Boulder, Colo.: Westview, 1980), p. 242.

66 For more on this argument, see Herrmann, *Perceptions and Behavior in Soviet Foreign Policy*, pp. 22–49.

67 Nathan Leites, *The Operational Code of the Politburo* (New York: McGraw-Hill, 1951).

68 Harry Gelman, *The Brezhnev Politburo and the Decline of Détente* (Ithaca: Cornell University Press, 1984); Robert Slusser, *The Berlin Crisis of 1961: Soviet-American Relations and the Struggle for Power in the Kremlin, June–November 1961* (Baltimore: Johns Hopkins University Press, 1973); and Richard Anderson, "Why Competitive Politics Inhibits Learning in Soviet Foreign Policy," in *Learning in U.S. and Soviet Foreign Policy*, ed. George W. Breslauer and Philip E. Tetlock (Boulder, Colo.: Westview, 1991).

69 Ulam, *Dangerous Relations*.

70 Jerry Hough, *The Soviet Union and Social Science Theory* (Cambridge: Harvard University Press, 1977), pp. 19–48.

71 Seweryn Bialer, *The Soviet Paradox: External Expansion, Internal Decline* (New York: Knopf, 1986); and idem, *Stalin's Successors: Leadership, Stability, and Change in the Soviet Union* (New York: Cambridge University Press, 1980).

72 Garthoff, *Détente and Confrontation*.

73 Robyn Dawes, "Prediction of the Future Versus an Understanding of

the Past: A Basic Asymmetry," *American Journal of Psychology* 106 (spring 1993): 1–24.

74 H. Gardner, *The Mind's New Science: A History of the Cognitive Revolution* (New York: Basic, 1985).

75 For instance, see Sarah Mendelson, "Internal Battles and External Wars: Politics, Learning, and the Soviet Withdrawal from Afghanistan," *World Politics* 45 (April 1993): 327–60.

76 Garthoff, *Détente and Confrontation*, pp. 887–965.

77 Richard K. Herrmann, "The Soviet Decision to Withdraw from Afghanistan: Changing Strategic and Regional Images." In *Dominoes and Bandwagons: Strategic Beliefs and Great Power Competition in the Eurasian Rimland*, ed. Robert Jervis and Jack Snyder (New York: Oxford University Press, 1991), pp. 220–49.

78 Ole Holsti and James Rosenau, *American Leadership in World Affairs: Vietnam and the Breakdown of Consensus* (Boston: Allen and Unwin, 1984).

79 See, e.g., George Kennan, *Russia, the Atom and the West* (New York: Harper, 1958); idem, *The Cloud of Danger: Current Realities of American Foreign Policy* (Boston: Little, Brown, 1977); and idem, *The Nuclear Delusion: Soviet-American Relations in the Atomic Age* (New York: Pantheon, 1982); William J. Fulbright, *Prospects for the West* (Cambridge: Harvard University Press, 1963); idem, *The Arrogance of Power* (New York: Random House, 1966); and idem, *The Crippled Giant: American Foreign Policy and Its Domestic Consequences* (New York: Random House, 1972). In "The Search for Accommodation: Gorbachev in Comparative Perspective," the seventh essay in this book, Ned Lebow spells out the very aggressive scenario he expected highly insecure states to adopt under pressure.

80 Herbert Simon, "Human Nature in Politics: The Dialogue of Psychology with Political Science," *American Political Science Review* 79 (June 1985): 293–304.

81 Stephen Walt, *The Origins of Alliances* (Ithaca: Cornell University Press, 1987), pp. 262–86.

82 See, e.g., Waltz, *Theory of International Relations*, p. 105; Joseph Grieco, *Cooperation Among Nations* (Ithaca: Cornell University Press, 1990), pp. 40–50; and Robert O. Keohane, "Institutionalist Theory and the Realist Challenge After the Cold War," paper presented at the Annual Meeting of the American Political Science Association, Chicago, September 3–6, 1992, pp. 10–17.

Index of Names

Acton, Lord, 136
Adenauer, Konrad, 183
Afheldt, Horst, 199
Aleksandrov-Agentov, Andrei, 240
Andropov, Yuri, 9, 129, 191, 226,
    228, 233, 238
Arbatov, Alexi, 200
Arbatov, Georgi, 198, 201, 241–42
Ash, Timothy Garton, 146

Bahr, Egon, 197–98, 200
Baker, James, 154–55
Beckman, Peter, 30–31
Begin, Menachem, 177
Beschloss, Michael, 147
Bethmann-Hollweg, Theobald von,
    101-2
Bialer, Seweryn, 117
Bismark, Otto von, 46, 157
Blacker, Coit, 130
Boserup, Anders, 199, 201
Brandt, Willy, 200, 270
Brazauskas, Algirdas, 154
Brezhnev, Leonid, 3, 9, 13, 36–38,
    40–41, 73, 128–29, 139, 144,
    145, 147, 149, 158, 175–77, 183,
    225, 227–28, 230, 234, 238,
    240–41, 270–71, 275
Bulganin, Nikolai Aleksandrovich, 9,
    10, 183
Bull, Hedley, 263, 266
Burlatsky, Fyodor, 152
Bush, George, 85–86, 133, 151, 155,
    156, 179, 189, 193

Carr. E. H., 50

Carter, Jimmy, 170, 176, 183
Ceauşescu, Nicolae, 177
Chase-Dunn, Christopher, 269
Checkel, Jeff, 74, 194–95
Chernenko, Konstantin, 9, 191, 226,
    228, 230, 233, 240
Clinton, Bill, 85
Combes, Emile, 172
Comisso, Ellen, 91

Darwin, Charles, 46
Dayan, Moshe, 177–78
de Gaulle, Charles, 44
Delcassé, Théophile, 172, 180
de Maizières, Lothar, 157
Deudney, Daniel, 192
Deutsch, Karl, 42, 44
Dienstbier, Jiri, 153
Djilas, Milovan, 140
Dobrynin, Anatoliy, 240
Douglass, Frederick, 89
Dreyfus, Alfred, 172
Drucker, Peter, 92
Dubček, Alexander, 154
Dulles, John Foster, 9, 10, 129, 183

Eisenhower, Dwight D., 9, 10, 62,
    183
Evangelista, Matthew, 193, 198

Falin, Valentin, 239
Frederick the Great, 46
Fukuyama, Francis, 90–91
Fulbright, Francis, 276

Gaddis, John, 3, 265

285

General Index

accommodation, 7, 10, 24, 36, 48,
171, 172, 173, 177, 178, 179,
181, 182, 226
Afghanistan, 76, 114, 171, 177, 275
American Academy of Arts and Sciences, 241
anarchy, 15, 24, 25, 41, 46, 49,
Anglo-French entente, 167, 173
Angola, 76, 270
Anti-Ballistic Missile (ABM), 196,
202, 203, 208
Armenia, 45
arms control, 5, 8, 35, 36, 41, 42,
48, 57, 85, 86, 151, 171, 176,
178, 179, 193, 195, 196, 197,
198, 202, 203, 204, 205, 208,
210, 225, 226, 227, 233, 234,
241, 242
Australia, 43, 44
Austria, 137, 155, 168
Austrianization, 146, 155, 157, 158
Azerbaijan, 45

balance of power, 16, 24, 113, 132,
136, 167, 203, 266, 268, 277
balance of threat, 277
Balkans, 34, 117
Baltic Republics, 32, 41, 114, 133,
153, 180
Berlin Crises, 4, 31, 40, 48, 143, 169
Berlin Wall, 204
bipolarity, 6–7, 15, 25, 26, 29, 30,
31, 32, 47, 62, 113, 129, 143,
265
Bosnia, 45
Bretton Woods, 121, 122

Brezhnev Doctrine, 13, 73, 128, 129,
139, 140, 144, 145, 146, 147,
149, 150, 152, 158
Brezhnevism, 9, 91
Bulgaria, 93, 94
Burma, 89

Cambodia, 270
Canada, 44, 239, 241
Caucasus, 117, 169, 263
Central Intelligence Agency (CIA), 61
chaos theory, 2
Cheka, 142
cognitive psychology, 10, 14, 210,
224, 228, 231, 232, 234, 278
common security, 14, 189, 190, 194,
196, 197, 198, 199, 200, 202,
204, 205, 206, 209
Commonwealth of Independent
States, 78, 132
constructivism, 128, 134–39, 145,
148
Council for Mutual Economic Assistance (CMEA), 70, 71, 72
Crimean War, 117
Croatia, 45
Cuba, 7, 8, 71
Cuban Missile Crisis, 3, 48, 167,
170
Cyprus, 42
Czechoslovakia, 31, 34, 40, 41, 73,
87, 93, 94, 100, 101, 144, 152,
153, 154, 169
Czech Republic, 44, 119

détente, 7, 38, 61, 62, 144, 145,